Certificate Paper

D0121335

2011 Syllabus

FUNDAMENTALS OF MANAGEMENT ACCOUNTING

For assessments in 2013 and 2014

CIMA

Study Text

In this October 2012 edition

- A **user-friendly format** for easy navigation

- Regular **fast forward** summaries emphasising the key points in each chapter

- **Assessment focus points** showing you what the assessor will want you to do

- **Questions** and **quick quizzes** to test your understanding

- **Question bank** containing objective test questions with answers

- A full index

BPP Learning Media's **i-Pass** product also supports this paper.

FOR ASSESSMENTS IN 2013 and 2014

First edition 2011
Second edition 2012

ISBN 9781 4453 6470 4
Previous ISBN 9781 4453 7776 6
eISBN 9781 4453 9111 3

British Library Cataloguing-in-Publication Data
A catalogue record for this book is available from the
British Library

Published by

BPP Learning Media Ltd
BPP House, Aldine Place
142-144 Uxbridge Road
London W12 8AA

www.bpp.com/learningmedia

Printed in the United Kingdom by Polestar Wheatons

Hennock Road
Marsh Barton
Exeter
EX2 8RP

Your learning materials, published by BPP Learning
Media Ltd, are printed on paper sourced from
sustainable, managed forests.

BPP
LEARNING MEDIA

Contents

The BPP Learning Media Study Text

Aims of this Study Text

> To provide you with the knowledge and understanding, skills and application techniques that you need if you are to be successful in your exams

This Study Text has been written to cover the 2011 **Fundamentals of Management Accounting** syllabus.

- It is **comprehensive**. It covers the syllabus content. No more, no less.

- It is written at the **right level**. Each chapter is written with CIMA's precise learning outcomes in mind.

- It is targeted to the **assessment**. We have taken account of guidance CIMA has given and the assessment methodology.

> To allow you to study in the way that best suits your learning style and the time you have available, by following your personal Study Plan (see page (vii))

You may be studying at home on your own until the date of the exam, or you may be attending a full-time course. You may like to (and have time to) read every word, or you may prefer to (or only have time to) skim-read and devote the remainder of your time to question practice. Wherever you fall in the spectrum, you will find the BPP Learning Media Study Text meets your needs in designing and following your personal Study Plan.

> To tie in with the other components of the BPP Learning Media Effective Study Package to ensure you have the best possible chance of passing the exam (see page (v))

Learning to Learn Accountancy

BPP Learning Media's ground-breaking **Learning to Learn Accountancy** book is designed to be used both at the outset of your CIMA studies and throughout the process of learning accountancy. It challenges you to consider how you study and gives you helpful hints about how to approach the various types of paper which you will encounter. It can help you **focus your studies on the subject and exam**, enabling you to **acquire knowledge, practise and revise efficiently and effectively**.

The BPP Learning Media Effective Study Package

Recommended period of use	The BPP Learning Media Effective Study Package
From the outset and throughout	**Learning to Learn Accountancy** Read this invaluable book as you begin your studies and refer to it as you work through the various elements of the BPP Learning Media Effective Study Package. It will help you to acquire knowledge, practise and revise, efficiently and effectively.
Three to twelve months before the assessment	**Study Text and Interactive Passcards** Use the Study Text and Interactive Passcards to acquire knowledge, understanding, skills and the ability to apply techniques.
Throughout	**i-Pass** **i-Pass**, our computer-based testing package, provides objective test questions in a variety of formats and is ideal for self-assessment.
One to six months before the assessment	**Practice & Revision Kit** Try the numerous assessment-format questions, for which there are full worked solutions where relevant prepared by BPP Learning Media's own authors. Then attempt the two mock assessments.
From three months before the assessment until the last minute	**Passcards** Work through these short, memorable notes which are focused on what is most likely to come up in the assessment you will be sitting.

Help yourself study for your CIMA assessment

Assessments for professional bodies such as CIMA are very different from those you have taken at college or university. You will be under **greater time pressure before** the assessment – as you may be combining your study with work. There are many different ways of learning and so the BPP Study Text offers you a number of different tools to help you through. Here are some hints and tips: they are not plucked out of the air, but **based on research and experience**. (You don't need to know that long-term memory is in the same part of the brain as emotions and feelings - but it's a fact anyway.)

The right approach

1   The right attitude

Believe in yourself	Yes, there is a lot to learn. Yes, it is a challenge. But thousands have succeeded before and you can too.
Remember why you're doing it	Studying might seem a grind at times, but you are doing it for a reason: to advance your career.

2   The right focus

Read through the Syllabus and learning outcomes	These tell you what you are expected to know and are supplemented by Assessment focus points in the text.

3   The right method

The whole picture	You need to grasp the detail - but keeping in mind how everything fits into the whole picture will help you understand better. • The **Introduction** of each chapter puts the material in context. • The **Syllabus content, Learning outcomes** and **Assessment focus points** show you what you need to **grasp**.
In your own words	To absorb the information (and to practise your written communication skills), it helps to **put it into your own words**. • **Take notes.** • Answer the **questions** in each chapter. You will practise your written communication skills, which become increasingly important as you progress through your CIMA assessments. • Draw **mindmaps**. • Try **'teaching' a subject** to a colleague or friend.
Give yourself cues to jog your memory	The BPP Learning Media Study Text uses **bold** to **highlight key points**. • Try **colour coding** with a highlighter pen. • Write **key points** on cards.

BPP LEARNING MEDIA

4   **The right review**

Review, review, review	It is a **fact** that regularly reviewing a topic in summary form can **fix it in your memory**. Because **review** is so important, the BPP Learning Media Study Text helps you to do so in many ways.
	• **Chapter roundups** summarise the 'fast forward' key points in each chapter. Use them to recap each study session.
	• The **Quick quiz** is another review technique you can use to ensure that you have grasped the essentials.
	• Go through the **Examples** in each chapter a second or third time.

Developing your personal Study Plan

BPP Learning Media's **Learning to Learn Accountancy** book emphasises the need to prepare (and use) a study plan. Planning and sticking to the plan are key elements of learning success.
There are four steps you should work through.

Step 1   **How do you learn?**

First you need to be aware of your style of learning. The BPP Learning Media **Learning to Learn Accountancy** book commits a chapter to this **self-discovery**. What types of intelligence do you display when learning? You might be advised to brush up on certain study skills before launching into this Study Text.

BPP Learning Media's **Learning to Learn Accountancy** book helps you to identify what intelligences you show more strongly and then details how you can tailor your study process to your preferences. It also includes handy hints on how to develop intelligences you exhibit less strongly, but which might be needed as you study accountancy.

Are you a **theorist** or are you more **practical**? If you would rather get to grips with a theory before trying to apply it in practice, you should follow the study sequence on page (viii). If the reverse is true (you like to know why you are learning theory before you do so), you might be advised to flick through Study Text chapters and look at examples, case studies and questions (Steps 8, 9 and 10 in the **suggested study sequence**) before reading through the detailed theory.

Step 2   **How much time do you have?**

Work out the time you have available per week, given the following.

- The standard you have set yourself
- The time you need to set aside later for work on the Practice & Revision Kit and Passcards
- The other exam(s) you are sitting
- Very importantly, practical matters such as work, travel, exercise, sleep and social life

Hours

Note your time available in box A.   A   [   ]

Step 3   **Allocate your time**

- Take the time you have available per week for this Study Text shown in box A, multiply it by the number of weeks available and insert the result in box B.

  B   [   ]

- Divide the figure in box B by the number of chapters in this text and insert the result in box C.

  C   [   ]

Remember that this is only a rough guide. Some of the chapters in this book are longer and more complicated than others, and you will find some subjects easier to understand than others.

Step 4   **Implement**

Set about studying each chapter in the time shown in box C, following the key study steps in the order suggested by your particular learning style.

This is your personal **Study Plan**. You should try and combine it with the study sequence outlined below. You may want to modify the sequence a little (as has been suggested above) to adapt it to your **personal style**.

BPP Learning Media's **Learning to Learn Accountancy** gives further guidance on developing a study plan, and deciding where and when to study.

Suggested study sequence

It is likely that the best way to approach this Study Text is to tackle the chapters in the order in which you find them. Taking into account your individual learning style, you could follow this sequence.

Key study steps	Activity
Step 1 **Topic list**	Each numbered topic is a numbered section in the chapter.
Step 2 **Introduction**	This gives you the big picture in terms of the context of the chapter, the learning outcomes the chapter covers, and the content you will read. In other words, it sets your objectives for study.
Step 3 **Fast forward**	Fast forward boxes give you a quick summary of the content of each of the main chapter sections. They are listed together in the roundup at the end of each chapter to provide you with an overview of the contents of the whole chapter.
Step 4 **Explanations**	Proceed methodically through the chapter, reading each section thoroughly and making sure you understand.
Step 5 **Key terms and Assessment focus points**	• Key terms can often earn you *easy marks* (and they are highlighted in the index at the back of the text). • Assessment focus points state how we think the examiner intends to examine certain topics.
Step 6 **Note taking**	Take brief notes, if you wish. Avoid the temptation to copy out too much. Remember that being able to put something into your own words is a sign of being able to understand it. If you find you cannot explain something you have read, read it again before you make the notes.

Key study steps	Activity
Step 7 **Examples**	Follow each through to its solution very carefully.
Step 8 **Questions**	Make a very good attempt at each one.
Step 9 **Answers**	Check yours against ours, and make sure you understand any discrepancies.
Step 10 **Chapter roundup**	Work through it carefully, to make sure you have grasped the significance of all the fast forward points.
Step 11 **Quick quiz**	When you are happy that you have covered the chapter, use the Quick quiz to check how much you have remembered of the topics covered and to practise questions in a variety of formats.
Step 12 **Question(s) in the question bank**	Either at this point, or later when you are thinking about revising, make a full attempt at the Question(s) suggested at the very end of the chapter. You can find these at the end of the Study Text, along with the Answers so you can see how you did.

Short of time: Skim study technique?

You may find you simply do not have the time available to follow all the key study steps for each chapter, however you adapt them for your particular learning style. If this is the case, follow the **skim study** technique below.

- Study the chapters in the order you find them in the Study Text.
- For each chapter:
    - Follow the key study steps 1-2
    - Skim-read through step 4, looking out for the points highlighted in the fast forward boxes (step 4)
    - Jump to step 10
    - Go back to step 5
    - Follow through step 7
    - Prepare outline answers to questions (steps 8/9)
    - Try the Quick quiz (step 11), following up any items you can't answer
    - Do a plan for the Question (step 12), comparing it against our answers
    - You should probably still follow step 6 (note-taking), although you may decide simply to rely on the BPP Leaning Media Passcards for this.

Moving on...

However you study, when you are ready to embark on the practice and revision phase of the BPP Learning Media Effective Study Package, you should still refer back to this Study Text, both as a source of **reference** (you should find the index particularly helpful for this) and as a way to **review** (the Fast forwards, Assessment focus points, Chapter roundups and Quick quizzes help you here).

And remember to keep careful hold of this Study Text – you will find it invaluable in your work.

More advice on Study Skills can be found in BPP Learning Media's **Learning to Learn Accountancy** book.

Learning outcomes and Syllabus

Syllabus overview

This paper is an introduction to management accounting for students with limited knowledge or no knowledge of the management accounting. While this paper focuses on the application of fundamental methods and techniques, students are also expected to have an understanding of when and when not to use them. Students must also appreciate the context of management accounting within an organisation.

Syllabus structure

The syllabus comprises the following topics and study weightings:

A	The context of management accounting	10%
B	Cost identification and behaviour	25%
C	Planning within organisations	30%
D	Accounting control systems	20%
E	Decision making	15%

Assessment strategy

There will be a two hour computer based assessment, comprising 50 compulsory questions, each with one or more parts. In addition, a 15 minute tutorial is available before the start of the assessment to help familiarise yourself with the software and assessment environment.

A variety of objective test question styles and types will be used within the assessment.

Learning outcomes and syllabus content

Learning Outcomes

On completion of their studies students should be able to:

Lead		Component		Level
A. The context of management accounting (10%)				
1	Explain the purpose of management accounting.	(a)	define management accounting;	1
		(b)	explain the importance of cost control and planning within organisations;	2
		(c)	describe how information can be used to identify performance within an organisation;	2
		(d)	explain the differences between financial information requirements for companies, public bodies and society.	2
2	Explain the role of the management accountant.	(a)	explain the role of the management accountant and activities undertaken;	2
		(b)	explain the relationship between the management accountant and the managers being served;	2
		(c)	explain the difference between placing management accounting within the finance function and a business partnering role within an organisation.	2
3	Explain the role of CIMA as a professional body for management accounting.	(a)	explain the background to the formation of CIMA;	2
		(b)	explain the role of CIMA in developing the practice of management accounting.	2

Learning Outcomes

On completion of their studies students should be able to:

Lead		Component		Level
B. Cost identification and behaviour (25%)				
1	Apply methods for identifying cost.	(a)	explain the concept of a direct cost and indirect cost;	2
		(b)	explain why the concept of a "cost" needs to be defined, in order to be meaningful;	2
		(c)	distinguish between the historical cost of an asset and the economic value of an asset to an organisation;	2
		(d)	prepare cost statements for allocation and apportionment of overheads, including reciprocal service departments;	3
		(e)	calculate direct, variable and full costs of products, services and activities using overhead absorption rates to trace indirect costs to cost units;	3
		(f)	apply cost information in pricing decisions.	3

2	Demonstrate cost behaviour.	(a)	explain how costs behave as product, service or activity levels increase or decrease;	2
		(b)	distinguish between fixed, variable and semi-variable costs;	2
		(c)	explain step costs and the importance of time-scales in their treatment as either variable or fixed;	2
		(d)	Calculate the fixed and variable elements of a semi-variable cost.	3

Learning Outcomes

On completion of their studies students should be able to:

Lead			Component	Level
C. Planning within organisations (30%)				
1	Prepare budgetary control statements.	(a)	explain why organisations set out financial plans in the form of budgets, typically for a financial year;	2
		(b)	prepare functional and budgets for capital expenditure and depreciation;	3
		(c)	prepare a master budget based on functional budgets;	3
		(d)	explain budget statements;	2
		(e)	identify the impact of budgeted cash surpluses and shortfalls on business operations;	2
		(f)	prepare a flexible budget;	3
		(g)	calculate budget variances;	3
		(h)	distinguish between fixed and flexible budgets;	2
		(i)	prepare a statement that reconciles budgeted contribution with actual contribution.	3
2	Prepare statements of variance analysis.	(a)	explain the difference between ascertaining costs after the event and planning by establishing standard costs in advance;	2
		(b)	explain why planned standard costs, prices and volumes are useful in setting a benchmark;	2
		(c)	calculate standard costs for the material, labour and variable overhead elements of a cost of a product or service;	3
		(d)	calculate variances for materials, labour, variable overhead, sales prices and sales volumes;	3
		(e)	prepare a statement that reconciles budgeted contribution with actual contribution;	3
		(f)	prepare variance statements.	3

Learning Outcomes
On completion of their studies students should be able to:

Lead		Component		Level
D. Accounting control systems (20%)				
1	Prepare integrated accounts in a costing environment.	(a)	explain the principles of manufacturing accounts and the integration of the cost accounts with the financial accounting system;	2
		(b)	Prepare a set of integrated accounts, showing standard cost variances;	3
		(c)	explain job, batch and process costing;	2
		(d)	prepare ledger accounts for job, batch and process costing system.	3
2	Prepare financial statements for managers.	(a)	prepare financial statements, that inform management;	3
		(b)	distinguish between managerial reports in a range of organisations including commercial enterprises, charities and public sector undertakings.	2

Learning Outcomes
On completion of their studies students should be able to:

Lead		Component		Level
E. Decision making (15%)				
1	Demonstrate the use of break-even analysis in making short-term decisions.	(a)	explain the contribution concept and its use in cost-volume profit (CVP) analysis;	2
		(b)	calculate the breakeven point, profit target, margin of safety and profit/volume ratio for a single product or service;	3
		(c)	prepare breakeven charts and profit/volume graphs for a single product or service.	3
2	Apply basic approaches for use in decision making.	(a)	explain relevant costs and cash flows;	2
		(b)	explain make or buy decisions;	2
		(c)	calculate the profit maximising sales mix using limiting factor analysis.	3
3	Demonstrate the use of investment appraisal techniques in making long-term decisions.	(a)	explain the process of valuing long-term investments;	2
		(b)	calculate the net present value, internal rate of return and payback for an investment.	3

The assessment

Format of computer-based assessment (CBA)

The CBA will not be divided into sections. There will be a total of fifty objective test questions and you will need to answer **ALL** of them in the time allowed.

Candidates **may not** take a calculator into their assessment. Instead, an onscreen calculator will be available in the assessment environment.

Frequently asked questions about CBA

Q   What are the main advantages of CBA?

A
- Assessments can be offered on a continuing basis rather than at six-monthly intervals
- Instant feedback is provided for candidates by displaying their results on the computer screen

Q   Where can I take CBA?

A
- CBA must be taken at a 'CIMA Accredited CBA Centre'. For further information on CBA, you can email CIMA at cba@cimaglobal.com.

Q   How does CBA work?

A
- Questions are displayed on a monitor
- Candidates enter their answers directly onto a computer
- The computer automatically marks the candidate's answers when the candidate has completed the examination
- Candidates are provided with some indicative feedback on areas of weakness if the candidate is unsuccessful

Q   What sort of questions can I expect to find in CBA?

A   Your assessment will consist entirely of a number of different types of **objective test question**. Here are some possible examples.

- **MCQs.** Read through the information on page (xv) about MCQs and how to tackle them.
- **Data entry.** This type of OT requires you to provide figures such as the correct figure for payables in a statement of financial position.
- **Multiple response.** These questions provide you with a number of options and you have to identify those which fulfil certain criteria.

This text provides you with **plenty of opportunities to practise** these various question types. You will find OTs **within each chapter** in the text and the **Quick quizzes** at the end of each chapter are full of them. The Question Bank contains more than one hundred and twenty objective test questions similar to the ones that you are likely to meet in your CBA.

Further information relating to OTs is given on page (xvi).

The **Practice and Revision Kit** for this paper was published in **December 2012** and is **full of OTs**, providing you with vital revision opportunities for the fundamental techniques and skills you will require in the assessment.

Tackling multiple choice questions

In a multiple choice question on your paper, you are given how many **incorrect** options?

A   Two
B   Three
C   Four
D   Five

The correct answer is B.

The MCQs in your assessment contain four possible answers. You have to **choose the option that best answers the question**. The three incorrect options are called distracters. There is a skill in answering MCQs quickly and correctly. By practising MCQs you can develop this skill, giving you a better chance of passing the exam.

You may wish to follow the approach outlined below, or you may prefer to adapt it.

Step 1   **Skim read** all the MCQs and **identify** what appear to be the easier questions.

Step 2   Attempt each question – **starting with the easier questions** identified in Step 1. Read the question thoroughly. You may prefer to work out the answer before looking at the options, or you may prefer to look at the options at the beginning. Adopt the method that works best for you.

Step 3   Read the four options and see if one matches your own answer. **Be careful with numerical questions**, as the distracters are designed to match answers that incorporate common errors. Check that your calculation is correct. Have you followed the requirement exactly? Have you included every stage of the calculation?

Step 4   You may **find that none of the options matches your answer**.

- Re-read the question to ensure that you understand it and are answering the requirement.

- Eliminate any obviously wrong answers.

- Consider which of the remaining answers is the most likely to be correct and select the option.

Step 5   If you are still **unsure** make a note **and continue to the next question**.

Step 6   **Revisit unanswered** questions. When you come back to a question after a break you often find you are able to answer it correctly straight away. If you are still unsure have a guess. You are not penalised for incorrect answers, so **never leave a question unanswered!**

Assessment focus. After extensive practice and revision of MCQs, you may find that you recognise a question when you sit the exam. Be aware that the detail and/or requirement may be different. If the question seems familiar read the requirement and options carefully – do not assume that it is identical.

> BPP Learning Media's i-Pass for this paper provides you with plenty of opportunity for further practice of MCQs.

Tackling objective test questions

The vast majority of the questions in your assessment will be multiple choice questions. However, there may be a small number of objective test questions.

What is an objective test question?

An **OT** is made up of some form of **stimulus**, usually a question, and a **requirement** to do something.

(a) Multiple choice questions

(b) Filling in blanks or completing a sentence

(c) Listing items, in any order or a specified order such as rank order

(d) Stating a definition

(e) Identifying a key issue, term, figure or item

(f) Calculating a specific figure

(g) Completing gaps in a set of data where the relevant numbers can be calculated from the information given

(h) Identifying points/zones/ranges/areas on graphs or diagrams, labelling graphs or filling in lines on a graph

(i) Matching items or statements

(j) Stating whether statements are true or false

(k) Writing brief (in a specified number of words) explanations

(l) Deleting incorrect items

(m) Choosing right words from a number of options

(n) Complete an equation, or define what the symbols used in an equation mean

OT questions in CIMA assessment

CIMA has offered the following **guidance** about OT questions in the assessment.

- Credit may be given for **workings** where you are asked to calculate a specific figure.

- If you **exceed a specified limit on the number of words** you can use in an answer, you will **not be awarded any marks**.

Examples of OTs are included within each chapter, in the **quick quizzes** at the end of each chapter and in the **objective test question bank**.

BPP Learning Media's i-Pass for this paper provides you with plenty of opportunity for further practice of OTs.

International terminology

Your Fundamentals of Management Accounting assessment will use international accounting terms and this text is written in international accounting terms as defined in IAS 1.

It is a good idea to start now getting used to these terms, so the table below provides a list of UK terms with their international equivalents.

UK term	International term
Profit and loss account	Income statement (statement of comprehensive income)
Profit and loss reserve (in balance sheet)	Accumulated profits
Balance sheet	Statement of financial position
Turnover	Revenue
Debtor account	Account receivable
Debtors (eg debtors have increased)	Receivables
Debtor	Customer
Creditor account	Account payable
Creditors (eg creditors have increased)	Payables
Creditor	Supplier
Debtors control account	Receivables control account
Creditors control account	Payables control account
Stock	Inventory
Fixed asset	Non-current asset (generally). Tangible fixed assets are also referred to as 'property, plant and equipment'.
Long term liability	Non-current liability
Provision (eg for depreciation)	Allowance (you will sometimes see 'provision' used too).
Nominal ledger	General ledger
VAT	Sales tax
Debentures	Loan notes
Preference shares/dividends	Preferred shares/dividends
Cash flow statement	Statement of cash flows

Part A
Cost determination and behaviour

Introduction to management accounting

Introduction

Welcome to BPP's Study Text for CIMA's Certificate Paper C01 **Fundamentals of Management Accounting.** This chapter will introduce the **subject of management accounting** and explain what management accounting is and what a **management accountant** does.

We will also cover **management information,** its uses and sources and also why information is different from data. There is also a short section on the background to **CIMA**.

Topic list	Syllabus references
1 What is accounting?	A1(a)
2 What do accountants do?	A1(a), A2(a)
3 Financial accounting versus management accounting	A1 (b)
4 Users of accounting information	A1 (c), (d)
5 The role of the management accountant	A2(a),(b),(c)
6 Management information	A1 (c),(d)
7 Sources and categories of information	A1(d)
8 Accounting bodies	A3(a),(b)

1 What is accounting?

Accounting is the process of collecting, recording, summarising and communicating financial information.
This information is essential to the efficient running of a business. It helps managers to control the use of resources, keep track of the assets and liabilities of the business and plan effectively for the future.

Accounts show where money came from and how it has been spent, this

- **aids** the efficient running of a business
- **indicates** how successfully managers are performing
- **provides information** about the resources and activities of a business

Accounting information **aids** the efficient running of a business in many ways.

(a) A business needs to pay bills for the goods and services it purchases, and collect money from its customers. It must, therefore, keep a record of such bills and invoices so that the correct amounts can be paid or collected at the correct times.

(b) Keeping records of a business's assets (eg its motor vehicles or computers) helps to keep them secure.

Accounts **indicate how successfully** the managers are performing.

Modern businesses are often complicated, they seldom have a single owner (some very large enterprises, such as J Sainsbury, may be owned by millions of shareholders). Frequently the owners are not involved in the day-to-day running of the business but appoint managers to act on their behalf. In addition, there are too many activities and assets for the managers to keep track of simply from personal knowledge and an occasional glance at the bank statement, so accounts which summarise transactions are very useful.

A business should **provide information** about its resources and activities because there are many groups of people who want or need that information.

2 What do accountants do?

Accountants undertake a **wide variety of tasks** and activities within a range of different types of organisations.

We will start this section by taking a look at some of the definitions of the work and the role of management accountants. Specifically the CIMA definition of the role of management accounting and the International Federation of Accountants (IFAC) definitions of the domain and the role of the professional accountant in business.

2.1 CIMA definition of the role of the management accountant

Chartered Management Accountants help organisations establish viable strategies and convert them into profit (in a commercial context) or into value for money (in a not-for-profit context). To achieve this they work as an integral part of multi-skilled management teams in carrying out the:

- Formulation of policy and setting of corporate objectives;

- Formulation of strategic plans derived from corporate objectives;

- Formulation of shorter-term operational plans;

- Acquisition and use of finance;

- Design of systems, recording of events and transactions and management of information systems;

- Generation, communication and interpretation of financial and operating information for management and other stakeholders;

- Provision of specific information and analysis on which decisions are based;

- Monitoring of outcomes against plans and benchmarks, financial and non-financial, quantitative and qualitative, for monitoring and control; and

- Improvement of business systems and processes through risk management and internal audit review.

Through these forward-looking roles and by application of their expert skills management accountants help organisations improve their performance, security, growth and competitiveness in an ever more demanding environment.

CIMA Official Terminology

2.2 IFAC definition of the role of the Professional Accountant in Business

The IFAC definition of the Professional Accountant in Business is:

A Professional Accountant in Business is someone that first meets the standards of a professional, defined as:

- Having skills, knowledge and expertise tested by examination and continuously developed in a structured and monitored context

- Committed to the values of accuracy, honesty, integrity, objectivity, transparency and reliability

- Subject to oversight by a body with disciplinary powers

This is similar to other professionals that achieve accreditation through exam, and maintain expertise via a commitment to on going continuing education.

Second, is recognised as being an accountant, defined as:

Belonging to a recognised accountancy body upholding professional standards and approaches in the discipline of recording, analysing, measuring, reporting, forecasting and giving advice in support of financial, management and strategic decisions.

And third, is in business, defined as:

- Working in an organisational entity of any size and ownership structure, or alone, whether or not operating for profit, other than engaged in external audit

- An integral member of, or support to, the management team striving to create and sustain value for stakeholders

Source IFAC

More than half of the 2.5 million professional accountants who are members of the bodies that make up IFAC work in business. They work in a wide variety of roles including: Internal Control, IT, Business Strategy, Financial Reporting and Risk Management. Many Professional Accountants in Business also have general management responsibilities later in their careers such as CEO, chairman or a non-executive director.

2.3 IFAC definition of the domain of the Professional Accountant in Business

The main activities, which are sometimes referred to collectively as 'management accounting' or 'financial management', can be analysed as:

- The generation or creation of value through the effective use of resources (financial and otherwise) through the understanding of the drivers of stakeholder value (which may include shareholders, customers, employees, suppliers, communities, and government) and organisational innovation

- The provision, analysis and interpretation of information to management for formulation of strategy, planning, decision making and control

- Performance measurement and communication to stakeholders, including the financial recording of transactions and subsequent reporting to stakeholders typically under national or international Generally Accepted Accounting Principles (GAAP)

- Cost determination and financial control, through the use of cost accounting techniques, budgeting and forecasting

- The reduction of waste in resources used in business processes through the use of process analysis and cost management

- Risk management and business assurance

These activities are carried out in different modes including directing, influencing, evaluating and informing. Many of the activities are forward looking in nature and have to deal with ambiguity.

Source IFAC

3 Management accounting versus financial accounting

FAST FORWARD In general terms, **management accounting** is for **internal** reporting whereas **financial accounting** is for **external** reporting.

The management accounting and financial accounting systems in a business both record the same basic data for income and expenditure, but each set of records may analyse the data in a different way. This is because each system has a **different purpose**.

(a)   **Management accounts** are prepared for **internal** managers of an organisation

(b)   **Financial accounts** are prepared for individuals **external** to an organisation eg shareholders, customers, suppliers, tax authorities and employees..

The data used to prepare management accounts and financial accounts is the same. The differences between the management accounts and the financial accounts arise because the data is analysed differently.

Management accounts	Financial accounts
Management accounts are used to aid management record, plan and control the organisation's activities and to help the decision-making process.	Financial accounts detail the performance of an organisation over a defined period and the state of affairs at the end of that period.
There is no legal requirement to prepare management accounts.	In many countries (including the UK), limited companies must, by law, prepare financial accounts.
The format of management accounts is entirely at management discretion: no strict rules govern the way they are prepared or presented. Each organisation can devise its own management accounting system and format of reports.	The format of published financial accounts is determined by law (mainly the Companies Acts), by Statements of Standard Accounting Practice and by Financial Reporting Standards. In principle the accounts of different organisations can therefore be easily compared.
Management accounts can focus on specific areas of an organisation's activities. Information may be produced to aid a decision rather than to be an end product of a decision.	Financial accounts concentrate on the business as a whole, aggregating revenues and costs from different operations, and are an end in themselves.
Management accounts incorporate non-monetary measures. Management may need to know, for example, tonnes of aluminium produced, monthly machine hours, or miles travelled by sales representatives.	Most financial accounting information is of a monetary nature.
Management accounts are both a historical record and a future planning tool.	Financial accounts present an essentially historical picture of past operations.

 Question

Information is provided for the use of managers within an organisation by: (tick one)

☐ **Financial accounting systems**

☐ **Management accounting systems**

Answer

☑ **Management accounting systems**

Financial accounting systems provide information to **external** users.

The **management accountant** is closer to the policy making and management process than the financial accountant. This is because the management accountant is not primarily interested in reporting to interested parties external to the organisation. After all, the requirements of external users of accounts may be different from those involved in managing and running the business in several respects.

- Aggregation of information
- Classification of data
- Level of detail
- The period covered

Internally, accountants therefore provide information for **planning, decision-making and controlling** the business.

Examples include:

- Competitors' performance
- Cost/profit centre performance
- Desirability of investments
- Past cost information

- Product profitability
- Sensitivity analysis
- Alternative options

The accountant provides information essential for the current management and decision-making of the business. If decisions are assessed in accounting terms, even in part, then the accountant will be involved in them. Accountants assess the future financial consequences of certain decisions.

Some of the information used for these decision may not be monetary. As mentioned in the table above, management accountants may need to collect and analyse non-monetary information in order to provide the decision support information. This could include information about staff competence and training needs, quality of raw material, competitors actions, customer satisfaction levels, etc.

4 Users of accounting information

FAST FORWARD

Accounting information is required for a wide range of users both within and outside the business.

The following people might be interested in financial information about a large public company.

User group	Comment
Managers of the company	People appointed by the company's owners to supervise the daily activities of the company need information about the company's current and expected future financial situation, to make **planning decisions**.
Shareholders of the company, ie the company's owners	Want to assess how effectively management is performing and how much profit they can withdraw from the business for their own use.
Trade contacts, ie suppliers of goods to the company on credit and customers	Suppliers want to know about the company's **ability** to **pay its debts**; customers need to know that the company is a secure source of supply and is in no danger of closing down.
Providers of finance to the company, ie lenders both short and long term	Lenders will want to ensure that the company is able to meet **interest payments**, and eventually to repay the amounts advanced.
The tax authorities	Want to know about business profits in order to **assess** the tax payable by the company.
Employees	Need to know about the company's financial situation because their **future** careers and the level of their wages and salaries depend on it.
Financial analysts and advisers	Need information for their clients. For example, stockbrokers need information to advise investors, credit agencies want information to advise potential suppliers of goods to the company, journalists need information for their reading public.
Government and their agencies	Interested in the allocation of resources and in the activities of enterprises. Also require information in order to provide a basis for national statistics.
The public	Want information because enterprises affect them in many ways, eg by providing jobs and using local suppliers, or by affecting the environment (eg pollution).

The following people might be interested in financial information about a public body or non governmental organisation.

User group	Comment
Managers of the organisation	People appointed by the Board or other governance structure to supervise the daily activities of the organisation need information about the current and expected future financial situation, to make **planning decisions**.
Funders (individuals, Trusts, government agencies, taxpayers etc)	Want to assess how effectively management is performing and how much value for money is being achieved.
Partner organisations, ie companies, charities,	Partners and suppliers want to know about the organisation's **ability** to **pay its debts**; commissioning agancies need to know that the company is a secure source of supply and is in no danger of closing down.
The governing bodies	Charities commission, Central government departments,
Employees	Need to know about the organisation's financial situation because their **future** careers and the level of their wages and salaries depend on it.
The public	Want information because the organisations affect them in many ways, eg by providing services to vulnerable groups, providing jobs and using local suppliers, or by affecting legislation, government spending, local services, the environment etc.
Government and their agencies	Interested in the allocation of resources and funding to organisations and in their activities. Also require information in order to provide a basis for national statistics, policy and operational planning.
Beneficiaries	Local residents will be interested in the services provided by their council, the beneficiaries of charities will be interested in the effectiveness of the interventions of a charity, even though they are not necessarily the people who pay for those services.

Question

Accounting information

It is easy to see how 'internal' people get hold of accounting information. A manager, for example, can ask the accounts department to prepare whatever accounting statements he needs. But external users of accounts cannot do this. How, in practice, can a business contact or a financial analyst access accounting information about a company?

Answer

Limited liability companies (though not other forms of business such as partnerships) are required to make certain accounting information public. They send copies of the required information to the Registrar of Companies at Companies House. The information filed at Companies House is available, at a fee, to any member of the public who asks for it. Other sources include financial comment in the press and company brochures.

5 The role of the management accountant

FAST FORWARD

The management accountant plays a critical role in providing information to management to assist in **planning, decision making and control.**

(a) **Planning**

    (i)   The finance function draws up **budgets** which direct and allocate resources.

    (ii)   The finance function also produces **forecasts** of anticipated future results.

(b) **Decision making**. The finance function is often involved in assessing and modelling the expenditure and cash flow implications of proposed decisions.

(c) **Control**

    (i)   **Budgets are also used to monitor performance.** The finance function regularly provides information comparing budgeted revenues and costs for a period, with **actual results** and with comparisons from previous months.

    (ii)   **Management accountants** are involved in assessing the contribution which products, services, processes and other operations make to overall profitability.

    (iii) **Costing based on predetermined standards** provides the information which enables managers to identify weaknesses and look for remedies all in a timely manner.

The success of management accountants in meeting their job objectives will depend upon two things.

- The **quality of the information** they provide
- Whether the information they provide to other managers is used properly

5.1 Cost accounting

Management accounting has its roots in cost accounting.

FAST FORWARD

Cost accounting is a management information system which analyses past, present and future data to provide the basis for managerial action.

5.2 The cost accountant

Who can provide the answers to the following questions?

- What was the cost of goods produced or services provided last period?
- What was the cost of operating a department last month?
- What revenues were earned last week?

Yes, you've guessed it, the cost accountant.

Knowing about costs incurred or revenues earned enables management to do the following.

(a) **Assess the profitability of a product**, a service, a department, or the whole organisation.

(b) Perhaps, **set selling prices** with some regard for the costs of sale.

(c) **Put a value on inventory** (raw materials, work in progress, finished goods) that are still held in store at the end of a period, for preparing a statement of financial position showing of the company's assets and liabilities.

That was quite easy. But who could answer the following questions?

(a) What are the future costs of goods and services likely to be?

(b)   How do actual costs compare with planned costs?

(c)   What information does management need in order to make sensible decisions about profits and costs?

Well, you may be surprised, but again it is the cost accountant.

5.3 Cost accounting and management accounting

FAST FORWARD

Management accounting, and nowadays **cost accounting**, provide management information for **planning**, **control** and **decision-making** purposes.

Originally cost accounting did deal with ways of accumulating historical costs and of charging these costs to units of output, or to departments, in order to establish inventory valuations, profits and statement of financial position items. It has since been extended into **planning**, **control** and **decision making**, so that the cost accountant is now able to answer the second set of questions. In today's modern industrial environment, the role of cost accounting in the provision of management information is therefore almost indistinguishable from that of management accounting, which is basically concerned with the **provision of information to assist management** with **planning**, **control** and **decision making**.

Key term

> **Cost accounting** is the 'gathering of cost information and its attachment to cost objects, the establishment of budgets, standard costs and actual costs of operations, processes, activities or products; and the analysis of variances, profitability or the social use of funds'.
> CIMA *Official Terminology*

Key term

> **Management accounting** is the application of the principles of accounting and financial management to create, protect, preserve and increase value for the stakeholders of for-profit and not-for-profit enterprises in the public and private sectors.
> Management accounting is an integral part of management. It requires the identification, generation, presentation, interpretation and use of relevant information to:
> - Inform strategic decisions and formulate business strategy
> - Plan long, medium and short-run operations
> - Determine capital structure and fund that structure
> - Design reward strategies for executives and shareholders
> - Inform operational decisions
> - Control operations and ensure the efficient use of resources
> - Measure and report financial and non-financial performance to management and other stakeholders
> - Safeguard tangible and intangible assets
> - Implement corporate governance procedures, risk management and internal policies   CIMA *Official Terminology*

So, as you can see, the management or cost accountant has his or her hands full! Don't worry about the terms mentioned in CIMA's definition – all will become clearer as you work through this Study Text.

5.4 Cost accounting systems

The managers of a business have the responsibility of planning and controlling the resources used. To carry out this task effectively they must be provided with **sufficiently accurate** and **detailed information**, and the cost accounting system should provide this. Indeed a costing system is the **basis of an organisation's internal financial information system for managers**.

Cost accounting systems are **not restricted to manufacturing operations**.

(a)   Cost accounting information is also used in service industries, government departments and welfare organisations.

(b)   Within a manufacturing organisation, the cost accounting system should be applied not only to manufacturing operations but also to administration, selling and distribution, research and development and so on.

Cost accounting is concerned with **providing information to assist** the following.

- **Establishing inventory valuations, profits and statement of financial position** items
- **Planning** (for example the provision of forecast costs at different activity levels)
- **Control** (such as the provision of actual and standard costs for comparison purposes)
- **Decision making** (for example, the provision of information about actual unit costs for the period just ended for pricing decisions).

5.5 The changing role of management accounting

Management accounting is now increasingly seen as a **support for management** by providing information for planning, control and decision-making rather than part of the finance function.

As you have seen earlier, the goals of management accounting information are quite different from those of financial accounting information.

In the past, management accountants have been able to successfully produce management accounting information using the general ledger system of financial accounting. This combination of management accounting and financial accounting information systems works as far as the goal of management accounting is strictly to track **cost information**.

However, changes in **organisational focus**, caused by factors such as **increased competition** in a worldwide market, mean that many organisations are competing on issues of quality and timeliness, as well as cost. This has led to a new role type in which the accountant acts more in an advisory capacity, integral to managerial decision-making, rather than solely as a provider of information.

The **current role** of the management accounting function is seen developing cost, quality and time-based information that **supports the management process** and seeks to **add value** to an organisation. As the management accountant is collecting so much information, there is an expectation that they may be the first one to notice an issue and it will be their responsibility to raise the issue with management.

5.5.1 Decision making and information

Decision-making operates at three levels in an organisation.

- Operational
- Management
- Strategic

The **strategic level** involves developing organisational goals and objectives and will require information as and when required. The information will be unstructured, forward looking and externally focussed.

The **management level** is concerned with implementing the strategy set from above, it involves monitoring resources and their effective and efficient use. These activities follow a regular pattern and require periodic information such as weekly, monthly or quarterly.

The **operational level** involves ensuring that specific tasks or activities are being carried out in an efficient and effective way. Operational information is required in real time so that issues are known as they arise and not at the end of a period. Operational information will be detailed, structured, numerical and internally focussed.

5.5.2 Management accounting as an aid to decision making

All **decision makers** in the organisation must understand how to use good management accounting information. Management accounting is also being significantly affected by dramatic improvements in computer technology. Current technology allows management to track performance information that goes beyond the cost-based information of historic general ledger systems. Good management accounting involves a responsibility to manage a wide variety of critical information.

Along with this new type of role, it is also predicted that the accountant's working methods will change, in particular with an increased emphasis on working **outside the finance function** and working in cross-functional teams.

Despite the consensus as to the broad change in the nature of the management accountant's role, studies have indicated that its translation into practice has so far been limited. Traditional responsibilities such as calculating variances, costing and budget preparation remain dominant in terms of demands on accountants' time.

There is a problem that it is **very difficult** to use the traditional financial reporting systems to track performance regarding quality and time. Information systems, specifically database systems, have progressed significantly in recent years so that it is possible for organisations to track just about any kind of information. Management accountants are required to organise the immense amount of data held and present it to managers so that it can be provided to support decision making. There is a balance to be struck between giving enough information to support decisions and overloading managers and executives with **unnecessary detail**.

Question   Good management information

Strategic planning is carried out by front-line managers.

☐ True

☐ False

Answer

☑ False

Strategic planning is carried out by senior management. Front line managers will be concerned with **operational planning**.

---

6 Management information

FAST FORWARD The purpose of **management information** is to help managers to manage resources efficiently and effectively, by planning and controlling operations and by allowing informed **decision-making**.

6.1 Introduction

Management is the term used for the people in charge of running a business (managers) or other organisation.

Management information can therefore be described as information that is given to the people who are in charge of running an organisation.

As we saw earlier, one of the main users of financial information are the managers of the company. In order to manage their resources, managers in any organisation need to know on a regular basis how their particular department or section is performing. They will also wish to know whether activities are going as planned and whether any problems have arisen.

The information required by a manager will vary according to the nature of the organisation and their individual responsibilities. Look at the following examples.

(a)   Senior management will usually be interested in the financial statements (statement of financial position and income statement), on a monthly basis.

(b)   A supervisor in a large factory may want a daily output report for every production shift.

(c)   A sales manager may want a weekly report of orders achieved by the sales team.

Management information is used for a wide variety of purposes. In a management accounting context, **planning**, **control** and **decision making** activities include:

*   Pricing
*   Valuing inventory
*   Assessing profitability
*   Deciding on the purchase of capital assets

In the present business environment where the rate of change is increasing, good management information systems are seen by many as the key to success. Although such systems give a basis for improved management decisions they do not guarantee good management. Poor information, however, is likely to reduce a manager's chances of success.

Key term	**Management information** is information supplied to managers for the purposes of planning, control and decision making.

Question
Helping management

The management accountant compares the profitability of two products, P and Q, and concludes that P is the best product to make. He writes a report of his findings for the board of directors. This report will primarily aid management in

A   Decision-making
B   Planning
C   Controlling
D   Implementing

Answer

A   A decision can be made as to which product should be made using this information.

Assessment focus point	You need to make sure that you understand the role of management and the purpose of management information.

7 Sources and categories of information

FAST FORWARD ▶▶   Raw **data** may be processed to produce meaningful **information**.

7.1 What is data?

Key term

> **Data** is a 'scientific' term for facts, figures, and measurements. Data are the raw materials for data processing.

Examples of data include the following.

- The number of tourists who visit Hong Kong each year
- The sales turnovers of all restaurants in Zambia
- The number of people who pass their driving test each year

Note that these examples are just collections of numbers which may not be particularly useful to the person who wants to use them. In order to be useful the data may have to be processed in some way. For example a French travel agent may be interested in the number of French tourists who visit Hong Kong each year. The data which contains all tourists would have to be analysed to obtain the number of French tourists. The analysed data is known as information because it is now meaningful to the person who wants to use it.

7.2 What is information?

Key term

> **Information** is data that has been processed in such a way as to be meaningful to the person who receives it. Information is anything that is communicated.

Information is sometimes referred to as processed data. The terms 'information' and 'data' are often used interchangeably. Let us consider the following situation in which data is **collected** and then **processed** in order to produce meaningful information.

Many companies providing a product or service research consumer opinion to ensure they provide what customers and potential customers want and will buy. A typical market research survey employs a number of researchers who request a sample of the public to answer questions relating to the product. Several hundred questionnaires may be completed. The questionnaires are usually input into a computer system for analysis.

Individually, a completed questionnaire would not tell the company very much, only the views of one consumer. In this case, the individual questionnaires are **data**. Once they have been processed, and analysed, the resulting report is **information**. The people who run the business can consider the report and use the information to make decisions regarding the product, such as whether to improve it or scrap it.

To run a business successfully depends upon making the right decisions. Information is vital to enable good decisions to be made. Examples of the some of the questions that management might wish to have answers to include:

- How much does it cost to produce the product(s) or service(s) they supply.
- How many product(s)/service(s) they sold last month.
- How much was spent on wages last year.
- How many staff the company currently employs.

Management information is often classified into two types:

- Financial information (measured in terms of money)
- Non-financial information (not measured in terms of money)

7.3 Management information

Management information reports might show the following.

- Comparisons between planned results (budgets) and actual results
- Year-to-date (cumulative information)
- Comparison of company results and competitor results
- Comparison between current year and previous year's results
- The profitability of a product or service or the whole organisation
- The value of inventories that are still held in store at the end of a period

7.4 The qualities of good information

FAST FORWARD

Good management information should be:

Accurate
Complete
Cost-beneficial
User-targeted
Relevant
Authoritative
Timely
Easy to use

Good management information helps managers makes informed decisions. The **qualities of good information** are outlined below in the form of a mnemonic 'accurate'.

Quality		Example
A	ccurate	Figures should **add up**, the degree of **rounding** should be appropriate, there should be **no mistakes**.
C	omplete	Information should include all relevant information – information that is correct but excludes something important is likely to be of little value. For example external data or comparative information may be required.
C	ost-beneficial	It should not **cost more** to obtain the information than the **benefit** derived from having it.
U	ser-targeted	The **needs of the user** should be borne in mind, for instance senior managers may require summaries.
R	elevant	Information that is **not relevant** should be omitted.
A	uthoritative	The **source** of the information should be reputable and reliable.
T	imely	The information should be available **when it is needed**.
E	asy to use	Information should be **clearly presented**, **not excessively long**, and sent using the **right communication channel** (e-mail, telephone, intranet, hard-copy report etc).

7.5 Internal information

Data and information come from sources both inside and outside an organisation. An information system should be designed so as to obtain - or **capture** - relevant information from whatever source. Capturing data/information from **inside** the organisation involves the following.

(a)   A **system** for collecting and/or measuring **transaction** data - for example sales, purchases, inventory turnover etc.

(b)   **Informal communication** of information between **managers and staff** (for example, by word-of-mouth or at meetings).

(c)   **Communication** between staff at all levels.

7.6 Internal data sources

FAST FORWARD

There are many **sources** of information (both internal and external) including accounting records, websites, staff, the staff of competitors, the government, the media and many others.

The accounting records include receivables ledgers, payables ledgers, general ledgers, cash books etc. These hold information that may be of great value outside the accounts department, for example, sales information for the **marketing** function.

To maintain the integrity of its accounting records, an organisation requires **controls** over transactions. These also give rise to valuable information. An inventory control system for example will include details of purchase orders, goods received notes, goods returned notes and so on, which can be analysed to provide management information about speed of delivery, say, or the quality of supplies.

Organisations record information to enable them to carry out operations and administrative functions.

(a)   Information about **personnel** will be held, possibly linked to the **payroll** system. Additional information may be obtained from this source if, say, a project is being costed and it is necessary to ascertain the availability and rate of pay of different levels of staff, or the need for and cost of recruiting staff from outside the organisation.

(b)   Much information will be produced by a **production** department about machine capacity, fuel consumption, movement of people, materials, and work in progress, set up times, maintenance requirements and so on.

(c)   Many **service** businesses, notably accountants and solicitors, need to keep detailed records of the **time spent** on various activities, both to justify fees to clients and to assess the efficiency and profitability of operations.

Staff themselves are one of the primary sources of internal information. Information may be obtained either informally in the course of day-to-day business or through meetings, interviews or questionnaires.

7.7 External information

Capturing information from **outside** the organisation might be a **routine** task entrusted to particular individuals, or might be collected on an 'informal' **non-routine** basis.

Routine formal collection of data from outside sources includes the following.

(a)   A company's **tax specialists** will be expected to gather information about changes in tax law and how this will affect the company.

(b)   Obtaining information about any new legislation on health and safety at work, or employment regulations, must be obtained - for example by the company's **legal expert** or **company secretary** - who must then pass on the information to other managers affected by it.

(c)   Research and development (R & D) work often relies on information about other R & D work being done by another organisation.

(d) **Marketing managers** need to know the attitudes and opinions of current and potential customers. To obtain this information, they might carry out market research exercises.

Non-routine, informal gathering of information from the environment **goes on all the time, both consciously and unconsciously.** For example, employees are exposed to newspapers, television reports, websites, meetings with business associates and trade publications.

7.8 External data sources

An organisation's files (paper and/or computerised) include information from external sources - such as invoices, e-mails, letters, advertisements and so on **received from customers and suppliers**. Sometimes additional external information is required – meaning an active search outside the organisation is necessary. The following sources may be identified.

(a) The government.

(b) Advice or information bureaux.

(c) Consultancies of all sorts.

(d) Newspaper and magazine publishers.

(e) There may be specific reference works which are used in a particular line of work.

(f) Libraries and information services.

(g) Increasingly businesses can use each other's systems as sources of information, for instance via electronic data interchange (EDI).

(h) Electronic sources of information are becoming ever more important, for example companies like **Reuters** offer access to a range of business related information.

(i) Many information provision services are now provided via the **Internet**. As the rate of Internet use increases, greater numbers of people and organisations are using it to source information on a vast range of topics.

Assessment focus point | Internal and external sources of information could easily be examined in a MCQ.

Question
Good management information

Good management information is

A   Relevant, regular and reliable
B   Timely, regular and sufficient
C   Reliable, timely and relevant
D   Relevant, convenient and material

Answer

C provides the most appropriate description

8 Accounting bodies

8.1 Professional accountancy bodies

FAST FORWARD

The global organisation for the accountancy profession is **IFAC**, the International Federation of Accountants.

IFAC is has 167 members and associates in 127 countries and jurisdictions. It represents about 2.5 million accountants across the public and private sectors. Some of the main accounting bodies operating in the UK are:

ACCA – The Association of Chartered Certified Accountants

CIPFA – The Chartered Institute of Public Finance and Accountancy

ICAEW – The Institute of Chartered Accountants in England and Wales

ICAS – The Institute of Chartered Accountants of Scotland

CIMA – The Chartered Institute of Management Accountants

These institutes were founding members of IFAC when it was established in 1977

FAST FORWARD

CIMA is a **global accounting body** which regulates its members in order to comply with best practice and to protect the public.

CIMA is global accounting body based in the UK. It is the world's largest professional body of management accountants. It has over 183,000 members and students in 168 countries.

8.2 The history of CIMA

CIMA was founded in 1919 as The Institute of Cost and Works Accountants (ICWA). It specialised in the development of accounting techniques for use in the internal control of manufacturing, service and public sector operations. It developed a position as the leading professional body in the areas of product costing, budgeting, management accounting, investment appraisal and business decision making.

The institute changed its name from ICWA to the Institute of Cost and Management Accountants (ICMA) in 1972 and subsequently to the Chartered Institute of Management Accountants (CIMA) in 1986, after the granting of a Royal Charter in 1975.

CIMA has played a role in founding other professional accounting bodies such as the Institute of Cost and Management Accountants of Pakistan, The Institute of Cost and Management Accountants of Bangladesh, Institute of Cost and Works Accountants of India and the Institute of Management Accountants (USA).

8.3 CIMA and the profession of management accounting

CIMA is recognised as a professional accounting body for various statutory purposes by UK and various overseas governments. The institute regulates the activities of its members by a code of practice, a discipline committee and a continuing education scheme. CIMA are committed to upholding the ethical and professional standards and to maintaining public confidence in management accounting.

CIMA regulates its members to ensure compliance with best practice and to protect the public. CIMA itself is overseen by a number of external regulators to ensure all students and members are working to the highest set of standards and ethical behaviour.

It is the responsibility of each student and member to ensure that they comply with both CIMA's regulations and any specific regulations and legislation as required by their country of residence. CIMA's professional standards and conduct department works towards upholding regulatory compliance and best practice by CIMA members.

Members and students must uphold the Code of Ethics and refrain from any conduct which might discredit the profession. They must have regard to these guidelines irrespective of their field of activity, their contract of employment or of any other professional memberships they may hold.

According to its Code of Ethics, CIMA's 5 fundamental ethical principles are:

Integrity – to be straightforward and honest in all professional and business relationships.

Objectivity – to not allow bias, conflict of interest or undue influence of others to override professional or business judgments.

Professional Competence and Due Care – to maintain professional knowledge and skill at the level required to ensure that a client or employer receives competent professional services based on current developments in practice, legislation and techniques and act diligently and in accordance with applicable technical and professional standards.

Confidentiality – to respect the confidentiality of information acquired as a result of professional and business relationships and, therefore, not disclose any such information to third parties without proper and specific authority, unless there is a legal or professional right or duty to disclose, nor use the information for the personal advantage of the professional accountant or third parties.

Professional Behavior – to comply with relevant laws and regulations and avoid any action that discredits the profession.

Chapter Roundup

- Accounting is the process of collecting, recording, summarising and communicating financial information.

- This information is essential to the efficient running of a business. It helps managers to control the use of resources, keep track of the assets and liabilities of the business and plan effectively for the future.

- Accountants undertake a wide variety of tasks and activities within a range of different types of organisations.

- In general terms, **management accounting** is for **internal** reporting whereas **financial accounting** is for **external** reporting.

- Accounting information is required for a wide range of users both within and outside the business.

- The management accountant plays a critical role in providing information to management to assist in planning, decision making and control.

- **Cost accounting** is a management information system which analyses past, present and future data to provide the basis for managerial action.

- **Management accounting**, and nowadays **cost accounting**, provide management information for **planning**, **control** and **decision-making** purposes.

- Management accounting is now increasingly seen as a **support for management** by providing information for planning, control and decision-making rather than part of the finance function.

- The purpose of **management information** is to help managers to manage resources efficiently and effectively, by planning and controlling operations and by allowing informed **decision-making**

- Raw **data** may be processed to produce meaningful **information**.

- Good management information should be:

    Accurate
    Complete
    Cost-beneficial
    User-targeted
    Relevant
    Authoritative
    Timely
    Easy to use

- There are many **sources** of information (both internal and external) including accounting records, websites, staff, the staff of competitors, the government, the media and many others.

- The global organisation for the accountancy profession is **IFAC**, the International Federation of Accountants.

- CIMA is a **global accounting body** which regulates its members in order to comply with best practice and to protect the public.

1   In general terms, financial accounting is for internal reporting whereas cost accounting is for external reporting.

    True ☐

    False ☐

2   Two statements follow about information:

    1.   Information is the scientific term for facts, figures and processing.

    2.   Management information is information that is given to the people who are in charge of running an organisation.

    Are the above statements true or false?

    A   Both statements are true
    B   Both statements are false
    C   Statement 1 is false but statement 2 is true
    D   Statement 1 is true but statement 2 is false

3   Which one of the following is not usually considered to be one of the purposes of management information?

    A   Implementing
    B   Planning
    C   Control
    D   Decision making

4   What is the main factor to consider when designing a management report?

    A   The needs of the user
    B   The length of the report
    C   Confidentiality
    D   Neat handwriting

5   Which one of the following 'qualities of information' does not appear in the mnemonic 'accurate'?

    A   Accurate
    B   Communication
    C   Complete
    D   User-targeted

6   Which one of the following sources of information would usually be an internal source of information for a business?

    A   The government
    B   Tax consultants
    C   The internet
    D   The receivables ledger

7   *Fill in the gaps*

    Management accounting is increasing being viewed as supporting .... rather than being part of the .... function.

8   **Data** which has been processed in such a way as to be meaningful is referred to as ☐

9   Management information is used for **planning**, **control** and ....

10   Non-financial information is relevant to management accounting

☐✓   True

☐   False

Answers to Quick Quiz

1   False. Cost accounting is mainly concerned with the preparation of management accounts for **internal** managers of an organisation. Financial accounts are prepared for individuals **external** to an organisation eg shareholders, customers and so on.

2   C   Statement 1 is false. It is **data** which is the term for facts, figures and processing. Statement 2 is true.

3   A   Implementing. The purpose of management information is to help managers to manage resources efficiently and effectively by planning and controlling operations and by allowing informed decision making.

4   A   The needs of the user. When considering the needs of the user you may also want to consider the length of the report and confidentiality but the first consideration should be the user's needs.

5   B   Communication. Communication is not a 'quality of information'. It is worth memorising the mnemonic for the exam.

6   D   The receivables ledger. The question says 'usually' because a tax specialist company would probably not need to use external tax consultants so their source of tax information would be internal.

7   Management accounting is increasing being viewed as supporting **management** rather than being part of the **finance** function.

8   Information

9   Decision making

10   ☑   True

    The management accountant may frequently have to take into account non-financial information.

Now try the questions below from the Question Bank

Question numbers
1–5

BPP
LEARNING MEDIA

Introduction to costing and performance measurement

Introduction

We will now turn our attention to **costs** and consider what cost actually is! We'll then look at some of the ways in which costs can be **classified** to assist the work of the cost accountant. Terms and concepts you encounter in these sections of the chapter are vitally important and will appear throughout this text and indeed all stages of your studies.

We will also consider some basic performance measures and the impact of **environmental and social concerns** on management accounting.

Topic list	Syllabus references
1 Some cost accounting concepts	A1(b)
2 The concept of cost	A1(b), B1(a),(b),(c)
3 Cost classification	B1(a)
4 Cost classification for inventory valuation and profit measurement	B1(a)
5 Cost classification for control	A1(c)
6 Performance measurement	A1(c)
7 Shareholder value and environmental and social concerns	A1(d)

1 Some cost accounting concepts

1.1 Functions and departments

An organisation, whether it is a manufacturing company, a provider of services (such as a bank or a hotel) or a public sector organisation (such as a hospital), may be divided into a number of different **functions** within which there are a number of **departments**. A manufacturing organisation might be structured as follows.

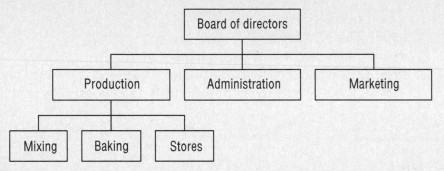

Suppose the organisation above produces chocolate cakes for a number of supermarket chains. The production function is involved with the making of the cakes, the administration department with the preparation of accounts and the employment of staff and the marketing department with the selling and distribution of the cakes.

Within the production function there are three departments, two of which are production departments (the mixing department and the baking department) which are actively involved in the production of the cakes and one of which is a service department (stores department) which provides a service or back-up to the production departments.

1.2 Cost objects

FAST FORWARD

If the users of accounting information want to know the cost of something, that something is called a **cost object**.

Examples of cost objects include:

- A product
- A service to a hotel guest
- A sales territory

Key term

> A **cost object** is 'for example a product, service, centre, activity, customer or distribution channel in relation to which costs are ascertained'.
> CIMA *Official Terminology*

In our example, cost objects include:

- Chocolate cakes
- The provision of supply to one of the supermarkets
- The administration department

1.3 Cost centres

Cost centres are collecting places for costs before they are further analysed.

In general, for cost accounting purposes, departments are termed **cost centres** and the product produced by an organisation is termed the **cost unit**. In our example, the cost centres of the production function could be the mixing department, the baking department and the stores department and the organisation's cost unit could be one chocolate cake.

When costs are incurred, they are generally allocated to a **cost centre**. Cost centres may include the following.

- A **department** (as in our example above)
- A **machine** or group of machines
- A **project** (eg the installation of a new computer system)
- A **new product** (to enable the costs of development and production to be identified)
- A **person** (eg a marketing director. Costs might include salary, company car and other expenses incurred by the director)

Assessment focus point

A typical objective testing (OT) question on the contents of this chapter might be to ask you to select appropriate cost centres from a number of suggestions for a particular organisation.

1.4 Cost units

Cost units are the **basic control units** for costing purposes.

Key term

A **cost unit** is a 'unit of product or service in relation to which costs are ascertained'.   CIMA *Official Terminology*

Once costs have been traced to cost centres, they can be further analysed in order to establish a **cost per cost unit**. Alternatively, some items of costs may be charged directly to a cost unit, for example direct materials and direct labour costs, which you will meet later in this text.

Different organisations use different cost units. Here are some suggestions.

Organisation	Possible cost unit
Steelworks	Tonne of steel produced Tonne of coke used
Hospital	Patient/day Operation Out-patient visit
Freight organisation	Tonne/kilometre
Passenger transport organisation	Passenger/kilometre
Accounting firm	Audit performed Chargeable hour
Restaurant	Meal served

Note that cost units can be tangible or non-tangible. Tangible cost units can be seen and touched, for example, a meal served. A chargeable hour is intangible.

1.5 Composite cost units

Notice that some of the cost units in this table are made up of **two parts**. For example the patient/day cost unit for the hospital. These two-part cost units are known as **composite cost units** and they are used most often in service organisations.

Composite cost units help to improve cost control. For example the measure of 'cost per patient' **might not be particularly useful for control purposes**. The cost per patient will vary depending on the length of the patient's stay, therefore monitoring costs using this basis would be difficult.

The cost per patient/day is not affected by the length of the individual patient's stay. Therefore it would be more useful for **monitoring and controlling costs**. Similarly, in a freight organisation the **cost per tonne/kilometre** (the cost of carrying one tonne for one kilometre) would be more meaningful for control than the cost per tonne carried, which would vary with the distance travelled.

| Question | Cost centres and cost units |

Identify the following as suitable cost centres or cost units for a hospital.

- Ward
- Operating theatre
- Bed/night
- Patient/day
- Outpatient visit
- Operating theatre hour

| Answer |

Cost unit	Cost Centre
Bed/night	Ward
Patient/day	Operating theatre
Operating theatre hour	
Outpatient visit	

2 The concept of cost

2.1 Cost measurement

FAST FORWARD

In practice most cost accounting transactions are recorded at **historic cost**, but costs can be measured in terms of **economic cost**.

Cost accounting transactions, indeed all accounting transactions, can be measured (or valued) on numerous bases. For example:

(a) Cost accounts kept on a historical cost basis use original/past values (i.e. the price that was paid).

(b) Cost accounts kept on a current cost basis use up-to-date market values.

Transactions can also be recorded at **economic cost**.

2.1.1 Economic cost

Economic cost, also referred to as **opportunity cost**, is the value of the best alternative course of action that was not chosen. In other words, it is **what could have been accomplished with the resources used in the course of action not chosen**. It represents opportunities forgone.

If a person has a job offer that pays $25 for an hour's work, and instead chooses to take a nap for an hour, the historical cost of the nap is zero; the person did not hand over any money in order to nap. The economic cost of the nap is the $25 that could have been earned working.

In practice **most cost accounting systems use historical cost as a measurement basis**.

2.2 Economic value

FAST FORWARD

Economic value is the amount someone is willing to pay.

The economic value of a particular item, for example a kilogram of rice, is measured by the maximum amount of other things that a person is willing to give up to have that kilogram of rice. If we simplify our example 'economy' so that the person only has two goods to choose from, rice and pasta, the value of a kilogram of rice would be measured by the amount of pasta that the person is willing to give up to have one more kilogram of rice.

Economic value is therefore measured by **the most someone is willing to give up in other products and services in order to obtain a product or service**. Dollars (or some other currency) are a universally accepted measure of economic value in many markets, because the number of **dollars** that a person is willing to pay for something tells how much of all other goods and services they are willing to give up to get that item. This is often referred to as 'willingness to pay'.

2.3 Qualifying the concept of cost

Key term

As a noun, **cost** is 'The amount of cash or cash equivalent paid ....'
As a verb, cost is 'To ascertain the cost of a specified thing or activity.
The word *cost* can rarely stand alone and should be qualified as to its nature and limitations.'

CIMA *Official Terminology*

Costs need to be **qualified or classified in some way** so that they can be **arranged into logical groups** in order to **facilitate** an efficient **system for collecting and analysing costs**.

As you work through this text you will encounter many different types of cost, each of which has its usefulness and limitations in various circumstances.

3 Cost classification

FAST FORWARD Before the cost accountant can plan, control or make decisions, all costs (whether labour, material or overheads) must be accurately **classified** and their destination in the costing system (cost units because they are direct costs or cost centres because they are indirect costs).

Key term | **Cost classification** is the 'arrangement of elements of cost into logical groups with respect to their nature (fixed, variable, value adding), function (production, selling) or use in the business of the entity'. CIMA *Official Terminology*

FAST FORWARD **Classification** can be by **nature (subjective)**, by **purpose (objective)**, by **behaviour** or by **responsibility**.

3.1 Classification by nature

Subjective classification of expenditure indicates the **nature** of the expenditure.

- Material
- Labour
- Expense

Each grouping may be subdivided. For example the materials classification may be subdivided into:

- Raw materials
- Components
- Consumables
- Maintenance materials such as spare parts

3.2 Classification by purpose

Objective classification of expenditure indicates the **purpose** of the expenditure, the reason why the expenditure has taken place, which might be for:

- Inventory valuation and profit measurement
- Decision making
- Control

We'll be looking at objective classification in the next few sections.

3.3 Classification by behaviour

Cost behaviour is the way in which a cost changes as activity level changes. Some costs are not affected by the level of activity and are known as **fixed costs**, other costs are affected by the level of activity and are known as **variable costs**. Chapter 3 covers cost behaviour at more length.

3.4 Classification by responsibility

Responsibility classification indicates who is responsible for the expenditure, and so is linked with objective classification for control. We'll look at this in detail in Section 5.

4 Cost classification for inventory valuation and profit measurement

4.1 Cost elements

For the purposes of inventory valuation and profit measurement, the cost accountant must calculate the cost of one unit. The total cost of a cost unit is made up of the following three **elements of cost**.

- Materials
- Labour
- Other expenses (such as rent and rates, interest charges and so on)

Key term

Cost elements are 'constituent parts of costs according to the factors upon which expenditure is incurred, namely material, labour and expenses'.   CIMA *Official Terminology*

Cost elements can be classified as **direct** costs or **indirect** costs.

4.2 Direct cost and prime cost

FAST FORWARD

A **direct cost** is a cost that can be traced in full to the product, service, or department that is being costed.

Usually the cost unit (which was covered earlier) is the **cost object** that direct costs can be attributed to.

Key term

A **direct cost** is 'expenditure that can be attributed to a specific cost unit, for example material that forms part of a product'.   CIMA *Official Terminology*

Direct costs are therefore **directly attributable to cost objects**.

(a) **Direct material costs** are the costs of materials that are known to have been used in making and selling a product (or providing a service).

(b) **Direct labour costs** are the specific costs of the workforce used to make a product or provide a service. Direct labour costs are established by measuring the time taken for a job, or the time taken in 'direct production work'.

(c) **Other direct expenses** are those expenses that have been incurred in full as a direct consequence of making a product, or providing a service, or running a department.

We look at these types of direct cost in more detail below.

FAST FORWARD

Prime cost = direct material cost + direct labour cost + direct expenses

Key term

Prime cost is the 'total of direct material, direct labour and direct expenses'.   CIMA *Official Terminology*

4.2.1 Direct material

Direct material is **all material becoming part of the product** (unless used in negligible amounts and/or having negligible cost).

Direct material costs are charged to the product as part of the **prime cost**. Examples of direct material are as follows.

(a) **Component parts** or other materials specially purchased for a particular job, order or process.

(b)   **Part-finished work** which is transferred from department 1 to department 2 becomes finished work of department 1 and a direct material cost in department 2.

(c)   **Primary packing materials** like cartons and boxes.

Materials used in negligible amounts and/or having negligible cost can be grouped under indirect materials as part of overhead (see Section 4.3).

4.2.2 Direct wages or direct labour costs

Direct wages are all **wages paid for labour** (either as basic hours or as overtime expended on work on the product itself).

Direct wages costs are charged to the product as part of the **prime cost**.

Examples of groups of labour receiving payment as direct wages are as follows.

(a)   Workers engaged in **altering** the condition, conformation or composition of the product.

(b)   Inspectors, analysts and testers **specifically required** for such production.

4.2.3 Direct expenses

Direct expenses are any expenses which are incurred on a specific product **other than direct material cost and direct wages**.

Direct expenses are charged to the product as part of the **prime** cost. Examples of direct expenses are as follows.

*   The cost of special designs, drawings or layouts
*   The hire of tools or equipment for a **particular** job

Direct expenses are also referred to as **chargeable expenses.**

4.3 Indirect cost/overhead

FAST FORWARD

An **indirect cost** (or **overhead**) is a cost that is incurred in the course of making a product, providing a service or running a department, but which cannot be traced directly and in full to the product, service or department.

Key terms

An **indirect cost** or **overhead** is 'expenditure on labour, materials or services that cannot be economically identified with a specific saleable cost unit'.

CIMA *Official Terminology*

Indirect costs are therefore **not directly attributable to cost objects**.

Examples of indirect costs might be the cost of supervisors' wages on a production line, cleaning materials and buildings insurance for a factory.

Total expenditure may therefore be **analysed** as follows.

Materials cost	=	Direct materials cost	+	Indirect materials cost
+		+		+
Labour cost	=	Direct labour cost	+	Indirect labour cost
+		+		+
Expenses	=	Direct expenses	+	Indirect expenses
Total cost	=	Direct cost/prime cost	+	Overhead cost

Question

Which of the following costs would be charged to the product as a prime cost?

A Component parts
B Part-finished work
C Primary packing materials
D Supervisor wages

Answer

A, B and C

A, B and C are all examples of direct material costs. The prime cost includes direct material, direct labour and direct expenses. D is an indirect labour cost.

4.3.1 Production overhead

Production (or factory) overhead includes all indirect material cost, indirect wages and indirect expenses **incurred in the factory from receipt of the order until its completion**, including:

(a) **Indirect materials** which cannot be traced in the finished product.

Consumable stores, eg material used in negligible amounts

(b) **Indirect wages**, meaning all wages not charged directly to a product.

Salaries of non-productive personnel in the production department, eg supervisor

(c) **Indirect expenses** (other than material and labour) not charged directly to production

(i) Rent, rates and insurance of a factory
(ii) Depreciation, fuel, power and maintenance of plant and buildings

4.3.2 Administration overhead

Administration overhead is all indirect material costs, wages and expenses **incurred in the direction, control and administration of an undertaking**, including:

- **Depreciation** of office equipment
- **Office salaries**, including the salaries of secretaries and accountants
- Rent, rates, insurance, telephone, heat and light cost of general offices

4.3.3 Selling overhead

Selling overhead is all indirect materials costs, wages and expenses **incurred in promoting sales and retaining customers**, including:

- **Printing** and **stationery**, such as catalogues and price lists
- **Salaries** and **commission** of sales representatives
- **Advertising** and **sales promotion**, market research
- Rent, rates and insurance for sales offices and showrooms

4.3.4 Distribution overhead

Distribution overhead is all indirect material costs, wages and expenses **incurred in making the packed product ready for despatch and delivering it to the customer**, including:

- Cost of packing cases
- Wages of packers, drivers and despatch clerks
- Depreciation and running expenses of delivery vehicles

Question

Direct and indirect labour costs

Classify the following labour costs as either direct or indirect.

(a)   The basic pay of direct workers (cash paid, tax and other deductions) is a ☐ cost.

(b)   The basic pay of indirect workers is a ☐ cost.

(c)   Overtime premium, ie the premium above basic pay, for working overtime is a ☐ cost.

(d)   Bonus payments under a group bonus scheme is a ☐ cost.

(e)   Employer's National Insurance contributions is a ☐ cost.

(f)   Idle time of direct workers, paid while waiting for work is a ☐ cost.

Answer

(a)   The basic pay of direct workers is a ☐ direct ☐ cost to the unit, job or process.

(b)   The basic pay of indirect workers is an ☐ indirect ☐ cost, unless a customer asks for an order to be carried out which involves the dedicated use of indirect workers' time, when the cost of this time would be a direct labour cost of the order.

(c)   Overtime premium paid to both direct and indirect workers is usually an ☐ indirect ☐ cost because it is 'unfair' to charge the items produced in overtime hours with the premium. Why should an item made in overtime be more costly just because, by chance, it was made after the employee normally clocks off for the day?

There are two particular circumstances in which the overtime premium might be a direct cost.

(i)   If overtime is worked at the specific request of a customer to get his order completed, the overtime premium paid is a direct cost of the order.

(ii)   If overtime is worked regularly by a production department in the normal course of operations, the overtime premium paid to direct workers could be incorporated into the (average) direct labour hourly rate.

(d)   Bonus payments are generally an ☐ indirect ☐ cost.

(e)   Employer's National Insurance contributions (which are added to employees' total pay as a wages cost) are normally treated as an ☐ indirect ☐ labour cost.

(f)   Idle time is an overhead cost, that is an ☐ indirect ☐ labour cost.

Question

A production worker is paid the following in week 5.

		$
(a)	Basic pay for normal hours worked, 36 hours at $4 per hour	144
(b)	Pay at the basic rate for overtime, 6 hours at $4 per hour	24
(c)	Overtime shift premium, with overtime paid at time-and-a-quarter	
	¼ × 6 hours × $4 per hour	6
(d)	A bonus payment under a group bonus (or 'incentive') scheme (bonus for the month)	30
(e)	Employer National Insurance	18
(f)	Idle time	14
	Total gross wages in week 5 for 42 hours of work	236

What is the direct labour cost for this employee in week 5?

A $144   B $168   C $230   D $236

Answer

The correct answer is B.

Let's start by considering a general approach to answering multiple choice questions (MCQs). In a numerical question like this, the best way to begin is to ignore the options and work out your own answer from the available data. If your solution corresponds to one of the four options then mark this as your chosen answer and move on. Don't waste time working out whether any of the other options might be correct. If your answer does not appear among the available options then check your workings. If it still does not correspond to any of the options then you need to take a calculated guess. **Never leave a question unanswered. CIMA does not penalise a wrong answer.**

Do not make the common error of simply selecting the answer which is closest to yours. The best thing to do is to first eliminate any answers which you know or suspect are incorrect. For example you could eliminate C and D because you should now know that costs such as group bonus schemes are usually indirect costs. You are then left with a choice between A and B, and at least you have now improved your chances if you really are guessing.

The correct answer is B because the basic rate for overtime is a part of direct wages cost. It is only the overtime premium that is usually regarded as an overhead or indirect cost.

Assessment focus point

Make sure you can distinguish between the various types of costs.

The examples in the diagram on the next page should help you get the costs types clear in your mind.

4.4 Product costs and period costs

FAST FORWARD

For the preparation of financial statements, costs are often classified as either **product costs** or **period costs**. Product costs are costs identified with goods produced or purchased for resale. Period costs are costs deducted as expenses during the current period.

A **product cost** is a 'cost of a finished product built up from its cost elements'.

A **period cost** is a 'cost relating to a time period rather than to the output of products or services'.

CIMA *Official Terminology*

Consider a retailer who acquires goods for resale without changing their basic form. The only product cost is therefore the purchase cost of the goods. Any unsold goods are held as inventory, valued at the lower of purchase cost and net realisable value and included as an asset in the statement of financial position. As the goods are sold, their cost becomes an expense in the form of 'cost of goods sold'. A retailer will also incur a variety of selling and administration expenses. Such costs are **period costs** because they are **deducted from revenue** without ever being regarded as part of the **value of inventory**.

Now consider a manufacturing firm in which direct materials are transformed into saleable goods with the help of direct labour and factory overheads. All these costs are **product costs** because they are allocated to the value of inventory until the goods are sold. As with the retailer, selling and administration expenses are regarded as **period costs.**

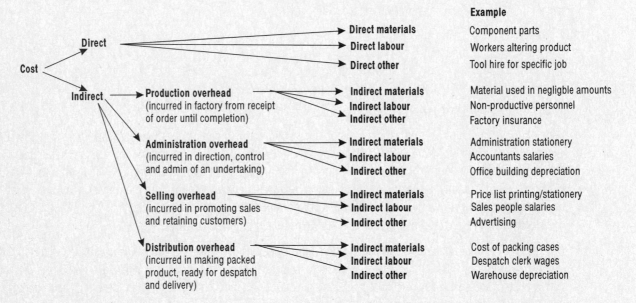

4.5 Functional costs

Classification by function involves classifying costs as production/manufacturing costs, administration costs or marketing/selling and distribution costs.

This way of classifying costs involves relating the costs to the activity causing the cost. In a 'traditional' costing system for a manufacturing organisation, costs are classified by function as follows.

* **Production or manufacturing** costs
* **Administration** costs
* **Marketing, or selling and distribution costs**

Many expenses fall comfortably into one or other of these three broad classifications. Other expenses that do not fall fully into one of these classifications might be categorised as **general overheads** or even classified on their own (for example **research and development costs**).

Within the costing system of a manufacturing company the following types of expense are incurred.

Reference number

1　Cost of oils used to lubricate production machinery
2　Motor vehicle licences for lorries
3　Depreciation of factory plant and equipment
4　Cost of chemicals used in the laboratory
5　Commission paid to sales representatives
6　Salary of the secretary to the finance director
7　Trade discount given to customers
8　Holiday pay of machine operatives
9　Salary of security guard in raw materials warehouse
10　Fees to advertising agency
11　Rent of finished goods warehouse
12　Salary of scientist in laboratory
13　Insurance of the company's premises
14　Salary of supervisor working in the factory
15　Cost of typewriter ribbons in the general office
16　Protective clothing for machine operatives

Required

Place each expense within the following classifications using the reference numbers above. Each type of expense should appear only once in your answer.

Classifications		Reference numbers of expenses
(a)	Production costs	1, 11, 14, 16
(b)	Selling and distribution costs	5, 7
(c)	Administration costs	2, 3, 6, 8, 9, 13, 15
(d)	Research and development costs	4, 12,

Answer

The reference number for each expense can be classified as follows.

Classifications		Reference numbers of expenses
(a)	Production costs	1, 3, 8, 9, 14, 16
(b)	Selling and distribution costs	2, 5, 7, 10, 11
(c)	Administration costs	6, 13, 15
(d)	Research and development costs	4, 12

5 Cost classification for control

FAST FORWARD

Classification by responsibility requires costs to be divided into those that are **controllable** and those that are **uncontrollable**. A system of **responsibility accounting** is therefore required.

There is little point allocating costs to products for the purposes of control as the production of a product, say, may consist of a number of operations, each of which is the responsibility of a different person. A product cost does not therefore provide a link between costs incurred and areas of responsibility. So costs (and revenues) must be traced in another way to the individuals responsible for their incurrence. This 'other way' is known as **responsibility accounting.**

5.1 Responsibility accounting and responsibility centres

Key terms

Responsibility accounting is a system of accounting that segregates revenue and costs into areas of personal responsibility in order to monitor and assess the performance of each part of an organisation.

A **responsibility centre** is a department or function whose performance is the direct responsibility of a specific manager.

Managers of responsibility centres should only be **held accountable** for costs over which they have **some influence**. From a motivation point of view this is important because it can be very demoralising for managers who feel that their performance is being judged on the basis of something over which they have no influence. It is also important from a control point of view in that control reports should ensure that information on costs is reported to the manager who is able to take action to control them.

Responsibility accounting attempts to associate costs, revenues, assets and liabilities with the managers most capable of controlling them. As a system of accounting, it therefore distinguishes between controllable and uncontrollable costs.

5.2 Controllable and uncontrollable costs

Key terms

A **controllable cost** is a cost which can be influenced by management decisions and actions.

An **uncontrollable cost** is a cost which cannot be affected by management within a given time span.

Most **variable costs** within a department are thought to be **controllable in the short term** because managers can influence the efficiency with which resources are used, even if they cannot do anything to raise or lower price levels.

A cost which is not controllable by a junior manager might be controllable by a senior manager. For example, there may be high direct labour costs in a department caused by excessive overtime working. The junior manager may feel obliged to continue with the overtime to meet production schedules, but his senior may be able to reduce costs by hiring extra full-time staff, thereby reducing the requirements for overtime.

A cost which is not controllable by a manager in one department may be controllable by a manager in another department. For example, an increase in material costs may be caused by buying at higher prices than expected (controllable by the purchasing department) or by excessive wastage (controllable by the production department) or by a faulty machine producing rejects (controllable by the maintenance department).

Some costs are **non-controllable**, such as increases in expenditure items due to inflation. Other costs are **controllable, but in the long term rather than the short term**. For example, production costs might be reduced by the introduction of new machinery and technology, but in the short term, management must attempt to do the best they can with the resources and machinery at their disposal.

5.2.1 The controllability of fixed costs

It is often assumed that all fixed costs are non-controllable in the short run. This is not so.

(a) **Committed fixed costs** are those costs arising from the possession of plant, equipment, buildings and an administration department to **support the long-term needs of the business**. These costs (depreciation, rent, administration salaries) are largely **non-controllable in the short term** because they have been committed by longer-term decisions affecting longer-term needs. When a company decides to cut production drastically, the long-term committed fixed costs will be reduced, but only after redundancy terms have been settled and assets sold.

(b) **Discretionary fixed costs**, such as advertising and research and development costs, are incurred as a result of a top management decision, but could be **raised or lowered at fairly short notice** (irrespective of the actual volume of production and sales).

5.2.2 Controllability and dual responsibility

Quite often a particular cost might be the **responsibility of two or more managers**. For example, raw materials costs might be the responsibility of the purchasing manager (prices) and the production manager (usage). A **reporting system must allocate responsibility appropriately**. The purchasing manager must be responsible for any increase in raw materials prices whereas the production manager should be responsible for any increase in raw materials usage.

Attention!

> You can see that there are **no clear cut rules** as to which costs are controllable and which are not. Each situation and cost must be reviewed separately and a decision taken according to the control value of the information and its behavioural impact.

5.2.3 Cost centres, profit centres and investment centres

Responsibility centres are usually divided into different categories. Cost centres were covered in section 1 of this chapter. Here we shall describe profit centres and investment centres.

A **profit centre** is any section of an organisation to which both revenues and costs are assigned, so that the profitability of the section may be measured.

Profit centre information is needed by managers who are responsible for both revenue and costs. For example, an individual branch of a hairdressing chain would incur costs and generate revenue.

The manager of the profit centre has some influence over both revenues and costs, that is, a say in both sales and production policies.

A profit centre manager is likely to be a fairly senior person within an organisation, and a profit centre is likely to cover quite a large area of operations. A profit centre might be an entire division within the organisation, or there might be a separate profit centre for each product, product range, brand or service that the organisation sells.

Investment centres refer to profit centres with additional responsibility for capital investment and possibly for financing.

Several profit centres might share the same capital items, for example the same buildings, stores or transport fleet, and so investment centres are likely to include several profit centres, and provide a basis for control at a very senior management level.

6 Performance measurement

Performance measurement aims to establish how well something or somebody is doing in relation to a planned activity.

6.1 Performance measures for cost centres

6.1.1 Productivity

This is the quantity of the product or service produced (**output**) **in relation to** the resources put in (**input**). For example so many units produced per hour, or per employee, or per tonne of material. It measures **how efficiently resources are being used**.

6.1.2 Cost per unit

Cost per unit is total costs ÷ number of units produced.

For the manager of a cost centre which is also a production centre one of the most important performance measures will be cost per unit. This is simply the total costs of production divided by the number of units produced in the period.

Example: cost per unit

The total costs and number of units produced for a production cost centre for the last two months are as follows:

	May	June
Production costs	$128,600	$143,200
Units produced	12,000	13,500
Cost per unit	$128,600	$143,200
	12,000	13,500
	= $10.72	$10.61

6.2 Performance measures for profit centres

Ratios and **percentages** are useful performance measurement techniques.
The **profit margin** (profit to sales ratio) is calculated as (profit ÷ sales) × 100%.

6.2.1 Profit margin

Key term

The **profit margin** (profit to sales ratio) is calculated as (profit ÷ sales) × 100%.

The profit margin provides a simple measure of performance for profit centres. Investigation of unsatisfactory profit margins enables control action to be taken, either by reducing excessive costs or by raising selling prices.

Profit margin is usually calculated using operating profit.

Key term

The **operating profit** is the difference between the value of sales (excluding sales tax) and the costs incurred during operations (total operating expenses).

6.2.2 Example: the profit to sales ratio

A company compares its year 2 results with year 1 results as follows.

	Year 2	Year 1
	$	$
Sales	160,000	120,000
Cost of sales		
Direct materials	40,000	20,000
Direct labour	40,000	30,000
Production overhead	22,000	20,000
Marketing overhead	42,000	35,000
	144,000	105,000
Operating profit	16,000	15,000
Profit to sales ratio	$\left(\dfrac{16,000}{160,000}\right) \times 100\%$	10%
	$\left(\dfrac{15,000}{120,000}\right) \times 100\%$	12½%

The above information shows that there is a decline in profitability in spite of the $1,000 increase in profit, because the profit margin is less in year 2 than year 1.

6.2.3 Gross profit margin

FAST FORWARD

The **gross profit margin** is calculated as gross profit ÷ sales × 100%

Key term

> **Gross profit** is the difference between the value of sales (excluding sales tax) and the cost of the goods sold.

The profit to sales ratio above was based on a profit figure which included non-production overheads. The gross profit margin calculates how efficiently a business is using its materials, labour and production overhead in the production process. It is calculated as (gross profit = turnover) ×100%.

For the company in section 6.2.2 the gross profit margin would be:

Year 2: $\left(\dfrac{(16,000 + 42,000)}{160,000}\right) \times 100\% = 36.25\%$

Year 1: $\left(\dfrac{(15,000 + 35,000)}{120,000}\right) \times 100\% = 41.67\%$

6.2.4 Cost/sales ratios

When target profits are not met, further ratios may be used to shed some light on the problem.

- Production cost of sales ÷ sales
- Distribution and marketing costs ÷ sales
- Administrative costs ÷ sales

Subsidiary ratios can be used to examine problem areas in greater depth. For example, for production costs the following ratios might be used.

- Material costs ÷ sales value of production
- Works labour costs ÷ sales value of production
- Production overheads ÷ sales value of production

6.2.5 Example: cost/sales ratios

Look back to the example in Section 6.2.2. A more detailed analysis would show that higher direct materials are the probable cause of the decline in profitability.

	Year 2	Year 1
Material costs/sales	$\left(\dfrac{40,000}{160,000}\right) \times 100\%$	25%
	$\left(\dfrac{20,000}{120,000}\right) \times 100\%$	16.7%

Other cost/sales ratios have remained the same or improved.

Question

Profit margins

Use the following summary income statement to answer the questions below

	$
Sales	3,000
Cost of sales	1,800
	1,200
Manufacturing expenses	300
Administrative expenses	200
Operating profit	700

1   The profit margin is

    A   60%
    B   40%
    C   30%
    D   23%

2   The gross profit margin is

    A   60%
    B   40%
    C   30%
    D   23%

Answer

1   D $\dfrac{700}{3,000} \times 100\% = 23\%$

The profit margin usually refers to operating profit / sales.

2   B $\dfrac{1,200}{3,000} \times 100\% = 40\%$

The gross profit margin takes the gross profit/sales.

6.2.6 Value added

Value added is calculated as sales – cost of bought in materials, components and services

Value added is a performance measure that looks at the wealth created by the activities of an organisation.

Sometimes used as a performance measure instead of profit, value added is useful since it indicates how effectivly an organisation creates wealth (value) from its inputs.

6.3 Performance measures for investment centres

Return on capital employed (ROCE) or return on investment (ROI) shows how much profit has been made in relation to the amount of resources invested.

6.3.1 Return on capital employed (ROCE)

Return on capital employed (ROCE) (also called Return on investment (ROI)) is calculated as (profit/capital employed) × 100% and shows how much profit has been made in relation to the amount of resources invested.

ROCE is generally used for measuring the performance of investment centres; profits alone do not show whether the return is sufficient when different values of assets are used. Thus if company A and company B have the following results, company B would have the better performance.

	A	B
	$	$
Profit	5,000	5,000
Sales	100,000	100,000
Capital employed	50,000	25,000
ROCE	10%	20%

The profit of each company is the same but company B only invested $25,000 to achieve that profit whereas company A invested $50,000.

ROCE may be calculated in a number of ways, but profit before interest and tax (that is, net profit) is usually used.

Similarly all assets of a non-operational nature (for example trade investments and intangible assets such as goodwill) should be excluded from capital employed.

Profits should be related to average capital employed. In practice many companies calculate the ratio using year-end assets. This can be misleading. If a new investment is undertaken near to the year end, the capital employed will rise but profits will only have a month or two of the new investment's contribution.

What does the ROCE tell us? What should we be looking for? There are two principal comparisons that can be made.

* The change in ROCE from one year to the next
* The ROCE being earned by other entities

6.3.2 Residual income (RI)

Residual income (RI) is an alternative way of measuring the performance of an investment centre. It is a measure of the centre's profits after deducting a notional or imputed interest cost.

An alternative way of measuring the performance of an investment centre, instead of using ROCE, is residual income (RI). **Residual income** is a **measure of the centre's profits after deducting a notional or imputed interest cost** (calculated on the whole of the capital employed - **not** just on borrowed funds).

Key term

> **Residual income (RI)** is pretax profits less a notional interest charge for invested capital.

Question

A division with capital employed of $400,000 currently earns a ROCE of 22%. It can make an additional investment of $50,000 for a 5 year life with nil residual value. The average net profit from this investment would be $12,000. A notional interest charge amounting to 14% of the amount invested is to be charged to the division each year.

The residual income of the division after the investment, will be

A $5,000
B $32,000
C $37,000
D $39,000

Answer

	$
C	
Divisional profit after investment ((400,000 × 22%) + 12,000))	100,000
Notional interest (450,000 × 0.14)	(63,000)
Residual income	37,000

6.3.3 Asset turnover

Asset turnover measures how efficiently the assets of the business are being used.

Key term

> **Asset turnover** is a measure of how well the assets of a business are being used to generate sales. It is calculated as (sales ÷ capital employed).

Suppose that two companies both have capital employed of $100,000. However Company A has sales revenue for the year of $150,000 and Company B has sales revenue for the year of $250,000. The asset turnover figure shows how much revenue is being earned for every $1 of capital employed:

$$\text{Company A} = \frac{\$150,000}{\$100,000} = 1.5$$

$$\text{Company B} = \frac{\$250,000}{\$100,000} = 2.5$$

This shows that Company B is earning $2.50 of sales revenue for every $1 invested compared to only $1.50 of sales revenue for Company A.

Note that the asset turnover figure is an absolute figure and not a percentage.

44   **2: Introduction to costing and performance measurement** │ Part A Cost determination and behaviour

BPP
LEARNING MEDIA

Asset turnover is an important figure in its own right as it shows how efficiently the assets or capital of the business is being used to create sales revenue. However, it is also important as it is one of the elements that make up return on capital employed.

Return on capital employed = Asset turnover × Net profit margin

$$\frac{\text{Net profit}}{\text{Capital employed}} = \frac{\text{Sales revenue}}{\text{Capital employed}} \times \frac{\text{Net profit}}{\text{Sales revenue}}$$

6.4 Example: return on capital employed, asset turnover and net profit margin

A company has the following figures:

	$
Sales revenue	540,000
Net profit	50,000
Capital employed	300,000

Return on capital employed $= \dfrac{\$50,000}{\$300,000} \times 100 = 16.67\%$

Asset turnover $= \dfrac{\$540,000}{\$300,000} = 1.8$

Net profit margin $= \dfrac{\$50,000}{\$540,000} \times 100 \quad = 9.26\%$

Return on capital employed	= Asset turnover	×	Net profit margin
16.67%	= 1.8	×	9.26%

This is an important relationship as it means that any changes in return on capital employed can be accounted for by changes in the profitability measured by net profit margin and in the efficiency of the use of the net assets measured by asset turnover.

Assessment focus point

One or more questions on any of these performance measures is likely in this assessment.

6.5 Not-for-profit organisations

Key term

Bois proposes that a **not-for-profit organisation** be defined as:' ... an organisation whose attainment of its prime goal is not assessed by economic measures. However, in pursuit of that goal it may undertake profit-making activities.'

The not-for-profit sector may involve a number of different kinds of organisation with, for example, differing legal status – charities, statutory bodies offering public transport or the provision of services such as leisure, health or public utilities such as water or road maintenance.

6.5.1 Value for money

FAST FORWARD

Value for money is getting the best possible combination of services from the least resources.

It is reasonable to argue that not-for-profit organisations **best serve society's interests** when the **gap** between the **benefits** they provide and the **cost** of providing those benefits is **greatest**. This is commonly termed **value for money** and is not dissimilar from the concept of profit maximisation, apart from the fact that society's interests are being maximised rather than profit.

Key term

> **Value for money** can be defined as getting the best possible combination of services from the least resources, which means maximising the benefits for the lowest possible cost.

This is usually accepted as requiring the application of economy, effectiveness and efficiency.

(a)   **Economy** (spending money frugally)

(b)   **Efficiency** (getting as much as possible for what goes in)

(c)   **Effectiveness** (doing what was supposed to be done)

More formally, these criteria can be defined as follows.

Key terms

> **Effectiveness** is the extent to which declared objectives/goals are met.
>
> **Efficiency** is the relationship between inputs and outputs.
>
> **Economy** is attaining the appropriate quantity and quality of inputs at lowest cost to achieve a certain level of outputs.

6.5.2 Example: Economy, efficiency, effectiveness

(a)   **Economy.** The economy with which a school purchases equipment can be measured by comparing actual costs with budgets, with costs in previous years, with government/ local authority guidelines or with amounts spent by other schools.

(b)   **Efficiency.** The efficiency with which a school's IT laboratory is used might be measured in terms of the proportion of the school week for which it is used.

(c)   **Effectiveness.** The effectiveness of a school's objective to produce quality teaching could be measured by the proportion of students getting good grades in their exams.

7 Shareholder value and environmental and social concerns

FAST FORWARD

> **Environmental costs** are important to the businesses for a number of reasons.
>
> - Identifying environmental costs associated with individual products and services can assist with **pricing** decisions.
> - Ensuring compliance with **regulatory standards**.
> - Potential for **cost savings**.

We said earlier that management accounting acts as support to management to add value to an organisation. One measure of value is **shareholder value.**

7.1 What does shareholder value mean?

Shareholder value is the **value delivered to shareholders** because of management's ability to grow earnings, dividends and share price. This means that shareholder value is created by the strategic decisions that affect a company.

Generating a healthy return on capital is a main driver of shareholder value. However, there is a fine line between **responsibly** growing shareholder value and pursuing the growth of profits above all other considerations. Decisions taken at the **expense of the environment**, for example, could cause shareholder value to decline.

Shareholder value is the total 'return to the shareholders in terms of both dividends and share price growth, calculated as the present value of future free cash flows of the business discounted at the weighted average cost of the capital of the business less the market value of its debt.'

CIMA Official Terminology

Environmental management accounting (EMA) is the generation and analysis of both financial and non-financial information in order to support internal environmental management processes.

7.2 Why are environmental costs important to the management accountant?

There are, of course, ethical reasons why environmental costs are important to the management accountant. For example, using energy generates carbon dioxide emissions and these contribute to climate change and threaten the future of our planet. Management accountants, however, should also consider environmental costs for the following reasons.

(a) Identifying environmental costs associated with individual products, services or processes helps with correct product or service **pricing**. **Correct pricing** helps to **increase profitability**.

(b) Poor environmental behaviour can result in **fines**, increased liability to **environmental taxes** and **damage** to the business's **reputation**.

(c) Recording environmental costs is important as some may require **regulatory compliance**. Most western countries now have laws to cover land-use planning, smoke emissions, water pollution and destruction of animals and natural habitats.

(d) Saving energy generally leads to cost savings.

Social accounting is a method of reporting whereby a business analyses the impact it has on society and the environment. **Environmental accounting** is a subset of social accounting. Environmental accounting involves preparation, presentation and communication of information about a business's interaction with the natural environment. It is a legal requirement in some countries such as Denmark and Australia.

7.3 Environmental concern and performance

Martin Bennett and Peter James ('The green bottom line: management accounting for environmental improvement and business benefit', *Management Accounting,* November 1998) looked at the **ways in which a company's concern for the environment can impact on its performance.**

(a) **Short-term savings** through waste minimisation and energy efficiency schemes can be substantial.

(b) Companies with poor environmental performance may face **increased cost of capital** because investors and lenders demand a higher risk premium.

(c) There are a number of **energy and environmental taxes**, such as the UK's landfill tax.

(d) **Pressure group campaigns** can cause damage to reputation and/or additional costs.

(e) Environmental legislation may cause the end of certain damaging products, but also present opportunities for **greener replacements**.

(f) The cost of processing input which becomes **waste** is equivalent to 5-10% of some organisations' revenue.

(g) The phasing out of CFCs has led to markets for alternative products.

Case Study

On 20 April 2010, multinational oil company BP's Deepwater Horizon rig exploded off the coast of the US state of Louisiana, killing 11 workers. BP chairman, Carl-Henric Svanberg was invited to meet US President Barack Obama amid concerns that the company did not have enough cash to pay for the clean-up operation and compensation for those affected – and agreed to set up a claims fund of $20 billion. The reputation of the global BP brand was seriously damaged.

7.3.1 Achieving business and environmental benefits

Bennett and James went on to suggest six main **ways in which business and environmental benefits can be achieved**.

(a)   **Integrating the environment into capital expenditure decisions** (by considering environmental opposition to projects which could affect cash flows, for example)

(b)   **Understanding and managing environmental costs**. Environmental costs are often 'hidden' in overheads and environmental and energy costs are often not allocated to the relevant budgets.

(c)   **Introducing waste minimisation schemes**

(d)   **Understanding and managing life cycle costs.** For many products, the greatest environmental impact occurs upstream (such as mining raw materials) or downstream from production (such as energy to operate equipment). This has led to producers being made responsible for dealing with the disposal of products such as cars, and government and third party measures to influence raw material choices. Organisations therefore need to identify, control and make provision for environmental life cycle costs and work with suppliers and customers to identify environmental cost reduction opportunities.

(e)   **Measuring environmental performance.** Business is under increasing pressure to measure all aspects of environmental performance, both for statutory disclosure reasons and due to demands for more environmental data from customers.

(f)   **Involving management accountants in a strategic approach to environment-related management accounting and performance evaluation.** A 'green accounting team' incorporating the key functions should analyse the strategic picture and identify opportunities for practical initiatives. It should analyse the short-, medium- and long-term impact of possible changes in the following.

   (i)   **Government policies**, such as on transport
   (ii)   **Legislation and regulation**
   (iii)   **Supply conditions**, such as fewer landfill sites
   (iv)   **Market conditions**, such as changing customer views
   (v)   **Social attitudes**, such as to factory farming
   (vi)   **Competitor strategies**

7.4 Social responsibility

Since organisations have an effect on their environment, it is arguable that they should act in a way which shows **social awareness and responsibility**.

Social responsibility is expected from all types of organisation.

(a)   **Local government** is expected to provide services to the local community, and to preserve or improve the character of that community, but at an acceptable cost to the ratepayers.

(b) **Businesses** are expected to provide goods and services, which reflect the needs of users and society as a whole. These needs may not be in harmony - arguably, the development of the Concorde aeroplane and supersonic passenger travel did not contribute to the public interest, and caused considerable inconvenience to residents near airports who suffered from excessive aircraft noise. A business should also be expected to anticipate the future needs of society; examples of socially useful products might be energy-saving devices and alternative sources of power.

(c) **Pollution control** is a particularly important example of social responsibility by Industrial organisations, and some progress has been made in the development of commercial processes for recycling waste material.

(d) **Universities and schools** are expected to produce students whose abilities and qualifications will prove beneficial to society. A currently popular view of education is that greater emphasis should be placed on vocational training for students.

(e) In some cases, **legislation** may be required to enforce social need, for example to regulate the materials used to make crash helmets for motor cyclists, or to regulate safety standards in motor cars and furniture. Ideally, however, organisations should avoid the need for legislation by taking **earlier self-regulating action**.

7.5 Environmental policy and management information

The means of codifying a company's attitude towards the environment is often the creation of a published **environmental policy document** or charter. This may be internally generated or it may be adopted from a standard environmental charter.

The problem here, as with other similar principles or charters, is that the commitment required from companies is generally too high and the fear exists that the principles may have legal status which could have a severe effect on a company's liability.

Chapter Roundup

- If the users of accounting information want to know the cost of something, that something is called a **cost object**.

- **Cost centres** are **collecting places** for costs before they are further analysed.

- **Cost units** are the **basic control units** for costing purposes.

- In practice most cost accounting transactions are recorded at **historic cost**, but costs can be measured in terms of **economic cost.**

- **Economic value** is the amount someone is willing to pay.

- Before the cost accountant can plan, control or make decisions, all costs (whether labour, material or overheads) must be accurately **classified** and their destination in the costing system (cost units because they are direct costs or cost centres because they are indirect costs).

- **Classification** can be by **nature** (**subjective**), by **purpose** (**objective**) or by **responsibility**.

- A **direct cost** is a cost that can be traced in full to the product, service or department that is being costed.

- **Prime cost** = direct material cost + direct labour cost + direct expenses

- An **indirect cost** (or **overhead**) is a cost that is incurred in the course of making a product, providing a service or running a department, but which cannot be traced directly and in full to the product, service or department.

- For the preparation of financial statements, costs are often classified as either **product costs** or **period costs**. Product costs are costs identified with goods produced or purchased for resale. Period costs are costs deducted as expenses during the current period.

- **Classification by function** involves classifying costs as production/manufacturing costs, administration costs or marketing/selling and distribution costs.

- **Classification by responsibility** requires costs to be divided into those that are **controllable** and those that are **uncontrollable**. A system of **responsibility accounting** is therefore required.

- **Performance measurement** aims to establish how well something or somebody is doing in relation to a planned activity.

- **Cost per unit** is total costs ÷ number of units produced.

- Performance measures for **materials** and **labour** include differences between actual and expected (budgeted) performance. Performance can also be measured using the **standard hour**.

- **Ratios** and **percentages** are useful performance measurement techniques.

- The **profit margin** (profit to sales ratio) is calculated as (profit ÷ sales) × 100%.

- The **gross profit margin** is calculated as gross profit ÷ sales × 100%

- **Return on capital employed (ROCE)** or **return on investment (ROI)** shows how much profit has been made in relation to the amount of resources invested.

- **Residual income (RI)** is an alternative way of measuring the performance of an investment centre. It is a measure of the centre's profits after deducting a notional or imputed interest cost.

- **Asset turnover** measures how efficiently the assets of the business are being used.

- **Value for money** is getting the best possible combination of services from the least resources.

- **Environmental costs** are important to the businesses for a number of reasons.

Identifying environmental costs associated with individual products and services can assist with **pricing** decisions.

Ensuring compliance with **regulatory standards**.

Potential for **cost savings**.

Quick Quiz

1   (a)   A .... is a unit of product or service to which costs can be related. It is the basic control unit for costing purposes.

     (b)   A .... acts as a collecting place for certain costs before they are analysed further.

     (c)   A .... is anything that users of accounting information want to know the cost of.

2   *Choose the correct words from those highlighted.*

     In practice, most cost accounting systems use **historical cost/economic cost/economic value/cost value** as a measurement basis.

3   Classification of expenditure into material, labour and expenses, say, is an example of:

     A   subjective classification
     B   objective classification
     C   classification by responsibility
     D   classification by behaviour

4   There are a number of different ways in which costs can be classified.

     (a)   .... and .... (or overhead) costs

     (b)   .... costs (production costs, distribution and selling costs, administration costs and financing costs)

5   Which of the following would be classified as indirect labour?

     A   Assembly workers in a company manufacturing televisions
     B   A stores assistant in a factory store
     C   Plasterers in a construction company
     D   An audit clerk in a firm of auditors

6   What is the main aim of performance measurement?

     A   To obtain evidence in order to dismiss someone
     B   To establish how well something or somebody is doing in relation to a planned activity
     C   To collect information on costs
     D   To award bonuses

7   Place the correct letters in the boxes.

     ROCE = ☐/☐ × 100%   Profit margin = ☐/☐ × 100%

     A   Profit
     B   Capital employed
     C   Sales

8   Which one of the following is the correct formula for asset turnover?

A   Sales ÷ capital employed
B   Net profit ÷ sales
C   Capital employed ÷ sales
D   Sales ÷ net profit

9   A company has to pay a $1 per unit royalty to the designer of a product which it manufactures and sells.

The royalty charge would be classified in the company's accounts as a (tick the correct answer):

☐   Direct expense
☐   Production overhead
☐   Administrative overhead
☐   Selling overhead

Answers to Quick Quiz

1   (a)   Cost unit
     (b)   Cost centre
     (c)   Cost object

2   Historical cost

3   A

4   (a)   Direct, indirect (overhead) costs
     (b)   Functional

5   B   The others are direct labour.

6   B   Note that the question said 'the **main** aim'. Performance measurement may well be used to decide on bonus levels but this is not the main aim.

7    $ROCE = \dfrac{A}{B} \times 100\%$ $Profit\ margin = \dfrac{A}{C} \times 100\%$

8   A   Asset turnover = sales ÷ capital employed. Net profit margin = net profit ÷ sales revenue

9   ☑   Direct expense

The royalty cost can be traced in full to the company's product, therefore it is a direct expense.

Now try the questions below from the Question Bank

Question numbers
6–10

BPP
LEARNING MEDIA

Cost behaviour

Introduction

This chapter examines the two-way split of **cost behaviour** into those that vary directly with changes in activity level (**variable costs**) and those that do not (**fixed costs**) and explains two methods of splitting total costs into these two elements, the **line of best fit** (or **scattergraph**) method and the **high-low** method.

You should study this chapter carefully as you will need to use the concepts explained here in the other chapters in this Study Text (particularly the next chapter) and in the remainder of your management accounting studies both at the Certificate stage and at future examination levels.

Topic list	Syllabus references
1 Cost behaviour and levels of activity	B2(a)
2 Cost behaviour patterns	B2(b),(c)
3 Determining the fixed and variable elements of semi-variable costs	B2(d)

1 Cost behaviour and levels of activity

Cost behaviour is the way in which a cost changes as activity level changes.

Cost behaviour is the 'Variability of input costs with activity undertaken. Cost may increase proportionately with increasing activity (the usual assumption for **variable cost**), or it may not change with increased activity (a **fixed cost**). Some costs (**semi-variable**) may have both variable and fixed elements. Other behaviour is possible; costs may increase more or less than in direct proportion, and there may be step changes in cost, for example. To a large extent, cost behaviour will be dependent on the timescale assumed.'   CIMA *Official Terminology*

1.1 Levels of activity

The level of activity refers to the amount of work done, or the number of events that have occurred. Depending on circumstances, the level of activity may refer to measures such as the following.

- The volume of production in a period
- The number of items sold
- The number of invoices issued
- The number of units of electricity consumed

1.2 Basic principle of cost behaviour

The basic principle of cost behaviour is that as the level of activity rises, costs will usually rise. It will probably cost more to produce 2,000 units of output than it will cost to produce 1,000 units; it will usually cost more to make five telephone calls than to make one call and so on. The problem for the accountant is to determine, for each item of cost, the way in which costs rise and by how much as the level of activity increases.

For our purposes in this chapter, the level of activity will generally be taken to be the volume of production/output.

2 Cost behaviour patterns

2.1 Fixed costs

Costs which are not affected by the level of activity are **fixed costs** or **period costs**.

A **fixed cost** is a 'cost incurred for an accounting period, that, within certain output or turnover limits, tends to be unaffected by fluctuations in the levels of activity (output or turnover)'.   CIMA *Official Terminology*

A **fixed cost** is a cost which tends to be unaffected by increases or decreases in the volume of output. Fixed costs are a **period charge**, in that they relate to a span of time; as the time span increases, so too will the fixed costs. A sketch graph of a fixed cost would look like this.

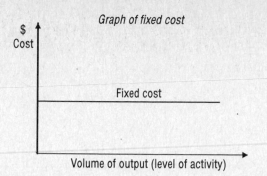

Graph of fixed cost

$ Cost

Fixed cost

Volume of output (level of activity)

2.1.1 Examples of fixed costs

- The salary of the managing director (per month or per annum)
- The rent of a single factory building (per month or per annum)
- Straight line depreciation of a single machine (per month or per annum)

Assessment focus point

You now know that fixed costs are the same, no matter how many units are produced. Note, however, that as the number of units increases, the fixed cost **per unit** actually decreases.

This concept may seem confusing at first and it's best to think in terms of numbers.

	20X1	*20X2*	
Fixed cost	$50,000	$50,000	
Number of units produced	500	1,000	◄── Units have increased
Fixed cost per unit ($50,000/no. of units)	$100	$50	◄── Cost per unit has decreased

Even though the costs are fixed, we still sometimes look at the cost per unit. Don't let this confuse you – total fixed costs are fixed and do not vary with activity levels.

2.2 Variable costs

FAST FORWARD

Variable costs increase or decrease with the level of activity.

Key term

A **variable cost** is a 'cost that varies with a measure of activity'. CIMA *Official Terminology*

We discussed variable costs earlier in this study text. A **variable cost** is a cost which tends to vary directly with the volume of output. The variable cost **per unit** is the same amount for each unit produced whereas **total** variable cost increases as volume of output increases. A sketch graph of a variable cost would look like this.

BPP LEARNING MEDIA

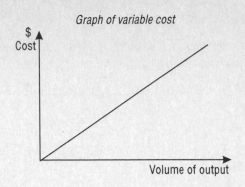

Graph of variable cost

2.2.1 Examples of variable costs

(a)   The cost of raw materials (where there is no discount for bulk purchasing since bulk purchase discounts reduce the unit cost of purchases).

(b)   Direct labour costs are, for very important reasons which you will study in Chapter 7, usually classed as a variable cost even though basic wages are often fixed.

(c)   Sales commission is variable in relation to the volume or value of sales.

2.3 Step costs

FAST FORWARD

A **step cost** is a cost which is fixed in nature but only within certain levels of activity. Depending on the time frame being considered, it may appear as fixed or variable.

Consider the depreciation of a machine which may be fixed if production remains below 1,000 units per month. If production exceeds 1,000 units, a second machine may be required, and the cost of depreciation (on two machines) would go up a step. A sketch graph of a step cost could look like this.

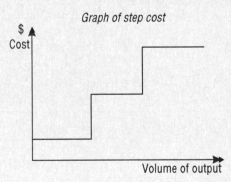

Graph of step cost

2.3.1 Examples of step costs

(a)   Rent is a step cost in situations where accommodation requirements increase as output levels get higher.

(b)   Basic pay of employees is nowadays usually fixed, but as output rises, more employees (direct workers, supervisors, managers and so on) are required.

2.3.2 The importance of time scale

The time scale over which we consider the behaviour of what appears to be a step cost can actually result in its classification as a fixed cost or a variable cost.

Over the short to medium term, a cost such as rent will appear as fixed, steps in the cost only occurring after a certain length of time.

Many **variable costs** also appear **fixed over a short period of time**. For example, spending on direct labour (traditionally classified as a variable cost) will be fixed in relation to changes in activity level as it takes time to respond to changes in activity and alter spending levels.

Over longer periods of time, however, say a number of years, **all costs will tend to vary in response to large changes in activity level**. For this reason **fixed costs** are sometimes called **long-term variable costs**. Costs traditionally classified as fixed will become step costs as no cost can remain unchanged forever. And so as the **time span increases**, **step costs become variable costs**, **varying with the passing of time**. For example, when considered over many years, rent will appear as a variable cost, varying in the long term with large changes in the level of activity.

2.4 Non-linear variable costs

Although variable costs are usually assumed to be linear, there are situations where variable costs are **curvilinear**. Have a look at the following graphs.

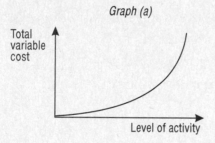

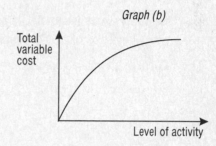

Graph (a) becomes steeper as levels of activity increase. Each additional unit of activity is adding more to total variable cost than the previous unit. Graph (b) becomes less steep as levels of activity increase. Each additional unit is adding less to total variable cost than the previous unit.

Question	Cost behaviour patterns

The cost of direct labour where employees are paid a bonus which increases as output levels increase might follow the cost behaviour pattern depicted in graph (a) above.

True ☐

False ☐

The cost of direct material where quantity discounts are available might follow the cost behaviour pattern in graph (b) above.

True ☐

False ☐

Graph (a)   ✓   True

Graph (b)   ✓   True

2.5 Semi-variable costs (or semi-fixed costs or mixed costs)

FAST FORWARD

Semi-variable, semi-fixed or **mixed costs** are costs which are part-fixed and part-variable and are therefore partly affected by a change in the level of activity.

Key term

A **semi-variable cost** is a 'cost containing both fixed and variable components and thus partly affected by a change in the level of activity'.

CIMA *Official Terminology*

2.5.1 Examples of semi-variable costs

(a)   **Electricity and gas bills**. There is a basic charge plus a charge per unit of consumption.

(b)   **Sales representative's salary**. The sales representative may earn a basic monthly amount of, say, $1,000 and then commission of 10% of the value of sales made.

The behaviour of a semi-variable cost can be presented graphically as follows.

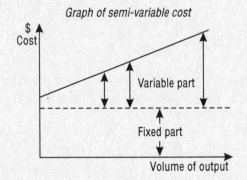

Graph of semi-variable cost

2.6 Cost behaviour and total and unit costs

If the variable cost of producing a unit is $5 per unit then it will remain at that cost per unit no matter how many units are produced. However if the business's fixed costs are $5,000 then the fixed cost **per unit** will decrease the more units are produced: one unit will have fixed costs of $5,000 per unit; if 2,500 are produced the fixed cost per unit will be $2; if 5,000 are produced the fixed cost per unit will be only $1. Thus as the level of activity increases the total costs **per unit** (fixed cost plus variable cost) will decrease.

In sketch graph form this may be illustrated as follows.

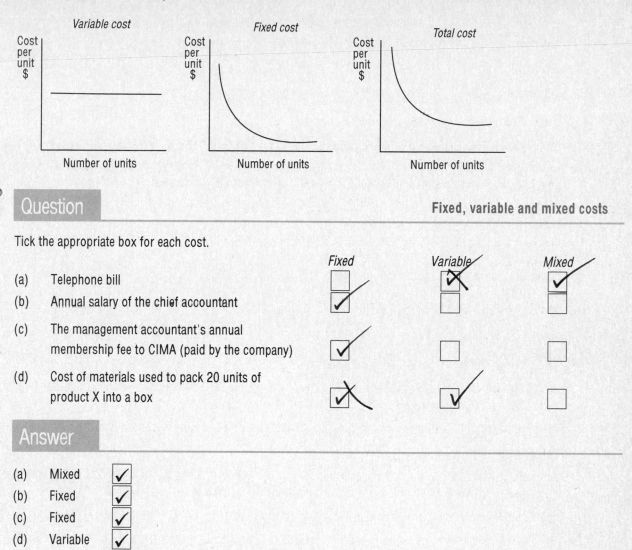

Question

Fixed, variable and mixed costs

Tick the appropriate box for each cost.

		Fixed	Variable	Mixed
(a)	Telephone bill	☐	☒	☑
(b)	Annual salary of the chief accountant	☑	☐	
(c)	The management accountant's annual membership fee to CIMA (paid by the company)	☑	☐	☐
(d)	Cost of materials used to pack 20 units of product X into a box	☒	☑	☐

Answer

(a)	Mixed	☑
(b)	Fixed	☑
(c)	Fixed	☑
(d)	Variable	☑

2.7 Assumption about cost behaviour

2.7.1 The relevant range

Key term

> The **relevant range** is 'activity levels within which assumptions about cost behaviour in breakeven analysis remain valid'.
> CIMA *Official Terminology*

The relevant range also broadly represents the **activity levels at which an organisation has had experience of operating at in the past** and for which **cost information is available**. It can therefore be dangerous to attempt to predict costs at activity levels which are outside the relevant range.

2.7.2 Assumptions

It is often possible to assume that, within the normal or relevant range of output, costs are either fixed, variable or semi-variable.

Question

Select the correct words in the following sentence.

The basic principle of cost behaviour is that as the level of activity rises, costs will usually (a) **rise/fall/stay the same**. In general, as activity levels rise, the variable cost per unit will (b) **rise/fall/stay the same**, the fixed cost per unit will (c) **rise/fall/stay the same** and the total cost per unit will (d) **rise/fall/stay the same**.

Answer

(a)   Rise
(b)   Stay the same
(c)   Fall
(d)   Fall

Question

Match the sketches (1) to (5) below to the listed items of expense. In each case the vertical axis relates to total cost, the horizontal axis to activity level.

(a)   Electricity bill: a standing charge for each period plus a charge for each unit of electricity consumed.

(b)   Supervisory labour.

(c)   Production bonus, which is payable when output in a period exceeds 10,000 units. The bonus amounts in total to $20,000 plus $50 per unit for additional output above 10,000 units.

(d)   Sales commission, which amounts to 2% of sales revenue.

(e)   Machine rental costs of a single item of equipment. The rental agreement is that $10 should be paid for every machine hour worked each month, subject to a maximum monthly charge of $480.

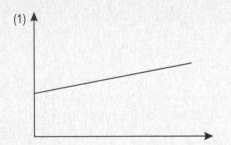

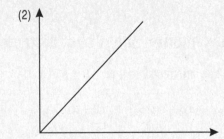

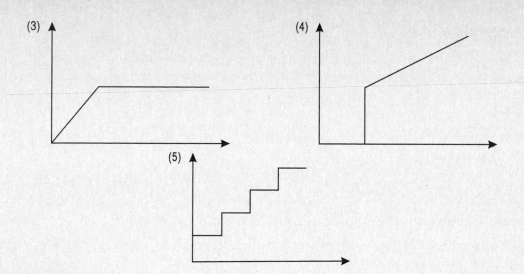

Answer

(a) Graph (1)
(b) Graph (5)
(c) Graph (4)
(d) Graph (2)
(e) Graph (3)

Question

Behaviour graph

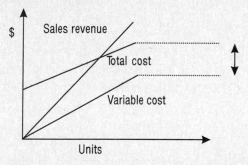

In the above graph, what does the arrow represent?

A   Fixed cost
B   Contribution
C   Profit
D   Breakeven quantity in units

Answer

A   Total cost = Variable cost + Fixed cost

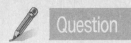
Question

The staff at Underworld Co are paid a basic minimum wage plus an amount per item of inventory produced. What type of cost are the staff wages?

A   Fixed
B   Variable
C   Semi-variable
D   Step

Answer

C   Semi-variable. The basic minimum wage is the fixed element and the extra amount per item of inventory is the variable element.

Assessment focus point

You may see graphical questions in your assessment. Always read the labels on the axes carefully before deciding what the graph represents.

3 Determining the fixed and variable elements of semi-variable costs

FAST FORWARD

The fixed and variable elements of semi-variable costs can be determined by the **high/low method** or the **'line of best fit'** **(scattergraph) method**.

There are several ways in which fixed cost elements and variable cost elements within semi-variable costs may be ascertained. Each method only gives an estimate, and can therefore give differing results from the other methods. The main methods that you need to know about for your assessment are the **high/low method** and the **line of best fit** **(scattergraph)** method.

3.1 High/low method

Key term

The **high/low method** is a 'method of estimating cost behaviour by comparing the total costs associated with two different levels of output. The difference in costs is assumed to be caused by variable costs increasing, allowing unit variable cost to be calculated. Following from this, since total cost is known, the fixed cost can be derived.'

CIMA *Official Terminology*

(a) Records of costs in previous periods are reviewed and the costs of the following two periods are selected.

    (i)   The period with the **highest** volume of activity

    (ii)   The period with the **lowest** volume of activity

(b) The difference between the total cost of these two periods will be the **variable cost** of the difference in activity levels (since the same fixed cost is included in each total cost).

(c) The variable cost per unit may be calculated from this (difference in total costs ÷ difference in activity levels), and the **fixed cost** may then be determined by substitution.

3.1.1 Example: the high/low method

The costs of operating the maintenance department of a computer manufacturer, Bread and Butter company, for the last four months have been as follows.

Month	Cost	Production volume
	$	Units
1	110,000	7,000
2	115,000	8,000
3	111,000	7,700
4	97,000	6,000

Required

Calculate the costs that should be expected in month five when output is expected to be 7,500 units. Ignore inflation.

Solution

(a)

	Units		$
High output	8,000	total cost	115,000
Low output	6,000	total cost	97,000
Variable cost of	2,000		18,000
Variable cost per unit	$18,000/2,000 = $9		

(b) Substituting in either the high or low volume cost:

		High		Low
		$		$
Total cost		115,000		97,000
Variable costs	(8,000 × $9)	72,000	(6,000 × $9)	54,000
Fixed costs		43,000		43,000

(c) Estimated maintenance costs when output is 7,500 units:

	$
Fixed costs	43,000
Variable costs (7,500 × $9)	67,500
Total costs	110,500

Assessment focus point

An assessment question will probably not tell you that you need to use the high low method. You need to get used to thinking for yourself, 'Can I use the high low method here?' Remember that you can use it to split out fixed and variable elements. So, for example, a question may talk about total costs and then ask you about the variable element.

Question

The Valuation Department of a large firm of surveyors wishes to develop a method of predicting its total costs in a period. The following past costs have been recorded at two activity levels.

	Number of valuations (V)	Total cost (TC)
Period 1	420	82,200
Period 2	515	90,275

The total cost model for a period could be represented as follows.

A   TC = $46,500 + 85V
B   TC = $42,000 + 95V
C   TC = $46,500 – 85V
D   TC = $51,500 – 95V

Answer

The correct answer is A.

Although we only have two activity levels in this question we can still apply the high/low method.

	Valuations V	Total cost $
Period 2	515	90,275
Period 1	420	82,200
Change due to variable cost	95	8,075

∴ Variable cost per valuation = $8,075/95 = $85.

Period 2: fixed cost   = $90,275 – (515 × $85)
                    = $46,500

Using good MCQ technique, you should have managed to eliminate C and D as incorrect options straightaway. The variable cost must be added to the fixed cost, rather than subtracted from it. Once you had calculated the variable cost as $85 per valuation (as shown above), you should have been able to select option A without going on to calculate the fixed cost (we have shown this calculation above for completeness).

Assessment focus point

> The high-low method was frequently tested in the form of multiple choice questions under the previous syllabus of this paper. The information in questions often relates to **two** activity levels only. The high-low method is still an appropriate method for identifying the fixed and variable elements of costs where two levels of activity are concerned – you still have a **high** and a **low** activity level.

3.2 'Line of best fit' or scattergraph method

A scattergraph of costs in previous periods can be prepared (with cost on the vertical axis and volume of output on the horizontal axis). A **line of best fit**, which is a line drawn **by judgement** to pass through the middle of the points, thereby having as many points above the line as below it, can then be drawn and the fixed and variable costs determined.

A scattergraph of the cost and volume data in Section 3.1.1 is shown below.

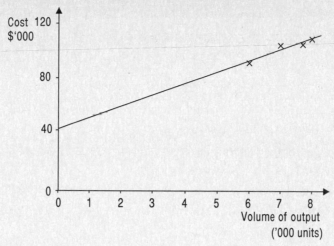

The point where the line cuts the vertical axis (approximately $40,000) is the fixed cost (the cost if there is no output). If we take the value of one of the plotted points which lies close to the line and deduct the fixed cost from the total cost, we can calculate the variable cost per unit.

Total cost for 8,000 units   = $115,000
Variable cost for 8,000 units   = $(115,000 – 40,000) = $75,000
Variable cost per unit   = $75,000/8,000 = $9.375

Note that both the high-low method and the scattergraph method use **historical data** to predict future costs. The problem with historical data is that it is **not necessarily representative** of future data. Management must remember this when using the results of the high-low or scattergraph method.

Assessment focus point

Although you would not actually be required to draw a scattergraph, you could perhaps be required to answer a multiple choice question about how the technique works, or its advantages and limitations.

Chapter Roundup

- **Cost behaviour** is the way in which a cost changes as activity level changes.

- Costs which are not affected by the level of activity are **fixed costs** or **period costs**.

- **Variable costs** increase or decrease with the level of activity.

- A **step cost** is a cost which is fixed in nature but only within certain levels of activity. Depending on the time frame being considered, it may appear as fixed or variable.

- **Semi-variable, semi-fixed** or **mixed costs** are costs which are part-fixed and part-variable and are therefore partly affected by a change in the level of activity.

- The fixed and variable elements of semi-variable costs can be determined by the **high-low method** or the **'line of best fit'** **(scattergraph) method**.

Quick Quiz

1   The basic principle of cost behaviour is that as the level of activity rises, costs will usually fall.

    True   ☐

    False   ☑

2   Fill in the gaps for each of the graph titles below.

    (a)

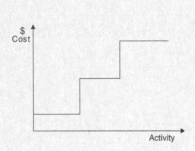

    Graph of a ......Stepped...... cost

    Example: Machine rental

    (b)

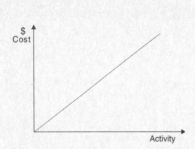

    Graph of a ...linear variable... cost

    Example:

(c)

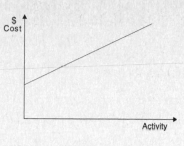

Graph of a _Semi variable_ cost

Example:

(d)

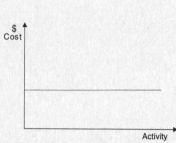

Graph of a _fixed_ cost

Example: _rent_

3   Costs are assumed to be either fixed, variable or semi-variable within the normal or relevant range of output.

True   [✓]

False   [ ]

4   The costs of operating the canteen at 'Eat a lot Company' for the past three months are as follows.

Month	Cost $	Employees
1	72,500	1,250
2	75,000	1,300
3	68,750	1,175

$$\frac{6250}{125} = 50$$ $50 \times 1500 = \frac{75000}{65000}$
$\overline{10000}$

Variable cost (per employee per month) =

Fixed cost per month = _10 000_

5   Pen Co produced the following units at the following costs during October, November and December.

Month	Number of units	Total Cost $
October	4,700	252,800
November	5,500	264,000
December	9,500	320,000

_133000_

The costs could be sub-divided into variable costs of $14 per unit and fixed costs of $...._187000_....
per month.

6   The management accountant at G Co is analysing some costs which have been entered onto the computer as 'miscellaneous staff expenses'.

No of staff	Cost per member of staff
20	$5
100	$5
150	$5
250	$5

What type of cost is the miscellaneous staff expense?

A   Fixed
B   Variable
C   Semi-variable
D   Non-linear

7   The costs of operating the canteen at 'Eat a lot Company' for the past three months is as follows.

Month	Cost	Employees
	$	
1	72,500	1,250
2	75,000	1,300
3	68,750	1,175

Variable cost (per employee per month) = $\frac{6250}{125}$ 50

Fixed cost per month = 10 000

8   A cost which is unaffected in total by increases and decreases in the volume of output is called?

A   Stepped-fixed
B   Variable
C   Constant
D   Fixed

9   Which one of the following is an example of a mixed cost?

A   Factory rent
B   Salaries
C   Telephone bill
D   Straight line depreciation

10   A particular cost is classified as being semi-variable.

What is the effect on the cost per unit if activity increases by 10%?
A   Decrease by 10%
B   Decrease by less than 10%
C   Increase by less than 10%
D   Remain constant

1   False. They will rise.

2   (a)   Step cost. Example: rent, supervisors' salaries
     (b)   Variable cost. Example: raw materials, direct labour
     (c)   Semi-variable cost. Example: electricity and telephone
     (d)   Fixed. Example: rent, depreciation (straight-line)

3   True

4   Variable cost = $50 per employee per month
     Fixed costs = $10,000 per month

	Activity	Cost $
High	1,300	75,000
Low	1,175	68,750
	125	6,250

Variable cost per employee = $6,250/125 = $50

For 1,175 employees, total cost = $68,750

Total cost	= variable cost + fixed cost
$68,750	= (1,175 × $50) + fixed cost
∴ Fixed cost	= $68,750 – $58,750
	= $10,000

5    $187,000

Using the high-low method we have:

	Units	Cost $
Highest	9,500	320,000
Lowest	4,700	252,800
Difference	4,800	67,200

Variable costs = 67,200/4,800 = $14/unit
Fixed costs = Total cost – variable cost
At 9,500 units, fixed cost = $320,000 – (9,500 × $14) = $187,000

6   B   Variable. Make sure you read the question carefully. Note that the $5 is **per staff member** so 100 staff would mean $500 in expenditure.

7   Variable cost = $50 per employee per month

Fixed costs = $10,000 per month

	Activity	Cost $
High	1,300	75,000
Low	1,175	68,750
	125	6,250

Variable cost per employee = $6,250/125 = $50

For 1,175 employees, total cost = $68,750

Total cost   = variable cost + fixed cost

$68,750   = (1,175 × $50) + fixed cost

∴Fixed cost   = $68,750 – $58,750

= $10,000

8   D   The name given to cost unaffected by increases and decreases in the volume of output is fixed costs.

9   C   Telephone bills usually have a fixed element (the line rental) and a variable element (the charge per call made). Options A, B and D are all usually fixed costs.

10   B   Only part of the cost is variable so a 10% increase in activity will lead to a less than 10% increase in the overall cost.

Now try the questions below from the Question Bank

Question numbers
11–15

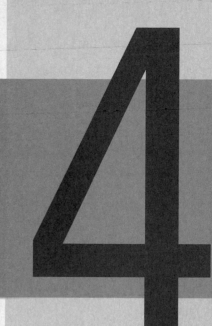

Overhead costs – absorption costing

Introduction

Here we study one method of dealing with overheads, **absorption costing**, which is defined in CIMA *Official Terminology* as a cost accounting method that 'assigns direct costs *and* all or part of overhead to cost units using one or more overhead absorption rates'. (It is sometimes referred to as **full costing**.)

Absorption costing is a method for sharing overheads between a number of different products on a fair basis. The chapter begins by looking at the three stages of absorption costing: **allocation, apportionment and absorption**. We then move on to the important issue of **over/under absorption**. Over/under absorption is very likely to be included in your assessment, so ensure you know how to deal with it.

In the next chapter we'll see an alternative approach to accounting for overheads – **marginal costing**.

Topic list	Syllabus references
1 Overheads	B1(d)
2 Overhead allocation	B1(d)
3 Overhead apportionment	B1(d)
4 Overhead absorption	B1(e)
5 Blanket absorption rates and departmental absorption rates	B1(e)
6 Over and under absorption of overheads	B1(e)
7 Activity based costing	B1(e)

1 Overheads

As explained in Chapter 2 costs can be described in terms of direct and indirect costs.

A direct cost is a cost that can be traced in full to the product or service or department, and an indirect cost, also known as an overhead, is a cost that is incurred in the course of making a product or delivering a service, but it cannot be traced in full to that product or service.

For example, in the case of a company that makes and sells cakes, flour and eggs are direct costs, as are the labour costs of the cooks. These costs can be directly attributed to the finished cake.

However, the rent of the company factory and offices also a cost, but not one that can be attributed to a cake or a department directly.

However, in order for the company to know how much each cake or department costs them to make, and if they are selling it at a profit or a loss, they need to have a way to attribute the overhead costs to the products and departments.

2 Overhead allocation

FAST FORWARD

> The first step in absorption costing is **allocation**. Allocation is the process by which whole cost items are charged direct to a cost unit or cost centre.

Key term

> **Allocation** is 'to assign a whole item of cost, or of revenue, to a single cost unit, centre, account or time period'.
>
> CIMA *Official Terminology*

Cost centres may be one of the following types.

(a)   A **production department**, to which production overheads are charged.

(b)   A **production area service department**, to which production overheads are charged.

(c)   An **administrative department**, to which administration overheads are charged.

(d)   A **selling** or a **distribution department**, to which sales and distribution overheads are charged.

(e)   An **overhead cost centre**, to which items of expense which are shared by a number of departments, such as rent and rates, heat and light and the canteen, are charged.

The following are examples of costs which would be charged direct to cost centres via the process of allocation.

(a)   The cost of a warehouse security guard will be charged to the warehouse cost centre.

(b)   Paper on which computer output is recorded will be charged to the computer department.

2.1 Example: overhead allocation

Consider the following costs of a company.

Wages of the supervisor of department A	$200
Wages of the supervisor of department B	$150
Indirect materials consumed in department A	$50
Rent of the premises shared by departments A and B	$300

The cost accounting system might include three cost centres.

Cost centre: 101 Department A
102 Department B
201 Rent

Overhead costs would be allocated directly to each cost centre, ie $200 + $50 to cost centre 101, $150 to cost centre 102 and $300 to cost centre 201. The rent of the factory will be subsequently shared between the two production departments, but for the purpose of day to day cost recording in this particular system, the rent will first of all be charged in full to a separate cost centre.

3 Overhead apportionment

FAST FORWARD

The second step in absorption costing is overhead **apportionment**. This involves apportioning general overheads to cost centres and then reapportioning the costs of service cost centres to production departments.

Key term

Apportion is 'to spread indirect revenues or costs over two or more cost units, centres, accounts or time periods'.
CIMA *Official Terminology*

3.1 First stage: apportioning general overheads

Overhead apportionment follows on from overhead allocation. The first stage of overhead apportionment is to identify all overhead costs as production department, production service department, administration or selling and distribution overhead. This means that the costs for heat and light, rent and rates, the canteen and so on (that is, costs which have been allocated to general overhead cost centres) must be shared out between the other cost centres.

3.1.1 Bases of apportionment

Overhead costs should be shared out on a fair basis. You will appreciate that because of the complexity of items of cost it is rarely possible to use only one method of apportioning costs to the various departments of an organisation. The bases of apportionment for the most usual cases are given below.

Overhead to which the basis applies	Basis
Rent, rates, heating and light, repairs and depreciation of buildings	Floor area occupied by each cost centre
Depreciation, insurance of equipment	Cost or book value of equipment
Personnel office, canteen, welfare, wages and cost offices, first aid	Number of employees, or labour hours worked in each cost centre
Heating, lighting (see above)	Volume of space occupied by each cost centre

 Question

Bases of apportionment

The following **bases of apportionment** are used by a factory.

A   Volume of cost centre
B   Value of machinery in cost centre
C   Number of employees in cost centre
D   Floor area of cost centre

Complete the table below using one of A to D to show the bases on which the **production overheads listed in the table** should be **apportioned**.

Production overheads	Basis
Rent	D
Heating costs	A
Insurance of machinery	B
Cleaning costs	D
Canteen costs	C

Answer

Production overheads	Basis
Rent	D
Heating costs	A
Insurance of machinery	B
Cleaning costs	D
Canteen costs	C

3.1.2 Example: overhead apportionment

McQueen Co has incurred the following overhead costs.

	$'000
Depreciation of factory	100
Factory repairs and maintenance	60
Factory office costs (treat as production overhead)	150
Depreciation of equipment	80
Insurance of equipment	20
Heating	39
Lighting	10
Canteen	90
	549

Information relating to the production and service departments in the factory is as follows.

	Department				
	Production 1	Production 2	Service 100	Service 101	Totals
Floor space (square metres)	1,200	1,600	800	400	4,000
Volume (cubic metres)	3,000	6,000	2,400	1,600	13,000
Number of employees	30	30	15	15	90
Book value of equipment	$30,000	$20,000	$10,000	$20,000	$80,000

Required

Determine how the overhead costs should be apportioned between the four departments.

Solution

Costs are apportioned using the following general formula.

$$\frac{\text{Total overhead cost}}{\text{Total value of apportionment base}} \times \text{value of apportionment base of cost centre}$$

For example, heating for department 1 = $\dfrac{\$39,000}{13,000} \times 3,000 = \$9,000$

Item of cost	Basis of apportionment	Total cost	To Department 1	2	100	101
		$	$	$	$	$
Factory depreciation	(floor area)	100	30.0	40	20.0	10.0
Factory repairs	(floor area)	60	18.0	24	12.0	6.0
Factory office costs	(number of employees)	150	50.0	50	25.0	25.0
Equipment depreciation	(book value)	80	30.0	20	10.0	20.0
Equipment insurance	(book value)	20	7.5	5	2.5	5.0
Heating	(volume)	39	9.0	18	7.2	4.8
Lighting	(floor area)	10	3.0	4	2.0	1.0
Canteen	(number of employees)	90	30.0	30	15.0	15.0
Total		549	177.5	191	93.7	86.8

Question   **Apportioning overheads**

Pippin Co has three production departments (forming, machines and assembly) and two service departments (maintenance and general).

The following is an analysis of budgeted overhead costs for a twelve-month period.

	$	$
Rent and rates		8,000
Power		750
Light, heat		5,000
Repairs, maintenance:		
Forming	800	
Machines	1,800	
Assembly	300	
Maintenance	200	
General	100	
		3,200
Departmental expenses:		
Forming	1,500	
Machines	2,300	
Assembly	1,100	
Maintenance	900	
General	1,500	
		7,300
Depreciation:		
Plant		10,000
Fixtures and fittings		250
Insurance:		
Plant		2,000
Buildings		500

Indirect labour:

Forming	3,000
Machines	5,000
Assembly	1,500
Maintenance	4,000
General	2,000
	15,500
	52,500

Other available data are as follows

	Floor area sq.ft	Plant value $	Fixtures & fittings $	Effective horse – power	Direct cost for year $	Labour hours worked	Machine hours worked
Forming	2,000	25,000	1,000	40	20,500	14,400	12,000
Machines	4,000	60,000	500	90	30,300	20,500	21,600
Assembly	3,000	7,500	2,000	15	24,200	20,200	2,000
Maintenance	500	7,500	1,000	5	–	–	–
General	500	–	500	–	–	–	–
	10,000	100,000	5,000	150	75,000	55,100	35,600

The overheads apportioned to:

(a)   Forming is $ [   ]

(b)   Machines is $ [   ]

(c)   Assembly is $ [   ]

(d)   Maintenance is $ [   ]

(e)   General is $ [   ]

Answer

(a)   **Forming $** [11,250]

(b)   **Machines $** [22,175]

(c)   **Assembly $** [8,025]

(d)   **Maintenance $** [6,750]

(e)   **General $** [4,300]

Workings

	Basis	Forming $	Machines $	Assembly $	Maint'nce $	General $	Total $
Directly allocated overheads:							
Repairs, maintenance		800	1,800	300	200	100	3,200
Departmental expenses		1,500	2,300	1,100	900	1,500	7,300
Indirect labour		3,000	5,000	1,500	4,000	2,000	15,500
Apportionment of other overheads:							
Rent, rates	1	1,600	3,200	2,400	400	400	8,000
Power	2	200	450	75	25	0	750
Light, heat	1	1,000	2,000	1,500	250	250	5,000
Dep'n of plant	3	2,500	6,000	750	750	0	10,000
Dep'n of F & F	4	50	25	100	50	25	250
Insurance of plant	3	500	1,200	150	150	0	2,000
Insurance of buildings	1	100	200	150	25	25	500
		11,250	22,175	8,025	6,750	4,300	52,500

Basis of apportionment:

1   Floor area
2   Effective horsepower
3   Plant value
4   Fixtures and fittings value

3.2 Second stage: service cost centre cost apportionment

The second stage of overhead apportionment concerns the treatment of **service cost centres**. A factory is divided into several production departments and also a number of service departments, but only the production departments are directly involved in the manufacture of the units. In order to be able to add production overheads to unit costs, it is necessary to have all the overheads charged to (or located in) the production departments. The next stage in absorption costing is, therefore, to apportion the costs of service cost centres to the production cost centres. Examples of possible apportionment bases are as follows.

Service cost centre	Possible basis of apportionment
Stores	Number of materials requisitions
Maintenance	Hours of maintenance work done for each cost centre
Production planning	Direct labour hours worked in each production cost centre

FAST FORWARD

There are two main methods of reapportioning the service department overheads to production departments.

* **Direct method** (ignores inter-service department work)
* **Repeated distribution method** (recognises inter-service department work)

Key term

Re-apportion is 'the re-spread of costs apportioned to service departments to production departments'.

CIMA *Official Terminology*

3.2.1 Example: service centre cost apportionment

A company has two production and two service departments (stores and maintenance). The following information about activity in the recent costing period is available.

	Production departments		Stores	Maintenance
	A	B	department	department
Overhead costs	$10,030	$8,970	$10,000	$8,000
Cost of material requisitions	$30,000	$50,000	–	$20,000
Maintenance hours needed	8,000	1,000	1,000	–

(a) *Direct method*

If service department overheads were apportioned **directly** to production departments, the apportionment would be as follows.

Service department	Basis of apportionment	Total cost		A		B
		$		$		$
Stores	Material requisitions	10,000	(3/8)	3,750	(5/8)	6,250
Maintenance	Maintenance hours	8,000	(8/9)	7,111	(1/9)	889
		18,000		10,861		7,139
Overheads of departments A and B		19,000		10,030		8,970
		37,000		20,891		16,109

(b) *Repeated distribution method*

If, however, recognition is made of the fact that the stores and maintenance department do work for each other, and the basis of apportionment remains the same, we ought to apportion service department costs as follows.

	Dept A	Dept B	Stores	Maintenance
Stores (100%)	30%	50%	–	20%
Maintenance (100%)	80%	10%	10%	–

This situation where the service departments do work for each other is known as **reciprocal servicing**. The re-apportionment of service department costs in this situation can be done using the **repeated distribution method of apportionment**.

	Production dept A	Production dept B	Stores	Maintenance
	$	$	$	$
Overhead costs	10,030	8,970	10,000	8,000
First stores apportionment (see note (a))	3,000	5,000	(10,000)	2,000
			0	10,000
First maintenance apportionment	8,000	1,000	1,000	(10,000)
			1,000	0
Second stores apportionment	300	500	(1,000)	200
Second maintenance apportionment	160	20	20	(200)
Third stores apportionment	6	10	(20)	4
Third maintenance apportionment	4	–	–	(4)
(see note (b))	21,500	15,500	0	0

Notes

(a)   The first apportionment could have been the costs of maintenance, rather than stores; there is no difference to the final results.

(b)   When the repeated distributions bring service department costs down to small numbers (here $4) the final apportionment to production departments is an approximate rounding.

Important!

You should note the difference in the final overhead apportionment to each production department using the different service department apportionment methods. Unless the difference is substantial, the **direct apportionment method** might be preferred because it is clerically simpler to use.

Question

Using your answer to the previous question (apportioning overheads) and the following information, apportion the overheads of the two service departments using the repeated distribution method.

Service department costs are apportioned as follows

	Maintenance %	General %
Forming	20	20
Machines	50	60
Assembly	20	10
General	10	–
Maintenance	–	10
	100	100

(a) The forming department overheads after service department apportionment are $ [   ]

(b) The machines department overheads after service department apportionment are $ [   ]

(c) The assembly department overheads after service department apportionment are $ [   ]

Answer

(a) **The forming department overheads after service department apportionment are $** | 13,705 |

(b) **The machines department overheads after service department apportionment are $** | 28,817 |

(c) **The assembly department overheads after service department apportionment are $** | 9,978 |

Workings

Apportionment of service department overheads to production departments, using the repeated distribution method.

	Forming $	Machines $	Assembly $	Maintenance $	General $	Total $
Overheads	11,250	22,175	8,025	6,750	4,300	52,500
Apportion maintenance (2:5:2:1)	1,350	3,375	1,350	(6,750)	675	
					4,975	
Apportion general (2:6:1:1)	995	2,985	498	497	(4,975)	
Apportion maintenance (2:5:2:1)	99	249	99	(497)	50	
Apportion general (2:6:1:1)	10	30	5	5	(50)	
Apportion maintenance (2:5:2:1)	1	3	1	(5)		
	13,705	28,817	9,978	0	0	52,500

Question
Reciprocal servicing

ABC Co has a production department in Block H of the building and another in Block F. There are also two service departments namely the canteen and the maintenance department. Fixed overheads are incurred as follows:

Department	Overheads $'000
H Block	400
F Block	700
Canteen	550
Maintenance	800

The canteen provides food for H Block (40%), F Block (40%) and the maintenance department (20%). Maintenance does work for H Block and F Block in the ratio 2:3.

What would be the total fixed overhead of H Block if all service department overheads are allocated to production departments?

A $546,000
B $364,000
C $984,000
D $1,466,000

Answer

C

	H Block $'000	F Block $'000	Canteen $'000	Maintenance $'000
Overheads	400	700	550	800
Canteen (2:2:1)	220	220	(550)	110
	620	920	–	910
Maintenance (2:3)	364	546		(910)
	984	1,466	–	–

4 Overhead absorption

4.1 Introduction

Having allocated and/or apportioned all overheads, the next stage in absorption costing is to add them to, or **absorb them into**, the cost of production or sales.

Production overheads are added to the prime cost (direct materials, labour and expenses), the total of the two being the factory cost, or full cost of production. Production overheads are therefore included in the value of inventories of finished goods.

4.2 Predetermined absorption rates

FAST FORWARD

In absorption costing, it is usual to add overheads into product costs by applying a **predetermined overhead absorption rate**. The predetermined rate is set annually, in the budget.

Key term

Overhead absorption rate is 'a means of attributing overhead to a product or service, based for example on direct labour hours, direct labour cost or machine hours'.

CIMA *Official Terminology*

Overheads are not absorbed on the basis of the actual overheads incurred but on the basis of estimated or budgeted figures (calculated prior to the beginning of the period). The rate at which overheads are included in cost of sales (**absorption rate**) is predetermined before the accounting period actually begins for a number of reasons.

(a) Goods are produced and sold throughout the year, but many actual overheads are not known until the end of the year. It would be inconvenient to wait until the year end in order to decide what overhead costs should be.

(b) An attempt to calculate overhead costs more regularly (such as each month) is possible, although estimated costs must be added for expenditures such as heating and lighting (incurred quarterly or annually). The difficulty with this approach would be that actual overheads from month to month would fluctuate randomly; therefore, overhead costs charged to production would depend on a certain extent on random events and charges. A unit made in one week might be charged with $4 of overhead, in a subsequent week with $5, and in a third week with $4.50. Only units made in winter would be charged with the heating overhead. Such charges are considered misleading for costing purposes and administratively inconvenient to deal with.

(c) Similarly, production output might vary each month. For example actual overhead costs might be $20,000 per month and output might vary from, say, 1,000 units to 20,000 units per month. The unit rate for overhead would be $20 and $1 per unit respectively, which would again lead to administration and control problems.

4.3 Calculating predetermined overhead absorption rates

FAST FORWARD

The **absorption rate** is calculated by dividing the budgeted overhead by the budgeted level of activity. For production overheads the level of activity is often budgeted direct labour hours or budgeted machine hours.

Overhead absorption rates are therefore predetermined as follows.

(a) The overhead **likely to be incurred** during the coming period is estimated.

(b) The total hours, units, or direct costs on which the overhead absorption rates are to be based (activity level) are estimated.

(c) The estimated overhead is divided by the budgeted activity level to arrive at an absorption rate.

4.4 Selecting the appropriate absorption base

FAST FORWARD

Management should try to establish an absorption rate that provides a **reasonably 'accurate' estimate** of overhead costs for jobs, products or services.

There are a number of different **bases of absorption** (or 'overhead **recovery** rates') which can be used. Examples are as follows.

- A percentage of direct materials cost
- A percentage of direct labour cost
- A percentage of prime cost
- A rate per machine hour
- A rate per direct labour hour
- A rate per unit

The choice of an absorption basis is a matter of judgement and common sense. There are no strict rules or formulae involved, although factors which should be taken into account are set out below. What is required is an absorption basis which realistically reflects the characteristics of a given cost centre and which avoids undue anomalies.

Many factories use a **direct labour hour rate** or **machine hour rate** in preference to a rate based on a percentage of direct materials cost, wages or prime cost.

(a)   A **direct labour** hour basis is most appropriate in a **labour intensive** environment.

(b)   A **machine hour** rate would be used in departments where production is controlled or dictated by **machines**. This basis is becoming more appropriate as factories become more heavily automated.

(c)   In a standard costing environment, both of these time-based methods would use **standard hours** as the absorption basis. We will return to study **standard labour hour** and **standard machine hour** absorption rates when we learn about standard costing.

Important!

A **rate per unit** would be effective only if all units were identical.

4.5 Example: overhead absorption bases

The budgeted production overheads and other budget data of Calculator Co are as follows.

Budget	Production dept 1	Production dept 2
Overhead cost	$36,000	$5,000
Direct materials cost	$32,000	
Direct labour cost	$40,000	
Machine hours	10,000	
Direct labour hours	18,000	
Units of production		1,000

Required

Calculate the production overhead absorption rate using the various bases of apportionment.

Solution

(a)   Department 1

(i)   Percentage of direct materials cost = $\dfrac{\$36,000}{\$32,000} \times 100\% = 112.5\%$

(ii)   Percentage of direct labour cost = $\dfrac{\$36,000}{\$40,000} \times 100\% = 90\%$

(iii)   Percentage of prime cost = $\dfrac{\$36,000}{\$72,000} \times 100\% = 50\%$

(iv)   Rate per machine hour = $\dfrac{\$36,000}{10,000 \text{ hrs}}$ = $3.60 per machine hour

(v)   Rate per direct labour hour = $\dfrac{\$36,000}{18,000 \text{ hrs}}$ = $2 per direct labour hour

(b)   The department 2 absorption rate will be based on units of output.

$$\frac{\$5,000}{1,000 \text{ units}} = \$5 \text{ per unit produced}$$

4.6 The impact of different absorption bases

The choice of the basis of absorption is significant in determining the cost of individual units, or jobs, produced. Using the previous example, suppose that an individual product has a material cost of $80, a labour cost of $85, and requires 36 labour hours and 23 machine hours to complete. The overhead cost of the product would vary, depending on the basis of absorption used by the company for overhead recovery.

(a)   As a percentage of direct materials cost, the overhead cost would be 112.5% × $80   = $90.00
(b)   As a percentage of direct labour cost, the overhead cost would be 90% × $85   = $76.50
(c)   As a percentage of prime cost, the overhead cost would be 50% × $165   = $82.50
(d)   Using a machine hour basis of absorption, the overhead cost would be 23 hrs × $3.60   = $82.80
(e)   Using a labour hour basis, the overhead cost would be 36 hrs × $2   = $72.00

In theory, each basis of absorption would be possible, but the company should choose a basis for its own costs which seems to be 'fairest'. In our example, this choice will be significant in determining the cost of individual products, as the following summary shows, but the **total cost** of production overheads is the budgeted overhead expenditure, no matter what basis of absorption is selected. It is the relative share of overhead costs borne by individual products and jobs which is affected by the choice of overhead absorption basis.

A summary of the product costs in the previous example is shown below.

	Basis of overhead recovery				
	Percentage of materials cost	Percentage of labour cost	Percentage of prime cost	Machine hours	Direct labour hours
	$	$	$	$	$
Direct material	80	80.00	80.00	80.00	80
Direct labour	85	85.00	85.00	85.00	85
Production overhead	90	76.50	82.50	82.80	72
Total production cost	255	241.50	247.50	247.80	237

Question   **Overhead absorption rates**

Using your answer to the previous question (repeated distribution method) and the following information, determine suitable overhead absorption rates for Pippin Co's three production departments.

	Forming	Machines	Assembly
Budgeted direct labour hours per annum	5,482	790	4,989
Budgeted machine hours per annum	1,350	5,240	147

(a)   The forming department rate is $ [   ] per direct labour hour/direct machine hour (delete as appropriate)

(b)   The machines department rate is $ [   ] per direct labour hour/direct machine hour (delete as appropriate)

(c)   The assembly department rate is $ [   ] per direct labour hour/direct machine hour (delete as appropriate)

(a)	Forming (labour intensive)	$\dfrac{\$13,705}{5,482}$	=	\$	2.50	per direct labour hour
(b)	Machines (machine intensive)	$\dfrac{\$28,817}{5,240}$	=	\$	5.50	per machine hour
(c)	Assembly (labour intensive)	$\dfrac{\$9,978}{4,989}$	=	\$	2	per direct labour hour

Question

Allocation, apportionment and absorption

B Co has five cost centres.

(a) Machining department
(b) Assembly department
(c) Finishing department
(d) Stores department
(e) Building occupancy – this cost centre is charged with all costs relating to the use of the building

In the cost accounting treatment of the costs of these cost centres, the total costs of building occupancy are apportioned before the stores department costs are apportioned.

Costs incurred and data available for Period 7 of the current year were as follows.

Allocated costs	*Total*	*Machining*	*Assembly*	*Finishing*	*Stores*
	\$	\$	\$	\$	\$
Indirect materials	2,800	500	1,700	600	–
Indirect wages	46,600	11,000	21,900	6,700	7,000
Other expenses	5,500	3,700	1,100	400	300
	54,900	15,200	24,700	7,700	7,300

Other costs	\$
Rent	3,000
Rates	800
Lighting and heating	200
Plant and equipment depreciation	19,800
Insurance on plant and equipment	1,980
Insurance on building	200
Company pension scheme	28,000
Factory administration	12,500
Contract costs of cleaning factory buildings	1,400
Building repairs	400
	68,280

General information

	Department			
	Machining	Assembly	Finishing	Stores
Area occupied (square metres)	3,000	4,000	2,000	1,000
Plant and equipment at cost ($'000)	1,400	380	150	50
Number of employees	100	350	150	25
Direct labour hours	24,000	80,000	35,000	–
Machine hours	52,725	20,500	10,200	
Direct wages ($)	24,000	89,400	36,000	–
Number of stores requisitions	556	1,164	270	–

Required

(a) The total of building occupancy costs for Period 7 is $ [   ]

(b) The cost accountant has begun work on the first stage of the analysis of overheads for Period 7. An extract from the working paper is shown below.

Overhead analysis sheet – first stage

	Basis	Total $	Machining $	Assembly $	Finishing $	Stores $
Allocated costs						
Indirect materials		2,800	500	1,700	600	0
Indirect wages		46,600	11,000	21,900	6,700	7,000
Other expenses		5,500	3,700	1,100	400	300
		54,900	15,200	24,700	7,700	7,300
Apportioned costs						
Plant depreciation	*	19,800	A			
Plant insurance	B					
Pension scheme	**	28,000		C		
Factory admin			2,000	7,000	D	500
Building occupancy	E					
		123,180	39,400	54,180	19,650	9,950

* Cost of plant and equipment
** Total labour cost

The entries to be shown as A to E in the boxes on the overhead analysis sheet are:

A $ [   ]

B   [   ]

C $ [   ]

D $ [   ]

E   [   ]

(c) After the re-apportionment of the stores cost to the production cost centres, the total cost centre overheads will be:

Machining $ [   ]

Assembly $ [   ]

Finishing $ [   ]

(d) Appropriate overhead absorption rates (to the nearest cent) for the three production cost centres are:

Machining $ [　　　] for each [　　　]

Assembly $ [　　　] for each [　　　]

Finishing $ [　　　] for each [　　　]

Answer

(a) The total of building occupancy costs for Period 7 is $ [6,000]

Workings

	$
Rent	3,000
Rates	800
Lighting and heating	200
Insurance on building	200
Contract costs of cleaning	1,400
Building repairs	400
	6,000

(b) A $14,000

B   Cost of plant and equipment

C $15,900

D $3,000

E   Area occupied

Workings

A   Total cost of plant and equipment ($'000) = 1,400 + 380 + 150 + 50 = 1,980

Apportioned cost of plant depreciation in Machinery $= \dfrac{1,400}{1,980} \times \$19,800$

$= \$14,000$

C   Total direct and indirect labour costs in the four departments:

	$
Direct wages (24,000 + 89,400 + 36,000)	149,400
Indirect wages	46,600
Total wages	196,000

Pension scheme costs (1/7 of wages cost) = $28,000

Apportioned pension cost to Assembly department:

	$
Direct wages	89,400
Indirect wages	21,900
	111,300

Apportioned cost = 1/7 × $111,300 = $15,900

D   Apportionment basis for factory administration costs = number of employees

$12,500 ÷ 625 employees = $20 per employee

Apportioned factory administration cost to finishing department = $20 × 150 = $3,000

(c) Machining $ ☐ 42,180

Assembly $ ☐ 60,000

Finishing $ ☐ 21,000

Workings: Overhead analysis sheet – second stage

	Total $	Machining $	Assembly $	Finishing $	Stores $
Allocated and apportioned overhead	123,180	39,400	54,180	19,650	9,950
Apportionment of stores costs (see note)		2,780	5,820	1,350	(9,950)
	123,180	42,180	60,000	21,000	0

Note. Stores costs are apportioned on the basis of the number of stores requisitions.

Stores cost $\dfrac{\$9,950}{(556 + 1,164 + 270)}$ = \$5 per requisition

(d) Machining: $ ☐ 0.80   for each **machine hour**

Assembly: $ ☐ 0.75   for each **direct labour hour**

Finishing: $ ☐ 0.60   for each **direct labour hour**

Workings

	Machining	Assembly	Finishing
Overhead cost	$42,180	$60,000	$21,000
Machine hours/direct labour hours	52,725	80,000	35,000
Absorption rate per machine hour/direct labour hour	$0.80	$0.75	$0.60

5 Blanket absorption rates and departmental absorption rates

The use of **separate departmental absorption rates** instead of **blanket (or single factory) absorption rates** will produce more realistic product costs.

5.1 Blanket absorption rates

A **blanket or single factory overhead absorption rate** is an absorption rate **used throughout a factory** and for all jobs and units of output irrespective of the department in which they were produced.

For example, if total overheads were $500,000 and there were 250,000 direct machine hours during the period, the **blanket overhead rate** would be $2 per direct machine hour and all units of output passing through the factory would be charged at that rate.

Such a rate is not appropriate, however, if there are a number of departments and units of output do not spend an equal amount of time in each department.

5.2 Are blanket overhead absorption rates 'fair'?

It is argued that if a single factory overhead absorption rate is used, some products will receive a higher overhead charge than they ought 'fairly' to bear, whereas other products will be under-charged. By using a separate absorption rate for each department, charging of overheads will be equitable and the full cost of production of items will be more representative of the cost of the efforts and resources put into making them. An example may help to illustrate this point.

5.3 Example: separate absorption rates

AB Co has two production departments, for which the following budgeted information is available.

	Department 1	Department 2	Total
Budgeted overheads	$360,000	$200,000	$560,000
Budgeted direct labour hours	200,000 hrs	40,000 hrs	240,000 hrs

If a single factory overhead absorption rate is applied, the rate of overhead recovery would be:

$$\frac{\$560,000}{240,000 \text{ hours}} = \$2.33 \text{ per direct labour hour}$$

If separate departmental rates are applied, these would be:

Department 1   Department 2

$$\frac{\$360,000}{200,000 \text{ hours}} = \$1.80 \text{ per direct labour hour} \qquad \frac{\$200,000}{40,000 \text{ hours}} = \$5 \text{ per direct labour hour}$$

Department 2 has a higher overhead cost per hour worked than department 1.

Now let us consider two separate products.

(a)   Product A has a prime cost of $100, takes 30 hours in department 2 and does not involve any work in department 1.

(b)   Product B has a prime cost of $100, takes 28 hours in department 1 and 2 hours in department 2.

What would be the factory cost of each product, using the following rates of overhead recovery.

(a)   A single factory rate of overhead recovery

(b)   Separate departmental rates of overhead recovery

Solution

			Product A		Product B
			$		$
(a)	**Single factory rate**				
	Prime cost		100		100
	Factory overhead (30 × $2.33)		70		70
	Factory cost		170		170
(b)	**Separate departmental rates**		$		$
	Prime cost		100		100.00
	Factory overhead: department 1		0	(28 × $1.80)	50.40
	department 2	(30 × $5)	150	(2 × $5)	10.00
	Factory cost		250		160.40

Using a single factory overhead absorption rate, both products would cost the same. However, since product A is done entirely within department 2 where overhead costs are relatively higher, whereas product B is done mostly within department 1, where overhead costs are relatively lower, it is arguable that product A should cost more than product B. This will occur if separate departmental overhead recovery rates are used to reflect the work done on each job in each department separately.

The following data relate to one year in department A.

Budgeted machine hours	25,000
Actual machine hours	21,875
Budgeted overheads	$350,000
Actual overheads	$350,000

Based on the data above, what is the machine hour absorption rate as conventionally calculated?

A $12   B $14   C $16   D $18

Answer

The correct answer is B.

Don't forget, if your calculations produce a solution which does not correspond with any of the options available, then eliminate the unlikely options and make a guess from the remainder. Never leave out an assessment question.

A common pitfall is to think 'we haven't had answer A for a while, so I'll guess that'. The computerised assessment does *not* produce an even spread of A, B, C and D answers. There is no reason why the answer to *every* question cannot be D!

The correct answer in this case is B.

$$\text{Overhead absorption rate} = \frac{\text{Budgeted overheads}}{\text{Budgeted machine hours}} = \frac{\$350,000}{25,000} = \$14 \text{ per machine hour}$$

6 Over and under absorption of overheads

FAST FORWARD

The rate of overhead absorption is based on **estimates** (of both numerator and denominator) and it is quite likely that either one or both of the estimates will not agree with what *actually* occurs. Actual overheads incurred will probably be either greater than or less than overheads absorbed into the cost of production.

(a)   **Over absorption** means that the overheads charged to the cost of production are greater than the overheads actually incurred.

(b)   **Under absorption** means that insufficient overheads have been included in the cost of production.

Key terms

Absorbed overhead is 'overhead attached to products or services by means of an absorption rate, or rates'.

Under or over absorbed overhead is 'the difference between overhead incurred and overhead absorbed, using an estimated rate, in a given period. If overhead absorbed is less than that incurred there is under-absorption, if overhead absorbed is more than that incurred there is over-absorption. Over- and under-absorptions are treated as period cost adjustments'.

CIMA *Official Terminology*

6.1 Example: over and under absorption of overheads

Suppose that the budgeted overhead in a production department is $80,000 and the budgeted activity is 40,000 direct labour hours. The overhead recovery rate (using a direct labour hour basis) would be $2 per direct labour hour.

Actual overheads in the period are, say $84,000 and 45,000 direct labour hours are worked.

	$
Overhead incurred (actual)	84,000
Overhead absorbed (45,000 × $2)	90,000
Over absorption of overhead	6,000

In this example, the cost of produced units or jobs has been charged with $6,000 more than was actually spent. An adjustment to reconcile the overheads charged to the actual overhead is necessary and the over-absorbed overhead will be written as a credit to the **income statement** at the end of the accounting period.

<table>
<tr><td>**Assessment focus point**</td><td>

You can always work out whether overheads are under- or over-absorbed by using the following rule.

- If **Actual** overhead incurred – **Absorbed** overhead = **NEGATIVE** (N), then overheads are **over-absorbed** (O) (NO)
- If **Actual** overhead incurred – **Absorbed** overhead = **POSITIVE** (P), then overheads are **under-absorbed** (U) (PU)

So, remember the **NOPU** rule when you go into your assessment and you won't have any trouble in deciding whether overheads are under- or over-absorbed!

</td></tr>
</table>

6.2 The reasons for under-/over-absorbed overhead

The overhead absorption rate is **predetermined from budget estimates** of overhead cost and the expected volume of activity. Under or over recovery of overhead will occur in the following circumstances.

- Actual overhead costs are different from budgeted overheads.
- The actual activity level is different from the budgeted activity level.
- Both actual overhead costs and actual activity level are different from budget.

6.3 Example: under and over absorption of overheads

Rex Co is a small company which manufactures two products, A and B, in two production departments, machining and assembly. A canteen is operated as a separate production service department.

The budgeted production and sales in the year to 31 March 20X3 are as follows.

	Product A	Product B
Sales price per unit	$50	$70
Sales (units)	2,200	1,400
Production (units)	2,000	1,500
Material cost per unit	$14	$12

	Product A Hours per unit	Product B Hours per unit
Direct labour:		
Machining department ($8 per hour)	2	3
Assembly department ($6 per hour)	1	2
Machine hours per unit:		
Machining department	3	4
Assembly department	1	2

Budgeted production overheads are as follows.

	Machining department $	Assembly department $	Canteen $	Total $
Allocated costs	10,000	25,000	12,000	47,000
Apportionment of other general production overheads	26,000	12,000	8,000	46,000
	36,000	37,000	20,000	93,000
Number of employees	30	20	1	51
Floor area (square metres)	5,000	2,000	500	7,500

Required

(a) Calculate an absorption rate for overheads in each production department for the year to 31 March 20X3 and the budgeted cost per unit of products A and B.

(b) Suppose that in the year to 31 March 20X3, 2,200 units of Product A are produced and 1,500 units of Product B. Direct labour hours per unit and machine hours per unit in both departments were as budgeted.

Actual production overheads are as follows.

	Machining department $	Assembly department $	Canteen $	Total $
Allocated costs	30,700	27,600	10,000	68,300
Apportioned share of general production overheads	17,000	8,000	5,000	30,000
	47,700	35,600	15,000	98,300

Calculate the under- or over-absorbed overhead in each production department and in total.

Solution

(a) **Choose absorption rates**

Since machine time appears to be more significant than labour time in the machining department, a machine hour rate of absorption will be used for overhead recovery in this department. On the other hand, machining is insignificant in the assembly department, and a direct labour hour rate of absorption would seem to be the basis which will give the fairest method of overhead recovery.

Apportion budgeted overheads

Next we need to apportion budgeted overheads to the two production departments. Canteen costs will be apportioned on the basis of the number of employees in each department. (Direct labour hours in each department are an alternative basis of apportionment, but the number of employees seems to be more directly relevant to canteen costs.)

	Machining department $	Assembly department $	Total $
Budgeted allocated costs	10,000	25,000	35,000
Share of general overheads	26,000	12,000	38,000
Apportioned canteen costs (30:20)	12,000	8,000	20,000
	48,000	45,000	93,000

Calculate overhead absorption rates

The overhead absorption rates are predetermined, using budgeted estimates. Since the overheads are production overheads, the budgeted activity relates to the volume of production, in units (the production hours required for volume of sales being irrelevant).

	Product A	Product B	Total
Budgeted production (units)	2,000	1,500	
Machining department: machine hours	6,000 hrs	6,000 hrs	12,000 hrs
Assembly department: direct labour hours	2,000 hrs	3,000 hrs	5,000 hrs

The overhead absorption rates will be as follows.

	Machining department	Assembly department
Budgeted overheads	$48,000	$45,000
Budgeted activity	12,000 hrs	5,000 hrs
Absorption rate	$4 per machine hour	$9 per direct labour hour

Determine a budgeted cost per unit

The budgeted cost per unit would be as follows.

	Product A		Product B	
	$	$	$	$
Direct materials		14		12
Direct labour:				
Machining department	16		24	
Assembly department	6		12	
		22		36
Prime cost		36		48
Production overhead:				
Machining department	12		16	
Assembly department	9		18	
		21		34
Full production cost		57		82

(b) **Apportion actual service department overhead to production departments**

When the actual costs are analysed, the 'actual' overhead of the canteen department ($15,000) would be split between the machining and assembly departments.

	Machining department $	Assembly department $	Total $
Allocated cost	30,700	27,600	58,300
Apportioned general overhead	17,000	8,000	25,000
Canteen (30:20)	9,000	6,000	15,000
	56,700	41,600	98,300

Establish the over- or under-absorption of overheads

There would be an over- or under-absorption of overheads as follows.

		Machining department $		Assembly department $	Total $
Overheads absorbed					
Product A (2,200 units)	(× $4 × 3hrs)	26,400	(× $9 × 1hr)	19,800	46,200
Product B (1,500 units)	(× $4 × 4hrs)	24,000	(× $9 × 2hrs)	27,000	51,000
		50,400		46,800	97,200
Overheads incurred		56,700		41,600	98,300
Over-/(under)-absorbed overhead		(6,300)		5,200	(1,100)

The total under-absorbed overhead of $1,100 will be written off to the income statement at the end of the year, to compensate for the fact that overheads charged to production ($97,200) were less than the overheads actually incurred ($98,300).

Question   Under and over absorption of overheads

Using your answer to an earlier question (entitled 'Overhead absorption rates') and the following information, determine whether the overhead in each of the three production departments of Pippin Co is under or over absorbed and by how much for the twelve-month period.

	Forming	Machines	Assembly
Actual direct labour hours	5,370	950	5,400
Actual machine hours	1,300	6,370	100
Actual overhead	$13,900	$30,300	$8,500

(a)   The overhead in the forming department is [   ] absorbed by $ [   ]

(b)   The overhead in the machines department is [   ] absorbed by $ [   ]

(c)   The overhead in the assembly department is [   ] absorbed by $ [   ]

Answer

(a)   [**Under**] absorbed by $ [**475**]

(b)   [**Over**] absorbed by $ [**4,735**]

(c)   [**Over**] absorbed by $ [**2,300**]

Working

Forming	$
Overhead absorbed ($2.50 × 5,370)	13,425
Overhead incurred	13,900
Under-absorbed overhead	475

Machines	$
Overhead absorbed ($5.50 × 6,370)	35,035
Overhead incurred	30,300
Over-absorbed overhead	4,735
Assembly	$
Overhead absorbed ($2 × 5,400)	10,800
Overhead incurred	8,500
Over-absorbed overhead	2,300

Important!

It is important that you should be completely confident in handling under and over absorption of overheads. This question will demonstrate that the techniques which you have just learned can also be applied in a service organisation.

Question   Budget overhead absorption rate

A management consultancy recovers overheads on chargeable consulting hours. Budgeted overheads were $615,000 and actual consulting hours were 32,150. Overheads were under-recovered by $35,000.

If actual overheads were $694,075 what was the budgeted overhead absorption rate per hour?

  A $19.13   B $20.50   C $21.59   D $22.68

Answer

The correct answer is B.

	$
Actual overheads	694,075
Under-recovered overheads	35,000
Overheads recovered for 32,150 hours at budgeted overhead absorption rate (x)	659,075

$$32,150x = 659,075$$

$$x = \frac{659,075}{32,150} = \$20.50$$

Assessment focus point

Absorption costing can seem quite daunting when you first study it. Don't panic if you are finding it difficult. Practise plenty of questions until it starts to sink in.

7 Activity based costing

FAST FORWARD

Activity based costing (ABC) is an alternative approach to absorption costing. It involves the identification of the factors (**cost drivers**) which cause the costs of an organisation's major activities.

7.1 The reasons for the development of ABC

7.1.1 In the past

Most organisations used to produce **only a few products**. **Direct labour costs** and **direct material costs** accounted for the **largest proportion** of total costs and so it was these variable costs that needed to be **controlled**.

Overhead costs were only a **very small fraction** of total costs and so it did not particularly matter what absorption costing bases were used to apportion overheads to products.

7.1.2 Nowadays

More **costs** tend to be **fixed** and **overheads huge**.

Manufacturing is **capital and machine intensive** rather than labour intensive and so direct labour might account for as little as 5% of a product's cost. For example, furniture is no longer made by skilled workers. Instead, complicated expensive machines are programmed with the necessary skills and workers become machine minders.

Advanced manufacturing technology (such as robotics) has had a significant impact on the level of overheads. For example, the marginal cost of producing a piece of computer software might be just a few pounds but the fixed (initial) cost of the software development might run into millions of pounds.

Many resources are used in **support activities** such as setting-up, production scheduling, first item inspection and data processing. These support activities help with the manufacture of a wide range of products and are **not**, in general, **affected by changes in production volume**. They tend to **vary** instead in the **long term** according to the **range** and **complexity** of the products manufactured.

The wider the range and the more complex the products, the more support services will be required. Suppose factory X produces 10,000 units of one product, the Alpha. Factory Y also produces 10,000 units, made up of 1,000 units each of ten slightly different versions of the Alpha. Consider the setting-up activity.

* Factory X will only need to set-up once.

* Factory Y will have to set-up the production run at least ten times for the ten different products and so will incur more set-up costs.

7.1.3 Problems of using absorption costing in today's environment

Overhead absorption rates might be 200% or 300% of unit labour costs. Unit **costs** are **distorted** and so cost information is **misleading**.

Overheads are **not controlled** because they are hidden within unit production costs rather than being shown as individual totals.

Products bear an arbitrary share of overheads which **do not reflect the benefits** they receive.

Absorption costing **assumes** all products **consume all resources** in **proportion** to their **production volumes**.

* It tends to **allocate too great a proportion** of overheads to **high volume products** (which cause relatively little diversity and hence use fewer support services).

* It tends to **allocate too small a proportion** of overheads to **low volume products** (which cause greater diversity and therefore use more support services).

Activity based costing (ABC) attempts to overcome these problems.

Activity based costing (ABC) is an 'approach to the costing and monitoring of activities which involves tracing resource consumption and costing final outputs. Resources are assigned to activities, and activities to cost objects based on consumption estimates. The latter utilise cost drivers to attach activity costs to outputs.'   CIMA *Official Terminology*

7.2 ABC and using it to calculate product costs

7.2.1 Major ideas behind ABC

Activities cause costs.	Activities include ordering and despatching.
The costs of an activity are caused or driven by factors known as **cost drivers**.	The cost of the ordering activity might be driven by the number of orders placed, the cost of the despatching activity by the number of despatches made.
The costs of an activity are assigned to products on the basis of the number of the activity's cost driver products generate.	If product A requires 5 orders to be placed, and product B 15 orders, ¼ (ie 5/(5 + 15)) of the ordering cost will be assigned to product A and ¾ (ie 15/(5 + 15)) to product B.

7.2.2 Cost drivers

A **cost driver** is 'a factor influencing the level of cost'.   CIMA *Official Terminology*

For those costs that **vary with production levels in the short term**, ABC uses **volume-related cost drivers** such as labour hours or machine hours. The cost of oil used as a lubricant on machines would therefore be added to products on the basis of the number of machine hours, since oil would have to be used for each hour the machine ran.

For costs that **vary with some other activity and not volume of production**, ABC uses **transaction-related cost drivers** such as the number of production runs for the production scheduling activity.

7.2.3 Calculating product costs using ABC

Step 1
Identify an organisation's major activities.

Step 2
Identify the factors (cost drivers) which cause the costs of the activities.

Step 3
Collect the costs associated with each activity into **cost pools**.

Cost pools are equivalent to cost centres used with traditional absorption costing.

Step 4
Charge the costs of activities to products on the basis of their usage of the activities. A product's usage of an activity is measured by the number of the activity's cost driver it generates.

Suppose the cost pool for the ordering activity totalled $100,000 and that there were 10,000 orders (orders being the cost driver). Each product would therefore be charged with $10 for each order it required. A batch requiring five orders would therefore be charged with $50.

7.2.4 Example: ABC

Suppose that Cooplan Co manufactures four products, W, X, Y and Z. Output and cost data for the period just ended are as follows.

	Output Units	No of production runs in the period	Material cost per unit $	Direct labour hours per unit	Machine hours per unit
W	10	2	20	1	1
X	10	2	80	3	3
Y	100	5	20	1	1
Z	100	5	80	3	3
		14			

Direct labour cost per hour is $5. Overhead costs are as follows.

	$
Short-run variable costs	3,080
Set-up costs	10,920
Production and scheduling costs	9,100
Materials handling costs	7,700
	30,800

Required

Calculate product costs using absorption costing and ABC.

Solution

Using absorption costing and an absorption rate based on either direct labour hours or machine hours, the product costs would be as follows.

	W	X	Y	Z	Total
	$	$	$	$	$
Direct material	200	800	2,000	8,000	11,000
Direct labour	50	150	500	1,500	2,200
Overheads *	700	2,100	7,000	21,000	30,800
	950	3,050	9,500	30,500	44,000
Units produced	10	10	100	100	
Cost per unit	$95	$305	$95	$305	

* $30,800 ÷ 440 hours = $70 per direct labour or machine hour

Using activity based costing and assuming that the number of production runs is the cost driver for set-up costs, production and scheduling costs and materials handling costs and that machine hours are the cost driver for short-run variable costs, unit costs would be as follows.

	W	X	Y	Z	Total
	$	$	$	$	$
Direct material	200	800	2,000	8,000	11,000
Direct labour	50	150	500	1,500	2,200
Short-run variable overheads (W1)	70	210	700	2,100	3,080
Set-up costs (W2)	1,560	1,560	3,900	3,900	10,920
Production and scheduling costs (W3)	1,300	1,300	3,250	3,250	9,100
Materials handling costs (W4)	1,100	1,100	2,750	2,750	7,700
	4,280	5,120	13,100	21,500	44,000
Units produced	10	10	100	100	
Cost per unit	$428	$512	$131	$215	

Workings

1	$3,080 ÷ 440 machine hours	=	$7 per machine hour
2	$10,920 ÷ 14 production runs	=	$780 per run
3	$9,100 ÷ 14 production runs	=	$650 per run
4	$7,700 ÷ 14 production runs	=	$550 per run

Summary

Product	Absorption costing Unit cost	ABC Unit cost	Difference
	$	$	$
W	95	428	+ 333
X	305	512	+ 207
Y	95	131	+ 36
Z	305	215	− 90

The figures suggest that the traditional volume-based absorption costing system is flawed.

- It under allocates overhead costs to low-volume products (here, W and X) and over allocates overheads to higher-volume products (here Z in particular).

- It under allocates overhead costs to less complex products (here W and Y with just one hour of work needed per unit) and over allocates overheads to more complex products (here X and particularly Z).

Having attended a course on activity based costing (ABC) you decide to experiment by applying the principles of ABC to the four products currently made and sold by your company. Details of the four products and relevant information are given below for one period.

Product	P1	P2	P3	P4
Output in units	120	100	80	120
Costs per unit:	$	$	$	$
Direct material	40	50	30	60
Direct labour	28	21	14	21

The four products are similar and are usually produced in production runs of 20 units.
The total of the production overhead for the period has been analysed as follows.

	$
Set up costs	5,250
Stores receiving	3,600
Inspection/quality control	2,100
Materials handling and despatch	4,620

You have ascertained that the following 'cost drivers' are to be used for the costs shown.

Cost	Cost driver
Set up costs	Number of production runs
Stores receiving	Requisitions raised
Inspection/quality control	Number of production runs
Materials handling and despatch	Orders executed

The number of requisitions raised on the stores was 20 for each product and the number of orders executed was 42, each order being for a batch of 10 of a product.

Required

(a)   The total costs for each product using activity based costing are:

      (i) $ ⬚ for P1   (iii) $ ⬚ for P3

      (ii) $ ⬚ for P2   (iv) $ ⬚ for P4

(b)   The unit costs are:

      (i) $ ⬚ for P1   (iii) $ ⬚ for P3

      (ii) $ ⬚ for P2   (iv) $ ⬚ for P4

(a) (i) $ | 12,480 | (iii) $ | 6,700 |

     (ii) $ | 10,850 | (iv) $ | 14,040 |

(b) (i) $ | 104 | (iii) $ | 83.75 |

     (ii) $ | 108.50 | (iv) $ | 117 |

Workings

	P1	P2	P3	P4
	$	$	$	$
Direct material	4,800	5,000	2,400	7,200
Direct labour	3,360	2,100	1,120	2,520
Production overhead *				
Set up costs	1,500	1,250	1,000	1,500
Stores receiving	900	900	900	900
Inspection/quality control	600	500	400	600
Material handling and despatch	1,320	1,100	880	1,320
(a) Total cost	12,480	10,850	6,700	14,040
(b) Unit costs	(÷120) $104	(÷ 100) $108.50	(÷ 80) $83.75	(÷ 120) $117

* Overhead costs will be divided in the following ratios, depending upon the number of production runs, requisitions or orders per product.

	P1	P2	P3	P4
Production runs	6	5	4	6
Requisitions raised	20	20	20	20
Orders executed	12	10	8	12

Chapter Roundup

- The first step in absorption costing is **allocation**. Allocation is the process by which whole cost items are charged direct to a cost unit or cost centre.

- The second step in absorption costing is overhead **apportionment**. This involves apportioning general overheads to cost centres and then reapportioning the costs of service cost centres to production departments.

- There are two main methods of reapportioning service department overheads to production departments.

    - **Direct method** (ignores inter-service department work)
    - **Repeated distribution method** (recognises inter-service department work)

- In absorption costing, it is usual to add overheads into product costs by applying a **predetermined overhead absorption rate**. The predetermined rate is set annually, in the budget.

- The **absorption rate** is calculated by dividing the budgeted overhead by the budgeted level of activity. For production overheads, the level of activity is often budgeted direct labour hours or budgeted machine hours.

- Management should try to establish an absorption rate that provides a **reasonably 'accurate' estimate** of overhead costs for jobs, products or services.

- The use of **separate departmental absorption rates** instead of **blanket (or single factory) absorption rates** will produce more realistic product costs.

- The rate of overhead absorption is based on **estimates** (of both numerator and denominator) and it is quite likely that either one or both of the estimates will not agree with what *actually* occurs. Actual overheads incurred will probably be either greater than or less than overheads absorbed into the cost of production.

    - **Over absorption** means that the overheads charged to the cost of production are greater than the overheads actually incurred.

    - **Under absorption** means that insufficient overheads have been included in the cost of production.

- **Activity based costing (ABC)** is an alternative approach to absorption costing. It involves the identification of the factors (**cost drivers**) which cause the costs of an organisation's major activities.

1   Allocation involves spreading overhead costs across cost centres.

    True   ☐

    False   ☐

2   Match the following overheads with the most appropriate basis of apportionment.

    Overhead   **Basis of apportionment**
    (a)   Depreciation of equipment   (1)   Direct machine hours
    (b)   Heat and light costs   (2)   Number of employees
    (c)   Canteen   (3)   Book value of equipment
    (d)   Insurance of equipment   (4)   Floor area

3   Which of the following departments are directly involved in production?

Department	Involved in production (✓)
Finished goods warehouse	
Canteen	
Machining department	
Offices	
Assembly department	

4   In relation to calculating total absorption cost, label the following descriptions in the correct order as Steps 1–5.

    Description   **Step**
    A   Apportion fixed costs over departments
    B   Establish the overhead absorption rate
    C   Choose fair methods of apportionment
    D   Apply the overhead absorption rate to products
    E   Reapportion service departments costs

5   In order to recognise the work service departments do for each other, the ………………….. method of reapportioning service department overheads should be used.

6   A direct labour hour basis is most appropriate in which of the following environments?

    A   Machine-intensive
    B   Labour-intensive
    C   When all units produced are identical
    D   None of the above

7   Over absorption occurs when absorbed overheads are greater than actual overheads.

    True   ☐

    False   ☐

8   *Choose the correct words from those highlighted.*

    Traditional costing systems tend to allocate **too great/too small** a proportion of overheads to high volume products and **too great/too small** a proportion of overheads to low volume products.

9   The following statements concern methods of absorbing fixed production overheads into units of production. Are they true or false?

	TRUE	FALSE
It is generally accepted that a time-based method should be used wherever possible (for example labour rate hours or machine rate hours).	☐	☐
Direct materials price percentage is not usually considered to be a suitable method because there is no reason why a higher material cost should lead to a cost unit incurring more overhead production overhead cost.	☐	☐

10   H Co bases its overhead absorption rate on labour hours. The following information is available for 20X9.

Budgeted overheads	$600,000
Actual overheads	$660,000
Budgeted labour hours	120,000
Actual labour hours	110,000

Calculate the over- or under-absorption of overheads for 20X9.

A $60,000 over-absorbed   B $60,000 under-absorbed

C $110,000 over-absorbed   D $110,000 under-absorbed

Answers to Quick Quiz

1   False. It is the process whereby whole cost items are charged direct to a cost unit or cost centre.

2   (a)   (3)
    (b)   (4)
    (c)   (2)
    (d)   (3)

3

Department	Involved in production (✓)
Finished goods warehouse	
Canteen	
Machining department	✓
Offices	
Assembly department	✓

4   A = 2
    B = 4
    C = 1
    D = 5
    E = 3

5   Repeated distribution method

6   B

7   True

8   Traditional costing systems tend to allocate **too great** a proportion of overheads to high volume products and **too small** a proportion of overheads to low volume products.

9   True. It is generally the case that overheads increase with time therefore a time-based approach is considered most sensible.

    True. This method is not particularly logical.

10 D $OAR = \dfrac{\text{Budgeted overheads}}{\text{Budgeted labour hours}} = \dfrac{\$600,000}{120,000} = \$5$ per labour hour

    Overheads absorbed   =   110,000 hours x $5
                         = $550,000

    Overheads absorbed – actual overheads   = $550,000 – $660,000
                                            = $110,000

    ∴ overheads were under-absorbed by $110,000.

Now try the questions below from the Exam Question Bank

Question numbers
16–20

Marginal costing and pricing decisions

Introduction

In Chapter 4 we saw how product costs are absorbed into the cost of units of output using absorption costing.

This chapter describes **marginal costing**, an alternative method of dealing with overheads. Whereas absorption costing recognises fixed costs (usually fixed production costs) as part of the cost of a unit of output and hence classifies them as product costs, marginal costing treats all fixed costs as period costs. (Remember we covered product costs and period costs in Chapter 2)

This chapter then goes on to cover how unit costs (whether full product costs derived using absorption costing, or marginal costs) can be used as the basis for setting **prices**.

Topic list	Syllabus references
1 Marginal cost	B1 (f)
2 Marginal costing	B1 (f)
3 Pricing decisions	B1 (f)

1 Marginal cost

FAST FORWARD ▶

Whereas fully absorbed product costs include fixed overhead, the **marginal cost** of a product usually consists of variable costs only.

1.1 Marginal cost

Key term

Marginal cost is 'part of the cost of one unit of product or service that would be avoided if the unit were not produced, or that would increase if one extra unit were produced'.   CIMA *Official Terminology*

The marginal production cost per unit of an item usually consists of the following.

- Direct materials
- Direct labour
- Variable production overheads

1.2 Contribution

FAST FORWARD ▶

Contribution is an important measure in marginal costing, and it is calculated as the difference between sales value and marginal or variable cost.

Key term

Contribution is '(sales value – variable cost of sales)'.   CIMA *Official Terminology*

The term 'contribution' is really short for 'contribution towards covering fixed overheads and making a profit'.

Question   Contribution

A particular electrical good is sold for $1,009.99. The direct material cost per unit is $320, the direct labour cost per unit is $192 and the variable production overhead cost per unit is $132. Fixed overheads per annum are $100,000 and the budgeted production level is 1,000 units.

The contribution per unit of the electrical good is $ [   ] .

Answer

The contribution per unit is $ | 365.99 |

Workings

	$	$
Selling price per unit		1009.99
Marginal cost per unit		
Direct material	320	
Direct labour	192	
Variable production overhead	132	
		644.00
Contribution per unit		365.99

We do *not* include absorbed fixed overheads in the calculation of marginal cost per unit and contribution per unit.

2 Marginal costing

Marginal costing is an alternative method of costing to absorption costing. In marginal costing, only variable costs are charged as a cost of sale and a contribution is calculated. Closing inventories of work in progress or finished goods are valued at marginal (variable) production cost. Fixed costs are treated as a period cost, and are charged in full against profit in the accounting period in which they are incurred.

Key term

Marginal (or **Variable**) **costing** 'assigns only variable costs to cost units while fixed costs are written off as period costs'.

CIMA *Official Terminology*

Fixed costs are a period charge and are the **same for any volume of sales and production** (within the relevant range). So, if an extra unit is sold, the following happens.

- Revenue will increase by the sales value of the item sold.
- Costs will increase by the variable cost per unit.
- Profit will increase by the **difference between sales value per unit and variable cost per unit (contribution).**

Therefore **only variable costs** are **charged** to the **cost of sales**.

Fixed costs are **deducted** from **total contribution** (the difference between sales revenue and the cost of sales) **to derive profit** for the period.

When a unit of product is made, the extra costs incurred in its manufacture are the variable production costs. Fixed costs are unaffected – no extra fixed costs are incurred when output is increased. The **valuation of units of output** and hence **closing inventory** is therefore at **variable production cost,** because these are the only costs properly attributable to the product.

Before explaining marginal costing principles any further it will be helpful to look at a numerical example.

2.1 Example: marginal costing

Water Co makes a product, the Splash, which has a variable production cost of $6 per unit and a sales price of $10 per unit. At the beginning of September 20X0 there were no opening inventories. Production during the month was 20,000 units. Fixed costs for the month were $45,000 (production, administration, sales and distribution). There were no variable marketing costs.

Required

Calculate at each of the following sales levels, the total contribution and total profit for September 20X0 and the contribution per unit and the profit/loss per unit, using marginal costing principles.

(a)   10,000 Splashes
(b)   15,000 Splashes
(c)   20,000 Splashes

Solution

The first stage in the profit calculation must be to identify the variable costs, and then the contribution. Fixed costs are deducted from the total contribution to derive the profit. All closing inventories are valued at marginal production cost ($6 per unit).

	10,000 Splashes		15,000 Splashes		20,000 Splashes	
	$	$	$	$	$	$
Sales (at $10)		100,000		150,000		200,000
Opening inventory	0		0		0	
Variable production cost	120,000		120,000		120,000	
	120,000		120,000		120,000	
Less value of closing inventory (at marginal cost)	60,000		30,000		–	
Variable cost of sales		60,000		90,000		120,000
Contribution		40,000		60,000		80,000
Less fixed costs		45,000		45,000		45,000
Profit/(loss)		(5,000)		15,000		35,000
Profit/(loss) per unit		$(0.50)		$1		$1.75
Contribution per unit		$4		$4		$4

The conclusions which may be drawn from this example are as follows.

(a)   The **profit per unit varies** at differing levels of sales, because the average fixed overhead cost per unit changes with the volume of output and sales.

(b)   The **contribution per unit is constant** at all levels of output and sales. Total contribution, which is the contribution per unit multiplied by the number of units sold, increases in direct proportion to the volume of sales.

(c)   Since the **contribution per unit does not change**, the most effective way of calculating the expected profit at any level of output and sales would be as follows.

(i)   First calculate the total contribution.

(ii)   Then deduct fixed costs as a period charge in order to find the profit.

(d)   In our example the expected profit from the sale of 17,000 Splashes would be as follows.

	$
Total contribution (17,000 × $4)	68,000
Less fixed costs	45,000
Profit	23,000

2.2 Profits, losses and breakeven point

(a)   If total contribution exceeds fixed costs, a profit is made.

(b)   If total contribution exactly equals fixed costs, no profit and no loss is made and breakeven point is reached.

(c)   If total contribution is less than fixed costs, there will be a loss.

PC company makes two products, the Loo and the Wash. Information relating to each of these products for April 20X1 is as follows.

	Loo	*Wash*
Opening inventory	nil	nil
Production (units)	15,000	6,000
Sales (units)	10,000	5,000
	$	$
Sales price per unit	20	30
Unit costs		
Direct materials	8	14
Direct labour	4	2
Variable production overhead	2	1
Variable sales overhead	2	3

Fixed costs for the month	$
Production costs	40,000
Administration costs	15,000
Sales and distribution costs	25,000

Using the approach set out in the answer to the example in Section 2.1 above, the marginal costing profit for April 20X1 is $ [   ].

Answer

The profit is $ | 10,000 |

Workings

	$
Contribution from Loos (unit contribution = $20 – $16 = $4 × 10,000)	40,000
Contribution from Washes (unit contribution = $30 – $20 = $10 × 5,000)	50,000
Total contribution	90,000
Fixed costs for the period	80,000
Profit	10,000

2.3 Inventory valuation using absorption costing and marginal costing

Marginal costing is significantly different from absorption costing. It is an **alternative method** of accounting for costs and profit, which rejects the principles of absorbing fixed overheads into unit costs.

(a)   **In marginal costing**

     (i)   Closing inventories are valued at **marginal production cost**.

     (ii)   Fixed costs are charged in full against the profit of the period in which they are incurred.

(b)   **In absorption costing**

   (i)   Closing inventories are valued at full production cost, and include a share of fixed production costs.

   (ii)   This means that the cost of sales in a period will include some fixed overhead incurred in a previous period (in opening inventory values) and will exclude some fixed overhead incurred in the current period but carried forward in closing inventory values as a charge to a subsequent accounting period.

With this in mind work through the following example.

2.4 Example: marginal and absorption costing

TLF Company manufactures a single product, the Claud. The following figures relate to the Claud for a one-year period.

Activity level	50%	100%
Sales and productions (units)	400	800
	$	$
Sales	8,000	16,000
Production costs: variable	3,200	6,400
fixed	1,600	1,600
Sales and distribution costs:		
variable	1,600	3,200
fixed	2,400	2,400

The normal level of activity for the year is 800 units. Fixed costs are incurred evenly throughout the year, and actual fixed costs are the same as budgeted.

There were no inventories of Claud at the beginning of the year.

In the first quarter, 220 units were produced and 160 units sold.

Required

(a)   Calculate the fixed production costs absorbed by Clauds in the first quarter if absorption costing is used.
(b)   Calculate the under/over recovery of overheads during the quarter.
(c)   Calculate the profit using absorption costing.
(d)   Calculate the profit using marginal costing.

Solution

(a) $$\frac{\text{Budgeted fixed production costs}}{\text{Budgeted output (normal level of activity)}} = \frac{\$1,600}{800\,\text{units}}$$

   Absorption rate = $2 per unit produced.

   During the quarter, the fixed production overhead absorbed was 220 units × $2 = $440.

(b)
	$
Actual fixed production overhead	400 (1/4 of $1,600)
Absorbed fixed production overhead	440
Over absorption of overhead	40

(c) **Profit for the quarter, absorption costing**

	$	$
Sales (160 × $20)		3,200
Production costs		
Variable (220 × $8)	1,760	
Fixed (absorbed overhead (220 × $2))	440	
Total (220 × $10)	2,200	
Less closing inventories (60 × $10)	600	
Production cost of sales	1,600	
Adjustment for over-absorbed overhead	40	
Total production costs		1,560
Gross profit		1,640
Less: sales and distribution costs		
variable (160 × $4)	640	
fixed (1/4 of $2,400)	600	
		1,240
Net profit		400

(d) **Profit for the quarter, marginal costing**

	$	$
Sales		3,200
Variable production costs	1,760	
Less closing inventories (60 × $8)	480	
Variable production cost of sales	1,280	
Variable sales and distribution costs	640	
Total variable costs of sales		1,920
Total contribution		1,280
Less:		
Fixed production costs incurred	400	
Fixed sales and distribution costs	600	
		1,000
Net profit		280

Now have a go at the following questions to assess whether or not you can use both absorption costing and marginal costing.

Question

Calculating profits

Suppose that a company makes and sells a single product. At the beginning of period 1, there are no opening inventories of the product, for which the variable production cost is $4 and the sales price is $6 per unit. Fixed costs are $2,000 per period, of which $1,500 are fixed production costs.

	Period 1	Period 2
Sales	1,200 units	1,800 units
Production	1,500 units	1,500 units

(a) Assuming normal output is 1,500 units per period, the absorption costing profit in each period and in total would be:

(i) Period 1 $ [   ]

(ii) Period 2 $ [   ]

(iii) Total $ [   ]

(b)   The marginal costing profit in each period and in total would be:

(i)   Period 1 $ [   ]

(ii)   Period 2 $ [   ]

(iii) Total $ [   ]

(a)   (i)   **Period 1** $ [**700**]

       (ii)   **Period 2** $ [**1,300**]

       (iii) **Total** $ [**2,000**]

Workings

The absorption rate for fixed production overhead is

$$\frac{\$1,500}{1,500 \text{ units}} = \$1 \text{ per unit}$$

	Period 1		Period 2		Total	
	$	$	$	$	$	$
Sales		7,200		10,800		18,000
Production costs						
Variable	6,000		6,000		12,000	
Fixed	1,500		1,500		3,000	
	7,500		7,500		15,000	
Add opening inventory b/f	–		1,500			
	7,500		9,000		15,000	
Less closing inventory c/f	(1,500)		–		–	
Production cost of sales	6,000		9,000		15,000	
(Under-)/over-absorbed						
overhead	–		–		–	
Total production costs		6,000		9,000		15,000
Gross profit		1,200		1,800		3,000
Other costs		500		500		1,000
Net profit		700		1,300		2,000

(b)   (i)   **Period 1** $ [**400**]

       (ii)   **Period 2** $ [**1,600**]

       (iii) **Total** $ [**2,000**]

Workings

	Period 1		Period 2		Total	
	$	$	$	$	$	$
Sales		7,200		10,800		18,000
Variable production cost	6,000		6,000		12,000	
Add opening inventory b/f	–		1,200		–	
	6,000		7,200		12,000	
Less closing inventory c/f	(1,200)		–		–	
Variable production cost						
of sales		4,800		7,200		12,000
Contribution		2,400		3,600		6,000
Fixed costs		2,000		2,000		4,000
Profit		400		1,600		2,000

Question | Two approaches to dealing with overheads

X Co commenced business on 1 March making one product only. The standard cost of one unit is as follows.

	$
Direct labour	5
Direct material	8
Variable production overhead	2
Fixed production overhead	5
Standard production cost	20

The fixed production overhead figure has been calculated on the basis of a budgeted normal output of 36,000 units per annum.

You are to assume that all the budgeted fixed expenses are incurred evenly over the year. March and April are to be taken as equal period months.

Selling, distribution and administration expenses are as follows.

Fixed	$120,000 per annum
Variable	15% of the sales value

The selling price per unit is $35 and the number of units produced and sold was as follows.

	March Units	April Units
Production	2,000	3,200
Sales	1,500	3,000

(a)   If a marginal costing system is in operation:

   (i)   The value of the closing inventory for each month will be:

   March $ [   ]

   April $ [   ]

   (ii)   The loss reported for March will be $ [   ]

   (iii) The profit reported for April will be $ [   ]

(b) If an absorption costing system is in operation:

(i) The value of the closing inventory for each month will be:

March $ [＿＿＿＿＿]

April $ [＿＿＿＿＿]

(ii) The production overhead for March will be [＿＿＿＿] absorbed by $ [＿＿＿＿]

(iii) The production overhead for April will be [＿＿＿＿] absorbed by $ [＿＿＿＿]

(iv) The loss reported for March will be $ [＿＿＿＿]

(v) The profit reported for April will be $ [＿＿＿＿]

Answer

(a) (i) **March $ 7,500** (500 units × $15)

April $ 10,500 (700 units × $15)

(ii) **The loss reported for March will be $ 2,875**

Workings

Contribution per unit:

	$ per unit
Selling price	35.00
Variable production cost	(15.00)
Variable selling expenses ($35 × 15%)	(5.25)
Contribution per unit	14.75

Loss for March:

	$
Contribution (1,500 × $14.75)	22,125
Fixed production overhead ($5 × 36,000 × 1/12)	(15,000)
Fixed selling expenses	(10,000)
Loss	(2,875)

(iii) **The profit reported for April will be $ 19,250**

Workings

	$
Contribution (3,000 × $14.75)	44,250
Fixed production overhead	(15,000)
Fixed selling expenses	(10,000)
	19,250

(b) (i) **March $ 10,000** (500 units × $20)

April $ 14,000 (700 units × $20)

(ii) **The production overhead for March will be** under **absorbed by $** 5,000

(iii) **The production overhead for April will be** | over | **absorbed by $** | 1,000 |

Workings

		March		April
		$		$
Overhead absorbed	(2,000 × $5)	10,000	(3,200 × $5)	16,000
Overhead incurred	($5 × 36,000 × 1/12)	15,000		15,000
Under/(over) absorbed		5,000		(1,000)

(iv) **The loss reported for March will be $** | 375 |

(v) **The profit reported for April will be $** | 20,250 |

Workings

	March	April
	$	$
Marginal costing (loss)/profit	(2,875)	19,250
Plus increase in inventory @ $5 fixed overhead per unit:		
500 units × $5	2,500	
200 units × $5		1,000
Absorption costing (loss)/profit	(375)	20,250

Assessment focus point

An assessment question may, for example, give you a marginal costing profit figure and ask you to use inventory figures and the overhead absorption rate to calculate the absorption costing profit. If inventory levels increase, absorption costing will report a higher profit than marginal costing. If inventory levels decrease, absorption costing will report the lower profit.

Question

Profit reconciliation

The following information is available for H Co.

20X9

Opening inventory	900 units
Closing inventory	300 units
Marginal costing profit	$100,000

Using an overhead absorption rate of $20 per unit, calculate what the profit would be if absorption costing were used.

Answer

	Units
Opening inventory	900
Closing inventory	300
Decrease	600 x $20 = $12,000 lower

Marginal profit	$100,000
	$12,000
Absorption profit	$88,000

3 Pricing decisions

3.1 Full cost plus pricing

FAST FORWARD

A price determined using **full cost plus pricing** is based on full cost plus a percentage mark-up for profit.

A traditional approach to pricing products is full cost plus pricing, whereby the sales price is determined by **calculating the full cost of the product and adding a percentage mark-up for profit.**

In full cost plus pricing, the full cost may be a fully absorbed *production* cost only, or it may include some absorbed administration, selling and distribution overhead.

A business might have an idea of the percentage profit margin it would like to earn and so might decide on an average profit mark-up as a general guideline for pricing decisions. This would be particularly **useful for** businesses that carry out a large amount of **contract work** or **jobbing work**, for which individual job or contract prices must be quoted regularly to prospective customers.

However, the **percentage profit mark-up** does not have to be fixed, but can be **varied to suit the circumstances**. In particular, the percentage mark-up can be varied to suit demand conditions in the market.

3.1.1 Problems with full cost plus pricing

(a) Prices must be adjusted to market and demand conditions, the decision cannot simply be made on a cost basis only. A company may need to match the prices of rival firms when these take a price-cutting initiative.

(b) A full cost plus basis for a pricing decision is a means of ensuring that, in the long run, a company succeeds in covering all its fixed costs and making a profit out of revenue earned. However, in the short term it is **inflexible**.

   (i) A firm tendering for a contract may quote a cost plus price that results in the contract going elsewhere, although a lower price would have been sufficient to cover all incremental costs and opportunity costs.

   (ii) In the short term, rapidly-changing environmental factors might dictate the need for lower (or higher) prices than long-term considerations would indicate.

(c) Where more than one product is sold by a company, the price decided by a cost plus formula depends on the method of apportioning fixed costs between the products.

3.1.2 Example: full cost plus pricing with more than one product

GL Company is attempting to decide sales prices for two products, Lyons and Tygers. The products are both made by the same workforce and in the same department. 30,000 direct labour hours are budgeted for the year. The budgeted fixed costs are $30,000 and it is expected that the department will operate at full capacity. Variable costs per unit are as follows.

		Lyons		*Tygers*
		$		$
Materials		4		4
Labour	(2 hours)	6	(3 hours)	9
Expenses	(1 machine hour)	2	(1 machine hour)	2
		12		15

Expected demand is 7,500 Lyons and 5,000 Tygers.

Required

Calculate the unit prices which give a profit of 20% on full cost if overheads are absorbed on the following bases.

(a)   On a direct labour hour basis
(b)   On a machine hour basis

Solution

(a)   **A direct labour hour basis**

$$\frac{\text{Budgeted fixed costs}}{\text{Budgeted labour costs}} = \frac{\$30,000}{(15,000+15,000)} = \$1$$

Absorption rate \$1 per direct labour hour

	Lyons	Tygers
	\$	\$
Variable costs	12.00	15.00
Overhead absorbed	2.00	3.00
	14.00	18.00
Profit (20%)	2.80	3.60
Price	16.80	21.60

The total budgeted profit would be \$(2.80 × 7,500) + (\$3.60 × 5,000) = \$39,000

(b)   **A machine hour basis**

$$\frac{\text{Budgeted fixed costs}}{\text{Budgeted machine hours}} = \frac{\$30,000}{(7,500+5,000)} = \frac{\$30,000}{12,500} = \$2.40$$

Absorption rate \$2.40 per machine hour

	Lyons	Tygers
	\$	\$
Variable costs	12.00	15.00
Overhead absorbed	2.40	2.40
Full cost	14.40	17.40
Profit (20%)	2.88	3.48
Price	17.28	20.88

The total budgeted profit would be \$(2.88 × 7,500) + (\$3.48 × 5,000) = \$39,000

(c)   The different bases for charging overheads result in different prices for both Lyons (difference of 48c per unit) and Tygers (difference of 72c per unit).

It is unlikely that the expected sales demand for the products would be the same at both sales prices. That means it would be unlikely that both (or either) product would achieve expected sales demand at the higher price. In other words, although the budgeted profit is \$39,000 whichever overhead absorption method is used, this assumes that budgeted sales would be achieved regardless of the unit price of each product. This is an unrealistic basis on which to make a decision.

3.1.3 Advantages of full cost plus pricing

(a)   Since the size of the profit margin can be varied at management's discretion, a decision based on a price in excess of full cost should ensure that a company working at normal capacity will cover all its fixed costs and make a profit. Companies may benefit from cost plus pricing in the following circumstances.

(i)   When they carry out large contracts which must make a sufficient profit margin to cover a fair share of fixed costs

(ii)   If they must justify their prices to potential customers (for example for government contracts)

(iii)   If they find it difficult to estimate expected demand at different sales prices

(b)   It is a **simple, quick and cheap** method of pricing which can be delegated to junior managers. This may be particularly important with jobbing work where many prices must be decided and quoted each day.

Question   Mark up

A company's product's full cost is $4.75 and it is sold at full cost plus 70%. A competitor has just launched a similar product selling for $7.99. The company needs to change the price of its product to match that of the competitor.

The margin of the first product should change to [   ] %.

Answer

The margin should change to [68.2] %

Workings

Margin in $ = $(7.99 − 4.75) = $3.24.
Margin as % of full cost = (3.24/4.75) × 100% = 68.2%.

3.1.4 Generating a return on sales or investment

Full cost plus pricing is a form of **target pricing**, which means setting a price so as to achieve a target return on sales or investment.

Let's start with looking at a **target return on sales**.

Suppose LM Company wishes to make a 20% **return on sales**. The full cost of product K is $100. The price that LM Company needs to set is therefore calculated as follows.

Let the selling price = P
P− full cost = 20% of P= 0.2P
Therefore P − 0.2P = full cost
Therefore 0.8P = full cost = $100
Therefore P = $100/0.8 = $125

Now let's look at a **target return on investment**. (ROI)

Suppose sales of product Z for the coming year are expected to be 500 units. A return of 15% in the coming year is required on the annual investment of $250,000 in product Z. The full cost of product Z is $175. The required selling price is calculated as follows.

Required return = 15% × $250,000 = $37,500
Expected cost = 500 × $175 = $87,500
Required revenue − expected cost = required return
Therefore expected revenue = $(37,500 + 87,500) = $125,000
Therefore selling price = $125,000/500 = $250

MM Company requires a 30% return on investment from its products. It will invest $800,000 in product B in the coming year, when it expects to sell 50,000 units.

If the full cost of product B is $100, the required selling price is $ ☐ .

Answer

The required selling price is $ 104.80

Workings

Required return = 30% × $800,000 = $240,000

Expected cost = 50,000 × $100 = $5,000,000

Required revenue = $(5,000,000 + 240,000) = $5,240,000

Selling price = $5,240,000/50,000 = $104.80

Assessment focus point

Watch out for OT questions in the assessment on this area in particular.

3.2 Marginal cost plus pricing

FAST FORWARD

Marginal cost plus prices are based on the marginal cost of production or the marginal cost of sales, plus a profit margin.

Instead of pricing products or services by adding a profit margin on to full cost, a business might **add a profit margin on to marginal cost (either the marginal cost of production or else the marginal cost of sales)**.

For example, if a company budgets to make 10,000 units of a product for which the variable cost of production is $3 a unit and the fixed production cost $60,000 a year, it might decide to fix a price by adding, say, $33^{1}/_{3}$% to full production cost to give a price of $9 × $1^{1}/_{3}$ = $12 a unit. Alternatively, it might decide to add a profit margin of, say, 250% on to the variable production cost, to give a price of $3 × 350% = $10.50.

3.2.1 Advantages of a marginal cost plus approach

(a) It is a **simple and easy** method to use.

(b) The **mark-up can be varied**, and so provided that a rigid mark-up is not used, mark-up pricing can be adjusted to reflect demand conditions.

(c) It draws management attention to contribution and the effects of higher or lower sales volumes on profit. This helps to **create a better awareness of** the concepts and implications of **marginal costing and breakeven analysis** (topics we cover in Chapters 4 and 6). For example, if a product costs $10 a unit and a mark-up of 150% is added to reach a price of $25 a unit, management should be clearly aware that every additional $1 of sales revenue would add 60c to contribution and profit.

(d) Mark-up pricing is **convenient where there is a readily identifiable basic variable cost. Retail industries** are the most obvious example, and it is quite common for the prices of goods in shops to be fixed by adding a mark-up (20% or 33¹/₃%, say) to the purchase cost. For example, a department store might buy in items of pottery at $3 each, add a mark-up of one third and resell the items at $4.

3.2.2 Drawbacks to marginal cost plus pricing

(a) Although the size of the mark-up can be varied in accordance with demand conditions, it does not ensure that sufficient attention is paid to demand conditions and competitors' prices.

(b) It ignores fixed overheads in the pricing decision, but the price must be high enough to ensure that a profit is made after covering fixed costs. Pricing decisions cannot ignore fixed costs altogether.

Question

Profit margin

A product has the following costs.

	$
Direct materials	5
Direct labour	3
Variable overhead	7

Fixed overheads are $10,000 per month. Budgeted sales for the month are 400 units.

The profit margin that needs to be added to marginal cost to break even is [   ] %

Answer

The profit margin is [167] **%**

Workings

Total costs for the month = variable costs + fixed costs

= ($15 × 400) + $10,000 = $16,000

∴ Sales revenue must equal $16,000

∴ Selling price per unit = $16,000/400 = $40

∴ Mark-up = $(40 − 15) = $25

Mark-up % = (25/15) × 100% = 167%

3.2.3 Margins and mark-ups

Consider the following **cost/profit/sales structure.**

	%
Cost	80
Profit	20
Sales	100

The **profit added** to the full cost or marginal cost of a product may be expressed in one of two ways.

- Percentage of **cost of sales**, such as **25%** ($^{20}/_{80}$) **mark-up**
- Percentage of **sales**, such as **20%** ($^{20}/_{100}$) **margin**

Alternatively, the **cost/profit/sales structure** could be:

	%
Cost	100
Profit	20
Sales	120

- Mark-up = $^{20}/_{100}$ = 20%
- Margin = $^{20}/_{120}$ = 16.7%

Question

(a) Product B's unit cost is $50. A selling price is set based on a margin of 15%. The selling price is $ [   ]

(b) Product L sells for $750. The mark-up is 10%. The unit cost of product L is $ [   ]

Answer

(a) **The selling price is $ [58.82]**

Workings

	$	%
Cost	50	85
Profit	?	15
Selling price	?	100

∴ Selling price = $50/0.85 = $58.82

(b) **The unit cost is $ [681.82]**

Workings

	$	%
Cost	?	100
Profit	?	10
Selling price	750	110

Cost = $750/1.1 = $681.82

Question

CTF Co uses a mark-up of 15% on full cost to price its product X. The indirect costs are 20% of the direct costs. What mark-up should be applied to direct costs to give the same selling price for product X?

A   138%
B   18%
C   38%
D   118%

C

Indirect costs are 20% of direct costs. Let D = direct costs and I = indirect costs.

So D + I	= Full cost
Therefore D + 20% D	= Full cost
Therefore 1.15 (D+ 0.2D)	= Selling price
Therefore 1.15 × 1.2D	= Selling price
Therefore 1.38D	= Selling price

So the mark-up on direct costs is 38%

Or, assume that direct costs are $100

	$		$
Direct costs	100		100
Indirect costs	20		
	120		
Mark-up (15%)	18	Mark-up (balancing figure)	38
Selling price	138	Selling price	138

Assessment focus point

If you struggle with percentage calculations you need to spend some time getting them clear in your head. Percentage calculations are vital for margin and mark-up questions.

Chapter Roundup

- Whereas fully absorbed product costs include fixed overhead, the **marginal cost** of a product usually consists of variable costs only.

- **Contribution** is an important measure in marginal costing, and it is calculated as the difference between sales value and marginal or variable cost.

- **Marginal costing** is an alternative method of costing to absorption costing. In marginal costing, only variable costs are charged as a cost of sale and a contribution is calculated. Closing inventories of work in progress or finished goods are valued at marginal (variable) production cost. Fixed costs are treated as a period cost, and are charged in full against profit in the accounting period in which they are incurred.

- A price determined using **full cost plus pricing** is based on full cost plus a percentage mark-up for profit.

- **Marginal cost plus prices** are based on the marginal cost of production or the marginal cost of sales, plus a profit margin.

Quick Quiz

1   Sales value – marginal cost of sales = …………………………………………………………..

2   Identify which of the following relate to either

A = Absorption costing
M = Marginal costing

		A or M
(a)	Closing inventories valued at marginal production cost	
(b)	Closing inventories valued at full production cost	
(c)	Cost of sales include some fixed overhead incurred in previous period in opening inventory values	
(d)	Fixed costs are charged in full against profit for the period	

3   Which of the following are arguments in favour of marginal costing?
(a)   It is simple to operate.
(b)   There is no under or over absorption of overheads.
(c)   Fixed costs are the same regardless of activity levels.
(d)   The information from this costing method may be used for decision making.

4   ABC Co plans to sell 1,200 units of product B. A 12% return is required on the $1,000,000 annual investment in product B. A selling price of $500 per unit has been set.

The full cost of product B is $ [   ].

5   XYZ Co produces a component W. The standard cost card for component W is as follows:

		$
Production costs	Fixed	255.70
	Variable	483.50
Selling costs	Fixed	124.80
	Variable	75.60
	Profit	60.40
	Selling price	1,000.00

(a)   Under an absorption costing system, what would be the value of inventory?

- $255.70
- $739.20
- $483.20
- $227.80

(b)   Under a variable costing system, what would be the value of inventory?

- $483.50
- $75.60
- $136.00
- $124.80

6   When comparing the profits reported under absorption costing and marginal costing during a period when the level of inventory increased:

A   Absorption costing profits will be higher and closing inventory valuations lower than those under marginal costing

B   Absorption costing profits will be higher and closing inventory valuations higher than those under marginal costing

C   Marginal costing profits will be higher and closing inventory valuations lower than those under absorption costing

D   Marginal costing profits will be higher and closing inventory valuations higher than those under absorption costing

7   What is a period cost in marginal costing?

8   Marginal costing and absorption costing are different techniques for assessing profit in a period. If there are changes in inventory during a period, marginal costing and absorption costing will report different profits.

Which of the following statements are true?

I   If inventory levels increase, marginal costing will report the higher profit.

II   If inventory levels decrease, marginal costing will report the lower profit.

III   If inventory levels decrease, marginal costing will report the higher profit.

IV   If the opening and closing inventory volumes are the same, marginal costing and absorption costing will report the same profit figure.

A   All of the above
B   I, II and IV
C   I and IV
D   III and IV

9   A product has the following costs:

	$/unit
Variable production costs	4.80
Total production costs	7.50
Total variable costs	5.90
Total costs	10.00

11,400 units of the product were manufactured in a period during which 11,200 units were sold.

What is the profit difference using absorption costing rather than marginal costing?

A   The profit for the period is $540 lower
B   The profit for the period is $540 higher
C   The profit for the period is $820 lower
D   The profit for the period is $820 higher

10   A company currently uses absorption costing. The following information relates to Product X for Month 1:

Opening inventory	Nil
Production	900 units
Sales	800 units

If the company had used marginal costing, which of the following combinations would be true?

	Profit	Inventory valuation
A	would be higher	would be higher
B	would be higher	would be lower
C	would be lower	would be higher
D	would be lower	would be lower

1   Contribution

2

		A or M
(a)	Closing inventory valued at marginal production cost	M
(b)	Closing inventory valued at full production cost	A
(c)	Cost of sales include some fixed overhead incurred in previous period in opening inventory values	A
(d)	Fixed costs are charged in full against profit for the period	M

3   All are arguments in favour of marginal costing.

4   Required return = 12% × $1,000,000 = $120,000

Expected revenue = 1,200 × $500 = $600,000

Expected cost = expected revenue − required return

∴ Expected cost = $(600,000 − 120,000) = $480,000

∴ Full cost per unit = $480,000/1,200 = $400

5   (a) $255.70 + $483.50 = $739.20

Selling costs are never included in inventory valuations. The valuation under absorption costing is the full production cost so it is the sum of the fixed production cost and the variable production cost.

(b) $483.50

Selling costs are never included in inventory valuations. The valuation under a variable costing system is the variable production cost.

6   B   Closing inventory valuation under absorption costing will always be higher than under marginal costing because of the absorption of fixed overheads into closing inventory values.

The profit under absorption costing will be greater because the fixed overhead being carried forward in closing inventory is greater than the fixed overhead being written off in opening inventory.

7   A fixed cost.

8   D   If inventory levels decrease, marginal costing will report the higher profit, if inventory levels increase, absorption costing will report the higher profit. The profit figures will be the same where inventory levels are unchanged.

9   B   200 units x ($7·50 − $4·80)/unit

10   D   Under marginal costing, closing inventory will be valued **lower** than under absorption costing. If production is greater than sales the inventory level has increased during the month. Absorption costing would therefore produce a higher profit than marginal costing.

Now try the questions below from the Question Bank

Question numbers
21–25

Breakeven analysis and limiting factor analysis

Introduction

You should by now realise that the cost accountant needs estimates of **fixed** and **variable costs**, and **revenues**, at various output levels. Cost accountants must also be fully aware of **cost behaviour** because, to be able to estimate costs, they must know what a particular cost will do given particular conditions.

An understanding of cost behaviour is not all that you may need to know, however. The application of **breakeven analysis**, which is based on cost behaviour principles and marginal costing ideas, is sometimes necessary so that the appropriate decision-making information can be provided. As you may have guessed, this chapter is going to look at that very topic.

We're also going to take a look at **limiting factor analysis**, another technique using marginal costing ideas. This one helps us to determine the profit-maximising production or sales mix.

Topic list	Syllabus references
1 Breakeven analysis and contribution	E1(a)
2 Breakeven point	E1(b)
3 The contribution/sales (C/S) ratio	E1(b)
4 The margin of safety	E1(b)
5 Breakeven arithmetic and profit targets	E1(b)
6 Breakeven charts and profit/volume graphs	E1(c)
7 Limitations of breakeven analysis	E1(c)
8 Limiting factor analysis	E2(c)

1 Breakeven analysis and contribution

Breakeven analysis or **cost-volume-profit (CVP) analysis** is the study of the interrelationships between costs, volume and profit at various levels of activity.

Key term

Cost-volume-profit analysis (CVP) is the 'study of the effects on future profit of changes in fixed cost, variable cost, sales price, quantity and mix'.

CIMA *Official Terminology*

1.1 Contribution

Contribution, a concept we encountered in Chapter 4, is fundamental to CVP analysis. As you know, contribution per unit is the difference between selling price per unit and variable costs per unit. The **total contribution** from the sales volume for a period can be **compared with the fixed costs** for the period. Any **excess of contribution** is **profit**, any **deficit** of contribution is a **loss**.

2 Breakeven point

The **breakeven point** occurs when there is neither a profit nor a loss and so fixed costs equal contribution.

Key term

The **breakeven point** is the 'level of activity at which there is neither profit nor loss'.

CIMA *Official Terminology*

The management of an organisation usually wishes to know the profit likely to be made if the aimed-for production and sales for the year are achieved. Management may also be interested to know the activity level at which there is neither profit nor loss. This is known as the **breakeven point**.

The breakeven point (BEP) can be calculated arithmetically.

Formula to learn

Breakeven point = Number of units of sale required to break even

$$= \frac{\text{Total fixed costs}}{\text{Contribution per unit}}$$

$$= \frac{\text{Contribution required to break even}}{\text{Contribution per unit}}$$

2.1 Example: breakeven point

Expected sales   10,000 units at $8 = $80,000
Variable cost $5 per unit
Fixed costs $21,000

Required

Compute the breakeven point.

Solution

The contribution per unit is $(8–5)	=	$3
Contribution required to break even	=	fixed costs = $21,000
Breakeven point (BEP)	=	21,000 ÷ 3
	=	7,000 units
In revenue, BEP	=	(7,000 × $8) = $56,000

Sales above $56,000 will result in profit of $3 per unit of additional sales and sales below $56,000 will mean a loss of $3 per unit for each unit by which sales fall short of 7,000 units. In other words, profit will improve or worsen by the amount of contribution per unit.

	7,000 units	7,001 units
	$	$
Revenue	56,000	56,008
Less variable costs	35,000	35,005
Contribution	21,000	21,003
Less fixed costs	21,000	21,000
Profit	0 (= breakeven)	3

3 The contribution/sales (C/S) ratio

FAST FORWARD

The **C/S ratio** (or **P/V ratio**) is a measure of how much contribution is earned from each $1 of sales.

3.1 C/S ratio and breakeven point

An alternative way of calculating the breakeven point to give an answer in terms of sales revenue and using the C/S ratio is as follows.

Formula to learn

Breakeven point = **Sales revenue** required to break even.

$$= \frac{\text{Contribution required to break even}}{\text{C/S ratio}}$$

$$= \frac{\text{Fixed costs}}{\text{C/S ratio}}$$

3.2 Example: C/S ratio

In the example in Section 2.1 the C/S ratio is $\frac{\$3}{\$8} = 37.5\%$

Breakeven is where sales revenue equals $\frac{\$21,000}{37.5\%} = \$56,000$. At a price of $8 per unit, this represents 7,000 units of sales.

The C/S ratio is a measure of how much contribution is earned from each $1 of sales. The C/S ratio of 37.5% in the above example means that for every $1 of sales, a contribution of 37.5c is earned. Thus, in order to earn a total contribution of $21,000 and if contribution increases by 37.5c per $1 of sales, sales must be:

$$\frac{\$1}{37.5c} \times \$21,000 = \$56,000$$

Important! The C/S (contribution/sales) ratio is sometimes called the **profit/volume or P/V ratio**.

Question

C/S ratio

The C/S ratio of product W is 20%. IB, the manufacturer of product W, wishes to make a contribution of $50,000 towards fixed costs.

If the selling price is $10 per unit, the number of units of W that must be sold is [   ]

Answer

The number of units that must be sold is [25,000].

Workings

$$\frac{\text{Required contribution}}{\text{C/S ratio}} = \frac{\$50,000}{20\%} = \$250,000$$

∴ Number of units = $250,000 ÷ $10 = 25,000.

4 The margin of safety

FAST FORWARD

The **margin of safety** is the difference in units between the budgeted sales volume and the breakeven sales volume. It is sometimes expressed as a percentage of the budgeted sales volume. Alternatively the margin of safety can be expressed as the difference between the budgeted sales revenue and breakeven sales revenue, expressed as a percentage of the budgeted sales revenue.

As well as being interested in the breakeven point, management may also be interested in the amount by which actual sales can fall below anticipated sales without a loss being incurred. This is the **margin of safety**.

Key term

The **margin of safety** 'indicates the percentage by which forecast revenue exceeds or falls short of that required to break even'.

CIMA *Official Terminology*

Formula to learn

$$\text{Margin of safety} = \frac{\text{Projected sales - breakeven point}}{\text{Projected sales}} \times 100$$

4.1 Example: margin of safety

Mal de Mer Co makes and sells a product which has a variable cost of $30 and which sells for $40. Budgeted fixed costs are $70,000 and budgeted sales are 8,000 units.

Required

Calculate the breakeven point and the margin of safety.

Solution

(a) Breakeven point $= \dfrac{\text{Total fixed costs}}{\text{Contribution per unit}} = \dfrac{\$70,000}{\$(40 - 30)}$

$= 7,000$ units

(b) Margin of safety $= 8,000 - 7,000$ units $= 1,000$ units

which may be expressed as $\dfrac{1,000 \text{ units}}{8,000 \text{ units}} \times 100\% = 12\tfrac{1}{2}\%$ of budget

(c) The margin of safety indicates to management that actual sales can fall short of budget by 1,000 units or 12½% before the breakeven point is reached and no profit at all is made.

5 Breakeven arithmetic and profit targets

5.1 Breakeven arithmetic

At the **breakeven point**, there is no profit or loss and so **sales revenue = total costs** or **total contribution = fixed costs**.

Formula to learn

At the **breakeven point**, sales revenue equals total costs and there is no profit.

$S = V + F$

where S $=$ Sales revenue
       V $=$ Total variable costs
       F $=$ Total fixed costs

Subtracting V from each side of the equation, we get:

$S - V = F$, that is, **total contribution = fixed costs**

5.2 Example: breakeven arithmetic

Butterfingers Company makes a product which has a variable cost of $7 per unit.

Required

If fixed costs are $63,000 per annum, calculate the selling price per unit if the company wishes to break even with a sales volume of 12,000 units.

Solution

			$
Contribution required to break even (= Fixed costs)	=	$63,000	
Volume of sales	=	12,000 units	
Required contribution per unit (S – V)	=	$63,000 ÷ 12,000	5.25
Variable cost per unit (V)	=		7.00
Required sales price per unit (S)	=		12.25

5.3 Target profits

FAST FORWARD

> The **target profit** is achieved when sales revenue equals variable costs plus fixed costs plus profit. Therefore the **total contribution required** for a target profit = **fixed costs + required profit.**

A similar formula may be applied where a company wishes to achieve a certain profit during a period. To achieve this profit, sales must cover all costs and leave the required profit.

Formula to learn

The **target profit** is achieved when: $S = V + F + P$,

Where S = Sales revenue
  V = Variable costs
  F = Fixed costs
  P = required profit

Subtracting V from each side of the equation, we get:

$S - V = F + P$, so

Total contribution required $= F + P$

5.4 Example: target profits

RB Co makes and sells a single product, for which variable costs are as follows.

	$
Direct materials	10
Direct labour	8
Variable production overhead	6
	24

The sales price is $30 per unit, and fixed costs per annum are $68,000. The company wishes to make a profit of $16,000 per annum.

Required

Determine the sales required to achieve this profit.

Solution

Required contribution = fixed costs + profit = $68,000 + $16,000 = $84,000

Required sales can be calculated in one of two ways.

(a) $\dfrac{\text{Required contribution}}{\text{Contribution per unit}}$ = $\dfrac{\$84,000}{\$(30-24)}$ = 14,000 units, or $420,000 in revenue

(b) $\dfrac{\text{Required contribution}}{\text{C/S ratio}}$ = $\dfrac{\$84,000}{20\%\,^*}$ = $420,000 of revenue, or 14,000 units.

* C/S ratio = $\dfrac{\$30-\$24}{\$30} = \dfrac{\$6}{\$30} = 0.2 = 20\%.$

Question

SLB Co wishes to sell 14,000 units of its product, which has a variable cost of $15 to make and sell. Fixed costs are $47,000 and the required profit is $23,000.

The required sales price per unit is $ ☐ .

Answer

The required sales price per unit is $ 20 .

Workings

Required contribution = fixed costs plus profit
= $47,000 + $23,000
= $70,000

Required sales = 14,000 units

	$
Required contribution per unit sold	5
Variable cost per unit	15
Required sales price per unit	20

Question

G Co has budgeted breakeven sales revenue of $600,000 and fixed costs of $210,000 for the month of September.

Calculate the sales revenue needed to achieve a profit of $75,250 in September.

Answer

$$\text{Sales revenue to breakeven} = \frac{\text{Fixed costs}}{\text{C/S ratio}}$$

$$\therefore \quad \$600,000 = \frac{\$210,000}{\text{C/S ratio}}$$

$$\therefore \quad \text{C/S ratio} = \$210,000/\$600,000$$
$$= 0.35$$

Total contribution for target profit = fixed costs + required profit
= $210,000 + $75,250
= $285,250

To convert this target contribution into target sales revenue, we use the C/S ratio

$285,250/0.35 = $815,000

5.5 Variations on breakeven and profit target calculations

You may come across variations on breakeven and profit target calculations in which you will be expected to consider the effect of altering the selling price, variable cost per unit or fixed cost.

5.5.1 Example: change in selling price

Stomer Cakes Co bakes and sells a single type of cake. The variable cost of production is 15c and the current sales price is 25c. Fixed costs are $2,600 per month, and the annual profit for the company at current sales volume is $36,000. The volume of sales demand is constant throughout the year.

The sales manager, Ian Digestion, wishes to raise the sales price to 29c per cake, but considers that a price rise will result in some loss of sales.

Required

Ascertain the minimum volume of sales required each month to raise the price to 29c.

Solution

The minimum volume of demand which would justify a price of 29c is one which would leave total profit at least the same as before, ie $3,000 per month. Required profit should be converted into required contribution, as follows.

	$
Monthly fixed costs	2,600
Monthly profit, minimum required	3,000
Current monthly contribution	5,600

Contribution per unit (25c – 15c) = 10c
Current monthly sales = 56,000 cakes

The minimum volume of sales required after the price rise will be an amount which earns a contribution of $5,600 per month, no worse than at the moment. The contribution per cake at a sales price of 29c would be 14c.

$$\text{Required sales} = \frac{\text{required contribution}}{\text{contribution per unit}} = \frac{\$5,600}{14c} = 40,000 \text{ cakes per month.}$$

5.5.2 Example: change in production costs

Close Brickett Co makes a product which has a variable production cost of $8 and a variable sales cost of $2 per unit. Fixed costs are $40,000 per annum, the sales price per unit is $18, and the current volume of output and sales is 6,000 units.

The company is considering whether to have an improved machine for production. Annual hire costs would be $10,000 and it is expected that the variable cost of production would fall to $6 per unit.

Required

(a) Determine the number of units that must be produced and sold to achieve the same profit as is currently earned, if the machine is hired.

(b) Calculate the annual profit with the machine if output and sales remain at 6,000 units per annum.

Solution

The current unit contribution is $(18 - (8+2)) = 8

(a)

		$
Current contribution (6,000 × $8)		48,000
Less current fixed costs		40,000
Current profit		8,000

With the new machine fixed costs will go up by $10,000 to $50,000 per annum. The variable cost per unit will fall to $(6 + 2) = $8, and the contribution per unit will be $10.

	$
Required profit (as currently earned)	8,000
Fixed costs	50,000
Required contribution	58,000

Contribution per unit = $10
Sales required to earn $8,000 profit = 5,800 units

(b) **If sales are 6,000 units**

	$	$
Sales (6,000 × $18)		108,000
Variable costs: production (6,000 × $6)	36,000	
sales (6,000 × $2)	12,000	
		48,000
Contribution (6,000 × $10)		60,000
Less fixed costs		50,000
Profit		10,000

Alternative calculation	$
Profit at 5,800 units of sale (see (a))	8,000
Contribution from sale of extra 200 units (× $10)	2,000
Profit at 6,000 units of sale	10,000

5.6 More applications of breakeven arithmetic

It may be clear by now that, given no change in fixed costs, **total profit is maximised when the total contribution is at its maximum**. Total contribution in turn depends on the unit contribution and on the sales volume.

An increase in the sales price will increase unit contribution, but sales volume is likely to fall because fewer customers will be prepared to pay the higher price. A decrease in sales price will reduce the unit contribution, but sales volume may increase because the goods on offer are now cheaper. The **optimum combination** of sales price and sales volume is arguably the one which **maximises total contribution**.

5.6.1 Example: profit maximisation

C Co has developed a new product which is about to be launched on to the market. The variable cost of selling the product is $12 per unit. The marketing department has estimated that at a sales price of $20, annual demand would be 10,000 units.

However, if the sales price is set above $20, sales demand would fall by 500 units for each 50c increase above $20. Similarly, if the price is set below $20, demand would increase by 500 units for each 50c stepped reduction in price below $20.

Required

Determine the price which would maximise C Co's profit in the next year.

Solution

At a price of $20 per unit, the unit contribution would be $(20 – 12) = $8. Each 50c increase (or decrease) in price would raise (or lower) the unit contribution by 50c. The total contribution is calculated at each sales price by multiplying the unit contribution by the expected sales volume.

Unit price	Unit contribution	Sales volume	Total contribution
$	$	Units	$
20.00	8.00	10,000	80,000

(a) Reduce price

19.50	7.50	10,500	78,750
19.00	7.00	11,000	77,000

(b) Increase price

20.50	8.50	9,500	80,750
21.00	9.00	9,000	81,000
21.50	9.50	8,500	80,750
22.00	10.00	8,000	80,000
22.50	10.50	7,500	78,750

The total contribution would be maximised, and therefore profit maximised, at a sales price of $21 per unit, and sales demand of 9,000 units.

Question

Breakeven point

Betty Battle Co manufactures a product which has a selling price of $20 and a variable cost of $10 per unit. The company incurs annual fixed costs of $29,000. Annual sales demand is 9,000 units.

New production methods are under consideration, which would cause a $1,000 increase in fixed costs and a reduction in variable cost to $9 per unit. The new production methods would result in a superior product and would enable sales to be increased to 9,750 units per annum at a price of $21 each.

If the change in production methods were to take place, the breakeven output level would be:

A	400 units higher	C	100 units higher
B	400 units lower	D	100 units lower

Answer

The correct answer is B.

	Current	Revised	Difference
	$	$	
Selling price	20	21	
Variable costs	10	9	
Contribution per unit	10	12	
Fixed costs	$29,000	$30,000	
Breakeven point (units)	2,900	2,500	400 lower

$$\text{Breakeven point (BEP)} = \frac{\text{Total fixed costs}}{\text{Contribution per unit}}$$

$$\text{Current BEP} = \frac{\$29,000}{\$10} = 2,900 \text{ units}$$

$$\text{Revised BEP} = \frac{\$30,000}{\$12} = 2,500 \text{ units}$$

Question   Breakeven point percentages

Chocco Co produces a single product and the following information is available.

	$
Selling price per unit	28
Variable cost per unit	13
Fixed overheads	105,000

The breakeven point was calculated using these figures but management have decided that the variable cost and selling price will rise by 1.9% and 5% respectively.

What will happen to the breakeven point when the new cost and price are taken into account?

A   It will rise by 7.14%   C   It will fall by 7.14%
B   It will rise by 1.14%   D   It will fall by 1.14%

Answer

C

	Now	Revised
	$	$
Selling price	28	29.40
Variable cost	13	13.25
Contribution	15	16.15
Breakeven volume	105,000/$15 = 7,000	$105,000/$16.15 = 6,500

Decrease in breakeven volume = (7,000 – 6,500)/7,000 = 7.14%

6 Breakeven charts and profit/volume graphs

6.1 Breakeven charts

FAST FORWARD

> The breakeven point can also be determined graphically using a **breakeven chart**.

Key term

> A **breakeven chart** is a chart that indicates approximate profit or loss at different levels of sales volume within a limited range.

A breakeven chart has the following axes.

- A **horizontal** axis showing the **sales/output** (in value or units)
- A **vertical axis** showing $ for **sales revenues** and **costs**

6.1.1 Lines on a breakeven chart

The following lines are drawn on the breakeven chart.

(a) The **sales line**

  (i) Starts at the origin
  (ii) Ends at the point signifying expected sales

(b) The fixed costs line

  (i) Runs parallel to the horizontal axis
  (ii) Meets the vertical axis at a point which represents total fixed costs

(c) The **total costs line**

  (i) Starts where the fixed costs line meets the vertical axis

  (ii) Ends at the point which represents anticipated sales on the horizontal axis and total costs of anticipated sales on the vertical axis

The **breakeven point** is the **intersection** of the **sales line** and the **total costs line**.

The distance between the **breakeven point** and the **expected (or budgeted) sales**, in units, indicates the **margin of safety**.

6.1.2 Example: a breakeven chart

The budgeted annual output of a factory is 120,000 units. The fixed overheads amount to $40,000 and the variable costs are 50p per unit. The sales price is $1 per unit.

Required

Construct a breakeven chart showing the current breakeven point and profit earned up to the present maximum capacity.

Solution

We begin by calculating the profit at the budgeted annual output.

	$
Sales (120,000 units)	120,000
Variable costs	60,000
Contribution	60,000
Fixed costs	40,000
Profit	20,000

The breakeven chart is shown on the following page.

The chart is drawn as follows.

(a)   The **vertical axis** represents **money** (costs and revenue) and the **horizontal axis** represents the **level of activity** (production and sales).

(b)   The fixed costs are represented by a **straight line parallel to the horizontal axis** (in our example, at $40,000).

(c)   The **variable costs** are added 'on top of' fixed costs, to give **total costs**. It is assumed that fixed costs are the same in total and variable costs are the same per unit at all levels of output.

The line of costs is therefore a straight line and only two points need to be plotted and joined up. Perhaps the two most convenient points to plot are total costs at zero output, and total costs at the budgeted output and sales.

(i)   At zero output, costs are equal to the amount of fixed costs only, $40,000, since there are no variable costs.

(ii)   At the budgeted output of 120,000 units, costs are $100,000.

	$
Fixed costs	40,000
Variable costs 120,000 × 50c	60,000
Total costs	100,000

(d)   The sales line is also drawn by plotting two points and joining them up.

(i)   At zero sales, revenue is nil.
(ii)   At the budgeted output and sales of 120,000 units, revenue is $120,000.

Breakeven chart

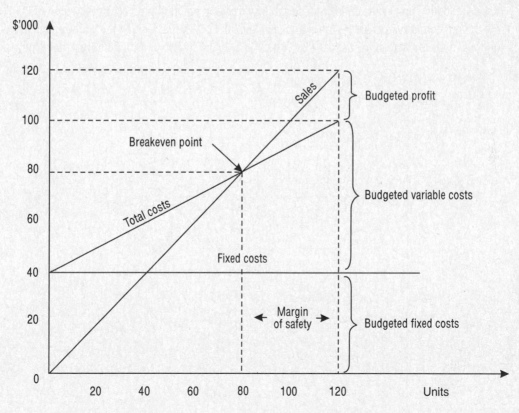

6.1.3 Interpreting the breakeven chart

The breakeven point is where total costs are matched exactly by total revenue. From the chart, this can be seen to occur at output and sales of 80,000 units, when revenue and costs are both $80,000. This breakeven point can be proved mathematically as:

$$\frac{\text{Required contribution } (= \text{fixed costs})}{\text{Contribution per unit}} = \frac{\$40,000}{50\text{c per unit}} = 80,000 \text{ units}$$

The margin of safety can be seen on the chart as the difference between the budgeted level of activity and the breakeven level.

6.1.4 The value of breakeven charts

Breakeven charts are used as follows.

*   To **plan** the production of a company's products
*   To **market** a company's products
*   To give a **visual display** of breakeven arithmetic

6.2 The contribution breakeven chart

FAST FORWARD

A **contribution breakeven chart** depicts variable costs, so that contribution can be read directly from the chart.

The main problem with the traditional breakeven chart is that it is not possible to read contribution directly from the chart.

The contribution breakeven chart remedies this by **drawing the variable cost line instead of the fixed cost line**. A contribution breakeven chart for the example in Section 6.1.2 would include the variable cost line passing through the origin and the total variable cost of $60,000 for 120,000 units. The contribution breakeven chart is shown below.

Contribution breakeven chart

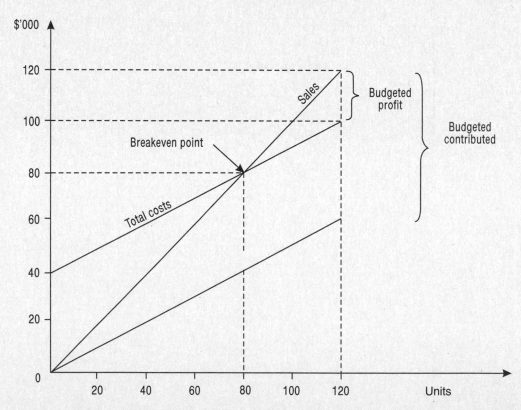

If you look back at the breakeven chart in Section 6.1.2(d) you will see that the breakeven point is the same, but that the budgeted contribution can now be read more easily from the chart.

6.3 The profit/volume (P/V) graph

FAST FORWARD

The **profit/volume (P/V) graph** is a variation of the breakeven chart and illustrates the relationship of profit to sales volume.

6.3.1 Construction of a profit/volume graph

A P/V graph is constructed as follows (look at the chart in the example that follows as you read the explanation).

(a)   'P' is on the y axis and actually comprises not only 'profit' but contribution to profit (in monetary value), extending above and below the x axis with a zero point at the intersection of the two axes, and the negative section below the x axis representing fixed costs. This means that at zero production, the firm is incurring a loss equal to the fixed costs.

(b)   'V' is on the x axis and comprises either volume of sales or value of sales (revenue).

(c)   The profit-volume line is a straight line drawn with its starting point (at zero production) at the intercept on the y axis representing the level of fixed costs, and with a gradient of contribution/unit (or the C/S ratio if sales value is used rather than units). The P/V line will cut the x axis at the breakeven point of sales volume. Any point on the P/V line above the x axis represents the profit to the firm (as measured on the vertical axis) for that particular level of sales.

6.3.2 Example: P/V graph

Let us draw a P/V graph for our example in Section 6.1.2. At sales of 120,000 units, total contribution will be 120,000 × $(1 − 0.5) = $60,000 and total profit will be $20,000.

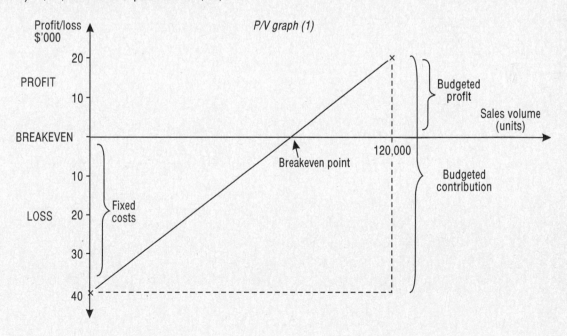

6.3.3 The advantage of the P/V graph

(a) If the budgeted selling price of the product in our example is increased to $1.20, with the result that demand drops to 105,000 units despite additional fixed costs of $10,000 being spent on advertising, we could add a line representing this situation to our P/V chart.

(b) At sales of 105,000 units, contribution will be 105,000 × $(1.20 – 0.50) = $73,500 and total profit will be $23,500 (fixed costs being $50,000).

(c) The diagram shows that if the selling price is increased, the breakeven point occurs at a lower level of sales revenue (71,429 units instead of 80,000 units), although this is not a particularly large decrease when viewed in the context of the projected sales volume. It is also possible to see that for sales above 50,000 units, the profit achieved will be higher (and the loss achieved lower) if the price is $1.20. For sales volumes below 50,000 units the first option will yield lower losses.

(d) The P/V graph is the clearest way of presenting such information; two conventional breakeven charts on one set of axes would be very confusing.

(e) Changes in the variable cost per unit or in fixed costs at certain activity levels can also be incorporated easily into a P/V graph. The profit or loss at each point where the cost structure changes should be calculated and plotted on the graph so that the profit/volume line becomes a series of straight lines.

(f) For example, suppose that in our example, at sales levels in excess of 120,000 units the variable cost per unit increases to $0.60 (perhaps because of overtime premiums that are incurred when production exceeds a certain level). At sales of 130,000 units, contribution would therefore be 130,000 × $(1 - 0.60) = $52,000 and total profit would be $12,000.

| Assessment focus point | Make sure that you can visualise what will happen to the graph if the breakeven point changes. The breakeven point will change if either fixed costs or contribution changes. |

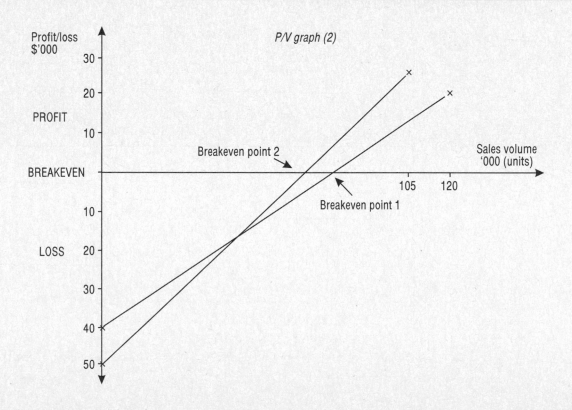

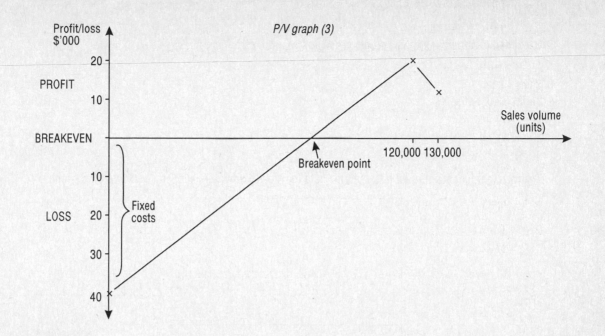

P/V graph (3)

Breakeven chart

Match the following labels to (a), (b), (c) and (d) marked on the breakeven chart below.

| Fixed costs | Margin of safety | Budgeted profit | Budgeted variable costs |

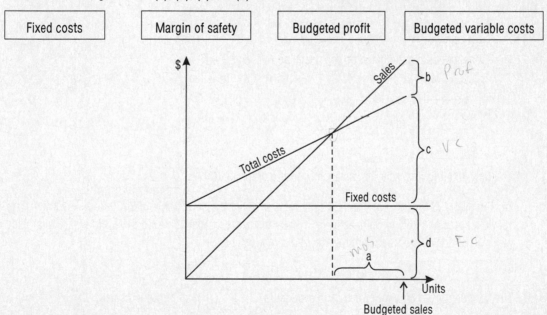

Answer

Fixed costs (d)   Budgeted profit (b)
Margin of safety (a)   Budgeted variable costs (c)

G Co manufactures and sells a single product. The profit statement for May is as follows.

	$
Sales value	80,000
Variable cost of sales	48,000
Contribution	32,000
Fixed costs	15,000
Profit	17,000

The management accountant has used the data for May to draw the following profit/volume graph.

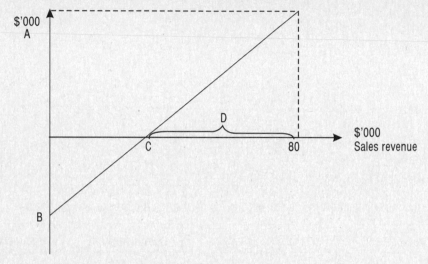

(a)   The monetary values indicated on the graph as A, B and C are:

A $ [   ]

B $ [   ]

C $ [   ]

(b)   The term used to describe the distance D on the graph is the [   ]

(c)   For the whole of the current year, G Co budgets to achieve a sales value of $900,000. Assuming that the unit variable costs and selling price achieved will be the same as that achieved during May, and that fixed costs for the year will be $180,000, the profit for the whole year will be

$ [   ]

(d)   The annual margin of safety for G Co's product is [   ] % of budgeted sales.

Answer

(a) **A** $17,000
 B   (–$15,000)
 C $37,500

Workings

A: profit achieved from $80,000 sales revenue = $17,000
B: loss at zero sales revenue = fixed costs = (–$15,000)
C: breakeven point = $37,500 sales revenue (see below)

C/S ratio = 32/80 = 40%

$$\text{Breakeven point} = \frac{\text{fixed costs}}{\text{C/S ratio}} = \frac{\$15,000}{0.4} = \$37,500 \text{ sales revenue}$$

(b) **The term used to describe the distance D on the graph is the** | **margin of safety** |.

This is the difference between the sales revenue budgeted or achieved, and the revenue required to break even.

(c) **The profit for the whole year will be $ | 180,000 |.**

Workings

Contribution achieved	=	sales revenue × C/S ratio
	=	$900,000 × 0.4
	=	$360,000
Fixed costs		$180,000
∴ Profit for whole year		$180,000

(d) **The annual margin of safety for G Co's product is | 50 | % of budgeted sales.**

Workings

$$\text{Annual breakeven point} = \frac{\text{fixed costs}}{\text{C/S ratio}} = \frac{\$18,000}{0.4} = \$450,000 \text{ sales revenue}$$

Margin of safety = $900,000 – $450,000   = $450,000 sales revenue
                                                              = 50% of budgeted sales

6.4 The economist's breakeven chart

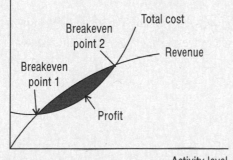

In economics, the lines on the breakeven chart are curved rather than straight. This is because economists assume that costs per unit and revenues per unit are not constant at every level of activity. Note that the total cost line falls initially and then rises again. This is because production is assumed to be more efficient as the number of goods being produced is increased. This is known as **economies of scale**.

7 Limitations of breakeven analysis

FAST FORWARD Despite the **advantages** of breakeven analysis, the technique has some serious **limitations**.

CVP analysis is a useful technique for managers. It can provide **simple** and **quick** estimates, and **breakeven charts** provide a **graphical representation** of breakeven arithmetic. It does, however, have a number of limitations.

- It **can only apply to a single product** or a single mix of a group of products.
- A breakeven chart may be **time-consuming** to prepare.
- It **assumes** fixed costs are constant at all levels of output.
- It **assumes** that **variable costs** are the **same** per unit at all levels of output.
- It **assumes** that **sales prices** are **constant** at all levels of output.
- It assumes **production** and **sales** are the **same** (inventory levels are ignored).
- It **ignores** the **uncertainty** in the estimates of fixed costs and variable cost per unit.

8 Limiting factor analysis

FAST FORWARD In a **limiting factor situation**, contribution will be maximised by earning the biggest possible contribution per unit of limiting factor.

8.1 Limiting factors

One of the more common problems faced by management is a situation where there are not enough resources to meet the potential sales demand, and so a decision has to be made about what mix of products to produce, using what resources there are as effectively as possible. The resource that limits the organisation's ability to meet sales demand is called a **limiting factor** or **key factor**.

Key term

> A **limiting factor** or **key factor** is 'anything which limits the activity of an entity. An entity seeks to optimise the benefit it obtains from the limiting factor. Examples are a shortage of supply of a resource or a restriction on sales demand at a particular price'.
>
> CIMA *Official Terminology*

A **limiting factor** could be sales if there is a limit to sales demand but any one of the organisation's resources (labour, materials and so on) may be insufficient to meet the level of production demanded.

It is assumed in limiting factor analysis that management wishes to maximise profit and that **profit will be maximised when contribution is maximised** (given no change in fixed cost expenditure incurred). In other words, **marginal costing ideas are applied**.

8.2 Limiting factor situations

For example if grade A labour is the limiting factor, contribution will be maximised by earning the biggest contribution from each hour of grade A labour worked.

The limiting factor decision therefore involves the determination of **the contribution earned by each different product from each unit of the limiting factor**.

8.2.1 Example: limiting factor

AB Co makes two products, the Ay and the Be. Unit variable costs are as follows.

	Ay $	Be $
Direct materials	1	3
Direct labour ($3 per hour)	6	3
Variable overhead	1	1
	8	7

The sales price per unit is $14 per Ay and $11 per Be. During July 20X2 the available direct labour is limited to 8,000 hours. Sales demand in July is expected to be 3,000 units for Ays and 5,000 units for Bes.

Required

Determine the profit-maximising production mix, assuming that monthly fixed costs are $20,000, and that opening inventories of finished goods and work in progress are nil.

Solution

Step 1 Confirm that the limiting factor is something other than sales demand.

	Ays	Bes	Total
Labour hours per unit	2 hrs	1 hr	
Sales demand	3,000 units	5,000 units	
Labour hours needed	6,000 hrs	5,000 hrs	11,000 hrs
Labour hours available			8,000 hrs
Shortfall			3,000 hrs

Labour is the limiting factor on production.

Step 2 Identify the contribution earned by each product per unit of limiting factor, that is, per labour hour worked.

	Ays $	Bes $
Sales price	14	11
Variable cost	8	7
Unit contribution	6	4
Labour hours per unit	2 hrs	1 hr
Contribution per labour hour (= unit of limiting factor)	$3	$4

Although Ays have a higher unit contribution than Bes, two Bes can be made in the time it takes to make one Ay. Because labour is in short supply it is more profitable to make Bes than Ays.

Step 3   Determine the **optimum production plan**. Sufficient Bes will be made to meet the full sales demand, and the remaining labour hours available will then be used to make Ays.

(a)

Product	Demand	Hours required	Hours available	Priority of manufacture
Bes	5,000	5,000	5,000	1st
Ays	3,000	6,000	3,000 (bal)	2nd
		11,000	8,000	

(b)

Product	Units	Hours needed	Contribution per unit $	Total $
Bes	5,000	5,000	4	20,000
Ays	1,500	3,000	3	9,000
		8,000		29,000
Less fixed costs				20,000
Profit				9,000

Conclusion

(a)   Unit contribution is *not* the correct way to decide priorities.

(b)   Labour hours are the scarce resource, and therefore contribution **per labour hour** is the correct way to decide priorities.

(c)   The Be earns $4 contribution per labour hour, and the Ay earns $3 contribution per labour hour. Bes therefore make more profitable use of the scarce resource, and should be manufactured first.

Assessment focus point

If an assessment question asks you to determine the optimum production plan, you might find it useful to follow the five-step approach used in the example above and shown below.

Step 1   Identify the limiting factor

Step 2   Calculate contribution per unit for each product

Step 3   Calculate contribution per unit of limiting factor

Step 4   Rank products (make product with highest contribution per unit of limiting factor first)

Step 5   Make products in rank order until scarce resource is used up (optimal production plan)

Question   Limiting factors

LF Co makes a single product for which the standard cost details are as follows.

	$
Direct material ($3 per kg)	12
Direct labour ($8 per hour)	72
Production overhead	18
Total production cost	102

Demand for next period will be 20,000 units. No inventories are held and only 75,000 kg of material and 190,000 hours of labour will be available. What will be the limiting factor next period?

A   Material only
B   Labour only
C   Material and labour
D   There will be no limiting factor next period

The correct answer is A.

Material required = 20,000 units × ($12/$3) = 80,000 kg

Material is therefore a limiting factor, since only 75,000 kg are available. This eliminates options B and D.

Labour required = 20,000 units × ($72/$8) = 180,000 hours.

Labour is not a limiting factor, since 190,000 labour hours are available. This eliminates option C.

 Question   POV Co

POV Co manufactures three products - X, Y and Z - that use the same machines. The budgeted income statements for the three products are as follows:

	X	Y	Z
	$'000	$'000	$'000
Sales	1,000	1,125	625
Prime costs	(500)	(562.5)	(437.5)
Variable overheads	(250)	(187.5)	(62.5)
Fixed overheads	(200)	(315)	(130)
Profit/(loss)	50	60	(5)
Annual sales demand (units)	5,000	7,500	2,500
Machine hours per unit	20	21	26

However, after the budget had been formulated, an unforeseen condition has meant that during the next period the available machine capacity has been limited to 296,500 hours.

(a)   The shortfall in available machine hours for next period is [   ] hours

(b)   The contribution earned per machine hour used on product X is $ [   ]

(c)   The management accountant has ranked the products in order of preference for production as follows:

1st   product X
2nd   product Y
3rd   product Z

The number of units of each product that should be manufactured next period is:

(i)   Product X   [   ] units

(ii)   Product Y   [   ] units

(iii) Product Z   [   ] units

(a) **The shortfall in available machine hours for next period is** | 26,000 | **hours.**

Workings

Machine hours required to satisfy annual sales demand:

		Hours
Product X	5,000 units × 20 hrs	100,000
Product Y	7,500 units × 21 hrs	157,500
Product Z	2,500 units × 26 hrs	65,000
Total machine hours required		322,500
Machine hours available		296,500
Shortfall in available machine hours		26,000

(b) **The contribution earned per machine hour used on product X is $** | 2.50 |.

Workings

	$'000
Sales revenue	1,000
Prime costs	(500)
Variable overheads	(250)
Contribution	250
Contribution per unit (÷ 5,000)	$50
Contribution per machine hour (÷ 20)	$2.50

(c) (i) **Product X** | 5,000 | **units**

(ii) **Product Y** | 7,500 | **units**

(iii) **Product Z** | 1,500 | **units**

Workings

Ranking	Product	Demand units	Hours required	Hours available	Production units
1st	X	5,000 (× 20)	100,000	100,000	5,000
2nd	Y	7,500 (× 21)	157,500	157,500	7,500
3rd	Z	2,500 (× 26)	65,000	39,000*	1,500
				296,500	

* Balance (296,500 – 100,000 – 157,500)

Chapter Roundup

- **Breakeven analysis** or **cost-volume-profit analysis (CVP) analysis** is the study of the interrelationships between costs, volume and profits at various levels of activity.

- The **breakeven point** occurs when there is neither a profit nor a loss and so fixed costs equal contribution.

- The **C/S ratio** (or **P/V ratio**) is a measure of how much contribution is earned from each $1 of sales.

- The **margin of safety** is the difference in units between the budgeted sales volume and the breakeven sales volume. It is sometimes expressed as a percentage of the budgeted sales volume. Alternatively the margin of safety can be expressed as the difference between the budgeted sales revenue and breakeven sales revenue, expressed as a percentage of the budgeted sales revenue.

- At the **breakeven point**, there is no profit or loss and so **sales revenue = total costs** or **total contribution = fixed costs.**

- The **target profit** is achieved when sales revenue equals variable costs plus fixed costs plus profit. Therefore the **total contribution required** for a target profit = **fixed costs + required profit.**

- The breakeven point can also be determined graphically using a **breakeven chart**.

- A **contribution breakeven chart** depicts variable costs, so that contribution can be read directly from the chart.

- The **profit/volume (P/V) graph** is a variation of the breakeven chart and illustrates the relationship of profit to sales volume.

- Despite the **advantages** of breakeven analysis, the technique has some serious **limitations**.

- In a **limiting factor situation**, contribution will be maximised by earning the biggest possible contribution per unit of limiting factor.

Quick Quiz

1   Use the following to make up four formulae which can be used to calculate the breakeven point.

| Contribution per unit |
| Contribution per unit |
| Fixed costs |
| Fixed costs |
| Contribution required to break even |
| Contribution required to break even |
| C/S ratio |
| C/S ratio |

(a)   Breakeven point (sales units)   =   _____

          or   _____

(b) Breakeven point (sales revenue) =

$$\boxed{}$$

or

$$\boxed{}$$

2   The P/V ratio is a measure of how much profit is earned from each $1 of sales.

      True   ☐

      False   ☐

3   Profits are maximised at the breakeven point.

      True   ☐

      False   ☐

4   At the breakeven point, total contribution = ...

5   The total contribution required for a target profit = ...

6   Breakeven charts show approximate levels of profit or loss at different sales volume levels within a limited range. Which of the following are true?

      I   The sales line starts at the origin
      II   The fixed costs line runs parallel to the vertical axis
      III   Breakeven charts have a horizontal axis showing the sales/output (in value or units)
      IV   Breakeven charts have a vertical axis showing $ for revenues and costs
      V   The breakeven point is the intersection of the sales line and the fixed cost line

      A   I and II
      B   I and III
      C   I, III and IV
      D   I, III, IV, and V

7   On a breakeven chart, the distance between the breakeven point and the expected (or budgeted) sales, in units, indicates the ....

8   Thornbury produces a single product X and has a contribution to sales ratio of 35%. The annual fixed costs are $157,500. In order to breakeven, how many units of X will Thornbury need to make and sell?

      A   196,000
      B   450,000
      C   60,000
      D   Cannot say without more information

9   The following information is available for product H.

      Breakeven point   70,000 units

      Contribution per unit $4.50

      Margin of safety   30%

      Calculate the budgeted profit

      A $100,000   C $315,000

      B $135,000   D $765,000

10   Give seven limitations of CVP analysis.

- ....
- ....
- ....
- ....
- ....
- ....
- ....

11   When determining the optimum production plan using limiting factor analysis, what five steps are involved?

Step 1...

Step 2...

Step 3...

Step 4...

Step 5...

Answers to Quick Quiz

1   (a)   Breakeven point (sales units) $=$ $\dfrac{\text{Fixed costs}}{\text{Contribution per unit}}$

or $\dfrac{\text{Contribution required to break even}}{\text{Contribution per unit}}$

(b)   Breakeven point (sales revenue) $=$ $\dfrac{\text{Fixed costs}}{\text{C/S ratio}}$

or $\dfrac{\text{Contribution required to break even}}{\text{C/S ratio}}$

2   False. The P/V ratio is a measure of how much **contribution** is earned from each $1 of sales.

3   False. At the breakeven point there is no profit.

4   At the breakeven point, total contribution = fixed costs

5   The total contribution required for a target profit = fixed costs + required profit

6   C   The fixed cost line runs parallel to the horizontal axis and the breakeven point is the intersection of the sales line and the total costs line

7   Margin of safety

8   D   The sales revenue can be calculated as $157,500/0.35 = $450,000. The number of units cannot be calculated with the information supplied.

9   B $135,000

$$\text{Breakeven point} = \frac{\text{Fixed costs}}{\text{Contribution/unit}}$$

$$\therefore 70,000 \text{ units} = \frac{\text{Fixed costs}}{\$4.50}$$

$$\therefore \text{Fixed costs} = 70,000 \text{ units} \times \$4.50$$
$$= \$315,000$$

$$\text{Margin of safety} = \frac{\text{Budgeted sales units} - \text{Breakeven sales units}}{\text{Budgeted sales units}}$$

$$\therefore 0.3 = \frac{\text{Budgeted sales units} - 70,000}{\text{Budgeted sales units}}$$

Let x = budgeted sales units

$$0.3 = \frac{x - 70,000}{x}$$

$\therefore 0.3x = x - 70,000$

$\therefore 70,000 = x - 0.3x$

$\therefore 70,000 = 0.7x$

$\therefore x = 100,000 = $ budgeted sales units

$$\text{Total profit} = \text{Contribution} - \text{fixed costs}$$
$$= (100,000 \text{ units} \times \$4.50) - \$315,000$$
$$= \$135,000$$

10   • It **can only apply to a single product** or a single mix of a group of products.
    • A breakeven chart may be **time-consuming** to prepare.
    • It **assumes** fixed costs are constant at all levels of output.
    • It **assumes** that **variable costs** are the **same** per unit at all levels of output.
    • It **assumes** that **sales prices** are **constant** at all levels of output.
    • It assumes **production** and **sales** are the **same** (inventory levels are ignored).
    • It **ignores** the **uncertainty** in the estimates of fixed costs and variable cost per unit.

11   **Step 1**   Identify the limiting factor

    Step 2   Calculate contribution per unit for each product

    Step 3   Calculate contribution per unit of limiting factor

    Step 4   Rank products (make product with highest contribution per unit of limiting factor first)

    Step 5   Make products in rank order until scarce resource is used up **(optimal production plan)**

Now try the questions below from the Question Bank

Question numbers
26–31

Part B
Standard costing

7

Standard costing

Introduction

Just as there are **standards** for most things in our daily lives (cleanliness in hamburger restaurants, educational achievement of nine year olds, number of trains running on time), there are standards for the costs of products and services. Moreover, just as the standards in our daily lives are not always met, the standards for the costs of products and services are not always met. We will not, however, be considering the standards of cleanliness of hamburger restaurants in this chapter but we will be looking at standards for **costs**, what they are used for and how they are set.

In the next chapter we will see how **standard costing** forms the basis of a process called **variance analysis**, a vital management control tool.

Topic list	Syllabus references
1 Standard costing	C2(a)
2 Preparation of standards	C2(a), (b)
3 Other aspects of standard costing	C2(b)
4 The standard hour	C2(c)
5 Standard labour costs	C2(c)

1 Standard costing

Standard costing is the preparation of standard costs to value inventories/cost products and/or to use in variance analysis, a key management control tool.

1.1 Standard cost

Key term

A **standard cost** is a 'planned unit cost of a product, component or service'.	CIMA *Official Terminology*

A **standard cost card** shows full details of the standard cost of each product.

The standard variable cost of product 1234 is set out below.

STANDARD COST CARD - PRODUCT 1234

	$	$
Direct materials		
Material X : 3 kg at $4 per kg	12	
Material Y : 9 litres at $2 per litre	18	
		30
Direct labour		
Grade A : 6 hours at $7 per hour	42	
Grade B : 8 hours at $8 per hour	64	
		106
Standard direct cost		136
Variable production overhead : 14 hours at $0.50 per hour		7
Standard variable cost of production		143
Fixed production overhead : 14 hours at $4.50 per hour		63
Standard full production cost		206
Administration and marketing overhead		15
Standard cost of sale		221
Standard profit		20
Standard sales price		241

Notice how the total standard cost is built up from standards for each cost element: standard quantities of materials at standard prices, standard quantities of labour time at standard rates and so on. It is therefore determined by management's estimates of the following.

- The expected prices of materials, labour and expenses
- Efficiency levels in the use of materials and labour
- Budgeted overhead costs and budgeted volumes of activity

1.2 The uses of standard costing

Standard costing has a variety of uses but its two principal ones are as follows.

(a) To **value inventories** and **cost production** for cost accounting purposes.

(b) To act as a **control device** by establishing standards (planned costs), highlighting (via **variance analysis** which we will cover in the next chapter) activities that are not conforming to plan and thus **alerting management** to areas which may be out of control and in need of corrective action.

B Company makes one product, the J. Two types of labour are involved in the preparation of a J, skilled and semi-skilled. Skilled labour is paid $10 per hour and semi-skilled $5 per hour. Twice as many skilled labour hours as semi-skilled labour hours are needed to produce a J, four semi-skilled labour hours being needed.

A J is made up of three different direct materials. Seven kilograms of direct material A, four litres of direct material B and three metres of direct material C are needed. Direct material A costs $1 per kilogram, direct material B $2 per litre and direct material C $3 per metre.

Variable production overheads are incurred at B Company at the rate of $2.50 per direct labour (skilled) hour.

A system of absorption costing is in operation at B Company. The basis of absorption is direct labour (skilled) hours. For the forthcoming accounting period, budgeted fixed production overheads are $250,000 and budgeted production of the J is 5,000 units.

Administration, selling and distribution overheads are added to products at the rate of $10 per unit.

A mark-up of 25% is made on the J.

Required

Using the above information complete the standard cost card below for the J.

STANDARD COST CARD – PRODUCT J

	$	$
Direct materials		
Direct labour		
Standard direct cost		
Variable production overhead		
Standard variable cost of production		
Fixed production overhead		
Standard full production cost		
Administration, selling and distribution overhead		
Standard cost of sale		
Standard profit		
Standard sales price		

STANDARD COST CARD - PRODUCT J

Direct materials	$	$
A 7 kgs × $1	7	
B 4 litres × $2	8	
C 3m × $3	9	
		24

Direct labour		
Skilled : 8 × $10	80	
Semi-skilled : 4 × $5	20	
		100

	$
Standard direct cost	124
Variable production overhead 8 × $2.50	20
Standard variable cost of production	144
Fixed production overhead 8 × $6.25 (W)	50
Standard full production cost	194
Administration, selling and distribution overhead	10
Standard cost of sale	204
Standard profit 25% × 204	51
Standard sales price	255

Working

Overhead absorption rate = $\dfrac{\$250,000}{5,000 \times 8}$ = $6.25 per skilled labour hour

Question

Profit calculations

Product P has the following standard cost card based on production and sales levels of 15,000 units.

	$
Production cost	
Variable	32.00
Fixed	45.50
Selling cost	
Variable	7.50
Fixed	29.00
Profit	5.00
Selling price	119.00

In the month of June, production was 16,000 units and sales were 15,000 units. Assuming all other factors remained the same, what was the profit for June?

$120,500

		$
Revenue	15,000 × $119.00	1,785,000
Cost of sales		
Fixed production cost	15,000 × $45.50	682,500
Fixed selling cost	15,000 × $29.00	435,000
Variable production cost	16,000 × $32.00	512,000
Variable selling cost	15,000 × $7.50	112,500
		1,742,000
Less closing inventory	1,000 × ($32 + $45.50)	77,500
		1,664,500
Profit		120,500

1.3 Standard costing as a control technique

Standard costing (for control) therefore involves the following.

- The establishment of predetermined estimates of the costs of products or services
- The collection of actual costs
- The comparison of the actual costs with the predetermined estimates.

The predetermined costs are known as **standard costs** and the difference between standard and actual cost is known as a **variance**. The process by which the total difference between standard and actual results is analysed is known as **variance analysis**.

1.4 Historical costs versus standard costs

A **focus on the future** is one of the principal **differences** between the **work of the cost and management accountant and the work of the financial accountant**.

(a)   Financial accountants are concerned with ensuring that the accounting records show a true and fair view of the organisation's operations over the accounting period (say 12 months).

(b) **Cost and management accountants**, on the other hand, are not so worried about the absolute validity, accuracy and verifiability of past events and transactions. Given their focus on planning, control and decision making they are more concerned with **what is likely to happen in the future**.

That's not to say that cost and management accounting is not concerned with the past. In the **final part of this text** we will look in depth at the **basic role of costing in accumulating, classifying, recording and ascertaining both historical unit costs and historical total costs of operations**. And it is only after basic cost accounting methods and processes have provided information about the historical costs of running an organisation that, the cost and management accounting role of providing information for planning, control and decision making can begin.

Standard costing is an integral part of an organisation's system of planning and control and is based on **standard costs** that are **established in advance**, before events and transactions occur. They represent what should happen rather than what has happened.

1.5 Standard costing and management by exception

Standard costs, when established, are **average expected unit costs**. Because they are only averages and **not a rigid specification**, **actual results will vary to some extent above or below the average**. Standard costs can therefore be viewed as **benchmarks** for comparison purposes, and **variances** (the differences between standard costs and actual costs) should only be **reported** and investigated if there is a **significant difference** between actual and standard. The problem is in deciding whether a variation from standard should be considered significant and worthy of investigation. **Tolerance limits** can be set and only variances that exceed such limits would require investigation.

Standard costing therefore enables the principle of **management by exception** to be practised.

Key term

> **Management by exception** is the 'Practice of concentrating on activities that require attention and ignoring those which appear to be conforming to expectations. Typically standard cost variances or variances from budget are used to identify those activities that require attention.'
>
> CIMA *Official Terminology*

2 Preparation of standards

FAST FORWARD

> **Standards** for each cost element are made up of a monetary component and a resources requirement component.

Standard costs may be used in both absorption costing and in marginal costing systems. We shall, however, confine our description to standard costs in marginal costing systems.

As we noted earlier, the standard cost of a product (or service) is made up of a number of different standards, one for each cost element, each of which has to be set by management.

2.1 Monetary parts of standards

2.1.1 Standard direct material prices

Direct material prices will be estimated by the purchasing department from their knowledge of the following.

- Purchase contracts already agreed
- Pricing discussions with regular suppliers
- The forecast movement of prices in the market
- The availability of bulk purchase discounts

Price inflation can cause difficulties in setting realistic standard prices. Suppose that a material costs $10 per kilogram at the moment and during the course of the next twelve months it is expected to go up in price by 20% to $12 per kilogram. What standard price should be selected?

- The current price of $10 per kilogram
- The average expected price for the year, say $11 per kilogram

Either would be possible, but neither would be entirely satisfactory.

(a)   If the **current price** were used in the standard, the reported price variance will become adverse as soon as prices go up, which might be very early in the year. If prices go up gradually rather than in one big jump, it would be difficult to select an appropriate time for revising the standard.

(b)   If an **estimated mid-year price** were used, price variances should be favourable in the first half of the year and adverse in the second half of the year, again assuming that prices go up gradually throughout the year. Management could only really check that in any month, the price variance did not become excessively adverse (or favourable) and that the price variance switched from being favourable to adverse around month six or seven and not sooner.

2.1.2 Standard direct labour rates

Direct labour rates per hour will be set by discussion with the personnel department and by reference to the payroll and to any agreements on pay rises with trade union representatives of the employees.

(a)   A separate hourly rate or weekly wage will be set for each different labour grade/type of employee.

(b)   An average hourly rate will be applied for each grade (even though individual rates of pay may vary according to age and experience).

Similar problems when dealing with inflation to those described for material prices can be met when setting labour standards.

2.2 Standard resource requirements

To estimate the materials required to make each product (**material usage**) and also the labour hours required (**labour efficiency**), **technical specifications** must be prepared for each product by production experts (either in the production department or the work study department).

(a)   The **'standard product specification'** for materials must list the quantities required per unit of each material in the product. These standard input quantities must be made known to the operators in the production department so that control action by management to deal with **excess material wastage** will be understood by them.

(b)   The **'standard operation sheet'** for labour will specify the expected hours required by each grade of labour in each department to make one unit of product. These standard times must be carefully set (for example by work study) and must be understood by the labour force. Where necessary, **standard procedures** or **operating methods** should be stated.

2.3 Standard variable overhead rates

Establishing the input of labour and material required for each unit of output is usually a fairly straightforward task. For example, if a unit of output requires five labour hours and each hour costs $10, the standard labour cost is $50.

It is not so easy to determine the cost of variable overhead resources per unit of output as there is no observable direct relationship between resources required and units of output. The relationship therefore has to be established using data from the past.

Variable overhead rates can be estimated by looking at **past relationships** between changes in costs and changes in activity level. The problem is in establishing which type of activity exerts the greatest influence on the cost (direct labour hours, machine hours, quantity of material used, units of output and so on).

Using one or more of a range of **statistical techniques** (including, at the basic level, the scattergraph and the high-low method which we looked at earlier in this text), the activity measure that best explains the variations in the level of costs should be selected.

In practice, direct labour hours and machine hours are the activity measures most frequently used.

The variable overhead rate per direct labour hour (or machine hour or whatever measure is selected) is then applied to the standard labour (or machine) usage per unit to derive a standard variable overhead cost per unit of output.

2.4 Performance standards

FAST FORWARD

> **Performance standards** are used to set efficiency targets. There are four types: **ideal**, **attainable**, **current** and **basic**.

The setting of standards raises the problem of **how demanding** the standard should be. Should the standard represent perfect performance or easily attainable performance?

There are four different types of **performance standard** that an organisation could aim for.

Key terms

> **Ideal standards** are based on the most favourable operating conditions, with no wastage, no inefficiencies, no idle time and no breakdowns. These standards are likely to have an unfavourable motivational impact, because employees will often feel that the goals are unattainable and not work so hard.
>
> **Attainable standards** are based on efficient (but not perfect) operating conditions. Some allowance is made for wastage, inefficiencies, machine breakdowns and fatigue. If well-set they provide a useful psychological incentive, and for this reason they should be introduced whenever possible. The consent and co-operation of employees involved in improving the standard are required.
>
> **Current standards** are standards based on current working conditions (current wastage, current inefficiencies). The disadvantage of current standards is that they do not attempt to improve on current levels of efficiency, which may be poor and capable of significant improvement.
>
> **Basic standards** are standards which are kept unaltered over a long period of time, and may be out-of-date. They are used to show changes in efficiency or performance over an extended time period. Basic standards are perhaps the least useful and least common type of standard in use.

2.5 Taking account of wastage and losses

If, during processing, the quantity of material input to the process is likely to reduce (due to wastage, evaporation and so on), the quantity input must be greater than the quantity in the finished product and a material standard must take account of this.

Suppose that the fresh raspberry juice content of a litre of Purple Pop is 100ml and that there is a 10% loss of raspberry juice during process due to evaporation. The standard material usage of raspberry juice per litre of Purple Pop will be:

$$100\text{ml} \times \frac{100\%}{(100-10)\%} = 100\text{ml} \times \frac{100\%}{90\%} = 111.11\text{ml}$$

Make sure that you understand how to account for wastage and losses when calculating standard costs. Assessment questions could well ask you to calculate the standard cost of a product given that there is loss due to evaporation or idle time and so on.

Question

A unit of product X requires 24 active labour hours for completion. It is anticipated that there will be 20% idle time which is to be incorporated into the standard times for all products. If the wage rate is $10 per hour, what is the standard labour cost of one unit of product X?

A $192   B $240   C $288   D $300

Answer

The correct answer is D.

The basic labour cost for 24 hours is $240. However with idle time it will be necessary to pay for more than 24 hours in order to achieve 24 hours of actual work. Therefore options A and B are incorrect.

Standard labour cost $= $ active hours for completion $\times \dfrac{125}{100} \times \$10 = 24 \times 1.25 \times \$10 = \$300$

Option C is incorrect because it results from simply adding an extra 20 per cent to the labour hours. However the idle hours are 20 per cent of the *total* hours worked, therefore we need to add 25 per cent to the required active hours, as shown in the working.

3 Other aspects of standard costing

FAST FORWARD

There are a number of **advantages** and **disadvantages** of standard costing.

3.1 Problems in setting standards

(a)   Deciding how to incorporate **inflation** into planned unit costs

(b)   Agreeing on a **performance standard** (attainable or ideal)

(c)   Deciding on the **quality** of materials to be used (a better quality of material will cost more, but perhaps reduce material wastage)

(d)   Estimating materials **prices** where seasonal price variations or bulk purchase discounts may be significant

(e)   Finding sufficient **time** to construct accurate standards as standard setting can be a **time-consuming process**

(f)   Incurring the **cost of setting up and maintaining a system** for establishing standards

(g)   Dealing with possible **behavioural problems**, managers responsible for the achievement of standards possibly resisting the use of a standard costing control system for fear of being blamed for any adverse variances

3.1.1 Standard costing and inflation

Note that standard costing is most difficult in times of inflation but it is still worthwhile.

(a) **Usage** and **efficiency** variances will still be meaningful.

(b) **Inflation is measurable**: there is no reason why its effects cannot be removed from the variances reported.

(c) Standard costs can be **revised** so long as this is **not done too frequently**.

3.2 The advantages of standard costing

(a) Carefully planned standards are an **aid to more accurate budgeting**.

(b) Standard costs provide a **yardstick** against which actual costs can be measured.

(c) The **setting of standards** involves determining the best materials and methods which may lead to cost **economies**.

(d) A **target of efficiency** is set for employees to reach and **cost consciousness** is stimulated.

(e) Variances can be calculated which enable the principle of '**management by exception**' to be operated. Only the variances which exceed acceptable tolerance limits need to be investigated by management with a view to control action.

(f) Standard costs **simplify the process of bookkeeping** in cost accounting, because they are easier to use than LIFO, FIFO and weighted average costs.

(g) Standard times **simplify the process of production scheduling**.

(h) Standard performance levels might provide an **incentive for individuals** to achieve targets for themselves at work.

3.3 The applicability of standard costing

FAST FORWARD Standard costing systems can be **adapted** to remain useful in the modern business environment.

3.3.1 Criticisms of standard costing

Critics of standard costing have argued that standard costing is not appropriate in the modern business environment.

(a) The use of standard costing relies on the existence of **repetitive operations** and relatively **homogeneous** output. Nowadays many organisations are forced continually to respond to customers' changing requirements, with the result that output and operations are not so repetitive.

(b) Standard costing systems were developed when the business environment was more stable and less prone to **change**. The current business environment is more dynamic and it is not possible to assume stable conditions.

(c) Standard costing systems assume that performance to standard is acceptable. Today's business environment is more focused on **continuous improvement**.

(d) Standard costing was developed in an environment of predominantly **mass production** and **repetitive assembly work**. It is not particularly useful in today's growing **service sector** of the economy.

3.3.2 Using standard costing today

This long list of criticisms of standard costing may lead you to believe that such systems have little use in today's business environment. However standard costing systems can be adapted to remain useful.

(a) Even when output is not standardised, it may be possible to identify a number of **standard components and activities** whose costs may be controlled effectively by the setting of standard costs and identification of variances.

(b) The use of computer power enables standards to be **updated rapidly** and more frequently, so that they remain useful for the purposes of control by comparison.

(c) The use of **ideal standards** and more demanding performance levels can combine the benefits of **continuous improvement** and standard costing control.

(d) Standard costing can be applied in **service industries**, where a **measurable cost unit** can be established. For example it is possible to set a standard cost for the following.

- Transport cost per tonne-mile
- Laundry cost per hotel room night
- Cost per chargeable consultant hour
- Cost per equivalent full time student
- Cost per medical examination

4 The standard hour

FAST FORWARD

> The **standard hour** can be used to overcome the problem of how to measure output when a number of dissimilar products are manufactured.

4.1 Example: standard hour

S Co manufactures plates, mugs and eggcups. Production during the first two quarters of 20X5 was as follows.

	Quarter 1	Quarter 2
Plates	1,000	800
Mugs	1,200	1,500
Eggcups	800	900

The fact that 3,000 products were produced in quarter 1 and 3,200 in quarter 2 does not tell us anything about S Co's performance over the two periods because plates, mugs and eggcups are so different. The fact that the production mix has changed is not revealed by considering the total number of units produced. This is where the concept of the standard hour is useful.

The standard hour (or standard minute) is the **amount of work achievable, at standard efficiency levels, in an hour or minute.**

(a) The standard time allowed to produce one unit of each of S Co's products is as follows.

	Standard time
Plate	$1/2$ hour
Mug	$1/3$ hour
Eggcup	$1/4$ hour

(b)   By measuring the standard hours of output in each quarter, a more useful output measure is obtained.

		Quarter 1		Quarter 2	
Product	Standard hours per unit	Production	Standard hours	Production	Standard hours
Plate	$^1/_2$	1,000	500	800	400
Mug	$^1/_3$	1,200	400	1,500	500
Eggcup	$^1/_4$	800	200	900	225
			1,100		1,125

The output level in the two quarters was therefore very similar.

5 Standard labour costs

FAST FORWARD **Bonus/incentive schemes** often incorporate labour standards as targets.

5.1 Remuneration methods

(a)   **Time-based systems**. These are based on the principle of paying an employee for the hours attended, regardless of the amount of work achieved (wages = hours worked × rate of pay per hour).

   (i)   Overtime premium = **extra** rate per hour for hours over and above the basic hours.
   (ii)   Quality of output is more important than quantity of output.
   (iii)   There is no incentive for improvements in employee performance.

(b)   **Piecework systems**. Here the employee is paid according to the output achieved (wages = units produced × rate of pay per unit).

(c)   **Incentive/bonus schemes**. There are a variety of these schemes, all of which are designed to encourage workers to be more productive.

We're going to be looking at piecework systems and incentive/bonus schemes and how standard labour costs can be used in them.

5.2 Piecework schemes

5.2.1 Straight piece rate schemes

A type of scheme where the employee is paid a constant rate per unit of output is called a straight piece rate scheme.

Suppose for example, an employee is paid $1 for each unit produced and works a 40 hour week. Production overhead is added at the rate of $2 per direct labour hour.

Weekly production Units	Pay (40 hours) $	Overhead $	Conversion cost $	Conversion cost per unit $
40	40	80	120	3.00
50	50	80	130	2.60
60	60	80	140	2.33
70	70	80	150	2.14

As the worker's output increases, their wage increases and at the same time unit costs of output are reduced.

These schemes can be unfair to employees if there are production problems, therefore many piecework schemes offer a **guaranteed minimum wage**, so that employees do not suffer loss of earnings when production is low through no fault of their own.

5.2.2 Schemes with standard time allowances

If an employee makes several different types of product, it may not be possible to add up the units for payment purposes. Instead, a **standard time allowance** is given for each unit to arrive at a total of piecework hours for payment.

For example, suppose an employee is paid $8 per piecework hour produced. In a 40 hour week the employee produces the following output.

	Piecework time allowed per unit
15 units of product X	0.5 hours
20 units of product Y	2.0 hours

Piecework hours produced are as follows.

Product X	15×0.5 hours	7.5 hours
Product Y	20×2.0 hours	40.0 hours
Total piecework hours		47.5 hours

Therefore employee's pay = $47.5 \times \$8 = \$380$ for the week.

5.2.3 Differential piecework schemes

Differential piecework schemes offer an incentive to employees to increase their output by paying higher rates for increased levels of production. For example:

up to and including 80 units, rate of pay per unit in this band = $1.00
81 to 90 units, rate of pay per unit in this band = $1.20
above 90 units, rate of pay per unit in this band = $1.30

An employee producing 97 units would therefore receive $(80 \times \$1.00) + (10 \times \$1.20) + (7 \times \$1.30) = \$101.10$.

Employers should obviously be careful to make it clear whether they intend to pay the increased rate on all units produced, or on the extra output only.

5.2.4 Piecework schemes – advantages and disadvantages

- They enjoy fluctuating popularity.
- They are occasionally used by employers as a means of increasing pay levels.
- They are frequently condemned as a means of driving employees to work too hard to earn a satisfactory wage.
- Careful inspection of output is necessary to ensure that quality is maintained as production increases.

Question

Match the descriptions of remuneration schemes to the graphs below.

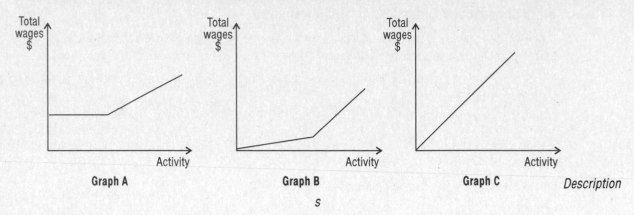

Graph A   Graph B   Graph C   *Description*
                    s

(a)   A basic hourly rate is paid for hours worked, with an overtime premium payable for hours worked in excess of 35 per week.

(b)   A straight piecework scheme is operated.

(c)   A straight piecework scheme is operated, with a minimum guaranteed weekly wage.

Answer

(a)   Graph B
(b)   Graph C
(c)   Graph A

5.3 Accounting for labour costs

The bookkeeping entries for wages will be covered in Chapter 11 but it is worth mentioning here that there is a distinction made between direct labour and indirect labour.

Assessment focus point

> Make sure that you read any assessment questions on wages very carefully. You may be required to calculate direct labour costs, indirect labour costs or both.

The basic distinction for classification of labour costs is that the labour costs of production workers are direct costs and the labour costs of other workers are indirect costs. However there are two specific areas where the costs of the production workers are often treated as indirect rather than direct.

When overtime is worked by employees they tend to be paid an additional premium over the general hourly rate, known as the **overtime premium.** The overtime premium is generally treated as an indirect cost rather than a direct cost of production. However there is an exception to this – if a customer requests that overtime is worked in order to complete a job earlier then the entire overtime payment will normally be treated as a direct cost of the job.

At some point during the working day it is entirely possible that production workers find that there is no work for them to do. This could be due to factors such as production scheduling problems or machine breakdowns. These hours which are paid for but during which no work is being done are known as **idle time.** The cost of idle time hours tends to be treated as an indirect labour cost.

During the week ending 30 June 20X3 the direct production workers in a factory worked for 840 hours in total. Of these hours 60 were idle time hours and 100 were overtime hours. The hourly rate of pay is $8.00 with overtime hours being paid at time and a half.

During the same week the indirect workers worked for 120 hours at a rate of $6.00 per hour with no overtime hours.

What is the direct labour cost and the indirect labour cost for the week?

	Direct labour cost	Indirect labour cost
A	$5,440	$2,400
B	$6,240	$1,600
C	$6,640	$1,200
D	$6,720	$1,120

Answer

Answer B

	$
Direct labour (840 – 60) × $8.00	6,240

	$
Indirect labour	
Indirect workers 120 × $6.00	720
Direct workers overtime premium	
100 hours × $4	400
Direct workers idle time	
60 hours × $8	480
	1,600

Chapter Roundup

- **Standard costing** is the preparation of standard costs to value inventories/cost products and/or to use in variance analysis, a key management control tool.

- **Standards** for each cost element are made up of a monetary component and a resources requirement component.

- **Performance standards** are used to set efficiency targets. There are four types: **ideal, attainable, current and basic**.

- There are a number of **advantages** and **disadvantages** of standard costing.

- Standard costing systems can be **adapted** to remain useful in the modern business environment.

- The **standard hour** can be used to overcome the problem of how to measure output when a number of dissimilar products are manufactured.

- **Bonus/incentive schemes** often incorporate labour standards as targets.

Quick Quiz

1   *Choose the correct words from those highlighted.*

A standard cost is a **planned/historical unit/total** cost.

2   The only use of standard costing is to value inventory.

True ☐

False ☐

3   A control technique which compares standard costs and revenues with actual results to obtain variances which are used to stimulate improved performance is known as:

A   Standard costing   C   Budgetary control
B   Variance analysis   D   Budgeting

4   Standard costs may only be used in absorption costing.

True ☐

False ☐

5   Four types of performance standard are

(a)   ....   (c)   ....
(b)   ....   (d)   ....

6   The formula for standard material cost per unit = ...

7   List three problems in setting standards.

(a)   ....

(b)   ....

(c)   ....

8   The standard time per unit of product W is five hours. Ten employees work a 40-hour week. Idle time is two hours per employee per week. Efficiency levels are 125%.

The weekly output is ⬚ units.

9   Which of the following are advantages of standard costing?

A   Standards are an aid to more accurate budgeting
B   Cost consciousness is stimulated
C   Inflation can be dealt with easily
D   The principle of management by exception can be operated

10   L Co has paid its staff for the following number of hours in September.

Basic pay   14,000 hours
Overtime   3,000 hours
Idle time   1,000 hours

Basic pay is paid at $20 per hour and overtime is paid at basic pay plus 20%

Calculate the indirect labour cost for September. $ ⬚

Answers to Quick Quiz

1   A standard cost is a **planned unit** cost.

2   False. It has a number of uses including:

(a)   To value inventory and cost production for cost accounting purposes.

(b)   To act as a control device by establishing standards and highlighting activities that are not conforming to plan and bringing these to the attention of management.

3   A

4   False

5   (a)   Ideal   (c)   Current
     (b)   Attainable   (d)   Basic

6   Standard material cost per unit = standard material usage × standard material price

7   (a)   Deciding how to incorporate **inflation** into planned unit costs

(b)   Agreeing on a **performance standard** (attainable or ideal)

(c)   Deciding on the **quality** of materials to be used (a better quality of material will cost more, but perhaps reduce material wastage)

(d)   Estimating materials **prices** where seasonal price variations or bulk purchase discounts may be significant

(e)   Finding sufficient **time** to construct accurate standards as standard setting can be a **time-consuming process**

(f)   Incurring the **cost of setting up and maintaining a system** for establishing standards

(g)   Dealing with possible **behavioural problems**, managers responsible for the achievement of standards possibly resisting the use of a standard costing control system for fear of being blamed for any adverse variances

8   Active hours = (40 − 2) × 10 = 380

Units produced = 380/5 × 125% = ⬚ 95 ⬚ units

9   A, B and D

If standards are planned carefully they can be an aid to more accurate budgeting. Cost consciousness can be stimulated when a target of efficiency is set for employees. Variances enable the principle of management by exception to be operated by setting tolerance limits.

10    $32.000

Idle time is treated as an indirect cost. The overtime premium (which means the 20% part only) is also treated as an indirect cost.

Overtime premium	=	$20 x 20%
	=	$4 per hour
Overtime: 3,000 x $4 =		$12,000
Idle time: 1,000 x $20 =		$20,000
Indirect labour cost =		$32,000

Now try the questions below from the Question Bank

Question numbers
32-36

Variance analysis

Introduction

The actual results achieved by an organisation during a reporting period (week, month, quarter, year) will, more than likely, be different from the expected results (the expected results being the standard costs and revenues which we looked at in the previous chapter). Such differences may occur between individual items, such as the cost of labour and the volume of sales, and between the total expected contribution and the total actual contribution.

Management will have spent considerable time and trouble setting standards. Actual results have differed from the standards. The wise manager will consider the differences that have occurred and use the results of these considerations to assist in attempts to attain the standards. The wise manager will use **variance analysis** as a method of **control**.

This chapter examines **variance analysis** and sets out the method of calculating the following variances.

- Direct material variances
- Direct labour variances
- Variable overhead variances
- Sales variances

We will then go on to look at the reasons for variances.

We will then build on the basics by introducing, among other things, operating statements.

Finally we will examine two further topics. We will consider how actual data can be derived from standard cost details and variances and we'll look at the interrelationship between various variances.

Topic list	Syllabus references
1 Variances	C2(d)
2 Direct material variances	C2(d)
3 Direct labour variances	C2(d)
4 Variable overhead variances	C2(d)
5 The reasons for cost variances	C2(e)
6 Sales variances	C2(d)
7 Operating statements	C2(e), (f)
8 Deriving actual data from standard cost details and variances	C1(d), C2(e)
9 Inter-relationships between variances	C2(e)

1 Variances

Variances measure the difference between actual results and expected results. The process by which the total difference between standard and actual results is analysed is known as **variance analysis**.

Key terms

A **variance** is 'the difference between a planned, budgeted, or standard cost and the actual cost incurred. The same comparisons may be made for revenues'.

Variance analysis is defined as the 'evaluation of performance by means of variances, whose timely reporting should maximise the opportunity for managerial action'.

CIMA *Official Terminology*

When actual results are better than expected results, we have a **favourable variance** (F). If, on the other hand, actual results are worse than expected results, we have an **adverse variance** (A).

2 Direct material variances

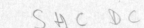

Key term

The **direct material total variance** is the 'measurement of the difference between the standard material cost of the output produced and the actual material cost incurred'.

CIMA *Official Terminology*

The **direct material total variance** (the difference between what the output actually cost and what it should have cost, in terms of material) can be divided into the **direct material price variance** and the **direct material usage variance**.

(a) **The direct material price variance**

This is the **difference between the standard cost and the actual cost for the actual quantity of material used or purchased.** In other words, it is the difference between what the material did cost and what it should have cost.

Key term

The **direct material price variance** is the 'difference between the actual price paid for the purchased materials and their standard cost'.

CIMA *Official Terminology*

(b) **The direct material usage variance**

This is the **difference between the standard quantity of materials that should have been used for the number of units actually produced, and the actual quantity of materials used, valued at the standard cost per unit of material**. In other words, it is the difference between how much material should have been used and how much material was used, valued at standard cost.

Key term

The **direct material usage variance** 'measures efficiency in the use of material, by comparing standard material usage for actual production with actual material used, the difference is valued at standard cost'. CIMA *Official Terminology*

2.1 Example: direct material variances

117000 − 98600
18,400

Product X has a standard direct material cost as follows.

> 10 kilograms of material Y at $10 per kilogram = $100 per unit of X.

During period 4, 1,000 units of X were manufactured, using 11,700 kilograms of material Y which cost $98,600.

Required

Calculate the following variances.

(a)   The direct material total variance
(b)   The direct material price variance
(c)   The direct material usage variance

Solution

(a)   **The direct material total variance**

This is the difference between what 1,000 units should have cost and what they did cost.

	$
1,000 units should have cost (× $100)	100,000
but did cost	98,600
Direct material total variance	1,400 (F)

The variance is **favourable** because the units cost less than they should have cost.

Now we can break down the direct material total variance into its two constituent parts: the direct material **price** variance and the direct material **usage** variance.

(b)   **The direct material price variance**

This is the difference between what 11,700 kgs should have cost and what 11,700 kgs did cost.

		$
11,700 kgs of Y should have cost (× $10)	SHC	117,000
but did cost		98,600
Material Y price variance		18,400 (F)

The variance is **favourable** because the material cost less than it should have.

(c)   **The direct material usage variance**

This is the difference between how many kilograms of Y should have been used to produce 1,000 units of X and how many kilograms were used, valued at the standard cost per kilogram.

1,000 units should have used (× 10 kgs)	10,000 kgs
but did use	11,700 kgs
Usage variance in kgs	1,700 kgs (A)
× standard cost per kilogram	× $10
Usage variance in $	$17,000 (A)

The variance is **adverse** because more material was used than should have been used.

(d)   **Summary**

	$
Price variance	18,400 (F)
Usage variance	17,000 (A)
Total variance	1,400 (F)

2.2 Materials variances and opening and closing inventory

Suppose that a company uses raw material P in production, and that this raw material has a standard price of $3 per metre. During one month 6,000 metres are bought for $18,600, and 5,000 metres are used in production. At the end of the month, inventory will have been increased by 1,000 metres. In variance analysis, the problem is to decide the

material price variance. Should it be calculated on the basis of **materials purchased** (6,000 metres) or on the basis of **materials used** (5,000 metres)? The answer to this problem depends on how **closing inventories** of the raw materials will be valued.

(a)   If closing inventories of raw materials are valued at **standard cost**, (1,000 units at $3 per unit) the price variance is calculated on material **purchases** in the period.

(b)   If closing inventories of raw materials are valued at **actual cost** (FIFO) (1,000 units at $3.10 per unit) the price variance is calculated on materials **used in production** in the period.

2.3 When to calculate the direct material price variance

> Since material inventories are usually valued at **standard cost** in a standard costing system, direct material price variances are usually extracted at the time of **receipt** of the materials, rather than at the time of usage.

A **full standard costing system** is usually in operation and therefore the price variance is usually calculated on **purchases** in the period. The variance on the full 6,000 metres will be written off to the costing income statement, even though only 5,000 metres are included in the cost of production.

There are two main advantages in extracting the material price variance at the time of **receipt**.

(a)   If variances are extracted at the time of receipt they will be **brought to the attention of managers earlier** than if they are extracted as the material is used. If it is necessary to correct any variances then management action can be more timely.

(b)   Since variances are extracted at the time of receipt, **all inventories will be valued at standard price**. This is administratively easier and it means that all issues from inventories can be made at standard price. If inventories are held at actual cost it is necessary to calculate a separate price variance on each batch as it is issued. Since issues are usually made in a number of small batches this can be a time-consuming task, especially with a manual system.

2.3.1 Calculation of the direct material price variance

The price variance would be calculated as follows.

	$
6,000 metres of material P purchased should cost (× $3)	18,000
but did cost	18,600
Price variance	600 (A)

Question	Material price variances

Select the correct words in each of the following sentences.

(a)   If material inventories are valued at standard cost, the material price variance should be based on the materials **purchased/used** in the period.

(b)   If material inventories are valued at actual cost, the material price variance should be based on the materials **purchased/used** in the period.

(a)   purchased
(b)   used

3 Direct labour variances

The calculation of **direct labour variances** is very similar to the calculation of direct material variances.

> The **direct labour total variance** (the difference between what the output should have cost and what it did cost, in terms of labour) can be divided into the **direct labour rate variance** and the **direct labour efficiency variance**.

Key term

> The **direct labour total variance** 'indicates the difference between the standard direct labour cost of the output which has been produced and the actual direct labour cost incurred'.   CIMA *Official Terminology*

(a)   **The direct labour rate variance**

This is similar to the direct material price variance. It is the **difference between the standard cost and the actual cost for the actual number of hours paid for.**

In other words, it is the difference between what the labour did cost and what it should have cost.

Key term

> The **direct labour rate variance** 'indicates the actual cost of any change from the standard labour rate of remuneration'.   CIMA *Official Terminology*

(b)   **The direct labour efficiency variance**

This is similar to the direct material usage variance. It is **the difference between the hours that should have been worked for the number of units actually produced, and the actual number of hours worked, valued at the standard rate per hour.**

In other words, it is the difference between how many hours should have been worked and how many hours were worked, valued at the standard rate per hour.

Key term

> The **direct labour efficiency variance** is the 'standard labour cost of any change from the standard level of labour efficiency'.   CIMA *Official Terminology*

3.1 Example: direct labour variances

The standard direct labour cost of product X is as follows.

2 hours of grade Z labour at $5 per hour = $10 per unit of product X.

During period 4, 1,000 units of product X were made, and the direct labour cost of grade Z labour was $8,900 for 2,300 hours of work.

Required

Calculate the following variances.

(a)   The direct labour total variance
(b)   The direct labour rate variance
(c)   The direct labour efficiency (productivity) variance

Solution

(a) **The direct labour total variance**

This is the difference between what 1,000 units should have cost and what they did cost.

	$
1,000 units should have cost (× $10)	10,000
but did cost	8,900
Direct labour total variance	1,100 (F)

The variance is **favourable** because the units cost less than they should have done.

Again we can analyse this total variance into its two constituent parts.

(b) **The direct labour rate variance**

This is the difference between what 2,300 hours should have cost and what 2,300 hours did cost.

	$
2,300 hours of work should have cost (× $5 per hr)	11,500
but did cost	8,900
Direct labour rate variance	2,600 (F)

The variance is **favourable** because the labour cost less than it should have cost.

(c) **The direct labour efficiency variance**

1,000 units of X should have taken (× 2 hrs)	2,000 hrs
but did take	2,300 hrs
Efficiency variance in hours	300 hrs (A)
× standard rate per hour	× $5
Efficiency variance in $	$1,500 (A)

The variance is **adverse** because more hours were worked than should have been worked.

(d) **Summary**

	$
Rate variance	2,600 (F)
Efficiency variance	1,500 (A)
Total variance	1,100 (F)

3.2 Idle time variance

FAST FORWARD If idle time arises, it is usual to calculate a separate **idle time variance**, and to base the calculation of the efficiency variance on **active hours** (when labour actually worked) only. It is always an **adverse** variance.

Key term

The **direct labour idle time variance** 'occurs when the hours paid exceed the hours worked and there is an extra cost caused by this idle time. Its computation increases the accuracy of the labour efficiency variance'.

CIMA *Official Terminology*

A company may operate a costing system in which any **idle time** is recorded. Idle time may be caused by machine breakdowns or not having work to give to employees, perhaps because of bottlenecks in production or a shortage of orders from customers. When idle time occurs, the labour force is still paid wages for time at work, but no actual work is

done. Time paid for without any work being done is unproductive and therefore inefficient. In variance analysis, **idle time is always an adverse efficiency variance**.

When idle time is recorded separately, it is helpful to provide control information which identifies the cost of idle time separately, and in variance analysis, there will be an idle time variance **as a separate part of the total labour efficiency variance**. The remaining efficiency variance will then relate only to the productivity of the labour force during the hours spent **actively working**.

3.2.1 Example: labour variances with idle time

Refer to the standard cost data in Section 3.1. During period 5, 1,500 units of product X were made and the cost of grade Z labour was $17,500 for 3,080 hours. During the period, however, there was a shortage of customer orders and 100 hours were recorded as idle time.

Required

Calculate the following variances.

(a)   The direct labour total variance
(b)   The direct labour rate variance
(c)   The idle time variance
(d)   The direct labour efficiency variance

Solution

(a)   **The direct labour total variance**

	$
1,500 units of product X should have cost (× $10)	15,000
but did cost	17,500
Direct labour total variance	2,500 (A)

Actual cost is greater than standard cost. The variance is therefore **adverse**.

(b)   **The direct labour rate variance**

The rate variance is a comparison of what the hours paid should have cost and what they did cost.

	$
3,080 hours of grade Z labour should have cost (× $5)	15,400
but did cost	17,500
Direct labour rate variance	2,100 (A)

Actual cost is greater than standard cost. The variance is therefore **adverse**.

(c)   **The idle time variance**

The idle time variance is the hours of idle time, valued at the standard rate per hour.

Idle time variance = 100 hours (A) × $5 = $500 (A)

Idle time is **always** an adverse variance.

(d)   **The direct labour efficiency variance**

The efficiency variance considers the hours actively worked (the difference between hours paid for and Idle time hours). In our example, there were (3,080 – 100) = 2,980 hours when the labour force was not idle. The variance is calculated by taking the amount of output produced (1,500 units of product X) and comparing the time it should have taken to make them, with the actual time spent **actively** making them (2,980 hours).

Once again, the variance in hours is valued at the **standard rate per labour hour.**

1,500 units of product X should take (× 2hrs)	3,000 hrs
but did take (3,080 – 100)	2,980 hrs
Direct labour efficiency variance in hours	20 hrs (F)
× standard rate per hour	× $5
Direct labour efficiency variance in $	$100 (F)

(e)   **Summary**

	$
Direct labour rate variance	2,100 (A)
Idle time variance	500 (A)
Direct labour efficiency variance	100 (F)
Direct labour total variance	2,500 (A)

Important! | Remember that, if idle time is recorded, the actual hours used in the efficiency variance calculation are the **active hours worked and not the hours paid for**.

 Question   Variances

Growler Co is planning to make 100,000 units per period of product AA. Each unit of AA should require 2 hours to produce, with labour being paid $11 per hour. Attainable work hours are less than clock hours, so 250,000 hours have been budgeted in the period.

Actual data for the period was:

Units produced	120,000
Direct labour cost	$3,200,000
Clock hours	280,000

(a)   The labour rate variance is $ ☐

(b)   The labour efficiency variance is $ ☐

(c)   The idle time variance is $ ☐

Answer

(a)   **The labour rate variance is $ | 120 (A) |**

(b)   **The labour efficiency variance is $ | 176,000 (F) |**

(c)   **The idle time variance is $ | 161,000 (A) |**

Workings

The information means that clock hours have to be multiplied by $\dfrac{200,000}{250,000}$ (80%) in order to arrive at a realistic efficiency variance.

(a)   **Labour rate variance**

	$'000
280,000 hours should have cost ($\times$ $11)	3,080
but did cost	3,200
Labour rate variance	120 (A)

(b)   **Labour efficiency variance**

120,000 units should have taken ($\times$ 2 hours)	240,000 hrs
but did take (280,000 $\times$ 80%)	224,000 hrs
	16,000 hrs (F)
	$\times$ $11
Labour efficiency variance	$176,000 (F)

(c)   **Idle time variance**

280,000 $\times$ 20%	56,000 hrs
	$\times$ $11
	$616,000 (A)

4 Variable overhead variances

The **variable overhead total variance** can be subdivided into the variable overhead **expenditure variance** and the variable overhead **efficiency variance** (**based on active hours**).

Key terms

The **variable production overhead total variance** 'measures the difference between variable overhead that should be used for actual output and variable production overhead actually used'.

The **variable production overhead expenditure variance** 'indicates the actual cost of any change from the standard rate per hour'.

The **variable production overhead efficiency variance** is the 'standard variable overhead cost of any change from the standard level of efficiency'.   CIMA *Official Terminology*

4.1 Example: variable overhead variances

Suppose that the variable production overhead cost of product X is as follows.

    2 hours at $1.50 = $3 per unit

During period 6, 400 units of product X were made. The labour force worked 820 hours, of which 60 hours were recorded as idle time. The variable overhead cost was $1,230.

Calculate the following variances.

(a)   The variable production overhead total variance
(b)   The variable production overhead expenditure variance
(c)   The variable production overhead efficiency variance

Since this example relates to variable production costs, the total variance is based on actual units of production. (If the overhead had been a variable selling cost, the variance would be based on sales volumes.)

		$
400 units of product X should cost (× $3)		1,200
but did cost		1,230
Variable production overhead total variance		30 (A)

4.2 Subdividing the variable overhead total variance

In many variance reporting systems, the variance analysis goes no further, and expenditure and efficiency variances are not calculated. However, the adverse variance of $30 may be explained as the sum of two factors.

(a)   The hourly rate of spending on variable production overheads was higher than it should have been, that is there is an **expenditure variance**.

(b)   The labour force worked inefficiently, and took longer to make the output than it should have done. This means that spending on variable production overhead was higher than it should have been, in other words there is an **efficiency (productivity) variance**. The variable production overhead efficiency variance is exactly the same, in hours, as the direct labour efficiency variance, and occurs for the same reasons.

It is usually assumed that **variable overheads are incurred during active working hours**, but are not incurred during idle time (for example the machines are not running, therefore power is not being consumed, and no direct materials are being used). This means in our example that although the labour force was paid for 820 hours, they were actively working for only 760 of those hours and so variable production overhead spending occurred during 760 hours.

4.2.1 The variable overhead expenditure variance

This is the difference between the amount of variable overhead that should have been incurred in the actual hours actively worked, and the actual amount of variable overhead incurred. Refer to the data in Section 4.1.

	$
760 hours of variable production overhead should cost (× $1.50)	1,140
but did cost	1,230
Variable production overhead expenditure variance	90 (A)

4.2.2 The variable overhead efficiency variance

If you already know the direct labour efficiency variance, the variable overhead efficiency variance is exactly the same in hours, but priced at the variable production overhead rate per hour. In the example in Section 4.1, the efficiency variance would be as follows.

400 units of product X should take (× 2hrs)	800 hrs
but did take (active hours)	760 hrs
Variable production overhead efficiency variance in hours	40 hrs (F)
× standard rate per hour	× $1.50
Variable production overhead efficiency variance in $	$60 (F)

4.2.3 Summary

	$
Variable production overhead expenditure variance	90 (A)
Variable production overhead efficiency variance	60 (F)
Variable production overhead total variance	30 (A)

5 The reasons for cost variances

Assessment focus point

This is not an exhaustive list and an assessment question might suggest other possible causes. You should review the information provided and select any causes that are consistent with the reported variances.

Variance	Favourable	Adverse
(a) Material price	Unforeseen discounts received More care taken in purchasing Change in material standard	Price increase Careless purchasing Change in material standard
(b) Material usage	Material used of higher quality than standard More effective use made of material Errors in allocating material to jobs	Defective material Excessive waste Theft Stricter quality control Errors in allocating material to jobs
(c) Labour rate	Use of apprentices or other workers at a rate of pay lower than standard	Wage rate increase Use of higher grade labour
(d) Idle time	The idle time variance is always adverse	Machine breakdown Non-availability of material Illness or injury to worker
(e) Labour efficiency	Output produced more quickly than expected because of work motivation, better quality of equipment or materials, or better methods. Errors in allocating time to jobs	Lost time in excess of standard allowed Output lower than standard set because of deliberate restriction, lack of training, or sub-standard material used Errors in allocating time to jobs
(f) Variable overhead expenditure	Change in types of overhead or their cost	Change in type of overhead or their cost
(g) Variable overhead efficiency	As for labour efficiency (if based on labour hours)	As for labour efficiency (if based on labour hours)

6 Sales variances

6.1 Sales price variance

Key term

The **sales price variance** is the 'change in revenue caused by the actual selling price differing from that budgeted'.

CIMA *Official Terminology*

Suppose that the standard selling price of product X is $15. Actual sales in 20X3 were 2,000 units at $15.30 per unit. The sales price variance is calculated as follows.

	$
Sales revenue from 2,000 units should have been (× $15)	30,000
but was	30,600
Sales price variance	600 (F)

The variance is favourable because the price was higher than expected.

6.2 Sales volume contribution variance

FAST FORWARD

The **sales volume variance** in units is the difference between the actual units sold and the budgeted quantity. This variance in units can be valued in one of three ways: in terms of standard revenue, standard gross margin or standard contribution margin.

The sales volume variance in units is calculated as the difference between the actual units sold and the budgeted quantity. This variance in units can be valued in one of three ways.

(a) At the **standard gross profit margin per unit**. This is the **sales volume profit variance** and it measures the change in profit (in an absorption costing system) caused by the sales volume differing from budget.

(b) At the **standard contribution per unit**. This is the **sales volume contribution variance** and it measures the change in profit (in a marginal costing system) caused by the sales volume differing from budget.

(c) At the **standard revenue per unit**. This is the **sales volume revenue variance** and it measures the change in sales revenue caused by sales volume differing from that budgeted.

Suppose that a company budgets to sell 8,000 units of product J for $12 per unit. The standard variable cost per unit is $4 and the standard full cost is $7 per unit. Actual sales were 7,700 units, at $12.50 per unit.

The sales volume variance in units is 300 units adverse (8,000 units budgeted – 7,700 units sold). The variance is adverse because actual sales volume was less than budgeted. The sales volume variance in units can be evaluated in the three ways described above.

(a) Sales volume profit variance = 300 units × standard gross profit margin per unit
= 300 units × $(12 – 7)
= $1,500 (A)

(b) Sales volume contribution variance = 300 units × standard contribution per unit
= 300 units × $(12 – 4)
= $2,400 (A)

(c) Sales volume revenue variance = 300 units × standard revenue per unit
= 300 units × $12
= $3,600 (A)

Note that the sales volume profit variance (in an absorption costing system) and the sales volume contribution variance (in a marginal costing system) can be derived from the sales volume revenue variance, if the profit margin percentage and the contribution to sales (C/S) ratio respectively are known.

In our example the profit margin percentage is 41.67% ($5/$12) and the C/S ratio is 66.67% ($8/$12).

Therefore the sales volume profit variance and the sales volume contribution variance, derived from the sales volume revenue variance, are as follows.

Sales volume profit variance = $3,600 (A) × 41.67% = $1,500 (A), as above
Sales volume contribution variance = $3,600 (A) × 66.67% = $2,400 (A), as above

Jasper has the following budget and actual figures for year 4.

	Budget	Actual
Sales units	600	620
Selling price per unit	€30	€29

Standard full cost of production = €28 per unit. Standard variable cost of production = €19 per unit

Calculate the following sales variances

(a) Selling price variance   (c) Sales volume contribution variance

(b) Sales volume profit variance (d) Sales volume revenue variance

Answer

(a)

	€
Sales revenue for 620 units should have been ($\times$ €30)	18,600
but was ($\times$ €29)	17,980
Selling price variance	620 (A)

(b)

Budgeted sales volume	600 units
Actual sales volume	620 units
Sales volume variance in units	20 units (F)

Sales volume profit variance = 20 units $\times$ €(30 − 28) = €40 (F)

(c) Sales volume contribution variance = 20 units $\times$ €(30 − 19) = €220(F)

(d) Sales volume revenue variance = 20 units $\times$ €30 = €600(F)

In this question you were asked to calculate both the sales volume profit variance and the sales volume contribution variance to give you some practice. However, the two variances would never be found together in the same system in a real situation. Either a marginal costing system is used, in which case the sale volume contribution variance is calculated, or an absorption costing system is used, in which case a sales volume profit variance is calculated.

Assessment focus point

You need to read the assessment question carefully to decide whether to value the sales volume variance at gross profit margin (in an absorption costing system), contribution (in a marginal costing system) or standard revenue. Remember that the **total** sales variance is the sum of the sales price variance and the sales volume variance.

7 Operating statements

FAST FORWARD

Operating statements show how the combination of variances reconcile budgeted contribution and actual contribution.

So far, we have considered how variances are calculated without considering how they combine to reconcile the difference between budgeted contribution and actual contribution during a period. This reconciliation is usually presented as a report to senior management at the end of each control period. The report is called an operating statement or statement of variances.

Let's have a look at an example. This will provide you with the opportunity to revise the variance calculations already described, and will also show you how to combine them into an operating statement.

7.1 Example: variances and operating statements

Sydney Co manufactures one product, and the entire product is sold as soon as it is produced. There are no opening or closing inventories and work in progress is negligible. The company operates a standard costing system and analysis of variances is made every month. The standard cost card for a product is as follows.

STANDARD COST CARD

		$
Direct materials	0.5 kilos at $4 per kilo	2.00
Direct wages	2 hours at $8.00 per hour	16.00
Variable overheads	2 hours at $0.30 per hour	0.60
Standard variable cost		18.60
Standard contribution		13.40
Standing selling price		32.00

Budgeted output for the month of June 20X7 was 5,100 units. Actual results for June 20X7 were as follows.

Production of 4,850 units was sold for $150,350.
Materials consumed in production amounted to 2,300 kgs at a total cost of $9,800.
Labour hours paid for amounted to 8,500 hours at a cost of $67,800.
Actual operating hours amounted to 8,000 hours.
Variable overheads amounted to $2,600.

Required

Calculate all variances and prepare an operating statement for the month ended 30 June 20X7.

Solution

(a)		$
	2,300 kg of material should cost (× $4)	9,200
	but did cost	9,800
	Material price variance	600 (A)
(b)	4,850 units should use (× 0.5 kgs)	2,425 kg
	but did use	2,300 kg
	Material usage variance in kgs	125 kg (F)
	× standard price per kg	× $4
	Material usage variance in $	$500 (F)
(c)		$
	8,500 hours of labour should cost (× $8)	68,000
	but did cost	67,800
	Labour rate variance	200 (F)
(d)	4,850 units should take (× 2 hrs)	9,700 hrs
	but did take (active hours)	8,000 hrs
	Labour efficiency variance in hours	1,700 hrs (F)
	× standard rate per hour	× $8
	Labour efficiency variance in $	$13,600 (F)
(e)	Idle time variance 500 hours (A) × $8	$4,000 (A)

(f)

	$
8,000 hours incurring variable o/hd expenditure should cost (× $0.30)	2,400
but did cost	2,600
Variable overhead expenditure variance	200 (A)

(g) Variable overhead efficiency variance in hours is the same as the labour efficiency variance:

1,700 hours (F) × $0.30 per hour $ 510 (F)

(h)

	$
Revenue from 4,850 units should be (× $32)	155,200
but was	150,350
Sales price variance	4,850 (A)

(i)

Budgeted sales volume	5,100 units
Actual sales volume	4,850 units
Sales volume contribution variance in units	250 units (A)
× standard contribution per unit	× $13.40
Sales volume contribution variance	$3,350 (A)

Now let's turn our attention to the operating statement.

There are several ways in which an operating statement can be presented. Perhaps the most common format is one which **reconciles budgeted contribution to actual contribution.**

- **Budgeted contribution** is adjusted by the **sales volume variance** to give the **budgeted contribution from actual sales.**

- The **sales price variance** is then included to give a figure representing the **actual sales revenue minus the standard variable cost of sales.**

- **Cost variances** are then taken into account to produce a figure for **actual contribution.**

SYDNEY CO – OPERATING STATEMENT JUNE 20X7

	$
Budgeted contribution ($13.40 × 5,100)	68,340
Sales volume variance	3,350 (A)
Budgeted contribution from actual sales	64,990
Sales price variance	4,850 (A)
Actual sales minus the standard variable cost of sales	60,140

Cost variances	(F)	(A)	
	$	$	
Material price		600	
Material usage	500		
Labour rate	200		
Labour efficiency	13,600		
Labour idle time		4,000	
Variable overhead expenditure		200	
Variable overhead efficiency	510		
	14,810	4,800	10,010 (F)
Actual contribution			70,150

Check	$	$
Sales		150,350
Materials	9,800	
Labour	67,800	
Variable overhead	2,600	
		80,200
Actual contribution		70,150

Question

NN Co manufactures a single product, the SK. The standard variable cost for this item is as follows.

	$	$
Direct materials:		
P (8 kg at $0.40 per kg)	3.20	
Q (4 kg at $0.70 per kg)	2.80	
		6.00
Direct labour (3 hours at $7.50)		22.50
Variable production overhead (3 hours at $0.50)		1.50
		30.00

The standard sales price per unit is $40. The budgeted production and sales for period 7 were 3,000 units.

Actual results for period 7 were as follows.

Sales and production	2,800 units
Sales revenue	$113,200

Direct materials purchased and used:

P	19,000 kg	Cost $7,500
Q	14,000 kg	Cost $10,250

Direct labour 8,600 hours Cost $67,100

It is known that 300 hours of this labour was recorded as idle time.

Variable production overhead $4,100

Complete the operating statement for period 7 shown below. You should insert each cost variance into the correct box according to whether it is adverse or favourable. For the sales variances, indicate in the box whether they are adverse (A) or favourable (F).

OPERATING STATEMENT FOR PERIOD 7

		$
	Budgeted contribution	30,000
(a)	Sales volume contribution variance	
(b)	Sales price variance	
	Actual sales less standard variable cost of sales	

Cost variances	$ Favourable	$ Adverse
(c) Direct material price		
(d) Direct material usage		
(e) Direct labour rate		
(f) Direct labour efficiency		
(g) Idle time		
(h) Variable production overhead expenditure		
(i) Variable production overhead efficiency		

Total cost variances

Actual contribution   24,250

Answer

OPERATING STATEMENT FOR PERIOD 7

		$	
	Budgeted contribution	30,000	
(a)	Sales volume contribution variance	2,000	(A)
(b)	Sales price variance	1,200	(F)
	Actual sales less standard variable cost of sales	29,200	

Cost variances	$ Favourable	$ Adverse
(c) Direct material price		350
(d) Direct material usage		600
(e) Direct labour rate		2,600
(f) Direct labour efficiency	750	
(g) Idle time		2,250
(h) Variable production overhead expenditure	50	
(i) Variable production overhead efficiency	50	

Total cost variances   4,950   (A)

Actual contribution   24,250

Workings

(a)   **Sales volume**

		$
Budgeted sales volume		3,000 units
Actual sales volume		2,800 units
Sales volume variance in units		200 units (A)
× standard contribution per unit ($(40 − 30))		× $10
Sales volume variance in $		$2,000 (A)

(b)   **Sales price**

		$
Revenue from 2,800 units should have been (× $40)		112,000
but was		113,200
Sales price variance		1,200 (F)

(c)   **Material price**

	$	$
19,000 kg of P should cost (× 40c)	7,600	
did cost	7,500	
Material P price variance		100 (F)
14,000 kg of Q should cost (× 70c)	9,800	
did cost	10,250	
Material Q price variance		450 (A)
Total material price variance		350 (A)

(d)   **Material usage**

Material P

2,800 units of SK should use (× 8 kgs)	22,400 kgs
did use	19,000 kgs
Material P usage variance in kgs	3,400 kgs (F)
× standard price per kg	× $0.40
Material P usage variance in $	$1,360 (F)

Material Q

2,800 units of SK should use (× 4 kgs)	11,200 kgs
did use	14,000 kgs
Material Q usage variance in kgs	2,800 kgs (A)
× standard price per kg	× $0.70
Material Q usage variance in $	$1,960 (A)
Total material usage variance ($1,960 − $1,360)	$600 (A)

(e)   **Direct labour rate**

	$
8,600 hours of labour should cost (× $7.50)	64,500
did cost	67,100
Direct labour rate variance	2,600

(f)   **Direct labour efficiency**

To make 2,800 units of SK should take (× 3 hrs)	8,400 hrs
did take (active hours)	8,300 hrs
Direct labour variance in hrs	100 hrs (F)
× standard rate per hour	× $7.50
Direct labour efficiency variance in $	$750 (F)

(g) **Idle time variance** 300 hours (A) × $7.50 = $2,250 (A)

(h) **Variable production overhead expenditure**

	$
8,300 worked hours should cost (× $0.50)	4,150
did cost	4,100
Variable overhead expenditure variance	50 (F)

(i) **Variable production overhead efficiency** (same as direct labour)
     100 hrs (F) × standard rate ($0.50) $50 (F)

Question   Further variance analysis

P Co, a manufacturing firm, operates a standard marginal costing system. It makes a single product, PG, using a single raw material.

Standard costs relating to PG have been calculated as follows.

Standard cost schedule – PG	Per unit
	$
Direct material, 100 kg at $5 per kg	500
Direct labour, 10 hours at $8 per hour	80
Variable production overhead, 10 hours at $2 per hour	20
	600

The standard selling price of a PG is $900 and P Co plan to produce and sell 1,020 units a month.

During December 20X0, 1,000 units of PG were produced and sold. Relevant details of this production are as follows.

Direct material

90,000 kgs costing $720,000 were bought and used.

Direct labour

8,200 hours were worked during the month and total wages were $63,000.

Variable production overhead

The actual cost for the month was $25,000.

Inventories of the direct material are valued at the standard price of $5 per kg.

Each PG was sold for $975.

(a) The variable production cost variance for December 20X0 is $ ☐

(b) (i)   The direct labour rate variance is $ ☐
     (ii) The direct labour efficiency variance is $ ☐

(c) (i)   The direct material price variance is $ ☐
     (ii) The direct material usage variance is $ ☐

(d) (i)   The variable production overhead expenditure variance is $ ☐
     (ii) The variable production overhead efficiency variance is $ ☐

(e)   (i)   The sales volume contribution variance is $ ☐

       (ii)   The sales price variance is $ ☐

Answer

(a)   **The variable production cost variance is $ 208,000 (A)**

Workings

This is simply a 'total' variance.

	$
1,000 units should have cost (× $600)	600,000
but did cost (see working)	808,000
Variable production cost variance	208,000 (A)

(b)   (i)   **The direct labour rate variance is $ 2,600 (F)**

Workings

	$
8,200 hours should cost (× $8)	65,600
but did cost	63,000
Direct labour rate variance	2,600 (F)

       (ii)   **The direct labour efficiency variance is $ 14,400 (F)**

Workings

1,000 units should take (× 10 hours)	10,000 hrs
but did take	8,200 hrs
Direct labour efficiency variance in hrs	1,800 hrs (F)
× standard rate per hour	× $8
Direct labour efficiency variance in $	$14,400 (F)

(c)   (i)   **The direct material price variance is $ 270,000 (A)**

Workings

	$
90,000 kg should cost (× $5)	450,000
but did cost	720,000
Direct material price variance	270,000 (A)

       (ii)   **The direct material usage variance is $ 50,000 (F)**

Workings

1,000 units should use (× 100 kg)	100,000 kg
but did use	90,000 kg
Direct material usage variance in kgs	10,000 kg (F)
× standard cost per kg	× $5
Direct material usage variance in $	$50,000 (F)

(d) (i) **The variable production overhead expenditure variance is $** ☐ **8,600 (A)**

Workings

	$
8,200 hours incurring o/hd should cost (× $2)	16,400
but did cost	25,000
Variable production overhead expenditure variance	8,600 (A)

   (ii) **The variable production overhead efficiency variance is $** ☐ **3,600 (F)**

Workings

Efficiency variance in hrs (from (b)(ii))	1,800 hrs (F)
× standard rate per hour	× $2
Variable production overhead efficiency variance	$3,600 (F)

(e) (i) **The sales volume contribution variance is $** ☐ **6,000 (A)**

Workings

Budgeted sales volume	1,020 units
Actual sales volume	1,000 units
Sales volume contribution variance in units	20 units (A)
× standard contribution per unit ($(900 – 600))	× $300
	$6,000 (A)

   (ii) **The sales price variance is $** ☐ **75,000 (F)**

Workings

	$
Revenue should have been (1,000 × $900)	900,000
but was (1,000 × $975)	975,000
	75,000 (F)

8 Deriving actual data from standard cost details and variances

FAST FORWARD

Variances can be **manipulated** so as to derive actual data from standard cost details.

8.1 Example: deriving actual data

The standard marginal cost card for the TR, one of the products made by P Co, is as follows.

	$
Direct material 16 kgs × $6 per kg	96
Direct labour 6 hours × $12 per hour	72
	168

P Co reported the following variances in control period 13 in relation to the TR.

Direct material price: $18,840 favourable
Direct material usage: $480 adverse
Direct labour rate: $10,598 adverse
Direct labour efficiency: $8,478 favourable

Actual direct wages cost $171,320. P Co paid $5.50 for each kg of direct material. There were no opening or closing inventories of the material.

Required

Calculate the following.

(a) Actual output   (c) Average actual wage rate per hour

(b) Actual hours worked   (d) Actual number of kilograms purchased and used

Solution

(a)

	$
Total direct wages cost	171,320
Adjust for variances:	
labour rate	(10,598)
labour efficiency	8,478
Standard direct wages cost	169,200

$\therefore$ Actual output = Total standard cost ÷ unit standard cost
              = $169,200 ÷ $72
              = 2,350 units

(b)

	$
Total direct wages cost	171,320.0
Less rate variance	(10,598.0)
Standard rate for actual hours	160,722.0
÷ standard rate per hour	÷ $12.0
Actual hours worked	13,393.5 hrs

(c) Average actual wage rate per hour = actual wages/actual hours = $171,320/13,393.5 = $12.79 per hour.

(d) Number of kgs purchased and used = x

	$
x kgs should have cost (× $6)	6.0x
but did cost (× $5.50)	5.5x
Direct material price variance	0.5x

$\therefore$ $0.5x = $18,840
$\therefore$ x = 37,680 kgs

Question   Actual rate of pay

XYZ Co uses standard costing. The following data relates to labour grade II.

Actual hours worked	10,400 hours
Standard allowance for actual production	8,320 hours
Standard rate per hour	$5
Rate variance (adverse)	$416

What was the actual rate of pay per hour?

A $4.95
B $4.96
C $5.04
D $5.05

Answer

The correct answer is C.

Rate variance per hour worked = $\dfrac{\$416}{10,400}$ = $0.04 (A)

Actual rate per hour = $(5.00 + 0.04) = $5.04.

You should have been able to eliminate options A and B because they are both below the standard rate per hour. If the rate variance is adverse then the actual rate must be above standard.

Option D is incorrect because it results from basing the calculations on standard hours rather than actual hours.

Question

Quantity of material X

The standard material content of one unit of product A is 10kgs of material X which should cost $10 per kilogram. In June 20X4, 5,750 units of product A were produced and there was an adverse material usage variance of $1,500.

The quantity of material X used in June 20X4 is ☐ kgs.

Answer

The quantity used is ☐ 57,650 ☐ kgs.

Workings

Let the quantity of material X used = Y

5,750 units should have used (× 10kgs)	57,500 kgs
but did use	Y kgs
Usage variance in kgs	(Y − 57,500) kgs
× standard price per kg	× $10
Usage variance in $	$1,500 (A)

∴   10(Y − 57,500) = 1,500
    Y − 57,500   = 150
∴   Y   = 57,650 kgs

Assessment focus point Make sure you can deal with this sort of variance analysis question as it is an ideal way of assessing your competence in this area.

9 Inter-relationships between variances

In many cases, individual variances should not be looked at in isolation. One variance might be inter-related with another, and much of it might have occurred only because the other, inter-related, variance occurred too.

FAST FORWARD When two variances are **interdependent (inter-related)** one will usually be adverse and the other one favourable.

Here are some examples of interdependent variables.

(a) **Materials price and usage**

It may be decided to purchase cheaper materials for a job in order to obtain a favourable price variance, possibly with the consequence that materials wastage is higher and an adverse usage variance occurs. If the cheaper materials are more difficult to handle, there might be an adverse labour efficiency variance too.

If a decision is made to purchase more expensive materials, which perhaps have a longer service life, the price variance will be adverse but the usage variance might be favourable.

(b) **Labour rate and efficiency**

If employees in a workforce are paid higher rates for experience and skill, using a highly skilled team to do some work would incur an adverse rate variance, but should also obtain a favourable efficiency variance. In contrast, a favourable rate variance might indicate a larger-than-expected proportion of inexperienced workers in the workforce, which could result in an adverse labour efficiency variance, and perhaps poor materials handling and high rates of rejects too (adverse materials usage variance).

(c) **Sales price and sales volume**

The possible interdependence between sales price and sales volume variances should (hopefully) be obvious to you. A reduction in the sales price might stimulate bigger sales demand, so that an adverse sales price variance might be offset by a favourable sales volume variance. Similarly a price rise would give a favourable price variance, but possibly at the cost of a fall in demand and an adverse sales volume variance.

(d) **Cost and sales variances**

(i) If there are **favourable cost variances** (perhaps cheaper labour or material have been used, say, so that there are favourable labour rate or material price variances), the possible drop in quality of the product could lead to an **adverse sales volume variance** because customers don't wish to buy the lower quality product.

(ii) If product quality is improved this might result in an **adverse cost variance**.

   – If more expensive material is used (adverse material price variance)

   – If labour are more careful in production of the product and hence take longer than standard (adverse labour efficiency variance)

   – If more skilled labour is used (adverse labour rate variance)

   But the change in quality might result in a **favourable sales volume variance**, customers wanting to buy more of the higher-quality product.

(iii) If costs have risen (resulting in **adverse labour rate, material price and variable overhead expenditure variances**), the sales price might have to be increased to cover the extra costs. This would result in a **favourable sales price variance**.

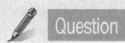
Question

Hey Co has been let down by its supplier and has had to buy from an alternative source. The alternative materials are of better quality but are more expensive than the original supplier's. What effect is this change in supplier likely to have on the variances at the month end?

(a)   Materials price variance   Favourable [   ]   Adverse [   ]

(b)   Materials usage variance   Favourable [   ]   Adverse [   ]

Answer

Adverse, Favourable

The materials are more expensive which will lead to an adverse price variance. They are however, better quality which means that the material usage variance should be favourable.

Chapter Roundup

- **Variances** measure the difference between actual results and expected results. The process by which the total difference between standard and actual results is analysed is known as **variance analysis**.

- The **direct material total variance** (the difference between what the output actually cost and what it should have cost, in terms of material) can be divided into the **direct material price variance** and the **direct material usage variance**.

- Since material inventories are usually valued at **standard cost** in a standard costing system, direct material price variances are usually extracted at the time of **receipt** of the materials, rather than at the time of usage.

- The **direct labour total variance** (the difference between what the output should have cost and what it did cost, in terms of labour) can be divided into the **direct labour rate variance** and the **direct labour efficiency variance**.

- If idle time arises, it is usual to calculate a separate **idle time variance**, and to base the calculation of the **efficiency variance** on **active hours** (when labour actually worked) only. It is always an **adverse** variance.

- The **variable overhead total variance** can be subdivided into the variable overhead **expenditure variance** and the variable overhead **efficiency variance (based on active hours).**

- There are a wide range of **reasons** for the occurrence of adverse and favourable cost **variances**.

- The **sales price variance** is a measure of the effect on expected contribution of a different selling price to standard selling price. It is calculated as the difference between what the sales revenue should have been for the actual quantity sold, and what it was.

- The **sales volume variance** in units is the difference between the actual units sold and the budgeted quantity. This variance in units can be valued in one of three ways: in terms of standard revenue, standard gross margin or standard contribution margin.

- **Operating statements** show how the combination of variances reconcile budgeted contribution and actual contribution.

- **Variances** can be **manipulated** so as to derive actual data from standard cost details.

- When two variances are **interdependent (inter-related)** one will usually be adverse and the other favourable.

1   Subdivide the following variances.

   (a)   Direct materials cost variance

   (b)   Direct labour cost variance

   (c)   Variable production overhead variance

2   What are the two main advantages in calculating the material price variance at the time of receipt of materials?

3   Adverse material usage variances might occur for the following reasons.

   I   Defective material
   II   Excessive waste
   III   Theft
   IV   Unforeseen discounts received

   A   I
   B   I and II
   C   I, II and III
   D   I, II, III and IV

4   Hat Co makes a product Kap which requires material budgeted at 50c per kg. During June, 6,200 kg were purchased for $3,224 and 6,000 kg were used. There was no opening inventory at the start of June. Inventory is valued at standard cost.

   (a)   Calculate the material price variance for June.

   A $224   C $244
   B $124   D $144

   (b)   Is the variance favourable or adverse?

        Favourable [   ]   Adverse [   ]

5   A regular report for management of actual cost and revenue, and usually comparing actual with budget (and showing variances) is known as

   A   Bank statement   C   Budget statement
   B   Variance statement   D   Operating statement

6   A favourable sales price variance can result from a combination of a lower than budgeted sales volume and a higher than standard selling price.

   True [   ]   False [   ]

7   If two variances are interdependent, both must be either favourable or adverse.

   True [   ]   False [   ]

8   The sales volume variance considers the difference between .... sales volume and .... sales volume.

Fill in the gaps using two of the following words.

- total
- incremental
- budgeted
- estimated
- actual
- past
- future
- confirmed

9   HF Co budgeted to produce 3,000 units of product K in June. The budgeted materials for product K were 1,500 kg at a cost of $3 per kg. The actual number of units produced was 2,200 and the material variances were as follows:

Direct material price variance $825(A)

Direct material efficiency varlance $1,650(A)

Calculate the actual direct material kgs used.

A   550 kg
B   1,100 kg
C   1,650 kg
D   4,950 kg

10   Using the information in question 9, calculate the actual direct material cost for June.

A $825
B $4,125
C $4,950
D $5,775

1   (a)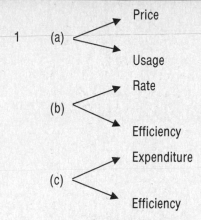
         Price

         Usage

    (b) Rate

         Efficiency

    (c) Expenditure

         Efficiency

2   (a) The earlier variances are extracted, the sooner they will be brought to the attention of managers.
    (b) All inventories will be valued at standard price which requires less administration effort.

3   C   Unforeseen discounts received would lead to a favourable price variance.

4   B $124 Adverse

	$
6,200 kg should have cost (× 50c)	3,100
But did cost	3,224
	124 (A)

5   D

6   True. The variance is favourable if the actual price is higher than standard.

7   False. Favourable material price and adverse material usage variances might be interdependent, for example.

8   The correct words are **budgeted** and **actual**.

9   C   First we write out the way we would normally calculate the material efficiency variance and fill in the figures that we know.

2,200 units should have used (x 3,000/1,500kg)	1,100	kg
But did use		(Q)
Material efficiency variance in kgs		(P)
x standard cost per kg	x $3	
	$1,650	(A)

Working backwards we can see that the efficiency variance in kg (box (P))

    = 1,650 ÷ $3
    = 550 kg

Now that we know the efficiency variance in kg, we can work out the number of kg that were actually used (box (Q))

    = 550 kg + 1,100 kg
    = 1,650 kg

10   D $5,775

1,650 kg should have cost (x $3)   4,950
But did cost

Materials price variance   825   (A)

Working backwards we can see that the actual cost must have been 825 + 4,950 = $5,775.

Now try the questions below from the Question Bank

Question numbers
37–46

Part C
Financial planning and control

Budget preparation

Introduction

This chapter is the first of two on a new topic, **budgeting**. It is a topic which you will meet at all stages of your examination studies so it is vital that you get a firm grasp of the basics now. The chapter begins by explaining the **reasons** why an organisation might prepare a budget and goes on to detail the **steps in the preparation of a budget**. The method of preparing and the relationship between the various **functional budgets** is then set out.

The chapter also considers the construction of **cash budgets** and **budgeted income statements and statements of financial position**, these three budgets making up what is known as a **master budget**.

In Chapter 10 we will build on the general awareness of budgeting gained in this chapter and look at more specific budgeting issues.

Topic list	Syllabus references
1 Why do organisations prepare budgets?	C1(a)
2 A framework for budgeting	C1(b)
3 Steps in the preparation of a budget	C1(b)
4 Functional budgets	C1(b)
5 Cash budgets	C1(c)
6 Master budgets	C1(e)
7 Capital expenditure budgets	C1(b)
8 Approaches to budgeting	C1(a)

1 Why do organisations prepare budgets?

Budgeting is a **multi-purpose activity**.

1.1 Reasons for preparing budgets

Here are some of the reasons why budgets are used.

Function	Detail
Compel planning	Budgeting forces management to look ahead, to set out detailed plans for achieving the targets for each department and (ideally) each manager. It helps management to predict problems.
Communicate ideas and plans	A formal system is necessary to ensure that each person affected by the plans is aware of what he or she is supposed to be doing. Communication might be one-way, with managers giving orders to subordinates, or there might be a two-way communication.
Coordinate activities	The activities of different departments need to be coordinated to ensure everyone in an organisation is working towards the same goals. This means, for example, that the purchasing department should base its budget on production requirements and that the production budget should in turn be based on sales expectations.
Provide a framework for responsibility accounting	Budgets require that managers are made responsible for the achievement of budget targets for the operations under their personal control.
Establish a system of control	Control over actual performance is provided by the comparisons of actual results against the budget plan. Departures from budget can then be investigated and the reasons for the departures can be divided into controllable and uncontrollable factors. Measure can then be put in place to bring performance back on track.
Provide a means of performance evaluation	Budgets provide targets which can be compared with actual outcomes in order to assess employee performance.
Motivate employees to improve their performance	The interest and commitment of employees can be retained if there is a system that lets them know how well or badly they are performing. The identification of controllable reasons for departures from budget with managers responsible provides an incentive for improving future performance.

Here's what the *Official Terminology* has to say:

Key term

> **Budget purposes**: 'Budgets may help in authorising expenditure, communicating objectives and plans, controlling operations, co-ordinating activities, evaluating performance, planning and rewarding performance. Often, reward systems involve comparison of actual with budgeted performance.'
> CIMA *Official Terminology*

1.2 Different things to different people

A **budget**, since it has different purposes, **might mean different things to different people**.

FAST FORWARD

A budget might be a **forecast**, a **means of allocating resources**, a **yardstick** or a **target.**

What it might mean	Detail
Forecast	It helps managers to plan for the future. Given uncertainty about the future, however, it is quite likely that a budget will become outdated as events occur and so the budget will cease to be a realistic forecast. New forecasts might be prepared that differ from the budget. (A **forecast** is **what is likely to happen**; a **budget** is **what an organisation wanted to happen**. These are not necessarily the same thing.)
Means of allocating resources	It can be used to decide how many resources are needed (cash, labour and so on) and how many should be given to each area of the organisation's activities. As we saw when we looked at limiting factor analysis, resource allocation is particularly important when some resources are in short supply. Budgets often set ceilings or limits on how much administrative departments and other service departments are allowed to spend in the period. Public expenditure budgets, for example, set spending limits for each government department.
Yardstick	By comparing it with actual performance, the budget provides a means of indicating where and when control action may be necessary (and possibly where some managers or employees are open to censure for achieving poor results).
Target	A budget might be a means of motivating the workforce to greater personal accomplishment, another aspect of control.

Key term

A **budget** is a 'quantitative expression of a plan for a defined period of time. It may include planned sales volumes and revenues; resource quantities, costs and expenses; assets, liabilities and cash flows.'   CIMA *Official Terminology*

2 A framework for budgeting

2.1 Budget committee

FAST FORWARD

The **budget committee** is the coordinating body in the preparation and administration of budgets.

The budget committee is usually headed up by the managing director (as chairman) and is assisted by a **budget officer** who is usually an accountant. Every part of the organisation should be represented on the committee, so there should be a representative from sales, production, marketing and so on. Functions of the budget committee include the following.

- Coordination and allocation of responsibility for the preparation of budgets
- Issuing of the budget manual
- Timetabling
- Provision of information to assist in the preparation of budgets
- Communication of final budgets to the appropriate managers
- Monitoring the budgeting process by comparing actual and budgeted results

2.2 The budget period

> A **budget period** is a 'period for which a budget is prepared, and used, which may then be sub-divided into control periods'.
>
> *CIMA Official Terminology*

Except for capital expenditure budgets, the budget period is usually the accounting year (sub-divided into 12 or 13 control periods).

2.3 Responsibility for budgets

FAST FORWARD

The manager responsible for preparing each budget should ideally be the manager responsible for carrying out the budget.

For example, the preparation of particular budgets might be allocated as follows.

(a)   The **sales manager** should draft the **sales budget** and the selling overhead cost centre budgets.

(b)   The **purchasing manager** should draft the **material purchases budget**.

(c)   The **production manager** should draft the **direct production cost budgets.**

Question

Budget committee

Which of the following is the budget committee *not* responsible for?

A   Preparing functional budgets
B   Timetabling the budgeting operation
C   Allocating responsibility for the budget preparation
D   Monitoring the budgeting process

Answer

The correct answer is A.

The manager responsible for implementing the budget that must prepare it, not the budget committee.

If you don't know the answer, remember not to fall for the common pitfall of thinking, 'Well, we haven't had a D for a while, so I'll guess that'. It is good practice to guess if you don't know the answer (never leave out an assessment question) but first eliminate some of the options if you can.

Since the committee is a co-ordinating body we can definitely say that they are responsible for B and D. Similarly, a co-ordinating body is more likely to allocate responsibility than to actually undertake the budget preparation, so eliminate C and select A as the correct answer.

2.4 The budget manual

The **budget manual** is a collection of instructions governing the responsibilities of persons and the procedures, forms and records relating to the preparation and use of budgetary data.

Key term

The **budget manual** is a 'detailed set of guidelines and information about the budget process typically including a calendar of budgetary events, specimen budget forms, a statement of budgetary objectives and desired results, listing of budgetary activities and budget assumptions, regarding, for example, inflation and interest rates'.

CIMA *Official Terminology*

A budget manual may contain the following.

(a) An explanation of the **objectives** of the budgetary process

    (i) The purpose of budgetary planning and control
    (ii) The objectives of the various stages of the budgetary process
    (iii) The importance of budgets in the long-term planning of the business

(b) **Organisational structures**

    (i) An organisation chart
    (ii) A list of individuals holding budget responsibilities

(c) An **outline of the principal budgets** and the **relationship between them**

(d) **Administrative details of budget preparation**

    (i) Membership and terms of reference of the budget committee
    (ii) The sequence in which budgets are to be prepared
    (iii) A timetable

(e) **Procedural matters**

    (i) Specimen forms and instructions for their completion
    (ii) Specimen reports
    (iii) Account codes (or a chart of accounts)
    (iv) The name of the budget officer to whom enquiries must be sent

3 Steps in the preparation of a budget

The first task in the budgetary process is to identify the **principal budget factor**. This is also known as the **key budget factor** or **limiting budget factor**. The principal budget factor is the factor which limits the activities of an organisation.

The procedures for preparing a budget will differ from organisation to organisation but the steps described below will be indicative of the steps followed by many organisations. The preparation of a budget may take weeks or months and the **budget committee** may meet several times before the **master budget** (budgeted income statement, budgeted statement of financial position and budgeted cash flow) is finally agreed. **Functional budgets** (sales budgets, production budgets, direct labour budgets and so on), which are amalgamated into the master budget, may need to be amended many times over as a consequence of discussions between departments, changes in market conditions and so on during the course of budget preparation.

3.1 Identifying the principal budget factor

> The **principal budget factor** 'limits the activities of an undertaking. Identification of the principal budget factor is often the starting point in the budget setting process. Often the principal budget factor will be sales demand but it could be production capacity or material supply.'
> CIMA *Official Terminology*

The **principal budget factor** is usually **sales demand**. A company is usually restricted from making and selling more of its products because there would be no sales demand for the increased output at a price which would be acceptable/profitable to the company. The principal budget factor may also be machine capacity, distribution and selling resources, the availability of key raw materials or the availability of cash. Once this factor is defined then the remainder of the budgets can be prepared. For example, if sales are the principal budget factor then the production manager can only prepare his budget after the sales budget is complete.

3.2 The order of budget preparation

Assuming that the principal budget factor has been identified as being sales, the stages involved in the preparation of a budget can be summarised as follows.

(a) The **sales budget** is prepared in units of product and sales value. The **finished goods inventory budget** can be prepared at the same time. This budget decides the planned increase or decrease in finished goods inventory levels.

(b) With the information from the sales and inventory budgets, the **production budget** can be prepared. This is, in effect, the sales budget in units plus (or minus) the increase (or decrease) in finished goods inventory. The production budget will be stated in terms of units.

(c) This leads on logically to budgeting the **resources for production**. This involves preparing a **materials usage budget, machine usage budget and a labour budget**.

(d) In addition to the materials usage budget, a **materials inventory budget** will be prepared, to decide the planned increase or decrease in the level of inventory held. Once the raw materials usage requirements and the raw materials inventory budget are known, the purchasing department can prepare a **raw materials purchases budget** in quantities and value for each type of material purchased.

(e) During the preparation of the sales and production budgets, the managers of the cost centres of the organisation will prepare their draft budgets for the department **overhead costs**. Such overheads will include maintenance, stores, administration, selling and research and development.

(f) From the above information a **budgeted income statement** can be produced.

(g) In addition several other budgets must be prepared in order to arrive at the **budgeted statement of financial position**. These are the **capital expenditure budget** (for non-current assets), the **working capital budget** (for budgeted increases or decreases in the level of receivables and accounts payable as well as inventories), and a **cash budget**.

Make sure that you understand the meaning of principal budget factor.

4 Functional budgets

> Functional/departmental budgets include budgets for sales, production, purchases and labour.

Key term

> A **departmental/functional budget** is a 'budget of income and/or expenditure applicable to a particular function frequently including sales budget, production cost budget (based on budgeted production, efficiency and utilisation), purchasing budget, human resources budget, marketing budget and research and development budget'.
>
> CIMA *Official Terminology*

Having seen the theory of budget preparation, let us look at **functional** (or **departmental**) budget preparation, which are best explained by means of an example.

4.1 Example: preparing a materials purchases budget

ECO Co manufactures two products, S and T, which use the same raw materials, D and E. One unit of S uses 3 litres of D and 4 kilograms of E. One unit of T uses 5 litres of D and 2 kilograms of E. A litre of D is expected to cost $3 and a kilogram of E $7.

Budgeted sales for 20X2 are 8,000 units of S and 6,000 units of T; finished goods in inventory at 1 January 20X2 are 1,500 units of S and 300 units of T, and the company plans to hold inventories of 600 units of each product at 31 December 20X2.

Inventories of raw material are 6,000 litres of D and 2,800 kilograms of E at 1 January and the company plans to hold 5,000 litres and 3,500 kilograms respectively at 31 December 20X2.

The warehouse and stores managers have suggested that a provision should be made for damages and deterioration of items held in store, as follows.

Product S: loss of 50 units   Material D: loss of 500 litres
Product T: loss of 100 units   Material E: loss of 200 kilograms

Required

Prepare a material purchases budget for the year 20X2.

Solution

To calculate material purchases requirements it is first necessary to calculate the material usage requirements. That in turn depends on calculating the budgeted production volumes.

	Product S Units	Product T Units
Production required		
To meet sales demand	8,000	6,000
To provide for inventory loss	50	100
For closing inventory	600	600
	8,650	6,700
Less inventory already in hand	1,500	300
Budgeted production volume	7,150	6,400

	Material D Litres	Material E Kgs
Usage requirements		
To produce 7,150 units of S	21,450	28,600
To produce 6,400 units of T	32,000	12,800
To provide for inventory loss	500	200
For closing inventory	5,000	3,500
	58,950	45,100
Less inventory already in hand	6,000	2,800
Budgeted material purchases	52,950	42,300
Unit cost	$3	$7
Cost of material purchases	$158,850	$296,100
Total cost of material purchases		$454,950

Important!

> The basics of the preparation of each functional budget are similar to those above. Work carefully through the following question which covers the preparation of a number of different types of functional budget.

Question
Functional budgets

XYZ company produces three products X, Y and Z. For the coming accounting period budgets are to be prepared based on the following information.

Budgeted sales

Product X   2,000 at $100 each
Product Y   4,000 at $130 each
Product Z   3,000 at $150 each

Budgeted usage of raw material

	RM11	RM22	RM33
Product X	5	2	–
Product Y	3	2	2
Product Z	2	1	3
Cost per unit of material	$5	$3	$4

Finished inventories budget

	Product X	Product Y	Product Z
Opening	500	800	700
Closing	600	1,000	800

Raw materials inventory budget

	RM11	RM22	RM33
Opening	21,000	10,000	16,000
Closing	18,000	9,000	12,000

	Product X	Product Y	Product Z
Expected hours per unit	4	6	8
Expected hourly rate (labour)	$9	$9	$9

Fill in the blanks.

(a) **Sales budget**

	Product X	Product Y	Product Z	Total
Sales quantity	☐	☐	☐	
Sales value	$ ☐	$ ☐	$ ☐	$ ☐

(b) **Production budget**

	Product X Units	Product Y Units	Product Z Units
Budgeted production	☐	☐	☐

(c) **Material usage budget**

	RM11 Units	RM22 Units	RM33 Units
Budgeted material usage	☐	☐	☐

(d) **Material purchases budget**

	RM11	RM22	RM33
Budgeted material purchases	$ ☐	$ ☐	$ ☐

(e) **Labour budget**

Budgeted total wages	$ ☐

Answer

(a) **Sales budget**

	Product X	Product Y	Product Z	Total
Sales quantity	2,000	4,000	3,000	
Sales price	$100	$130	$150	
Sales value	$ 200,000	$ 520,000	$ 450,000	$ 1,170,000

(b) **Production budget**

	Product X Units	Product Y Units	Product Z Units
Sales quantity	2,000	4,000	3,000
Closing inventories	600	1,000	800
	2,600	5,000	3,800
Less opening inventories	500	800	700
Budgeted production	2,100	4,200	3,100

(c) **Material usage budget**

	Production Units	RM11 Units	RM22 Units	RM33 Units
Product X	2,100	10,500	4,200	–
Product Y	4,200	12,600	8,400	8,400
Product Z	3,100	6,200	3,100	9,300
Budgeted material usage		29,300	15,700	17,700

(d) **Material purchases budget**

	RM11 Units	RM22 Units	RM33 Units
Budgeted material usage	29,300	15,700	17,700
Closing inventories	18,000	9,000	12,000
	47,300	24,700	29,700
Less opening inventories	21,000	10,000	16,000
Budgeted material purchases	26,300	14,700	13,700
Standard cost per unit	$5	$3	$4
Budgeted material purchases	$ 131,500	$ 44,100	$ 54,800

(e) **Labour budget**

Product	Production Units	Hours required per unit	Total hours	Rate per hour $	Cost $
X	2,100	4	8,400	9	75,600
Y	4,200	6	25,200	9	226,800
Z	3,100	8	24,800	9	223,200
Budgeted total wages					525,600

Assessment focus point

You may get an assessment question which asks you to work out one budgeted figure from another. For example you may be given the sales budget and asked to work out the production budget. Make sure that you learn this formula.

Units made = units sold + units in closing inventory – units in opening inventory.

The business must produce enough to cover its sales volume and to leave enough in closing inventory, but it gets a 'head start' from opening inventory. This is why opening inventory is deducted.

You can apply this principle to other areas of budgeting. For example,

Materials purchases = materials usage + closing inventory material – opening inventory material.

Question

The following information is available for B Co.

Budgeted annual sales	100,000 units
Opening inventory	25,000 units
Closing inventory	27,500 units

What is the number of units of production for the year?

A	72,500	C	100,000
B	97,500	D	102,500

Answer

D   102,500

Units made = units sold + closing inventory units – opening inventory units
            = 100,000 + 27,500 – 25,000
            = 102,500

5 Cash budgets

FAST FORWARD

A **cash budget** is a statement in which estimated future cash receipts and payments are tabulated in such a way as to show the forecast cash balance of a business at defined intervals.

Key term

A **cash budget** is a 'detailed budget of estimated cash inflows and outflows incorporating both revenue and capital items'.
CIMA *Official Terminology*

5.1 Preparing cash budgets

For example, in December 20X2 an accounts department might wish to estimate the cash position of the business during the three following months, January to March 20X3. A cash budget might be drawn up in the following format.

	Jan $	Feb $	Mar $
Estimated cash receipts			
From accounts payable	14,000	16,500	17,000
From cash sales	3,000	4,000	4,500
Proceeds on disposal of non-current assets		2,200	
Total cash receipts	17,000	22,700	21,500

Estimated cash payments			
To suppliers of goods	8,000	7,800	10,500
To employees (wages)	3,000	3,500	3,500
Purchase of non-current assets		16,000	
Rent and rates			1,000
Other overheads	1,200	1,200	1,200
Repayment of loan	2,500		
	14,700	28,500	16,200
Net surplus/(deficit) for month	2,300	(5,800)	5,300
Opening cash balance	1,200	3,500	(2,300)
Closing cash balance	3,500	(2,300)	3,000

In this example (where the figures are purely for illustration) the accounts department has calculated that the cash balance at the beginning of the budget period, 1 January, will be $1,200. Estimates have been made of the cash which is likely to be received by the business (from cash and credit sales, and from a planned disposal of non-current assets in February). Similar estimates have been made of cash due to be paid out by the business (payments to suppliers and employees, payments for rent, rates and other overheads, payment for a planned purchase of non-current assets in February and a loan repayment due in January).

From these estimates it is a simple step to calculate the excess of cash receipts over cash payments in each month. In some months cash payments may exceed cash receipts and there will be a **deficit** for the month; this occurs during February in the above example because of the large investment in non-current assets in that month.

The last part of the cash budget above shows how the business's estimated cash balance can then be rolled along from month to month. Starting with the opening balance of $1,200 at 1 January a cash surplus of $2,300 is generated in January. This leads to a closing January balance of $3,500 which becomes the opening balance for February. The deficit of $5,800 in February throws the business's cash position into **overdraft** and the overdrawn balance of $2,300 becomes the opening balance for March. Finally, the healthy cash surplus of $5,300 in March leaves the business with a favourable cash position of $3,000 at the end of the budget period.

5.2 The usefulness of cash budgets

FAST FORWARD

The **usefulness of cash budgets** is that they enable management to make any **forward planning decisions** that may be needed, such as advising their bank of estimated overdraft requirements or strengthening their credit control procedures to ensure that customers pay more quickly.

The cash budget is one of the most important planning tools that an organisation can use. It shows the **cash effect of all plans made within the budgetary process** and hence its preparation can lead to a **modification of budgets** if it shows that there are insufficient cash resources to finance the planned operations.

It can also give management an indication of **potential problems** that could arise and allows them the opportunity to take action to avoid such problems. A cash budget can show **four positions**. Management will need to take appropriate action depending on the potential position.

5.3 Potential cash positions

Cash position	Appropriate management action
Short-term surplus	• Pay suppliers early to obtain discount • Attempt to increase sales by increasing receivables and inventories • Make short-term investments
Short-term shortfall	• Increase accounts payable • Reduce receivables • Arrange an overdraft
Long-term surplus	• Make long-term investments • Expand • Diversify • Replace/update non-current assets
Long-term shortfall	• Raise long-term finance (such as via issue of share capital) • Consider shutdown/disinvestment opportunities

Question

Cash budget

Tick the boxes to show which of the following should be included in a **cash** budget.

	Include	Do not include
Funds from the receipt of a bank loan		
Revaluation of a non-current asset		
Receipt of dividends from outside the business		
Depreciation of distribution vehicles		
Bad debts written off		
Share dividend paid		

Answer

Any item that is a **cash** flow will be included. Non-cash items are excluded from a cash budget.

	Include	Do not include
Funds from the receipt of a bank loan	✓	
Revaluation of a non-current asset		✓
Receipt of dividends from outside the business	✓	
Depreciation of distribution vehicles		✓
Bad debts written off		✓
Share dividend paid	✓	

5.4 Example: cash budgets again

Peter Blair has worked for some years as a sales representative, but has recently been made redundant. He intends to start up in business on his own account, using $15,000 which he currently has invested with a building society. Peter maintains a bank account showing a small credit balance, and he plans to approach his bank for the necessary additional finance. Peter asks you for advice and provides the following additional information.

(a)   Arrangements have been made to purchase non-current assets costing $8,000. These will be paid for at the end of September and are expected to have a five-year life, at the end of which they will possess a nil residual value.

(b)   Inventories costing $5,000 will be acquired on 28 September and subsequent monthly purchases will be at a level sufficient to replace forecast sales for the month.

(c)   Forecast monthly sales are $3,000 for October, $6,000 for November and December, and $10,500 from January 20X4 onwards.

(d)   Selling price is fixed at the cost of inventory plus 50%.

(e)   Two months' credit will be allowed to customers but only one month's credit will be received from suppliers of inventory.

(f)   Running expenses, including rent but excluding depreciation of non-current assets, are estimated at $1,600 per month.

(g)   Blair intends to make monthly cash drawings of $1,000.

Required

Prepare a cash budget for the six months to 31 March 20X4.

Solution

The opening cash balance at 1 October will consist of Peter's initial $15,000 less the $8,000 expended on non-current assets purchased in September. In other words, the opening balance is $7,000. Cash receipts from credit customers arise two months after the relevant sales.

Payments to suppliers are a little more tricky. We are told that cost of sales is 100/150 × sales. Thus for October cost of sales is 100/150 × $3,000 = $2,000. These goods will be purchased in October but not paid for until November. Similar calculations can be made for later months. The initial inventory of $5,000 is purchased in September and consequently paid for in October. **Depreciation is not a cash flow and so is *not* included in a cash budget.**
The cash budget can now be constructed.

CASH BUDGET FOR THE SIX MONTHS ENDING 31 MARCH 20X4

	Oct $	Nov $	Dec $	Jan $	Feb $	Mar $
Payments						
Suppliers	5,000	2,000	4,000	4,000	7,000	7,000
Running expenses	1,600	1,600	1,600	1,600	1,600	1,600
Drawings	1,000	1,000	1,000	1,000	1,000	1,000
	7,600	4,600	6,600	6,600	9,600	9,600
Receipts						
Receivables	–	–	3,000	6,000	6,000	10,500
Surplus/(shortfall)	(7,600)	(4,600)	(3,600)	(600)	(3,600)	900
Opening balance	7,000	(600)	(5,200)	(8,800)	(9,400)	(13,000)
Closing balance	(600)	(5,200)	(8,800)	(9,400)	(13,000)	(12,100)

Question

You are presented with the budgeted data shown in Annex A for the period November 20X1 to June 20X2 by your firm. It has been extracted from the other functional budgets that have been prepared.

You are also told the following.

(a)   Sales are 40% cash, 60% credit. Credit sales are paid two months after the month of sale.
(b)   Purchases are paid the month following purchase.
(c)   75% of wages are paid in the current month and 25% the following month.
(d)   Overheads are paid the month after they are incurred.
(e)   Dividends are paid three months after they are declared.
(f)   Capital expenditure is paid two months after it is incurred.
(g)   The opening cash balance at 1 January 20X2 is $15,000.

Annex A

	Nov X1 $	Dec X1 $	Jan X2 $	Feb X2 $	Mar X2 $	Apr X2 $	May X2 $	June X2 $
Sales	80,000	100,000	110,000	130,000	140,000	150,000	160,000	180,000
Purchases	40,000	60,000	80,000	90,000	110,000	130,000	140,000	150,000
Wages	10,000	12,000	16,000	20,000	24,000	28,000	32,000	36,000
Overheads	10,000	10,000	15,000	15,000	15,000	20,000	20,000	20,000
Dividends		20,000						40,000
Capital expenditure			30,000			40,000		

The net cash balance carried forward at the end of June 20X2 is $ ☐ .

Answer

The net cash balance carried forward at the end of June 20X2 is $ (156,000) .

Workings

	January $'000	February $'000	March $'000	April $'000	May $'000	June $'000
Receipts						
Sales revenue						
Cash	44	52	56	60	64	72
Credit	48	60	66	78	84	90
	92	112	122	138	148	162
Payments						
Purchases	60	80	90	110	130	140
Wages						
75%	12	15	18	21	24	27
25%	3	4	5	6	7	8
Overheads	10	15	15	15	20	20
Dividends			20			
Capital expenditure			30			40
	85	114	178	152	181	235
Net cash flow	7	(2)	(56)	(14)	(33)	(73)
b/f	15	22	20	(36)	(50)	(83)
c/f	22	20	(36)	(50)	(83)	(156)

Question

The following information is available for ABC Co.

	May $	June $
Budgeted sales	30,000	40,000
Gross profit as a percentage of sales	30%	30%
Closing trade payables as a percentage of cost of sales	50	50%
Opening inventory	nil	nil
Closing inventory	nil	nil

How much money should be budgeted for supplier payments in June?

A $10,500
B $14,000
C $24,500
D $30,000

Answer

C

	May $	June $
Sales	30,000	40,000
Gross profit (@ 30%)	9,000	12,000
Cost of sales (sales – GP)	21,000	28,000
Closing trade payables (@ 50%)	10,500	14,000

	$
June opening payables	10,500
Increase in amounts owing (COS)	28,000
June closing payables	(14,000)
Amount paid in June	24,500

5.5 Example: using cash budgets

Suppose that a bank overdraft with a ceiling of $50,000 has been arranged to accommodate the increased inventory levels and wage bill for overtime required to support the rising sales shown in Annex A in the question above.

What advice might be offered, given the cash budget prepared in answering the question?

Solution

The overdraft arrangements are quite inadequate to service the cash needs of the business over the six month period. If the figures are realistic then action should be taken now to avoid difficulties in the near future. The following are possible courses of action.

(a)   Activities could be curtailed.

(b)   Other sources of cash could be explored, for example a long-term loan to finance the capital expenditure and a factoring arrangement to provide cash due from customers more quickly.

(c)   Efforts to increase the speed of debt collection could be made.

(d)   Payments to suppliers could be delayed.

(e)   The dividend payments could be postponed (the figures indicate that this is a small company, possibly owner-managed).

(f)   Staff might be persuaded to work at a lower rate in return for, say, an annual bonus or a profit-sharing agreement.

(g)   Extra staff might be taken on to reduce the amount of overtime paid.

(h)   The stockholding policy should be reviewed: it may be possible to meet demand from current production and minimise cash tied up in inventories.

Assessment focus point

> Questions on functional and cash budget preparation are likely to appear in your assessment.

6 Master budgets

FAST FORWARD

> The **master budget** provides a consolidation of all the subsidiary budgets and normally consists of a budgeted income statement, budgeted statement of financial position, and a cash budget.

As well as wishing to forecast its cash position, a business might want to estimate its profitability and its financial position for a coming period. This would involve the preparation of a budgeted income statement and statement of financial position, both of which form a part of the **master budget**.

6.1 Example: preparing a budgeted income statement and statement of financial position

Using the information in Section 5.4, you are required to prepare Peter Blair's budgeted income statement for the six months ending on 31 March 20X4 and a budgeted statement of financial position as at that date.

Solution

The income statement is straightforward. The first figure is sales, which can be computed very easily from the information in Section 5.4(c). It is sufficient to add up the monthly sales figures given there; for the income statement there is no need to worry about any closing receivables. Similarly, cost of sales is calculated directly from the information on gross margin contained in Section 5.4(d).

FORECAST TRADING AND INCOME STATEMENT
FOR THE SIX MONTHS ENDING 31 MARCH 20X4

	$	$
Sales $(3,000 + (2 \times 6,000) + (3 \times 10,500))$		46,500
Cost of sales $(2/3 \times \$46,500)$		31,000
Gross profit		15,500
Expenses		
Running expenses $(6 \times \$1,600)$	9,600	
Depreciation $(\$8,000 \times 20\% \times 6/12)$	800	
		10,400
Net profit		5,100

Items will be shown in the statement of financial position as follows.

(a)   Inventory will comprise the initial purchases of $5,000.
(b)   Receivables will comprise sales made in February and March (not paid until April and May respectively).
(c)   Accounts payable will comprise purchases made in March (not paid for until April).
(d)   The bank overdraft is the closing cash figure computed in the cash budget.

STATEMENT OF FINANCIAL POSITION
FORECAST AT 31 MARCH 20X4

	$	$
Non-current assets $(8,000 – 800)		7,200
Current assets		
Inventories	5,000	
Receivables (2 × $10,500)	21,000	
	26,000	
Current liabilities		
Bank overdraft	12,100	
Trade suppliers (March purchases)	7,000	
	19,100	
Net current assets		6,900
		14,100
Proprietor's interest		
Capital introduced		15,000
Profit for the period	5,100	
Less drawings	(6,000)	
Deficit retained		(900)
		14,100

We have now prepared all of the elements of Peter Blair's **master budget**: the budgeted income statement and statement of financial position, and the budgeted cash flow from Section 5.4

6.2 A few hints

Budget questions are often accompanied by a large amount of sometimes confusing detail. This should not blind you to the fact that many figures can be entered very simply from the logic of the trading situation described. For example in the case of Blair you might feel tempted to begin a T-account to compute the closing receivables figure. This kind of working is rarely necessary, since you are told that receivables take two months to pay. Closing receivables will equal total credit sales in the last two months of the period.

Similarly, you may be given a simple statement that a business pays rates at $1,500 a year, followed by a lot of detail to enable you to calculate a prepayment at the beginning and end of the year. If you are preparing a budgeted income statement for the year do not lose sight of the fact that the rates expense can be entered as $1,500 without any calculation at all.

7 Capital expenditure budgets

Because of the monetary amounts involved in capital expenditure, the **capital expenditure budget** is one of the principal subsidiary budgets.

7.1 Steps in the preparation of capital expenditure budgets

The steps in the preparation of such a budget are as follows.

Step 1 An **accountant or budget officer should be responsible** for the capital expenditure budget. Their tasks should include communicating between interested parties, providing necessary data to assist in budget preparation, drawing up a timetable to ensure that proper consultation takes place and so on.

Step 2 Sales, production and related budgets cover, in general, a 12-month period. A detailed **capital expenditure budget should be prepared for the budget period but additional budgets should be drawn up for both the medium and long term.** This requires an in-depth consideration of the organisation's requirements for land, buildings, plant, machinery, vehicles, fixtures and fittings and so on for the short, medium and long term.

Step 3 The **budget covering the 12 month period** should be **broken down into monthly** or **quarterly spending**, and details incorporated into the cash budget.

Step 4 Suitable **financing** must be arranged as necessary.

Step 5 The capital expenditure budget should **take account of the principal budget factor**. If available funds are limiting the organisation's activities then they will more than likely limit capital expenditure.

Step 6 As part of the overall budget coordination process, the capital expenditure budget must be **reviewed in relation to the other budgets**. Proposed expansion of production may well require significant non-current asset expenditure which should be reflected in the budget.

Step 7 The capital expenditure budget should be **updated on a regular basis** since both the timing and amount of expenditure can change at short notice.

7.2 Example of a capital expenditure budget

A capital expenditure budget might appear as follows.

XYZ Company: Capital expenditure budget – 20X4

Project	Description/detail of capital investment items	Month	$'000
LV45	Installation of new personal computers and flat screen monitors throughout office and factory	April	100
LV46	Plant replacement of obsolete packing equipment by new automated and electronic machinery	October	500
Budgeted capital expenditure			600

7.3 Depreciation

Any depreciation on budgeted capital expenditure will need to be incorporated into the budgeted income statement, along with depreciation on existing non-current assets. The depreciation on planned disposals of non-current assets also needs to be taken into consideration.

7.3.1 Example: budgeted depreciation.

Suppose, for simplicity, XYZ Company (whose capital expenditure budget is shown above) applies a 10% straight-line depreciation policy to all non-current assets. All non-current assets are under ten years old. Non-current assets had a cost value of $4,000,000 at the beginning of 20X4. Budgeted additions to non-current assets are shown above. The plant being replaced by project LV46 has a cost value of $200,000, and will be disposed of at the very end of September (the new plant becoming operational on 1 October 20X4).

The budgeted depreciation charge for the year is:

	$
Depreciation on non-current assets held at 1 January 20X4 ($4,000,000 × 10%)	400,000
Less: depreciation not charged on disposals (3/12 × 10% × $200,000)	(5,000)
Plus: depreciation on additions	
LV45 (9/12 × 10% × $100,000)	7,500
LV46 (3/12 × 10% × $500,000)	12,500
Budgeted depreciation charge for 20X4	415,000

8 Approaches to budgeting

FAST FORWARD

There are several different approaches to budgeting. These include **incremental budgeting**, **zero-based budgeting**, **rolling budgeting** and **participative budgeting.**

8.1 Incremental budgeting

The **traditional approach** to budgeting is to **base next year's budget on the current year's results plus an extra amount for estimated growth or inflation next year**. This approach is known as **incremental budgeting** since it is concerned mainly with the increments in costs and revenues which will occur in the coming period.

Advantages of incremental budgets	Disadvantages
Simple and cheap to prepare	Past inaccuracies are carried forward and current market conditions are ignored
In stable market and operational conditions, it can give a good indication of the outcome and enables comparability between years to show departments/products that are over or under-performing against their peers	In times of change the outcome could be very different from the budget, due to factors outside the managers control
Increased certainty and lack of change means that longer term planning can take place	Focus is on the past and discourages innovation and risk taking

8.2 Zero-based budgeting

Zero-based budgeting involves preparing a budget for each cost centre from a zero base. Every item of expenditure has then to be justified in its entirety in order to be included in the next year's budget.

ZBB rejects the assumption inherent in incremental budgeting that next year's budget can be based on this year's costs.

Advantages of ZBB	Disadvantages
Based on planned activity rather than what was done last year, and so should be more realistic	Time consuming and expensive to operate
Involvement in setting means that there is greater motivation to achieve the budget	Large volume of work can be off putting for managers
Managers are forced to justify their budgets and the	May encourage a short-termist attitude

competition for funds should mean that there is great efficiency in allocating funds	Comparison between activities may be difficult
Less waste	More uncertainty for staff and managers about what activities will be undertaken from year to year

8.3 Rolling budgets

As an organisation and the environment it operates in are dynamic (always changing) management may decide to introduce a system of **rolling budgets** (also called **continuous budgets**).

A **rolling budget** is a budget which is continuously updated by adding a further accounting period (a month or quarter) when the earlier accounting period has expired.

This is in contract to the more traditional **periodic budget** which is prepared for a set period of time, often the financial year.

Advantages of rolling budgets	Disadvantages
Regular assessment leads to greater accuracy	Time consuming and expensive to operate
Motivation of managers is increased as changes in market conditions are reflected in the budget	Large volume of work can be off-putting for managers
More realistic as budgets focus on the near-term where there is more certainty	
Focus is on the future and encourages forward planning	

8.4 Participative budgeting

Participative budgeting is 'A budgeting system in which all budget holders are given the opportunity to participate in setting their own budgets'. (CIMA *Official* Terminology)

Advantages of participative budgets	Disadvantages
Prepared by those closer to the delivery and so should be more realistic	Time consuming and expensive to operate
Involvement in setting means that there is greater motivation to achieve the budget	Large volume of work can be off putting for managers

8.5 Budget slack

Budget slack is the 'Intentional overestimation of expenses and/or underestimation of revenues during the budget setting'. (CIMA *Official* Terminology)

Chapter Roundup

- Budgeting is a **multi-purpose activity**.

- A budget might be a **forecast**, a **means of allocating resources,** a **yardstick** or a **target.**

- The **budget committee** is the coordinating body in the preparation and administration of budgets.

- The manager responsible for preparing each budget should ideally be the manager responsible for carrying out the budget.

- The **budget manual** is a collection of instructions governing the responsibilities of persons and the procedures, forms and records relating to the preparation and use of budgetary data.

- The first task in the budgetary process is to identify the **principal budget factor**. This is also known as the **key budget factor** or **limiting budget factor**. The principal budget factor is the factor which limits the activities of an organisation.

- **Functional/departmental budgets** include budgets for sales, production, purchases and labour.

- A **cash budget** is a statement in which estimated future cash receipts and payments are tabulated in such a way as to show the forecast cash balance of a business at defined intervals.

- The **usefulness of cash budgets** is that they enable management to make any **forward planning decisions** that may be needed, such as advising their bank of estimated overdraft requirements or strengthening their credit control procedures to ensure that customers pay more quickly.

- The **master budget** provides a consolidation of all the subsidiary budgets and normally consists of a budgeted income statement, budgeted statement of financial position and a cash budget.

- Because of the monetary amounts involved in capital expenditure, the **capital expenditure budget** is one of the principal subsidiary budgets.

- There are several different approaches to budgeting. These include **incremental budgeting**, **zero-based budgeting**, **rolling budgeting** and **participative budgeting**.

1   Budgets have a number of purposes. Fill in the key words which are missing from the statements below.

    (a)   To .... the activities of different departments towards a single plan.

    (b)   To .... targets to managers responsible for achieving them.

    (c)   To establish a system of .... by comparing budgeted and actual results.

    (d)   To compel ....

2   Which of the following is unlikely to be contained with a budget manual?

    A   Organisational structures
    B   Objectives of the budgetary process
    C   Selling overhead budget
    D   Administrative details of budget preparation

3   The factor which limits the activities of an organisation is known as:

| I | The key budget factor | III | The principal budget factor |
| II | The limiting budget factor | IV | The main budget factor |

    A   I, II and IV   C   II and III
    B   I and III   D   I, II and III

4   If the principal budget factor is sales demand, in which order would the following budgets be prepared?

Materials usage	Materials purchase	Production	Sales	Cash

1st   [   ]

2nd   [   ]

3rd   [   ]

4th   [   ]

5th   [   ]

5   Match the following cash positions with the appropriate management action.

Short-term surplus	Increase payables
Long-term surplus	Replace/update non-current assets
Short-term shortfall	Issue share capital
Long-term shortfall	Increase receivables and inventory

6   Depreciation has an effect on net profit and is therefore included in a cash budget.

    True   [ ]

    False   [ ]

7   Which of the following are included in the master budget?
   I   Budgeted income statement
   II   Budgeted statement of financial position
   III   Budgeted cash flow
   IV   Functional budgets

   A   I, II and III
   B   II and III
   C   II, III and IV
   D   IV only

8   The following information is available for Biscuit Co.

	Jan	Feb
	$	$
Budgeted sales	60,000	80,000
Gross profit as a percentage of sales	40%	40%
Closing trade payables as a percentage of cost of sales	50%	50%
Opening inventory	nil	nil
Closing inventory	nil	nil

   Note that all cost of sales are paid for on credit.

   How much money should be budgeted for supplier payments in February?

   A $10,500   C $24,500
   B $14,000   D $42,000

9   Jay Co produces a product called the Bee. There has been a surge in Bee sales as a result of an advertising campaign and so Jay Co is paying its staff overtime to build up the inventory levels.

Labour hours per unit	3
Basic wage rate per hour	$20
Overtime premium	25%
Normal number of labour hours per month	340,000 hours

   Jay Co expects sales of 100,000 units in September and wants to have closing inventory at the end of September of 20,000 units. There will be no opening inventory on 1st September.

   Calculate the budgeted labour cost. $ [   ]

10   *Fill in the blanks.*

   When preparing a production budget, the quantity to be produced is equal to sales .... opening inventory .... closing inventory.

1   (a)   Coordinate   (c)   Control
    (b)   Communicate   (d)   Planning

2   C

3   D

4   1st | Sales |

    2nd | Production |

    3rd | Material usage |

    4th | Material purchase |

    5th | Cash |

5   Short term surplus ─────────────→ Increase payables

    Long-term surplus ─────────────→ Replace/update non-current assets

    Short-term shortfall ─────────────→ Issue share capital

    Long-term shortfall ─────────────→ Increase receivables and inventory

6   False. Only cash flow items are included in cash budgets. Depreciation is not a cash flow and so is not included in a cash budget.

7   A

8   D

	Jan	Feb
	$	$
Sales	60,000	80,000
Gross profit (@ 40%)	24,000	32,000
Cost of sales (sales – GP)	36,000	48,000
Closing trade payables (@ 50%)	18,000	24,000

	$
Feb opening payables	18,000
Increase in amounts owing (COS)	48,000
Feb closing payables	(24,000)
Amount paid in Feb	42,000

9    $7,300,000

Jay Co needs to produce 100,000 + 20,000 = 120,000 units in September.

Labour hours required = 120,000 units x 3 hours
                       = 360,000 hours

Only 340,000 hours are usually worked so there will need to be overtime of 360,000 – 340,000 = 20,000 hours.

	$
360,000 hours at basic rate (x $20)	7,200,000
20,000 hours at premium (x $20 x 25%)	100,000
Budgeted labour cost	7,300,000

10   When preparing a production budget, the quantity to be produced is equal to sales **minus** opening inventory **plus** closing inventory.

Now try the questions below from the Question Bank

Question numbers
47–51

Flexible budgeting

Introduction

You should now be able to **prepare functional budgets, a cash budget and a master budget** and have some idea of the **budgeting process**. This chapter takes the budgeting theme further.

We begin by looking at **flexible budgets**, a vital management planning and control tool. This part of the chapter relies on your understanding of **cost behaviour** covered in Chapter 3.

We'll also take a look at the way in which budgets can be used in a system of reward strategies for managers.

Topic list	Syllabus references
1 Flexible budgets	C1(f)
2 Flexible budgets and control	C1(f),(h)

1 Flexible budgets

1.1 Fixed budgets versus flexible budgets

- A **fixed budget** is a budget which is set for a single activity level.

- A **flexible budget** is a budget which recognises different cost behaviour patterns and is designed to change as volume of activity changes.

Master budgets are based on planned volumes of production and sales but do not include any provision for the event that actual volumes may differ from the budget. In this sense they may be described as **fixed budgets**.

Key term

A **fixed budget** is a 'budget set prior to the control period and not subsequently changed in response to changes in activity, costs or revenue. It may serve as a benchmark in performance evaluation.' CIMA *Official Terminology*

Assessment focus point

Make sure you are clear on the difference between fixed and flexible budgets.

1.2 Advantages of flexible budgets

A **flexible budget** has two advantages.

(a) At the **planning** stage, it may be helpful to know what the effects would be if the actual outcome differs from the prediction. For example, a company may budget to sell 10,000 units of its product, but may prepare flexible budgets based on sales of, say, 8,000 and 12,000 units. This would enable **contingency plans** to be drawn up if necessary.

(b) At the end of each month or year, actual results may be compared with the relevant activity level in the flexible budget as a **control** procedure.

1.3 Preparation of flexible budgets

Step 1 The first step in the preparation of a flexible budget is the **determination of cost behaviour patterns**, which means **deciding whether costs are fixed, variable or semi-variable**.

- Fixed costs are easy to spot. They remain constant as activity levels change.

- For non-fixed costs, divide each cost figure by the related activity level. If the cost is a variable cost, the cost per unit will remain constant. If the cost is a semi-variable cost, the unit rate will reduce as activity levels increase.

Step 2 The second step in the preparation of a flexible budget is to calculate the **budget cost allowance** for each cost item.

Budget cost allowance = budgeted fixed cost* + (number of units × variable cost per unit)**

* nil for variable cost
** nil for fixed cost

Semi-variable costs therefore need splitting into their fixed and variable components so that the budget cost allowance can be calculated.

Budget flexing involves 'flexing variable costs from original budgeted levels to the allowances permitted for actual volume achieved while maintaining fixed costs at original budget levels'. CIMA *Official Terminology*

1.3.1 Splitting semi-variable costs

One method for splitting semi-variable costs is the high/low method, which we covered in Chapter 3. Attempt the following question to make sure you remember how to do this.

Question
Cost estimation

The cost of factory power has behaved as follows in past years.

	Units of output produced	Cost of factory power $
20X1	7,900	38,700
20X2	7,700	38,100
20X3	9,800	44,400
20X4	9,100	42,300

Budgeted production for 20X5 is 10,200 units.

Ignoring inflation, the cost of factory power which will be incurred is estimated to be $ _____ .

Answer

The cost of factory power is estimated to be $ 45,600 .

Workings

	Units	$
20X3 (highest output)	9,800	44,400
20X2 (lowest output)	7,700	38,100
	2,100	6,300

The variable cost per unit is therefore $6,300/2,100 = $3.

The level of fixed cost can be calculated by looking at any output level.

	$
Total cost of factory power in 20X3	44,400
Less variable cost of factory power (9,800 × $3)	29,400
Fixed cost of factory power	15,000

An estimate of costs is 20X5 is as follows.

	$
Fixed cost	15,000
Variable cost of budgeted production (10,200 × $3)	30,600
Total budgeted cost of factory power	45,600

Now you are ready to prepare a flexible budget.

1.4 Example: preparing a flexible budget

(a) Prepare a budget for 20X6 for the direct labour costs and overhead expenses of a production department flexed at the activity levels of 80%, 90% and 100%, using the information listed below.

    (i)   The direct labour hourly rate is expected to be $3.75.

    (ii)   100% activity represents 60,000 direct labour hours.

    (iii) Variable costs

Indirect labour	$0.75 per direct labour hour
Consumable supplies	$0.375 per direct labour hour
Canteen and other welfare services	6% of direct and indirect labour costs

    (iv) Semi-variable costs are expected to relate to the direct labour hours in the same manner as for the last five years.

Year	Direct labour hours	Semi-variable costs $
20X1	64,000	20,800
20X2	59,000	19,800
20X3	53,000	18,600
20X4	49,000	17,800
20X5	40,000 (estimate)	16,000 (estimate)

    (v)   *Fixed costs*

	$
Depreciation	18,000
Maintenance	10,000
Insurance	4,000
Rates	15,000
Management salaries	25,000

    (vi) Inflation is to be ignored.

(b) Calculate the budget cost allowance (ie expected expenditure) for 20X6 assuming that 57,000 direct labour hours are worked.

Solution

(a)

	80% level 48,000 hrs $'000	90% level 54,000 hrs $'000	100% level 60,000 hrs $'000
Direct labour	180.00	202.50	225.0
Other variable costs			
Indirect labour	36.00	40.50	45.0
Consumable supplies	18.00	20.25	22.5
Canteen etc	12.96	14.58	16.2
Total variable costs ($5.145 per hour)	246.96	277.83	308.7
Semi-variable costs (W)	17.60	18.80	20.0
Fixed costs			
Depreciation	18.00	18.00	18.0
Maintenance	10.00	10.00	10.0
Insurance	4.00	4.00	4.0
Rates	15.00	15.00	15.0
Management salaries	25.00	25.00	25.0
Budgeted costs	336.56	368.63	400.7

Working

Using the high/low method:

	$
Total cost of 64,000 hours	20,800
Total cost of 40,000 hours	16,000
Variable cost of 24,000 hours	4,800
Variable cost per hour ($4,800/24,000)	$0.20

	$
Total cost of 64,000 hours	20,800
Variable cost of 64,000 hours (× $0.20)	12,800
Fixed costs	8,000

Semi-variable costs are calculated as follows.

		$
60,000 hours	(60,000 × $0.20) + $8,000	20,000
54,000 hours	(54,000 × $0.20) + $8,000	18,800
48,000 hours	(48,000 × $0.20) + $8,000	17,600

(b)   The budget cost allowance for 57,000 direct labour hours of work would be as follows.

		$
Variable costs	(57,000 × $5.145)	293,265
Semi-variable costs	($8,000 + (57,000 × $0.20))	19,400
Fixed costs		72,000
		384,665

Assessment focus point

You must be able to analyse the fixed and variable elements of semi-variable costs in order to be able to produce a flexible budget.

---

2 Flexible budgets and control

FAST FORWARD

Control involves **comparing a flexible budget** (based on the actual activity level) with **actual results**. The **differences** between the flexible budget figures and the actual results are **budget variances**.

2.1 Flexible budgets for control

Suppose W Co manufactures a single product, the CL. Budgeted results and actual results for June 20X2 are shown below.

	Budget	Actual results	Variance
Production and sales of the CL (units)	2,000	3,000	
	$	$	$
Sales revenue (a)	20,000	30,000	10,000 (F)
Direct materials	6,000	8,500	2,500 (A)
Direct labour	4,000	4,500	500 (A)
Maintenance	1,000	1,400	400 (A)
Depreciation	2,000	2,200	200 (A)
Rent and rates	1,500	1,600	100 (A)
Other costs	3,600	5,000	1,400 (A)
Total costs (b)	18,100	23,200	5,100
Profit (a) – (b)	1,900	6,800	4,900 (F)

(a)   In this example, the variances are meaningless for purposes of control. Costs were higher than budget because the **volume of output was also higher**; variable costs would be expected to increase above the budgeted costs in the fixed budget. There is no information to show whether control action is needed for any aspect of costs or revenue.

(b)   For control purposes, it is necessary to know the answers to questions such as the following.

   (i)   Were actual costs higher than they should have been to produce and sell 3,000 CLs?
   (ii)   Was actual revenue satisfactory from the sale of 3,000 CLs?

2.1.1 The correct approach to control

Important!

The **correct approach** to control is as follows.

- Identify fixed and variable costs.
- Produce a **flexible budget** based on the **actual activity level**.

In the previous example of W Co, let us suppose that we have the following estimates of cost behaviour.

(a)   Direct materials, direct labour and maintenance costs are variable.
(b)   Rent and rates and depreciation are fixed costs.
(c)   Other costs consist of fixed costs of $1,600 plus a variable cost of $1 per unit made and sold.

The control analysis should therefore be based on a flexible budget as follows.

	Fixed budget (a)	Flexible budget (b)	Actual results (c)	Budget variance (c)–(b)	
Production and sales (units)	2,000	3,000	3,000		
	$	$	$	$	
Sales revenue	20,000	30,000	30,000	0	
Variable costs					
Direct materials	6,000	9,000	8,500	500	(F)
Direct labour	4,000	6,000	4,500	1,500	(F)
Maintenance	1,000	1,500	1,400	100	(F)
Semi-variable costs					
Other costs	3,600	4,600	5,000	400	(A)
Fixed costs					
Depreciation	2,000	2,000	2,200	200	(A)
Rent and rates	1,500	1,500	1,600	100	(A)
Total costs	18,100	24,600	23,200	1,400	(F)
Profit	1,900	5,400	6,800	1,400	(F)

$3,500 (F)
Volume variance

$1,400 (F)
Expenditure variance

$4,900 (F)
Total variance

Notice that the total variance has not altered. It is still $4,900 (F) as in Section 2.1. The flexible budget comparison merely analyses the total variance into two separate components.

Important!

Variances are calculated by comparing actual results and the flexible budget, *not* actual results and the original budget.

BPP
LEARNING MEDIA

2.1.2 Interpretation of the control statement

We can analyse the above as follows.

(a)   In selling 3,000 units the expected profit should have been, not the fixed budget profit of $1,900, but the flexible budget profit of $5,400. Instead, actual profit was $6,800 ie $1,400 more than we should have expected. This is the $1,400 favourable expenditure variance. The reason for this $1,400 improvement is that, given output and sales of 3,000 units, overall costs were lower than expected (and sales revenue was exactly as expected). For example the direct material cost was $500 lower than expected.

(b)   Another reason for the improvement in profit above the fixed budget profit is the **sales volume**. W Co sold 3,000 units of CL instead of 2,000, with the following result.

	$	$
Budgeted sales revenue increased by		10,000
Budgeted variable costs increased by:		
direct materials	3,000	
direct labour	2,000	
maintenance	500	
variable element of other costs	1,000	
Budgeted fixed costs are unchanged		6,500
Budgeted profit increased by		3,500

Budgeted profit was therefore increased by $3,500 because sales volume increased. This is the $3,500 favourable volume variance.

(c)   A full variance analysis statement would be as follows.

	$	$
Fixed budget profit		1,900
Variances		
Sales volume		3,500 (F)
Direct materials cost	500 (F)	
Direct labour cost	1,500 (F)	
Maintenance cost	100 (F)	
Other costs	400 (A)	
Depreciation	200 (A)	
Rent and rates	100 (A)	
Total expenditure variance		1,400 (F)
Actual profit		6,800

Important! | If management believes that any of these variances are large enough to justify it, they will investigate the reasons for them to see whether any corrective action is necessary.

WL Co manufactures and sells a single product, R. Since the R is highly perishable, no inventories are held at any time. WL Co's management uses a flexible budgeting system to control costs. Extracts from the flexible budget are as follows.

	4,000	5,500
Output and sales (units)		
Budget cost allowances	$	$
Direct material	16,000	22,000
Direct labour	20,000	24,500
Variable production overhead	8,000	11,000
Fixed production overhead	11,000	11,000
Selling and distribution overhead	8,000	9,500
Administration overhead	7,000	7,000
Total expenditure	70,000	85,000

Production and sales of product R amounted to 5,100 units during period 5.

The total budget cost allowances in the flexible budget for period 5 will be:

(a)   Direct material $ [   ]

(b)   Direct labour $ [   ]

(c)   Variable production overhead $ [   ]

(d)   Fixed production overhead $ [   ]

(e)   Selling and distribution overhead $ [   ]

(f)   Administration overhead $ [   ]

(g)   Production and sales of product R in period 6 amounted to 5,500 units. Budgeted output for the period was 4,000 units. Actual total expenditure was $82,400.

   (i)   The total expenditure variance for period 6 was $ [   ] favourable/adverse (delete as necessary)

   (ii)   The volume variance for period 6 was $ [   ] favourable/adverse (delete as necessary)

Answer

(a)   Direct material $ [20,400]

(b)   Direct labour $ [23,300]

(c)   Variable production overhead $ [10,200]

(d)   Fixed production overhead $ [11,000]

(e)   Selling and distribution overhead $ [9,100]

(f)   Administration overhead $ [700]

(g)   (i)   The total expenditure variance for period 6 was $ [2,600] favourable/~~adverse~~

   (ii)   The volume variance for period 6 was $ [15,000] ~~favourable~~/adverse

Workings

(a) Direct material is a variable cost of $16,000/4,000 = $4 per unit
     Budget cost allowance for 5,100 units = 5,100 × $4 = $20,400

(b) Direct labour is a semi-variable cost which can be analysed using the high-low method.

	Output Units	$
High	5,500	24,500
Low	4,000	20,000
Change	1,500	4,500

Variable cost per unit = $4,500/1,500 = $3
Substituting in high output, fixed cost = $24,500 − (5,500 × $3)
                                        = $8,000

Budget cost allowance for 5,100 units:

	$
Variable cost = 5,100 × $3	15,300
Fixed cost	8,000
	23,300

(c) Variable production overhead per unit = $8,000/4,000 = $2 per unit

     Budget cost allowance for 5,100 units = 5,100 × $2 = $10,200

(d) Fixed production overhead cost allowance is fixed at $11,000.

(e) Selling and distribution is a semi-variable cost which can be analysed using the high-low method.

	Output Units	$
High	5,500	9,500
Low	4,000	8,000
Change	1,500	1,500

Variable cost per unit = $1,500/1,500 = $1
Substituting in high output, fixed cost = $9,500 − (5,500 × $1)
                                        = $4,000

Budget cost allowance for 5,100 units:

	$
Variable cost = 5,100 × $1	5,100
Fixed cost	4,000
	9,100

(f) Administration overhead cost allowance is fixed at $7,000.

(g) The budgeted and actual output volumes correspond to the two activity levels provided in the question data. The total budget cost allowance for each activity level can be used as the basis for the variance calculations.

   (i)   Expenditure variance = budget cost allowance for 5,500 units − actual expenditure for 5,500 units
                             = $85,000 − $82,400
                             = $2,600 favourable

   (ii) Volume variance = budget cost allowance for original budget of 4,000 units − budget cost allowance for actual volume of 5,500 units

         = $70,000 − $85,000 = $15,000 adverse

Question

The following extract is taken from the production cost budget of Zebra Co:

Production units	4,000	6,000
Production cost	$35,529	$41,280

The budget cost allowance for an activity level of 8,000 units is $ [   ]

Answer

	4,000	6,000	*Change*
Production units	4,000	6,000	2,000
Production cost	$35,520	$41,280	$5,760

Variable cost per unit = $\dfrac{\$5,760}{2,000}$ = $2.88

Fixed costs = $35,520 − (4,000 × $2.88) = $24,000

Therefore, budget cost allowance for activity level of 8,000 units = $24,000 + (8,000 × $2.88)

= $47,040

A flexible budget is designed at the planning stage to vary with activity levels. A **flexed** budget is a revised budget that reflects the actual activity levels achieved in the budget period.

Chapter Roundup

- A **fixed budget** is a budget which is set for a single activity level.

- A **flexible budget** is a budget which recognises different cost behaviour patterns and is designed to change as volume of activity changes.

- **Control** involves **comparing a flexed budget** (based on the actual activity level) with **actual results**. The **differences** between the flexed budget figures and the actual results are **budget variances**.

Quick Quiz

1 *Fill in the blanks with the word 'fixed' or the word 'flexible'.*

   (a) At the planning stage, a .... budget can show what the effects would be if the actual outcome differs from the prediction.

   (b) At the end of each period, actual results may be compared with the relevant activity level in the .... budget as a control procedure.

   (c) Master budgets are .... budgets.

2 Flexible budgets are normally prepared on a marginal costing basis.

   True ☐

   False ☐

3 *Fill in the gaps.*

   Budget cost allowance = ... + (......................... × ....)

4 What are the disadvantages of using a fixed budget for budgetary control?

5 How should budgetary control be approached using a flexible budget?

6 Distinguish between a fixed budget and a flexible budget.

7 What are the two main reasons for differences between a fixed budget profit and actual profit?

8 *Fill in the gaps*

   A flexible budget is a budget which, by recognising ...., is designed to .... as the level of activity changes.

9 A flexible budget is

   ☐ a budget which by recognising different cost behaviour patterns is designed to change as the volume of activity changes

   ☐ a budget for a defined period of time which includes planned revenues, expenses, assets, liabilities and cash flow

   ☐ a budget which is prepared for a period of one year which is reviewed monthly, whereby each time actual results are reported, a further forecast period is added and the intermediate period forecasts are updated

   ☐ a budget of semi-variable production costs only

10   Which one of the following statements about a fixed budget is/are correct? A fixed budget is:

☐   A budget which ignores inflation

☐   A budget for fixed assets

☐   A budget which is most generally used for planning purposes

☐   A budget for a single level of activity

☐   A budget for fixed costs

Answers to Quick Quiz

1   (a)   At the planning stage, a **flexible** budget can show what the effects would be if the actual outcome differs from the prediction.

(b)   At the end of each period, actual results may be compared with the relevant activity level in the **flexible** budget as a control procedure.

(c)   Master budgets are **fixed** budgets.

2   True

3   Budget cost allowance = budgeted fixed cost + (number of units × variable cost per unit)

4   Using a fixed budget at the planning stage means that only one activity level scenario is planned for. Management is not forced to think of contingency plans for different activity levels.

When actual results are compared against a fixed budget. the variances that are due to different activity levels can produce a misleading impression of performance.

5   •   To identify fixed and variable costs
•   To produce a flexible budget using marginal costing techniques

6   A **fixed budget** is a budget which is designed to remain unchanged regardless of the volume of output or sales achieved.

A **flexible budget** is a budget which, by recognising different cost behaviour patterns, is designed to change if volumes of output change.

7   A fixed budget profit might differ from an actual profit because costs were higher or lower than expected given the actual output and/or sales volumes were different to the level expected.

8   cost behaviour patterns

flex/change

9   ☑   A budget which by recognising different cost behaviour patterns is designed to change as the volume of activity changes.

A flexible budget shows the budgeted costs and revenues at different levels of activity. The budgeted variable costs and revenues are **increased or decreased in line with changes in activity,** and the budgeted fixed cost remains **unaltered**.

10   ☑   A budget which is most generally used for planning purposes

☑   A budget for a single level of activity

Fixed budgets are prepared for a single level of activity and do not include any provision for the event that actual volumes may differ from the budget. They are generally used for planning purposes because they use a single level of activity for coordination and resource allocation.

Now try the questions below from the Question Bank

Question numbers
52–56

10: Flexible budgeting | Part C Financial planning and control

Part D
Costing and accounting systems

11

Cost bookkeeping

Introduction

In Part A of this Study Text you saw how to determine the major elements of the cost of a unit of product - **material**, **labour**, **overhead** - and how to build up these elements into a total cost. In Chapters 12 and 13 you will see how costs are recorded depending on the costing method adopted by an organisation. But what you need to know first is how to account for costs within a cost accounting system. This chapter will teach you. It will teach you **cost bookkeeping**.

The overall bookkeeping routine will vary from organisation to organisation but either an **integrated** or an **interlocking** system will be used. For the purposes of this Paper C1 syllabus you **only need to know about integrated systems**, however.

In the last part of this chapter we will look at how a standard costing system is used in conjunction with an integrated system of cost bookkeeping.

Topic list	Syllabus references
1 Accounting for costs	D1(a)
2 Integrated systems	D1(a),(b)
3 Standard cost bookkeeping	D1(b)

1 Accounting for costs

> **Cost bookkeeping** is based on the principles of **double entry**, the **golden rule** of which is that for **every entry made in one account, there must be a corresponding balancing entry in another account.**

1.1 Cost accounting systems

There are **no statutory requirements** to keep detailed cost records and so some small firms only keep traditional financial accounts and prepare cost information in an ad-hoc fashion. This approach is, however, unsatisfactory for all but the smallest organisations: most firms therefore maintain some form of cost accounting system.

Cost accounting systems range from simple analysis systems to computer based accounting systems. Often systems are tailored to the users' requirements and therefore incorporate unique features. All systems will incorporate a number of common aspects and all records will be maintained using the **principles of double entry**.

1.2 Principles of double entry bookkeeping

The principles of double entry bookkeeping are not described in this chapter, but if you have not yet begun your studies of basic financial accounting, you may not be familiar with the concept of 'debits and credits'. Nevertheless you may still be able to follow the explanations below, provided that you remember the 'golden rule' of double entry bookkeeping, that for every entry made in one account, there must be a corresponding balancing entry in another account.

2 Integrated systems

> **Integrated systems** combine both financial and cost accounts in one system of ledger accounts.

Key term

> **Integrated accounts** are a 'set of accounting records that integrates both financial and cost accounts using a common input of data for all accounting purposes'. CIMA *Official Terminology*

2.1 The principal accounts in a system of integrated accounts

(a) **The resources accounts**

   (i) Materials control account or stores control account
   (ii) Wages (and salaries) control account
   (iii) Production overhead control account
   (iv) Administration overhead control account
   (v) Selling and distribution overhead control account

(b) **Accounts which record the cost of production items from the start of production work through to cost of sales**

   (i) Work in progress control account
   (ii) Finished goods control account
   (iii) Cost of sales control account

(c) Sales account

(d) Income statement

2.2 Accounting entries in an integrated system

The basic entries in an integrated system are as follows:

- **Expenditure** on materials, wages and overheads

    DR   Resources account
    CR   Cash or accounts payable

- **Work in progress**

    DR   WIP (for overhead, this is **overhead absorbed**)
    CR   Resources account (for overhead, this is **overhead absorbed**)

- **Finished goods**

    DR   Finished goods
    CR   WIP

- **Cost of sales**

    DR   Cost of sales
    CR   Finished goods

The accounting entries in an integrated system can be confusing and it is important to keep in mind some general principles.

2.2.1 Materials, wages and overheads expenditure

When **expenditure** is incurred on materials, wages or overheads, the actual amounts paid or payable are debited to the appropriate **resources accounts**. The credit entries are made in the cash or accounts payable accounts.

2.2.2 Work in progress

When production begins, **resources are allocated to work in progress**. This is recorded by crediting the resources accounts and debiting the work in progress account. In the case of production overheads, the amount credited to the overhead account and debited to work in progress should be the amount of overhead absorbed. If this differs from the amount of overhead incurred, there will be a difference on the overhead control account; this should be written off to an under-/over-absorbed overhead account. (One other point to remember is that when **indirect** materials and labour are allocated to production, the entries are to credit the materials and wages accounts and debit **production overhead account**.)

2.2.3 Finished goods

As **finished goods** are produced, work in progress is reduced. This is recorded by debiting the finished goods control account and crediting the work in progress control account.

2.2.4 Cost of sales

At the end of the period, the cost of goods sold is transferred from the finished goods account to the cost of sales account, and from there to the income statement.

2.2.5 Non-production overheads

The balances on the administration overhead control account and the selling and distribution overhead control account are usually transferred direct to the income statement at the period end.

2.2.6 Sales

Sales are debited to the receivables control account and credited to the sales account.

2.2.7 Profits

Profit is established by transferring to the income statement the balances on the sales account, cost of sales account and under-/over-absorbed overhead account.

2.3 Accounting entries in full costing and marginal costing systems

Cost bookkeeping can appear quite daunting to begin with. You may find it useful to study the two diagrams on the following pages, which illustrate the (simplified) operation of integrated systems using absorption costing and marginal costing. Follow the entries through the various control accounts and note the differences between the two diagrams. You will then be ready to work through an example.

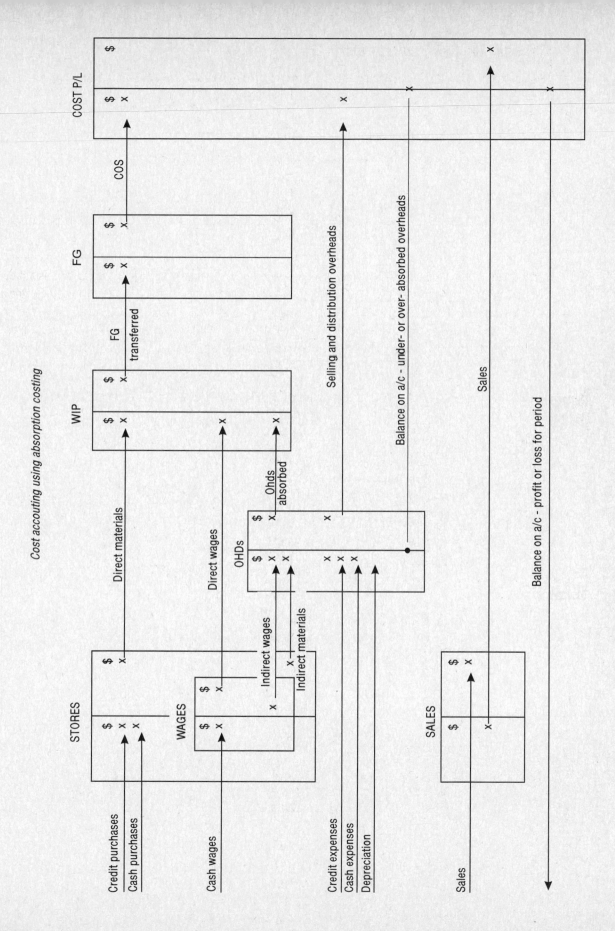

Cost accouting using absorption costing

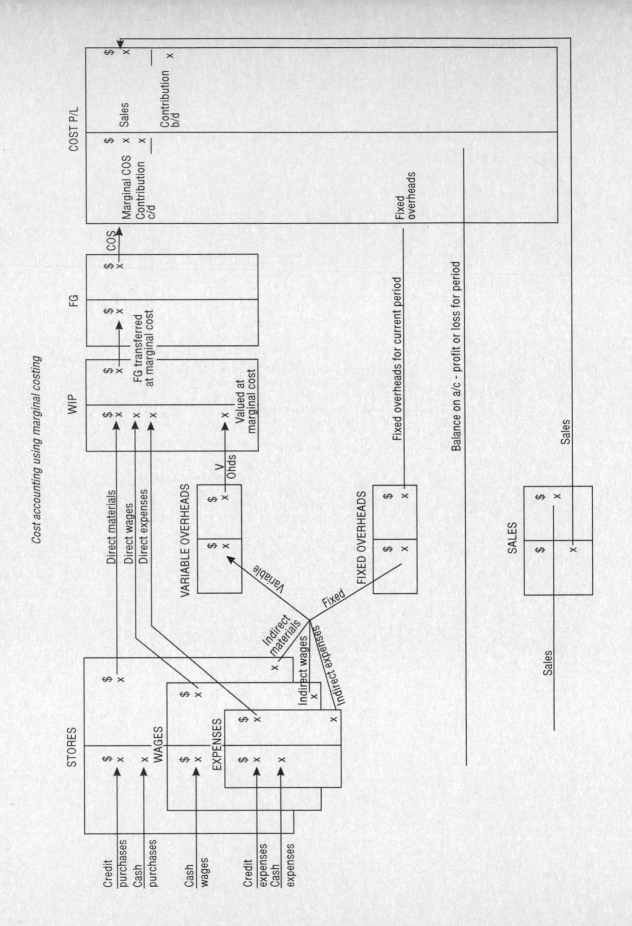

Cost accounting using marginal costing

2.4 Example: integrated accounts

Using the information given below for October, you are required to prepare the following accounts.

- Raw materials control
- Work in progress control
- Finished goods control
- Production overhead control
- Wages and salaries control
- Selling and administration overhead control
- Cost of sales
- Trading and income statement

Balances as at 1 October

	$'000
Raw materials control	10
Work in progress control	15
Finished goods control	18

Transactions for October

	$'000
Materials received from suppliers on credit	50
Materials issued to production	42
Materials issued to production service departments	5
Direct wages incurred	30
Production indirect wages incurred	13
Selling and administration salaries incurred	12
Production expenses paid as incurred	8
Selling and administration expenses paid as incurred	9
Allowance for depreciation: production equipment	3
selling and administration equipment	2
Wages and salaries paid: direct wages	28
production indirect wages	13
selling and administration salaries	12
Production completed and transferred to finished goods store	90
Production cost of goods sold	97
Sales on credit	145

Production overhead is absorbed at the rate of 80 per cent of direct wages incurred.

Solution

The figures in brackets refer to the explanations which follow after the ledger accounts.

RAW MATERIALS CONTROL

	$'000		$'000
Balance b/d	10	Work in progress (1)	42
Accounts payable	50	Production overhead control (1)	5
		Balance c/d	13
	60		60
Balance b/d	13		

WORK IN PROGRESS CONTROL

	$'000		$'000
Balance b/d	15	Finished goods control (4)	90
Raw materials control (1)	42	Balance c/d (4)	21
Wages and salaries control (2)	30		
Production overhead control (3)	24		
	111		111
Balance b/d	21		

FINISHED GOODS CONTROL

	$'000		$'000
Balance b/d	18	Cost of sales (5)	97
Work in progress control (4)	90	Balance c/d (5)	11
	108		108
Balance b/d	11		

PRODUCTION OVERHEAD CONTROL

	$'000		$'000
Raw materials control (1)	5	Work in progress control (3)	24
Wages and salaries control (2)	13	Under absorption to income	
Bank (6)	8	statement (8)	5
Allowance for depreciation (6)	3		
	29		29

WAGES AND SALARIES CONTROL

	$'000		$'000
Bank (7)	53	Work in progress control (2)	30
Balance c/d (7)	2	Production overhead control (2)	13
		Selling and admin o/h control (2)	12
	55		55
		Balance b/d	2

SELLING AND ADMINISTRATION OVERHEAD CONTROL

	$'000		$'000
Bank (6)	9	Income statement	23
Wages and salaries control (2)	12		
Allowance for depreciation (6)	2		
	23		23

COST OF SALES

	$'000		$'000
Finished goods control (5)	97	Income statement	97

TRADING AND INCOME STATEMENT

	$'000		$'000
Cost of sales (5)	97	Sales – receivables	145
Gross profit c/d	48		
	145		145
Under-absorbed overhead (8)	5	Gross profit b/d	48
Selling and admin o/h	23		
Net profit for October	20		
	48		48

Notes

1. The materials issued to production are charged as **direct materials** to work in progress. The materials issued to production service departments are **indirect materials**. The cost of indirect materials is 'collected' in the production overhead control account, pending its later absorption, along with all the other production overheads, into the value of work in progress.

2. The wages and salaries **incurred** are debited to the relevant control accounts:

    *   direct wages to work in progress
    *   indirect wages to production overhead control
    *   selling and administration salaries to selling and administration overhead control

    The credit entry for wages **incurred** is made in the wages and salaries control account.

3. Once the direct material and direct wages have been debited to work in progress, the next step is to **absorb production overheads**, using the predetermined overhead absorption rate. The work in progress account is charged with 80 per cent of wages incurred: $30,000 × 80% = $24,000.

4. Now that all of the elements of production cost have been charged to work in progress, the **production cost of goods completed** can be transferred to the finished goods control account.

5. The **production cost of goods sold** is transferred from the finished goods account to the cost of sales account. The balance on the finished goods account represents the inventory at the end of October.

6. The production expenses incurred and the depreciation on production machinery are debited in the production overhead control account. Thus they are 'collected' with the other production overheads, for later **absorption into work in progress**.

7. The total amount of wages **paid** ($28,000 + $13,000 + $12,000) is debited to the wages and salaries control account. The balance remaining on the account is the difference between the wages paid and the wages incurred. This represents a $2,000 accrual for wages, which is carried down into next month's accounts.

8. The balance remaining on the production overhead control account is the difference between the production overhead incurred, and the amount absorbed into work in progress. On this occasion the overhead is **underabsorbed** and is transferred as a debit in the income statement.

2.5 Bookkeeping entries for wages

Accounting for wages often causes difficulties for students, so let's look at another example. This example shows you how to deal with deductions for income tax, national insurance and so on.

2.5.1 Example: the wages control account

The following details were extracted from a weekly payroll for 750 employees at a factory.

	Direct workers $	Indirect workers $	Total $
Analysis of gross pay:			
Ordinary time	36,000	22,000	58,000
Overtime: basic wage	8,700	5,430	14,130
premium	4,350	2,715	7,065
Shift allowance	3,465	1,830	5,295
Sick pay	950	500	1,450
Idle time	3,200	–	3,200
	56,665	32,475	89,140
Net wages paid to employees	$45,605	$24,220	$69,825

Required

Prepare the wages control account for the week.

Solution

(a) The **wages control account** acts as a sort of 'collecting place' for net wages paid and deductions made from gross pay. The gross pay is then analysed between direct and indirect wages.

(b) The first step is to determine which wage costs are direct and which are indirect. The direct wages will be debited to the work in progress account and the indirect wages will be debited to the production overhead account.

(c) There are in fact only two items of direct wages cost in this example - the ordinary time ($36,000) and the basic overtime wage ($8,700) paid to direct workers. All other payments (including the overtime premium) are indirect wages.

(d) The net wages paid are debited to the control account, and the balance then represents the deductions which have been made for income tax, national insurance, and so on.

WAGES CONTROL ACCOUNT

	$		$
Bank: net wages paid	69,825	Work in progress – direct labour	44,700
Deductions control accounts*		Production overhead control:	
($89,140 – $69,825)	19,315	Indirect labour	27,430
		Overtime premium	7,065
		Shift allowance	5,295
		Sick pay	1,450
		Idle time	3,200
	89,140		89,140

* In practice there would be a separate deductions control account for each type of deduction made (such as income tax, National Insurance).

Question — Raw materials inventory control account

The following information relates to E Co for March.

Opening balance of raw materials	$12,000
Raw materials purchased on credit	$80,000
Raw materials issued: to production	$73,000
to production maintenance	$8,000
Raw materials returned to supplier	$2,000

The balance c/d at the end of March on the raw materials inventory control account is $ ☐ .

Answer

The balance c/d is $ 9,000 .

Workings

RAW MATERIALS INVENTORY CONTROL

	$		$
Balance b/d	12,000	Work in progress	73,000
Accounts payable	80,000	Production overhead control	8,000
		Accounts payable	2,000
		Balance c/d	9,000
	92,000		92,000
Balance b/d	9,000		

Question

Wages control account

	$		$
Bank	310,000	Work in progress control	239,000
Income tax payable	45,000	Production overhead control	179,000
Employees national insurance payable	31,000		
Employers national insurance payable	32,000		
	418,000		418,000

How much are the gross wages, the indirect wages and the direct wages for the period?

Answer

Gross wages = net wages paid + income tax + national insurance
= $310,00 + $45,000 + $63,000
= $418,000

Indirect wages are transferred to the production overhead control account = $179,000

Direct wages are transferred to the work in progress control account = $239,000

2.6 Manufacturing accounts

FAST FORWARD

The **ledger accounts related to production** can be consolidated into a **manufacturing account**.

Suppose an organisation has the following ledger accounts for control period 2.

RAW MATERIALS CONTROL

	$'000		$'000
Balance b/d	50	WIP	250
Purchases	275	Balance c/d	75
	325		325

WIP CONTROL

	$'000		$'000
Balances b/d	40	Finished goods control	810
Raw materials control	250		
Wages and salaries control	380		
Production overhead control	200	Balance c/d	60
	870		870

The **manufacturing** account is as follows.

MANUFACTURING ACCOUNT

	$'000		$'000
Raw materials (opening inventory)	50	Raw materials consumed	250
Purchases	275	Raw materials (closing inventory)	75
	325		325
WIP (opening inventory)	40	WIP (closing inventory)	60
Raw materials consumed	250	Manufacturing (or factory or production)	
Wages and salaries	380	cost of goods produced	810
Production overheads	200		
	870		870

2.7 The advantage and disadvantage of integrated systems

(a)   The **advantage** of integrated systems over systems which have separate systems for cost and financial accounting is the **saving in administrative effort**. Only one set of accounts needs to be maintained instead of two and the possible confusion arising from having two sets of accounts with different figures (such as for inventory values and profits) does not exist.

(b)   The **disadvantage** of integrated accounts is that one set of accounts is expected to fulfil two different purposes.

(i)   Stewardship of the business, and external reporting
(ii)   Provision of internal management information

(c)   At times, these different purposes may conflict; for example, the valuation of inventories in an integrated system will conform to statutory requirements, whereas for management information purposes it might be preferable to value closing inventories at, say, marginal cost or replacement cost.

(d)   In practice, however, computers have overcome these disadvantages and most modern cost accounting systems are integrated systems, incorporating coding systems which allow basic data to be analysed and presented in different ways for different purposes.

Question | **Production overhead control account**

The following information relates to Jamboree Co.

Production overheads incurred	$50,000
Labour hours worked	5,000
Production overhead absorption rate	$11 per labour hour

Delete the incorrect words and fill in the missing figure in the statement below.

The production overhead is **under/over** absorbed by $ [   ] . This amount is a **debit/credit** to the production overhead control account.

The production overhead is **over** absorbed by $ [5,000] . This amount is a **debit** to the production overhead control account.

Workings

PRODUCTION OVERHEAD CONTROL ACCOUNT

	$		$
Cash/payables	50,000	Work in progress control	
Over-absorbed overhead to income		(5,000 hr × $11)	55,000
statement	5,000		
	55,000		55,000

Question

Accounting entries

At the end of a period, in an integrated cost and financial accounting system, the accounting entries for $18,000 overheads under-absorbed would be

A	Debit work-in-progress control account	Credit overhead control account
B	Debit income statement	Credit work-in-progress control account
C	Debit income statement	Credit overhead control account
D	Debit overhead control account	Credit income statement

Answer

The correct answer is C.

Eliminate the incorrect options first. The only overhead charge made to work in progress (WIP) is the overhead absorbed into production based on the predetermined rate. Under or over absorption does not affect WIP. This eliminates A and B. Under-absorbed overhead means that overhead charges have been too low therefore there must be a further debit to income statement. This eliminates D, and the correct answer is C.

3 Standard cost bookkeeping

When an organisation runs a standard costing system, the variances need to be included in the ledger accounts. This is known as standard cost bookkeeping.

3.1 Basic principles

There are some possible variations in accounting method between one organisation's system and others, especially in the method of recording overhead variances, but the following are the basic principles.

3.1.1 Where the variances are recorded

FAST FORWARD

In a **standard cost bookkeeping system**, the variances are recorded as follows:

- The **material price variance** is recorded in the **stores control account**.

- The **labour rate variance** is recorded in the **wages control account**.

- The following variances are recorded in the **work in progress account**.

  - Material usage variance
  - Idle time variance
  - Labour efficiency variance
  - Variable overhead efficiency variance

- The **production overhead expenditure variance** will be recorded in the **production overhead control account**.

- The **production overhead volume variance** may be recorded in the **fixed production overhead account**. (*Note.* Alternatively, you may find the volume variance recorded in the **work in progress account**.)

- **Sales variances do not appear in the books of account.** Sales are recorded in the sales account at actual invoiced value.

- The balance of variances in the variance accounts at the end of a period may be **written off to the income statement.**

3.1.2 When the variances are recorded

FAST FORWARD

The general principle in standard cost bookkeeping is that cost variances should be recorded as **early as possible**. They are recorded in the relevant account **in which they arise** and the appropriate double entry is taken to a variance account.

(a) **Material price variances** are apparent when materials are purchased, and they are therefore recorded in the **stores account**. If a price variance is adverse, we should credit the stores account and debit a variance account with the amount of the variance.

(b) **Material usage variances** do not occur until output is actually produced in the factory, and they are therefore recorded in the **work in progress account**. If a usage variance is favourable, we should debit the work in progress account and credit a variance account with the value of the variance.

3.1.3 Adverse and favourable variances

FAST FORWARD

Adverse variances are **debited** to the relevant variance account; **favourable** variances are **credited** in the relevant variance account.

The actual process is best demonstrated with an example. Work carefully through the one which follows, ensuring that you look at how the various variances are recorded.

3.2 Example: cost bookkeeping and variances

Zed Co operates an integrated accounting system and a standard marginal costing system and prepares its final accounts monthly. You are provided with the following information.

Balances as at 1 October

	$'000
Plant and machinery, at cost	600
Inventory – raw materials	520
Wages payable	40
Inventory – finished goods	132

Data for the month of October

Materials purchased on credit	400,000 kgs at $4.90 per kg
Issued to production	328,000 kgs
Direct wages incurred	225,000 hours at $4.20 per hour
Direct wages paid	$920,000
Variable overhead incurred	$1,385,000
Sales	$4,875,000
Production and sales	39,000 units

Additional data

Inventories of raw materials and finished goods are maintained at standard cost.

Standard data

Direct material price	$5.00 per kg
Direct material usage	8 kgs per unit
Direct wages	$4.00 per hour
Direct labour	6 hours per unit
Variable overhead	6 labour hours per unit at $6 per hour
Budgeted output	10,000 units per week

Required

(a)   Calculate the appropriate cost variances for October.

(b)   Show the following ledger accounts for October.

(i)   Stores ledger control account
(ii)   Direct wages control account
(iii)   Variable overhead control account
(iv)   Work in progress control account
(v)   Finished goods control account

(vi)   Cost of sales control account
(vii)   Sales account
(viii) Variances account
(ix)   Income statement

Solution

(a)   We will begin by determining the standard unit cost and calculating the variances.

	$
Standard marginal cost per unit	
Direct materials (8 kgs × $5)	40
Direct labour (6 hrs × $4)	24
Variable production overhead (6 hrs × $6)	36
	100

	$'000
Direct material price variance	
400,000 kgs should cost (× $5)	2,000
but did cost (400,000 × $4.90)	1,960
	40 (F)

Direct material usage variance	
39,000 units should use (× 8)	312,000 kgs
but did use	328,000 kgs
Variance in kg	16,000 kgs (A)
× standard price per kg	× $5
	$80,000 (A)

	$'000
Direct labour rate variance	
225,000 hours should cost (× $4)	900
but did cost (225,000 × $4.20)	945
	45 (A)

Direct labour efficiency variance	
39,000 units should take (× 6 hrs)	234,000 hrs
but did take	225,000 hrs
Variance in hours	9,000 hrs (F)
× standard rate per hour	× $4
	$36,000 (F)

	$
Variable overhead expenditure variance	
225,000 hours should cost (× $6)	1,350,000
but did cost	1,385,000
	35,000 (A)

Variable overhead efficiency variance	
Labour efficiency variance in hours	9,000 hrs (F)
× standard rate per hour	× $6
	$54,000 (F)

(b)   (i)

STORES LEDGER CONTROL ACCOUNT

	$'000		$'000
Balance b/f	520	Work in progress	
Payables		(328,000 × $5)	1,640
(400,000 × $4.90)	1,960	Balance c/d	880
Material price variance	40		
	2,520		2,520
Balance b/d	880		

Notes

(1) Materials are issued from store at standard price.

(2) The material price variance is recorded in this account. It is a favourable variance, therefore it is recorded as a credit in the variance account.

(ii)

DIRECT WAGES CONTROL ACCOUNT

	$'000		$'000
Bank	920	Balance b/f	40
Balance c/d	65	Work in progress	
		(225,000 hrs × $4)	900
		Labour rate variance	45
	985		985
		Balance b/d	65

Notes

(1) Labour hours are charged to work in progress at the standard rate per hour.

(2) The labour rate variance is recorded in this account. It is an adverse variance, therefore it is recorded as a debit in the variance account.

(iii)

VARIABLE OVERHEAD CONTROL ACCOUNT

	$'000		$'000
Payables	1,385	Variable overhead expenditure	
		variance	35
		Work in progress	
		(225,000 × $6)	1,350
	1,385		1,385

Notes

(1) Variable overhead is charged to work in progress at the standard rate per hour.

(2) The variable overhead expenditure variance is recorded in this account. It is an adverse variance and so is a debit in the variance account.

(iv)

WORK IN PROGRESS CONTROL ACCOUNT

	$'000		$'000
Stores ledger control	1,640	Finished goods	
Direct wages control	900	(39,000 × $100)	3,900
Variable overhead control	1,350	*Direct material usage*	
Direct labour		*variance*	80
efficiency variance	36		
Variable overhead efficiency	54		
	3,980		3,980

Notes

(1) Output is transferred to the finished goods account at standard marginal production cost.
(2) The efficiency variances appear in this account.

(v)

FINISHED GOODS CONTROL ACCOUNT

	$'000		$'000
Balance b/f	132	Cost of sales (39,000 × $100)	3,900
Work in progress	3,900	Balance c/d	132
	4,032		4,032
Balance b/d	132		

(vi)

COST OF SALES CONTROL ACCOUNT

	$'000		$'000
Finished goods	3,900	Income statement	3,900

(vii)

SALES ACCOUNT

	$'000		$'000
Income statement	4,875	Bank/receivables	4,875

(viii)

VARIANCES ACCOUNT

	$'000		$'000
Wages (labour rate)	45	Stores (material price)	40
WIP (o/hd expenditure)	35	WIP (labour efficiency)	36
WIP (material usage)	80	WIP (o/hd efficiency)	54
		Income statement	30
	160		160

Assessment focus point

The variances are recorded in a variances account as part of the double entry system. The balance on the account at the end of the period is written off to the income statement. Sometimes a separate account is used for each variance, but the double entry principles would be the same. An adverse variance is debited in the relevant variance account; a favourable variance is credited in the variance account.

(ix)

INCOME STATEMENT

	$'000		$'000
Cost of sales	3,900	Sales	4,875
Variances	30		
Gross profit for month	945		
	4,875		4,875

3.3 Example: journal entries

Suppose that 4 kgs of material A are required to make one unit of product TS, each kilogram costing $10. It takes direct labour 5 hours to make one unit of product TS. The labour force is paid $4.50 per hour.

During the period the following results were recorded.

Material A: 8,200 kgs purchased on credit *	$95,000
Material A: kgs issued to production*	8,200 kgs
Units of product TS produced*	1,600
Direct labour hours worked*	10,000
Cost of direct labour*	$32,000

Required

(a)   Calculate the following variances for the period.

(i)   Material price variance
(ii)   Material usage variance
(iii)   Labour rate variance
(iv)   Labour efficiency variance

(b)   Prepare journal entries for the transactions marked * above, together with the variances calculated in (a).

Note. You should make the following assumptions.

(i)   An integrated accounting system is maintained.
(ii)   There are no opening or closing inventories of work in progress.

Solution

(a)

(i)		$
	8,200 kgs should cost (× $10)	82,000
	but did cost	95,000
	Material price variance	13,000 (A)

(ii)		
	1,600 units of TS should use (× 4 kgs)	6,400 kgs
	but did use	8,200 kgs
	Usage variance in kgs	1,800 kgs (A)
	× standard price per kg	× $10
	Material usage variance	$18,000 (A)

(iii)		$
	10,000 hours should cost (× $4.50)	45,000
	but did cost	32,000
	Labour rate variance	13,000 (F)

(iv)		
	1,600 units of TS should take (× 5 hrs)	8,000 hrs
	but did take	10,000 hrs
	Efficiency variance in hrs	2,000 hrs (A)
	× standard rate per hour	× $4.50
	Labour efficiency variance	$9,000 (A)

(b)

(i)		$	$
	Stores ledger control account (8,200 kgs × $10)	82,000	
	Material price variance	13,000	
	Payables		95,000
	The purchase of materials on credit		

(ii)		$	$
	Work in progress control account	82,000	
	Stores ledger control account		82,000
	The issue of material A to production		

(iii)			
	Material usage variance	18,000	
	Work in progress control account		18,000
	The recording of the material A usage variance		

(iv)	Work in progress control account (10,000 hrs × $4.50)	45,000	
	Direct labour control account		32,000
	Direct labour rate variance		13,000
	The charging of labour to work in progress		
(v)	Direct labour efficiency variance	9,000	
	Work in progress control account		9,000
	The recording of the labour efficiency variance		
(vi)	Finished goods control account (1,600 × $62.50 (W))	100,000	
	Work in progress control account		100,000
	The transfer of finished goods from work in progress		

Working

Standard cost of product TS

	$
Material A (4 kgs × $10)	40.00
Direct labour (5 hrs × $4.50)	22.50
	62.50

Question

A company uses raw material J in production. The standard price for material J is $3 per metre. During the month 6,000 metres were purchased for $18,600, of which 5,000 metres were issued to production.

Required

Show the journal entries to record the above transactions in integrated accounts in the following separate circumstances.

(a) When raw material inventory is valued at standard cost, that is the direct materials price variance is extracted on receipt.

(b) When raw materials inventory is valued at actual cost, that is the direct materials price variance is extracted as the materials are used.

Answer

(a)		$	$
	Raw material inventory (6,000 × $3)	18,000	
	Direct material price variance	600	
	Payables		18,600
	Purchase on credit of 6,000 metres of material J		
	Work in progress (5,000 × $3)	15,000	
	Raw material inventory		15,000
	Issue to production of 5,000 metres of J		

(b)		$	$
	Raw material inventory	18,600	
	Payables		18,600
	Purchase on credit of 6,000 metres of material J		
	Work in progress	15,000	
	Direct material price variance (5,000 × $(3.10 − 3.00))	500	
	Raw material inventory		15,500
	Issue to production of 5,000 metres of material J		

Note that in both cases the material is charged to work in progress at standard price. In (b) the price variance is extracted only on the material which has been used up, the inventory being valued at actual cost.

Question

A firm uses standard costing and an integrated accounting system. The double entry for an adverse material usage variance is

A	DR stores control account	CR work-in-progress control account
B	DR material usage variance account	CR stores control account
C	DR work-in-progress control account	CR material usage variance account
D	DR material usage variance account	CR work-in-progress control account

Answer

The correct answer is D.

The usage variance arises during production therefore the correct account to be credited is work-in-progress. Option D is correct.

An adverse variance is debited to the relevant variance account. Therefore we can eliminate the incorrect options A and C.

Option B has the correct debit entry for the adverse variance but the credit entry is incorrect.

Chapter Roundup

- **Cost bookkeeping** is based on the principles of **double entry**, the **golden rule** of which is that for **every entry made in one account, there must be a corresponding balancing entry in another account**.

- **Integrated systems** combine both financial and cost accounts in one system of ledger accounts.

- The basic entries in an integrated system are as follows:

  Expenditure on materials, wages and overheads

  DR   Resources account
  CR   Cash or accounts payable

  Work in progress

  DR   WIP (for overhead, this is overhead absorbed)
  CR   Resources accounts (for overhead, this is **overhead absorbed**)

  Finished goods

  DR   Finished goods
  CR   WIP

  Cost of sales

  DR   Cost of sales
  CR   Finished goods

- The **ledger accounts related to production** can be consolidated into a **manufacturing account**.

- In a **standard cost bookkeeping system**, the variances are recorded as follows:

  - The **material price variance** is recorded in the **stores control account**.

  - The **labour rate variance** is recorded in the **wages control account**.

  - The following variances are recorded in the **work in progress account**.

    Material usage variance
    Idle time variance
    Labour efficiency variance
    Variable overhead efficiency variance

  - The **production overhead expenditure variance** will be recorded in the **production overhead control account**.

  - The **production overhead volume variance** may be recorded in **the fixed production overhead account**. (Note. Alternatively, you may find the volume variance recorded in the **work in progress account**.)

  - **Sales variances do not appear in the books of account**. Sales are recorded in the sales account at actual invoiced value.

  - The balance of variances in the variance accounts at the end of a period may be **written off to the income statement**.

- The general principle in standard cost bookkeeping is that cost variances should be recorded as **early as possible**. They are recorded in the relevant account **in which they arise** and the appropriate double entry is taken to a variance account.

- **Adverse** variances are **debited** to the relevant variance account; **favourable** variances are **credited** in the relevant variance account.

1 What is the double entry for the following in an integrated accounts system?

   (a)   Production overhead absorbed in the cost of production

   (b)   Completed work transferred from the production process to inventory

2 GF Co bought $100,000 worth of materials and issued $75,000 to production. An entry was made to trade creditors for the purchase, which of the three following entries completes the correct bookkeeping treatment?

I	Dr	Raw materials	$75,000
II	Dr	Raw materials	$100,000
III	Cr	Work-in-progress	$75,000
IV	Cr	Raw materials	$75,000
V	Cr	Raw materials	$100,000
VI	Dr	Work-in-progress	$75,000
VII	Dr	Work-in-progress	$100,000

3 The wages control account for X Co for October looks like this.

WAGES CONTROL ACCOUNT

	$'000		$'000
Bank	110	Work in progress	101
		Production overhead	7
		Balance c/d	2
	110		110

Indicate whether the following statements are true or false.

		True	False
I	Total wages incurred during October was $110,000	☐	☐
II	Indirect wages incurred during October was $7,000	☐	☐
III	Wages accrued at the end of October were $2,000	☐	☐

4 The material usage variance is recorded in the raw materials control account.

True   ☐

False   ☐

5 What is the double entry for recording sales variances in cost accounts?

6 Indicate whether the following statements are true or false.

		True	False
I	Integrated systems conform to statutory requirements	☐	☐
II	Integrated systems are preferable to two systems because they conform to statutory requirements	☐	☐
III	Integrated systems reduce the number of account reconciliations	☐	☐
IV	Systems with separate cost and financial accounting systems can aid provision of internal management information	☐	☐

7   Which three of the following variances are recorded in the work-in-progress control account in a standard cost bookkeeping system?

☐   Material price variance

☐   Material usage variance

☐   Labour rate variance

☐   Variable overhead efficiency variance

☐   Sales variance

☐   Idle time variance

8   A company operates an integrated accounting system. The accounting entries for the issue to production of indirect materials from inventory would be:

	Debit	Credit
A	Work in progress account	Stores control account
B	Stores control account	Overhead control account
C	Overhead control account	Stores control account
D	Cost of sales account	Stores control account

9   Which of the following descriptions correctly describes a control account?

A   An account for pooling costs before they are recharged
B   Contra to cash
C   An account which records total cost as opposed to individual costs
D   A type of suspense account

10   In a cost bookkeeping system what would be the entry for the absorption of production overhead?

	Debit	Credit
A	Cost Ledger Control Account	Production Overhead Account
B	Production Overhead Account	Work-in-Progress Account
C	Work-in-Progress Account	Cost Ledger Control Account
D	Work-in-Progress Account	Production Overhead Account

1   (a)   Dr   Work in progress control account
          Cr   Production overhead account

    (b)   Dr   Finished goods control account
          Cr   Work in progress control account

2   II
    IV
    VI

    Costs incurred are debited to the materials account, and those issued as direct materials to production are credited to the materials account and subsequently debited to the work-in-progress account.

3   I   False. Total wages *paid* was $110,000.
    II   True. Indirect wages of $7,000 were charged to production overhead.
    III   False. Wages were prepaid at the end of October

4   False. Material usage variances are recorded in the WIP account.

5   Sales variances do not appear in the books of account.
    Sales are recorded in the sales account at actual invoiced value.

6   I   True

    II   False. This is one of the disadvantages of an integrated system. It must conform to statutory requirements but this is not necessarily useful for management purposes.

    III   True. Having one set of accounts instead of two eliminates the need to reconcile the two systems.

    IV   True. As mentioned above the integrated system must conform to statutory requirements. Internal management information does not need to conform to statutory requirement and in some cases it is more useful if it doesn't.

7   Material usage variance, variable overhead efficiency variance and idle time variance. The material price variance is recorded in the stores control account. The labour rate variance is recorded in the wages control account. The sales variances do not appear in the books of account.

8   C   The cost of indirect materials issued is **credited to the stores account** and 'collected' in the overhead control account **pending its absorption into work in progress**. Therefore the correct answer is C.

9   C   An account which records total cost as opposed to individual costs.

10 D   **Debit** Work in Progress Account **Credit** Production Overhead Account

Now try the questions below from the Question Bank

Question numbers
57–64

Process costing

12

Introduction

We will look at **costing systems** in this part of the Study Text. These costing systems are used to cost goods or services and which method is used depends on the way in which the goods or services are produced. In Chapter 13 we will look at job and batch costing. In this chapter we will consider **process costing**. Process costing is applied when output consists of a continuous stream of **identical units**. We will begin from basics and look at how to account for the most simple of processes. We will then move on to how to account for any **losses** which might occur, as well as what to do with any **scrapped units** which are sold. Next we will consider how to deal with **closing work in progress** before examining situations involving closing work in progress and losses. We will then go on to have a look at situations involving **opening work in progress** and finally we shall consider how to deal with situations where we have both opening and closing work in progress and losses.

Topic list	Syllabus references
1 The distinguishing features of process costing	D1(c)
2 The basics of process costing	D1(c)
3 Dealing with losses in process	D1(c),(d)
4 Accounting for scrap	D1(c),(d)
5 Valuing closing work in progress	D1(c),(d)
6 Valuing opening work in progress	D1(c),(d)

1 The distinguishing features of process costing

FAST FORWARD

> **Process costing** is a costing method used where it is not possible to identify separate units of production, or jobs, usually because of the continuous nature of the production processes involved.

Process costing is used where there is a continuous flow of identical units and it is common to identify it with **continuous production** such as the following.

- Oil refining
- The manufacture of soap
- Paint manufacture
- Food and drink manufacture

Key term

> **Process costing** is a 'form of costing applicable to continuous processes where process costs are attributed to the number of units produced. This may involve estimating the number of equivalent units in stock at the start and end of the period under consideration.'
> CIMA *Official Terminology*

The meaning of the term 'equivalent units' will become clear as you work through this chapter.

The **features of process costing** which make it different from other methods of costing such as job or batch costing are as follows.

(a)   The continuous nature of production in many processes means that there will usually be **closing work in progress which must be valued**. In process costing it is not possible to build up cost records of the cost of each individual unit of output because production in progress is an **indistinguishable homogeneous mass**.

(b)   There is often a **loss in process** due to spoilage, wastage, evaporation and so on.

(c)   The **output** of one process becomes the **input** to the next until the finished product is made in the final process.

2 The basics of process costing

2.1 Process accounts

Costs incurred in processes are recorded in what are known as process accounts.

FAST FORWARD

> A process account has **two sides**, and on **each side there are two columns** – one for **quantities** (of raw materials, work in progress and finished goods) and one for **costs**.

(a)   On the **left hand side** of the process account we record the **inputs** to the process and the **cost of these inputs**. So we might show the quantity of material input to a process during the period and its cost, the cost of labour and the cost of overheads.

(b)   On the right hand side of the process account we record what happens to the inputs by the end of the period.

   (i)   Some of the input might be converted into **finished goods**, so we show the units of finished goods and the cost of these units.

   (ii)   Some of the material input might evaporate or get spilled or damaged, so there would be **losses**. So we record the loss units and the cost of the loss.

   (iii)   At the end of a period, some units of input might be in the process of being turned into finished units so would be work in progress (**WIP**). We record the units of WIP and the cost of these units.

The **quantity columns on each side of the account** should total to the **same amount**. Why? Well think about it. If we put 100 kgs of material in to a process (which we record on the left hand side of the account) we should know what has happened to those 100 kgs. Some would be losses maybe, some would be WIP, some would be finished units, but the total should be 100 kgs.

Likewise the **cost of the inputs to the process during a period** (ie the total of the costs recorded on the left hand side of the account) is the **cost of the outputs of the process**. If we have recorded material, labour and overhead costs totalling $1,000 and at the end of the process we have 100 finished units (and no losses or WIP), then that output cost $1,000.

Here's a very simple example of a process account.

PROCESS ACCOUNT

	Units	$		Units	$
Material	1,000	11,000	Closing WIP	200	2,000
Labour		4,000	Finished units	800	16,000
Overhead		3,000			
	1,000	18,000		1,000	18,000

As you can see, the **quantity columns on each side balance** (ie they are the same), **as do the monetary columns**. (Don't worry at this stage about how the costs are split between WIP and finished units.)

2.2 Example: basics of process costing

Suppose that Purr and Miaow Co make squeaky toys for cats. Production of the toys involves two processes, shaping and colouring. During the year to 31 March 20X3, 1,000,000 units of material worth $500,000 were input to the first process, shaping. Direct labour costs of $200,000 and production overhead costs of $200,000 were also incurred in connection with the shaping process. There were no opening or closing inventories in the shaping department. The process account for shaping for the year ended 31 March 20X3 is as follows.

PROCESS 1 (SHAPING) ACCOUNT

	Units	$		Units	$
Direct materials	1,000,000	500,000	Output to Process 2	1,000,000	900,000
Direct labour		200,000			
Production overheads		200,000			
	1,000,000	900,000		1,000,000	900,000

Assessment focus point

> When preparing process accounts, balance off the quantity columns (ie ensure they total to the same amount on both sides) **before** attempting to complete the monetary value columns since they will help you to check that you have missed nothing out. This becomes increasingly important as more complications are introduced into questions.

When using process costing, if a **series of separate processes** is needed to manufacture the finished product, the **output of one process becomes the input to the next** until the final output is made in the final process. In our example, all output from shaping was transferred to the second process, colouring, during the year to 31 March 20X3. An additional 500,000 units of material, costing $300,000, were input to the colouring process. Direct labour costs of $150,000 and production overhead costs of $150,000 were also incurred. There were no opening or closing inventories in the colouring department. The process account for colouring for the year ended 31 March 20X3 is as follows.

PROCESS 2 (COLOURING) ACCOUNT

	Units	$		Units	$
Materials from process 1	1,000,000	900,000	Output to finished		
Added materials	500,000	300,000	goods	1,500,000	1,500,000
Direct labour		150,000			
Production overhead		150,000			
	1,500,000	1,500,000		1,500,000	1,500,000

Assessment focus point

Direct labour and production overhead may be treated together in an assessment question as **conversion cost**.

Added materials, labour and overhead in Process 2 are usually **added gradually** throughout the process. Materials from Process 1, in contrast, will often be **introduced in full at the start of the second process**.

2.3 Framework for dealing with process costing

FAST FORWARD

Use our suggested **four-step approach** when dealing with process costing questions.

Step 1	Determine output and losses
Step 2	Calculate cost per unit of output, losses and WIP
Step 3	Calculate total cost of output, losses and WIP
Step 4	Complete accounts

Process costing is centred around **four key steps**. The exact work done at each step will depend on the circumstances of the question, but the approach can always be used. Don't worry about the terms used. We will be looking at their meaning as we work through the chapter.

Step 1   **Determine output and losses**

- Determine expected output.
- Calculate normal loss and abnormal loss and gain.
- Calculate equivalent units if there is closing work in progress.

Step 2   **Calculate cost per unit of output, losses and WIP**

Calculate cost per unit or cost per equivalent unit.

Step 3   **Calculate total cost of output, losses and WIP**

In some examples this will be straightforward. In cases where there is work in progress, a **statement of evaluation** will have to be prepared.

Step 4   **Complete accounts**

- Complete the process account.
- Write up the other accounts required by the question.

Assessment focus point

It always saves time in an assessment if you don't have to think too long about how to approach a question before you begin. This four-step approach can be applied to any process costing question so it would be a good idea to learn it now. It will be useful as a framework for any workings that you may need to do.

3 Dealing with losses in process

> **Losses** may occur in process. If a certain level of loss is expected, this is known as **normal loss**. If losses are greater than expected, the extra loss is **abnormal loss**. If losses are less than expected, the difference is known as **abnormal gain**.

3.1 Losses

During a production process, a loss may occur.

Key terms

Normal loss is 'expected loss, allowed for in the budget, and normally calculated as a percentage of the good output, from a process during a period of time. Normal losses are generally either valued at zero or at their disposal values.'

Abnormal loss is 'any loss in excess of the normal loss allowance'.

Abnormal gain is 'improvement on the accepted or normal loss associated with a production activity'.

CIMA *Official Terminology*

Losses may occur due to wastage, spoilage, evaporation, and so on.

Since normal loss is not given a cost, the cost of producing these units is borne by the 'good' units of output.

Abnormal loss and gain units are valued at the same unit rate as 'good' units. Abnormal events do not therefore affect the cost of good production. Their costs are **analysed separately** in an **abnormal loss or abnormal gain account**.

3.1.1 The bookkeeping

(a) In an **abnormal loss account**, the **debit** entry shows the **units (and their value) from the process account**. The credit entry shows the **impact on the income statement**.

(b) In an **abnormal gain account**, the **debit** entry shows the **effect on the income statement**, while the **credit** entry shows the **units (and their value) from the process account**.

3.2 Example: abnormal losses and gains

Suppose that input to a process is 1,000 units at a cost of $4,500. Normal loss is 10% and there are no opening or closing inventories. Determine the accounting entries for the cost of output and the cost of the loss if actual output were as follows.

(a) 860 units (so that actual loss is 140 units)
(b) 920 units (so that actual loss is 80 units)

Solution

Before we demonstrate the use of the 'four-step framework' we will summarise the way that the losses are dealt with.

(a) Normal loss is given no share of cost.

(b) The cost of output is therefore based on the **expected** units of output, which in our example amount to 90% of 1,000 = 900 units.

(c) Abnormal loss is given a cost, which is written off to the income statement via an abnormal loss/gain account.

(d) **Abnormal gain** is treated in the same way, except that being a gain rather than a loss, it appears as a **debit** entry in the process account (as it is a **sort of input**, being additional unexpected units), whereas a **loss** appears as a **credit** entry in this account (as it is a **sort of output**).

(a)   **Output is 860 units**

Step 1   **Determine output and losses**

If actual output is 860 units and the actual loss is 140 units:

	Units
Actual loss	140
Normal loss (10% of 1,000)	100
Abnormal loss	40

Step 2   **Calculate cost per unit of output and losses**

The cost per unit of output and the cost per unit of abnormal loss are based on expected output.

$$\frac{\text{Costs incurred}}{\text{Expected output}} = \frac{\$4,500}{900 \text{ units}} = \$5 \text{ per unit}$$

Step 3   **Calculate total cost of output and losses**

Normal loss is not assigned any cost.

	$
Cost of output (860 × $5)	4,300
Normal loss	0
Abnormal loss (40 × $5)	200
	4,500

Step 4   **Complete accounts**

PROCESS ACCOUNT

	Units	$		Units		$
Cost incurred	1,000	4,500	Normal loss	100		0
			Output (finished goods a/c)	860	(× $5)	4,300
			Abnormal loss	40	(× $5)	200
	1,000	4,500		1,000		4,500

ABNORMAL LOSS ACCOUNT

	Units	$		Units	$
Process a/c	40	200	Income statement	40	200

(b)   **Output is 920 units**

Step 1   **Determine output and losses**

If actual output is 920 units and the actual loss is 80 units:

	Units
Actual loss	80
Normal loss (10% of 1,000)	100
Abnormal gain	20

Step 2   **Calculate cost per unit of output and losses**

The cost per unit of output and the cost per unit of abnormal gain are based on **expected** output.

$$\frac{\text{Costs incurred}}{\text{Expected output}} = \frac{\$4,500}{900 \text{ units}} = \$5 \text{ per unit}$$

(Whether there is abnormal loss or gain does not affect the valuation of units of output. The figure of $5 per unit is exactly the same as in the previous paragraph, when there were 40 units of abnormal loss.)

Step 3 Calculate total cost of output and losses

		$
Cost of output (920 × $5)		4,600
Normal loss		0
Abnormal gain (20 × $5)		(100)
		4,500

Step 4 Complete accounts

PROCESS ACCOUNT

	Units	$		Units	$
Cost incurred	1,000	4,500	Normal loss	100	0
Abnormal gain a/c	20	(× $5) 100	Output (finished goods a/c)	920	(× $5) 4,600
	1,020	4,600		1,020	4,600

ABNORMAL GAIN

	Units	$		Units	$
Income statement	20	100	Process a/c	20	100

3.3 Example: abnormal losses and gains again

During a four-week period, period 3, costs of input to a process were $29,070. Input was 1,000 units, output was 850 units and normal loss is 10%.

During the next period, period 4, costs of input were again $29,070. Input was again 1,000 units, but output was 950 units.

There were no units of opening or closing inventory.

Required

Prepare the process account and abnormal loss or gain account for each period.

Solution

Step 1 Determine output and losses

Period 3

	Units
Actual output	850
Normal loss (10% × 1,000)	100
Abnormal loss	50
Input	1,000

Period 4

	Units
Actual output	950
Normal loss (10% × 1,000)	100
Abnormal loss	(50)
Input	1,000

Step 2 Calculate cost per unit of output and losses

For each period the cost per unit is based on expected output.

$$\frac{\text{Cost of input}}{\text{Expected units of output}} = \frac{\$29,070}{900} = \$32.30 \text{ per unit}$$

Step 3   Calculate total cost of output and losses

Period 3	$
Cost of output (850 × $32.30)	27,455
Normal loss	0
Abnormal loss (50 × $32.30)	1,615
	29,070

Period 4	$
Cost of output (950 × $32.30)	30,685
Normal loss	0
Abnormal gain (50 × $32.30)	1,615
	29,070

Step 4   Complete accounts

PROCESS ACCOUNT

	Units	$		Units	$
Period 3					
Cost of input	1,000	29,070	Normal loss	100	0
			Finished goods a/c (× $32.30)	850	27,455
			Abnormal loss a/c (× $32.30)	50	1,615
	1,000	29,070		1,000	29,070
Period 4					
Cost of input	1,000	29,070	Normal loss	100	0
Abnormal gain a/c (× $32.30)	50	1,615	Finished goods a/c (× $32.30)	950	30,685
	1,050	30,685		1,050	30,685

ABNORMAL LOSS OR GAIN ACCOUNT

	$		$
Period 3		**Period 4**	
Abnormal loss in process a/c	1,615	Abnormal gain in process a/c	1,615
Abnormal loss in process a/c	1,615	Abnormal gain in process a/c	1,615

There is a zero balance on this account at the end of period 4.

Question   **Cost of output**

Charlton Co manufactures a product in a single process operation. Normal loss is 10% of input. Loss occurs at the end of the process. Data for June are as follows.

Opening and closing inventories of work in progress	Nil
Cost of input materials (3,300 units)	$59,100
Direct labour and production overhead	$30,000
Output to finished goods	2,750 units

The full cost of finished output in June was

A $74,250
B $81,000
C $82,500
D $89,100

The correct answer is C.

Step 1   **Determine output and losses**

	Units
Actual output	2,750
Normal loss (10% × 3,300)	330
Abnormal loss	220
	3,300

Step 2   **Calculate cost per unit of output and losses**

$$\frac{\text{Cost of input}}{\text{Expected units of output}} = \frac{\$89,100}{3,300 - 330} = \$30 \text{ per unit}$$

Step 3   **Calculate total cost of output and losses**

	$
Cost of output (2,750 × $30)	82,500
Normal loss	0
Abnormal loss (220 × $30)	6,600
	89,100

If you had to make an educated guess, you could have eliminated option D. This is simply the total input cost, with no attempt to apportion some of the cost to the abnormal loss.

Option A is incorrect because it results from allocating a full unit cost to the normal loss: remember that normal loss does not carry any of the process cost.

Option B is incorrect because it results from calculating a 10% normal loss based on *output* of 2,750 units (275 units normal loss), rather than on *input* of 3,300 units.

Question   **Abnormal gain**

Zed Co makes a product Emm which goes through several processes. The following information is available for the month of June.

	Kg
Opening WIP	5,200
Closing WIP	3,500
Input	58,300
Normal loss	400
Transferred to finished goods	59,900

What was the abnormal gain in June?

A   260 kg
B   300 kg
C   400 kg
D   560 kg

B

Process account

Dr		Cr	
Opening WIP	5,200	Output	59,900
Input	58,300	Normal loss	400
Abnormal gain		Closing WIP	3,500
	63,800		63,800

The abnormal gain is the balancing figure. 63,800 – 5,200 – 58,300 = 300

4 Accounting for scrap

Key term

> **Scrap** is 'discarded material having some value'.
>
> CIMA *Official Terminology*

4.1 Basic rules for accounting for scrap

(a) **Revenue from scrap** is treated, not as an addition to sales revenue, but as a **reduction in costs**.

FAST FORWARD

> The **valuation of normal loss is either at scrap value or nil**. It is conventional for the **scrap value of normal loss to be deducted from the cost of materials** before a cost per equivalent unit is calculated.

(b) The scrap value of **normal loss** is therefore used to reduce the material costs of the process.

DEBIT   Scrap account
CREDIT   Process account

with the scrap value of the normal loss.

FAST FORWARD

> Abnormal losses and gains never affect the cost of good units of production. The scrap value of abnormal losses is not credited to the process account, and the abnormal loss and gain units **carry the same full cost as a good unit of production**.

(c) The scrap value of **abnormal loss** is used to reduce the cost of abnormal loss.

DEBIT   Scrap account
CREDIT   Abnormal loss account

with the scrap value of abnormal loss, which therefore reduces the write-off of cost to the income statement.

(d) The scrap value of abnormal gain arises because the actual units sold as scrap will be less than the scrap value of normal loss. Because there are fewer units of scrap than expected, there will be less revenue from scrap as a direct consequence of the abnormal gain. The abnormal gain account should therefore be debited with the scrap value.

DEBIT   Abnormal gain account
CREDIT   Scrap account

with the scrap value of abnormal gain.

(e) The **scrap account** is completed by recording the **actual cash received** from the sale of scrap.

DEBIT   Cash received
CREDIT   Scrap account

with the cash received from the sale of the actual scrap.

Important!

> The same basic principle therefore applies that only **normal losses** should affect the cost of the good output. The scrap value of **normal loss only** is credited to the process account. The scrap values of abnormal losses and gains are analysed separately in the abnormal loss or gain account.

4.2 Example: scrap and abnormal loss or gain

A factory has two production processes. Normal loss in each process is 10% and scrapped units sell for $0.50 each from process 1 and $3 each from process 2. Relevant information for costing purposes relating to period 5 is as follows.

Direct materials added:	Process 1	Process 2
units	2,000	1,250
cost	$8,100	$1,900
Direct labour	$4,000	$10,000
Production overhead	150% of direct labour cost	120% of direct labour cost
Output to process 2/finished goods	1,750 units	2,800 units
Actual production overhead	$17,800	

Required

Prepare the accounts for process 1, process 2, scrap, abnormal loss or gain.

Solution

Step 1   **Determine output and losses**

	Process 1	Process 2
	Units	Units
Output	1,750	2,800
Normal loss (10% of input)	200	300
Abnormal loss	50	-
Abnormal gain	-	(100)
	2,000	3,000*

* 1,750 units from Process 1 + 1,250 units input to process.

Step 2 **Calculate cost per unit of output and losses**

		Process 1 $		Process 2 $
Cost of input				
– material		8,100		1,900
– from Process 1		–	(1,750 × $10)	17,500
– labour		4,000		10,000
– overhead	(150% × $4,000)	6,000	(120% × $10,000)	12,000
		18,100		41,400
Less: scrap value of				
normal loss	(200 × $0.50)	(100)	(300 × $3)	(900)
		18,000		40,500
Expected output				
90% of 2,000		1,800		
90% of 3,000				2,700
Cost per unit				
$18,000 ÷ 1,800		$10		
$40,500 ÷ 2,700				$15

Step 3 **Calculate total cost of output and losses**

	Process 1 $		Process 2 $
Output (1,750 × $10)	17,500	(2,800 × $15)	42,000
Normal loss (200 × $0.50)*	100	(300 × $3)*	900
Abnormal loss (50 × $10)	500		–
	18,100		42,900
Abnormal gain	–	(100 × $15)	(1,500)
	18,100		41,400

* Remember that normal loss is valued at scrap value only.

Step 4 **Complete accounts**

PROCESS 1 ACCOUNT

	Units	$		Units	$
Direct material	2,000	8,100	Scrap a/c (normal loss)	200	100
Direct labour		4,000	Process 2 a/c	1,750	17,500
Production			Abnormal loss a/c	50	500
overhead a/c		6,000			
	2,000	18,100		2,000	18,100

PROCESS 2 ACCOUNT

	Units	$		Units	$
Direct materials					
From process 1	1,750	17,500	Scrap a/c (normal loss)	300	900
Added materials	1,250	1,900	Finished goods a/c	2,800	42,000
Direct labour		10,000			
Production o'hd		12,000			
	3,000	41,400			
Abnormal gain	100	1,500			
	3,100	42,900		3,100	42,900

ABNORMAL LOSS ACCOUNT

	$		$
Process 1 (50 units)	500	Scrap a/c: sale of scrap of extra loss (50 units)	25
		Income statement	475
	500		500

ABNORMAL GAIN ACCOUNT

	$		$
Scrap a/c (loss of scrap revenue due to abnormal gain,		Process 2 abnormal gain (100 units)	1,500
100 units × $3)	300		
Income statement	1,200		
	1,500		1,500

SCRAP ACCOUNT

	$		$
Scrap value of normal loss		Cash a/c - cash received	
Process 1 (200 units)	100	Loss in process 1 (250 units)	125
Process 2 (300 units)	900	Loss in process 2 (200 units)	600
Abnormal loss a/c (process 1)	25	Abnormal gain a/c (process 2)	300
	1,025		1,025

Question   Process accounts

Parks Co operates a processing operation involving two stages, the output of process 1 being passed to process 2. The process costs for period 3 were as follows.

Process 1

Material 3,000 kg at $0.25 per kg
Labour $120

Process 2

Material 2,000 kg at $0.40 per kg
Labour $84

General overhead for period 3 amounted to $357 and is absorbed into process costs at a rate of 375% of direct labour costs in process 1 and 496% of direct labour costs in process 2.

The normal output of process 1 is 80% of input and of process 2, 90% of input. Waste matter from process 1 is sold for $0.20 per kg and that from process 2 for $0.30 per kg.

The output for period 3 was as follows.

Process 1 2,300 kgs
Process 2 4,000 kgs

There was no inventory of work in progress at either the beginning or the end of the period and it may be assumed that all available waste matter had been sold at the prices indicated.

Required

Show how the foregoing data would be recorded in process, scrap and abnormal loss/gain accounts by completing the proformas below. (**Hint.** Not all boxes require entries.)

PROCESS 1 ACCOUNT

	kg	$		kg	$
Material	☐	☐	Normal loss to scrap a/c	☐	☐
Labour		☐	Production transferred to process 2		
General overhead		☐		☐	☐
Abnormal gain account	☐	☐	Abnormal loss a/c	☐	☐
	☐	☐		☐	☐

PROCESS 2 ACCOUNT

	kg	$		kg	$
Transferred from process 1	☐	☐	Normal loss to scrap a/c	☐	☐
Material added	☐	☐	Production transferred to		
Labour		☐	finished inventory	☐	☐
General overhead		☐	Abnormal loss	☐	☐
Abnormal gain	☐	☐			
	☐	☐		☐	☐

SCRAP ACCOUNT

	kg	$		kg	$
Normal loss (process 1)	☐	☐	Abnormal gain (process 1)	☐	☐
Normal loss (process 2)	☐	☐	Abnormal gain (process 2)	☐	☐
Abnormal loss (process 1)	☐	☐	Cash	☐	☐
Abnormal loss (process 2)	☐	☐			
	☐	☐		☐	☐

ABNORMAL LOSS AND GAIN ACCOUNT

	kg	$		kg	$
Process 1 (loss)	☐	☐	Scrap value of abnormal		
Process 2 (loss)	☐	☐	loss	☐	☐
Scrap value of abnormal gain	☐	☐	Process 1 (gain)	☐	☐
Income statement		☐	Process 2 (gain)	☐	☐
	☐	☐		☐	☐

Step 1   Determine output and losses

	Process 1 kgs		Process 2 kgs
Output	2,300		4,000
Normal loss (20% of 3,000 kgs)	600	(10% of 4,300)	430
Abnormal loss	100		–
Abnormal gain	–		(130)
	3,000		4,300*

* From process 1 (2,300 kgs) + 2,000 kgs added

Step 2   Determine cost per unit of output and losses

	Process 1 $		Process 2 $
Material (3,000 × $0.25)	750	(2,000 × $0.40)	800
From process 1	×	(2,300 × $0.50)	1,150
Labour	120		84
Overhead (375% × $120)	450	(496% × $84)	417
Less: scrap value of **normal** loss			
(600 × $0.20)	(120)	(430 × $0.3)	(129)
	1,200		2,322

Expected output

	Process 1		Process 2
3,000 × 80%	2,400	4,300 × 90%	3,870
Cost per unit $\left(\dfrac{\$1,320-\$120}{3,000-600} \right)$	$0.50	$\left(\dfrac{\$2,451-\$129}{4,300-430} \right)$	$0.60

Step 3   Determine total cost of output and losses

	Process 1 $		Process 2 $
Output (2,300 × $0.50)	1,150	(4,000 × $0.60)	2,400
Normal loss (scrap)			
(600 × $0.20)	120	(430 × $0.30)	129
Abnormal loss (100 × $0.50)	50		–
	1,320		2,529
Abnormal gain	–	(130 × $0.60)	(78)
	1,320		2,451

Step 4   Complete accounts

PROCESS 1 ACCOUNT

	kg	$		kg	$
Material	3,000	750	Normal loss to scrap a/c		
Labour		120	(20%)	600	120
General overhead		450	Production transferred to		
			process 2	2,300	1,150
			Abnormal loss a/c	100	50
	3,000	1,320		3,000	1,320

PROCESS 2 ACCOUNT

	kg	$		kg	$
Transferred from					
process 1	2,300	1,150	Normal loss to scrap a/c		
Material added	2,000	800	(10%)	430	129
Labour		84	Production transferred to		
General overhead		417	finished inventory	4,000	2,400
	4,300	2,451			
Abnormal gain	130	78			
	4,430	2,529		4,430	2,529

SCRAP ACCOUNT

	kg	$		kg	$
Normal loss (process 1)	600	120	Abnormal gain (process 2)	130	39
Normal loss (process 2)	430	129	Cash	1,000	230
Abnormal loss					
(process 1)	100	20			
	1,130	269		1,130	269

ABNORMAL LOSS AND GAIN ACCOUNT

	kg	$		kg	$
Process 1 (loss)	100	50	Scrap value of		
Scrap value of abnormal			abnormal loss	100	20
gain	130	39	Process 2 (gain)	130	78
Income statement		9			
	230	98		230	98

(*Note.* In this answer, a single account has been prepared for abnormal loss/gain. It is also possible to separate this single account into two separate accounts, one for abnormal gain and one for abnormal loss.)

5 Valuing closing work in progress

FAST FORWARD

When units are partly completed at the end of a period (ie when there is **closing work in progress**) it is necessary to calculate **the equivalent units of production** in order to determine the cost of a completed unit.

In the examples we have looked at so far we have assumed that opening and closing inventories of work in process have been nil. We must now look at more realistic examples and consider how to allocate the costs incurred in a period between completed output (ie finished units) and partly completed closing inventory.

Some examples will help to illustrate the problem, and the techniques used to share out (apportion) costs between finished output and closing work in progress.

5.1 Example: valuation of closing inventory

Trotter Co Is a manufacturer of processed goods. In March 20X3, in one process, there was no opening inventory, but 5,000 units of input were introduced to the process during the month, at the following cost.

	$
Direct materials	16,560
Direct labour	7,360
Production overhead	5,520
	29,440

Of the 5,000 units introduced, 4,000 were completely finished during the month and transferred to the next process. Closing inventory of 1,000 units was only 60% complete with respect to materials and conversion costs.

Solution

(a) The problem in this example is to **divide the costs of production** ($29,440) between the finished output of 4,000 units and the closing inventory of 1,000 units. It is argued, with good reason, that a division of costs in proportion to the number of units of each (4,000:1,000) would not be 'fair' because closing inventory has not been completed, and has not yet 'received' its full amount of materials and conversion costs, but only 60% of the full amount. The 1,000 units of closing inventory, being only 60% complete, are the equivalent of 600 fully worked units.

(b) To apportion costs fairly and proportionately, units of production must be converted into the equivalent of completed units, ie into **equivalent units of production**.

Key term

> **Equivalent units** are 'notional whole units representing incomplete work. Used to apportion costs between work in progress and completed output …'
> CIMA *Official Terminology*

Step 1 Determine output

For this step in our framework we need to prepare a statement of equivalent units.

STATEMENT OF EQUIVALENT UNITS

	Total units	Completion	Equivalent units
Fully worked units	4,000	100%	4,000
Closing inventory	1,000	60%	600
	5,000		4,600

Step 2 Calculate cost per unit of output, and WIP

For this step in our framework we need to prepare a statement of costs per equivalent unit because equivalent units are the basis for apportioning costs.

STATEMENT OF COSTS PER EQUIVALENT UNIT

$$\frac{\text{Total costs}}{\text{Equivalent units}} = \frac{\$29,440}{4,600}$$

Cost per equivalent unit $6.40

Step 3 Calculate total cost of output and WIP

For this step in our framework a statement of evaluation may now be prepared, to show how the costs should be apportioned between finished output and closing inventory.

STATEMENT OF EVALUATION

Item	Equivalent units	Cost per equivalent unit	Valuation
			$
Fully worked units	4,000	$6.40	25,600
Closing inventory	600	$6.40	3,840
	4,600		29,440

Step 4   Complete accounts

The process account would be shown as follows.

PROCESS ACCOUNT

	Units	$		Units	$
Direct materials	5,000	16,560	Output to next process	4,000	25,600
Direct labour		7,360	Closing inventory c/f	1,000	3,840
Production o'hd		5,520			
	5,000	29,440		5,000	29,440

5.2 A few hints on preparing accounts

When preparing a process account, it might help to make the entries as follows.

(a)   **Enter the units first**. The units columns are simply memorandum columns, but they help you to make sure that there are no units unaccounted for (for example as loss).

(b)   **Enter the costs of materials, labour and overheads next**. These should be given to you.

(c)   **Enter your valuation of finished output and closing inventory next**. The value of the credit entries should, of course, equal the value of the debit entries.

5.3 Different rates of input

In many industries, materials, labour and overhead may be added at **different rates** during the course of production.

(a)   Output from a previous process (for example the output from process 1 to process 2) may be introduced into the subsequent process all at once, so that closing inventory is 100% complete in respect of these materials.

(b)   Further materials may be **added gradually** during the process, so that closing inventory is only **partially complete** in respect of these added materials.

(c)   Labour and overhead may be 'added' at yet another different rate. When production overhead is absorbed on a labour hour basis, however, we should expect the degree of completion on overhead to be the same as the degree of completion on labour.

When this situation occurs, equivalent units, and a cost per equivalent unit, should be **calculated separately for each type of material, and also for conversion costs**.

5.4 Example: equivalent units and different degrees of completion

Suppose that Shaker Co is a manufacturer of processed goods, and that results in process 2 for April 20X3 were as follows.

Opening inventory	nil
Material input from process 1	4,000 units

Costs of input:

	$
Material from process 1	6,000
Added materials in process 2	1,080
Conversion costs	1,720

Output is transferred into the next process, process 3.

Closing work in process amounted to 800 units, complete as to:

	%
Process 1 material	100
Added materials	50
Conversion costs	30

Required

Prepare the account for process 2 for April 20X3.

Solution

Step 1 Determine output and losses

STATEMENT OF EQUIVALENT UNITS (OF PRODUCTION IN THE PERIOD)

			Equivalent units of production					
			Process 1 material		Added materials		Labour and overhead	
Input	*Output*	*Total*						
Units		Units	Units	%	Units	%	Units	%
4,000	Completed prod n	3,200	3,200	100	3,200	100	3,200	100
	Closing Inventory	800	800	100	400	50	240	30
4,000		4,000	4,000		3,600		3,440	

Step 2 Calculate cost per unit of output, losses and WIP

STATEMENT OF COST (PER EQUIVALENT UNIT)

Input	*Cost*	*Equivalent production in units*	*Cost per unit*
	$		$
Process 1 material	6,000	4,000	1.50
Added materials	1,080	3,600	0.30
Labour and overhead	1,720	3,440	0.50
	8,800		2.30

Step 3 Calculate total cost of output, losses and WIP

STATEMENT OF EVALUATION (OF FINISHED WORK AND CLOSING INVENTORIES)

Production	*Cost element*	*Number of equivalent units*	*Cost per equivalent unit*	*Total*	*Cost*
			$	$	$
Completed production		3,200	2.30		7,360
Closing inventory:	process 1 material	800	1.50	1,200	
	added material	400	0.30	120	
	labour and overhead	240	0.50	120	
				1,440	
				8,800	

Step 4   Complete accounts

PROCESS ACCOUNT

	Units	$		Units	$
Process 1 material	4,000	6,000	Process 3 a/c	3,200	7,360
Added material		1,080	(finished output)		
Conversion costs		1,720	Closing inventory c/f	800	1,440
	4,000	8,800		4,000	8,800

5.5 Closing work in progress and losses

The previous sections have dealt separately with the following.

(a)   The treatment of loss and scrap.

(b)   The use of equivalent units as a basis for apportioning costs between units of output and units of closing inventory.

We must now look at a situation where both problems occur together. We shall begin with an example where loss has no scrap value.

The rules are as follows.

(a)   Costs should be divided between finished output, closing inventory and abnormal loss/gain using **equivalent units** as a basis of apportionment.

(b)   Units of abnormal loss/gain are often taken to be **one full equivalent unit each**, and are valued on this basis, ie they carry their full 'share' of the process costs.

(c)   **Abnormal loss units are an addition** to the total equivalent units produced but **abnormal gain units are subtracted** in arriving at the total number of equivalent units produced.

(d)   Units of **normal loss are valued at zero equivalent units**, ie they do not carry any of the process costs.

5.6 Example: changes in inventory level and losses

The following data have been collected for a process.

Opening inventory	none	Output to finished goods	2,000 units
Input units	2,800 units	Closing inventory	450 units, 70% complete
Cost of input	$16,695	Total loss	350 units
Normal loss	10%; nil scrap value		

Required

Prepare the process account for the period.

Solution

Step 1   **Determine output and losses**

STATEMENT OF EQUIVALENT UNITS

	Total units		Equivalent units of work done this period
Completely worked units	2,000	(× 100%)	2,000
Closing inventory	450	(× 70%)	315
Normal loss	280		0
Abnormal loss	70	(× 100%)	70
	2,800		2,385

Step 2   **Calculate cost per unit of output, losses and WIP**

STATEMENT OF COST PER EQUIVALENT UNIT

$$\frac{\text{Costs incurred}}{\text{Equivalent units of work done}} = \frac{\$16,695}{2,385}$$

Cost per equivalent unit   = $7

Step 3   **Calculate total cost of output, losses and WIP**

STATEMENT OF EVALUATION

	Equivalent units	$
Completely worked units	2,000	14,000
Closing inventory	315	2,205
Abnormal loss	70	490
	2,385	16,695

Step 4   **Complete accounts**

PROCESS ACCOUNT

	Units	$		Units	$
Opening inventory	–	–	Normal loss	280	0
Input costs	2,800	16,695	Finished goods a/c	2,000	14,000
			Abnormal loss a/c	70	490
			Closing inventory c/d	450	2,205
	2,800	16,695		2,800	16,695

5.7 Closing work in progress, loss and scrap

When loss has a **scrap value**, the accounting procedures are the same as those previously described. However, if the equivalent units are a different percentage (of the total units) for materials, labour and overhead, it is a convention that the **scrap value of normal loss** is **deducted from the cost of materials** before a cost per equivalent unit is calculated.

BPP
LEARNING MEDIA

Complete the process account below from the following information.(**Hint.** Not all boxes require entries.)

Opening inventory	Nil
Input units	10,000
Input costs	
Material	$5,150
Labour	$2,700
Normal loss	5% of input
Scrap value of units of loss	$1 per unit
Output to finished goods	8,000 units
Closing inventory	1,000 units
Completion of closing inventory	80% for material
	50% for labour

PROCESS ACCOUNT

	Units	$		Units	$
Material	☐	☐	Completed production	☐	☐
Labour		☐	Closing inventory	☐	☐
Abnormal gain	☐	☐	Normal loss	☐	☐
			Abnormal loss	☐	☐
	☐	☐		☐	☐

Answer

Step 1   **Determine output and losses**

STATEMENT OF EQUIVALENT UNITS

	Total Units	Equivalent units Material %	Units	Labour %	Units
Completed production	8,000	100	8,000	100	8,000
Closing inventory	1,000	80	800	50	500
Normal loss	500				
Abnormal loss	500	100	500	100	500
	10,000		9,300		9,000

Step 2   **Calculate cost per unit of output, losses and WIP**

STATEMENT OF COST PER EQUIVALENT UNIT

	Cost $	Equivalent units	Cost per equivalent unit $
Material ($(5,150 – 500))	4,650	9,300	0.50
Labour	2,700	9,000	0.30
	7,350		0.80

Step 3 Calculate total cost of output, losses and WIP

STATEMENT OF EVALUATION

	Equivalent units	Cost per equivalent unit		Total
		$	$	$
Completed production	8,000	0.80		6,400
Closing inventory: material	800	0.50	400	
labour	500	0.30	150	
				550
Abnormal loss	500	0.80		400
				7,350

Step 4 Complete accounts

PROCESS ACCOUNT

	Units	$		Units	$
Material	10,000	5,150	Completed production	8,000	6,400
Labour		2,700	Closing inventory	1,000	550
Abnormal gain	0	0	Normal loss	500	500
			Abnormal loss	500	400
	10,000	7,850		10,000	7,850

6 Valuing opening work in progress

FAST FORWARD

The **weighted average cost method of valuing opening WIP** makes no distinction between units of opening WIP and new units introduced to the process during the current period.

6.1 Weighted average cost method

The weighted average cost method of inventory valuation is a inventory valuation method that calculates a weighted average cost of units produced from both opening inventory and units introduced in the current period.

Important!

With the weighted average cost method no distinction is made between units of opening WIP and new units introduced to the process during the current period. The cost of opening WIP is added to costs incurred during the period, and completed units of opening WIP are each given a value of one full equivalent unit of production.

6.2 Example: weighted average cost method

Magpie Co produces an item which is manufactured in two consecutive processes. Information relating to Process 2 during September 20X3 is as follows.

Opening inventory 800 units
Degree of completion:

	%	$
process 1 materials	100	4,700
added materials	40	600
conversion costs	30	1,000
		6,300

During September 20X3, 3,000 units were transferred from process 1 at a valuation of $18,100. Added materials cost $9,600 and conversion costs were $11,800.

Closing inventory at 30 September 20X3 amounted to 1,000 units which were 100% complete with respect to process 1 materials and 60% complete with respect to added materials. Conversion cost work was 40% complete.

Magpie Co uses a weighted average cost system for the valuation of output and closing inventory.

Required

Prepare the Process 2 account for September 20X3.

Solution

Step 1   Determine output and losses

Opening inventory units count as a full equivalent unit of production when the weighted average cost system is applied. Closing inventory units are assessed in the usual way.

STATEMENT OF EQUIVALENT UNITS

	Total units		Process 1 material		Added material		Conversion costs
Output to finished goods*	2,800	(100%)	2,800		2,800		2,800
Closing inventory	1,000	(100%)	1,000	(60%)	600	(40%)	400
	3,800		3,800		3,400		3,200

* 3,000 units from Process 1 minus closing inventory of 1,000 units plus opening inventory of 800 units.

Step 2   Calculate cost per unit of output and WIP

The cost of opening inventory is added to costs incurred in September 20X3, and a cost per equivalent unit is then calculated.

STATEMENT OF COSTS PER EQUIVALENT UNIT

	Process 1 material $	Added materials $	Conversion costs $
Opening inventory	4,700	600	1,000
Added in September 20X3	18,100	9,600	11,800
Total cost	22,800	10,200	12,800
Equivalent units	3,800 units	3,400 units	3,200 units
Cost per equivalent unit	$6	$3	$4

Step 3   Calculate total cost of output and WIP

STATEMENT OF EVALUATION

	Process 1 material $	Added materials $	Conversion costs $	Total cost $
Output to finished goods (2,800 units)	16,800	8,400	11,200	36,400
Closing inventory	6,000	1,800	1,600	9,400
				45,800

Step 4   Complete accounts

PROCESS 2 ACCOUNT

	Units	$		Units	$
Opening inventory b/f	800	6,300	Finished goods a/c	2,800	36,400
Process 1 a/c	3,000	18,100			
Added materials		9,600			
Conversion costs		11,800	Closing inventory c/f	1,000	9,400
	3,800	45,800		3,800	45,800

Assessment focus point

You must be prepared to deal with assessment questions which have opening WIP, closing WIP **and** losses all occurring together in the same process.

6.3 A final question

The following question involves the following process costing situations.

- Normal loss (with and without sale of scrap)
- Abnormal loss
- Abnormal gain
- Opening work in progress
- Closing work in progress

Take time to work through this question carefully and to check your workings against the answer given below. This is an excellent question which should help you to consolidate all of the process costing knowledge that you have acquired while studying this chapter.

Question   Watkins Co

W Co has a financial year which ends on 30 April. It operates in a processing industry in which a single product is produced by passing inputs through two sequential processes. A normal loss of 10% of input is expected in each process.

The following account balances have been extracted from its ledger at 31 March 20X0.

	Debit	Credit
	$	$
Process 1 (Materials $4,400; Conversion costs $3,744)	8,144	
Process 2 (Process 1 $4,431; Conversion costs $5,250)	9,681	
Abnormal loss	1,400	
Abnormal gain		300
Overhead control account		250
Sales		585,000
Cost of sales	442,500	
Finished goods inventory	65,000	

W Co uses the weighted average method of accounting for work in process.

During April 20X0 the following transactions occurred.

Process 1			
	Materials input (kg, $)	4,000 kg	22,000
	Labour cost		$12,000
	Transfer to process 2	2,400 kg	

Process 2   Transfer from process 1   2,400 kg
             Labour cost $15,000
             Transfer to finished goods   2,500 kg
Overhead costs incurred amounted to $54,000
Sales to customer were $52,000

Overhead costs are absorbed into process costs on the basis of 150% of labour cost.

The losses which arise in process 1 have no scrap value: those arising in process 2 can be sold for $2 per kg.

Details of opening and closing work in process for the month of April 20X0 are as follows.

	Opening	Closing
Process 1	3,000 kg	3,400 kg
Process 2	2,250 kg	2,600 kg

In both processes closing work in process is fully complete as to material cost and 40% complete as to conversion cost.

Inventories of finished goods at 30 April 20X0 were valued at cost of $60,000.

Required

(a)   In an account for process 1, the monetary and quantity values for:

    (i)   transfers to process 2 are [   ] kgs at $ [   ]

    (ii)   normal loss are [   ] kgs at $ [   ]

    (iii) abnormal loss are [   ] kgs at $ [   ]

    (iv)   abnormal gain are [   ] kgs at $ [   ]

    (v)   WIP materials are [   ] kgs at $ [   ]

    (vi)   WIP conversion costs are [   ] kgs at $ [   ]

(b)   In an account for process 2, the monetary and quantity values for:

    (i)   finished goods are [   ] kgs at $ [   ]

    (ii)   normal loss are [   ] kgs at $ [   ]

    (iii) WIP from process 1 are [   ] kgs at $ [   ]

    (iv)   WIP from process 2 are [   ] kgs at $ [   ]

Answer

(a)   **Process 1**

STATEMENT OF EQUIVALENT UNITS

		Equivalent units	
	Total units	*Material costs*	*Conversion costs*
Transfers to process 2	2,400	2,400	2,400
Closing WIP	3,400	(100%) 3,400	(40%) 1,360
Normal loss (10% × 4,000)	400	0	0
Abnormal loss	800	800	800
	7,000	6,600	4,560

STATEMENT OF COSTS PER EQUIVALENT UNIT

$$\frac{\text{Costs incurred}}{\text{Equivalent units}} = \text{Cost per equivalent unit}$$

$$\therefore \text{Materials cost per equivalent unit} = \frac{\$4,400 + \$22,000}{6,600}$$

$$= \frac{\$26,400}{6,600} = \$4$$

$$\therefore \text{Conversion costs per equivalent unit} = \frac{\$3,744 + \$12,000 + \$18,000}{4,560}$$

$$= \frac{\$33,744}{4,560} = \$7.40$$

STATEMENT OF EVALUATION

	Materials $	Conversion costs $	Total $
Transfers to process 2	9,600	17,760	27,360
Abnormal loss	3,200	5,920	9,120
Closing WIP	13,600	10,064	23,664
	26,400	33,744	60,144

PROCESS 1 ACCOUNT

	Kg	$		Kg	$
WIP materials	3,000	4,400	Process 2	2,400	27,360
WIP conversion costs	–	3,744	Normal loss	400	–
Materials	4,000	22,000	Abnormal loss	800	9,120
Labour	–	12,000	WIP materials	3,400	13,600
Overhead	–	18,000	WIP conversion costs	–	10,064
	7,000	60,144		7,000	60,144

The monetary and quantity values for:

(i)   **transfer to process 2 are** [2,400] **kgs at $** [27,360]

(ii)   **normal loss are** [400] **kgs at $** [0]

(iii)   **abnormal loss are** [800] **kgs at $** [9,120]

(iv)   **abnormal gain are** [0] **kgs at $** [0]

(v)   **WIP materials are** [3,400] **kgs at $** [13,600]

(vi)   **WIP conversion costs are** [0] **kgs at $** [10,064]

(b) **Process 2**

STATEMENT OF EQUIVALENT UNITS

	Total units	Process 1	Conversion costs
Finished goods	2,500	2,500	2,500
Normal loss	240	0	0
Abnormal gain	(690)	(690)	(690)
Closing WIP	2,600*	2,600	1,040 **
	4,650	4,410	2,850

* Total input units = opening WIP + input = 2,250 + 2,400 = 4,650

  Total output units = finished goods + closing WIP + normal loss − abnormal gain

  = 2,500 + 2,600 + 240 − 690

  = 4,650

** 2,600 × 40% = 1,040

STATEMENT OF COSTS PER EQUIVALENT UNIT

$$\text{Process 1} = \frac{\$4,431 + \$27,360 - 480}{4,410} = \$7.10$$

$$\text{Conversion costs} = \frac{\$5,250 + \$15,000 + \$22,500}{2,850} = \$15.00$$

STATEMENT OF EVALUATION

	Process 1	Conversion costs	Totals
	$	$	$
Finished goods	17,750	37,500	55,250
Abnormal gain	(4,899)	(10,350)	(15,249)
Closing WIP	18,460	15,600	34,060

PROCESS 2 ACCOUNT

	Kg	$		Kg	$
WIP Process 1	2,250	4,431	Finished goods	2,500	55,250
WIP conversion costs	–	5,250	Normal loss	240	480
Process 1	2,400	27,360	WIP Process 1	2,600	18,460
Labour	–	15,000	WIP conversion costs	–	15,600
Overhead	–	22,500			
Abnormal gain	690	15,249			
	5,340	89,790		5,340	89,790

The monetary and quantity values for:

(i) finished goods are | 2,500 | kgs at $ | 55,250 |

(ii) normal loss are | 240 | kgs at $ | 480 |

(iii) WIP from process 1 are | 2,600 | kgs at $ | 18,460 |

(iv) WIP from process 2 are | 0 | kgs at $ | 15,600 |

Assessment focus point

Many students find process costing difficult. The best ways to improve your understanding are to memorise the step approach and to practise as many questions as possible.

Chapter Roundup

- **Process costing** is a costing method used where it is not possible to identify separate units of production, or jobs, usually because of the continuous nature of the production processes involved.

- A process account has **two sides**, and on **each side there are two columns** – one for **quantities** (of raw materials, work in progress and finished goods) and one for **costs**.

- Use our suggested **four-step approach** when dealing with process costing questions.

    Step 1   Determine output and losses

    Step 2   Calculate cost per unit of output, losses and WIP

    Step 3   Calculate total cost of output, losses and WIP

    Step 4   Complete accounts

- **Losses** may occur in process. If a certain level of loss is expected, this is known as **normal loss**. If losses are greater than expected, the extra loss is **abnormal loss**. If losses are less than expected, the difference is known as **abnormal gain**.

- The **valuation of normal loss is either at scrap value or nil**. It is conventional for the **scrap value of normal loss to be deducted from the cost of materials** before a cost per equivalent unit is calculated.

- Abnormal losses and gains never affect the cost of good units of production. The scrap value of abnormal losses is not credited to the process account, and the abnormal loss and gain units **carry the same full cost as a good unit of production**.

- When units are partly completed at the end of a period (ie when there is **closing work in progress**) it is necessary to calculate the **equivalent units of production** in order to determine the cost of a completed unit.

- The **weighted average cost** method of valuing opening WIP makes no distinction between units of opening WIP and new units introduced to the process during the current period.

1   *Choose the correct words from those highlighted.*

     Process costing is likely to be used in **the construction of large buildings/ paint manufacture/ a supermarket**.

2   There are four key steps to approaching process costing. What are they?

     Step 1   ....

     Step 2   ....

     Step 3   ....

     Step 4   ....

3   Abnormal gains result when actual loss is less than normal or expected loss.

     True   ☐

     False   ☐

4   *Match the types of loss with the correct method of valuation.*

     Normal loss (no scrap value)   Same value as good output (positive cost)

     Abnormal loss   **?**   No value

     Abnormal gain   Same value as good output (negative cost)

5   How is revenue from scrap treated?

     A   As an addition to sales revenue
     B   As a reduction in costs of processing
     C   As a bonus to employees
     D   Any of the above

6   When there is closing WIP at the end of a process, the first step in the four-step approach to process costing questions is to draw up a statement of evaluation.

     True   ☐

     False   ☐

7   *Choose the correct words from those highlighted.*

     The weighted average cost method of inventory valuation **makes no distinction/makes a distinction** between units of opening WIP and new units introduced to the process during the current period.

8   Yum Co makes a fizzy drink which passes through several processes. The normal loss is 5% of the input from the previous period and can be sold at $0.50 per litre. The equivalent cost per litre has been calculated as $9.50 per complete litre.

The following information is available for June.

	Opening Inventory	From previous period	To next period	Closing inventory
Litres	200	1,000	1,150	160

Are the following statements true or false?

	True	False
Yum Co would make an abnormal loss	☐	☐
The level of abnormal loss/gain is 40 litres	☐	☐

9   A factory operates a processing operation which has a normal loss of 10%. Scrapped units sell for $2 per kg. The following information is available for June.

Materials used   2,000 kg @ $4 per kg

Output   1,700 kg

What is the scrap value for the abnormal loss?

A   Nil

B $200

What would the double entry be for the scrap value of the abnormal loss?

C   Dr   Scrap value
       Cr   Abnormal loss account

D   Dr   Scrap value
       Cr   Process account

Answers to Quick Quiz

1   Process costing is likely to be used in **paint manufacture**.

2   **Step 1**   Determine output and losses

    Step 2   Calculate cost per unit of output, losses and WIP

    Step 3   Calculate total cost of output, losses and WIP

    Step 4   Complete accounts

3   True

4   Normal loss (no scrap value)   Same value as good output (positive cost)

    Abnormal loss   No value

    Abnormal gain   Same value as good output (negative cost)

5   B

6   False. The first step is to calculate the equivalent units of production by drawing up a statement of equivalent units.

7   The weighted average cost method of inventory valuation **makes no distinction** between units of opening WIP and new units introduced to the process during the current period.

8   False, False

Process account

Dr		Cr	
Opening WIP	200	Output	1,150
Input	1,000	Normal loss	50
Abnormal gain	[ ]	Closing WIP	____
	1,360		1,360

The balancing figure is a debit therefore an abnormal gain. 1,360 – 200 – 1,000 = 160.

9   B & C

Determine output and losses:

	Process Kg
Output	1,700
Normal loss (10% of input)	200
Abnormal loss (balancing figure)	100
	2,000

Scrap value of abnormal loss = 100 kg x $2

                                = $200

Now try the questions below from the Question Bank

Question numbers
65–76

BPP
LEARNING MEDIA

13

Job and batch costing

Introduction

A **costing method** is designed to suit the way goods are processed or manufactured or the way services are provided. Each organisation's costing method will therefore have unique features but costing methods of firms in the same line of business will more than likely have common aspects. We've already looked at process costing, which is used when production is a continuous flow of identical units.

In this chapter we will be looking at **specific order costing** methods, specific order costing being the 'basic cost accounting method applicable if work consists of separately identifiable batches, contracts or jobs' (CIMA *Official Terminology*).

This chapter begins by covering **job costing** and then moves on to **batch costing**, the procedure for which is similar to job costing.

Topic list	Syllabus references
1 Job costing	D1(c)
2 Job costing example	D1(c),(d)
3 Job costing for internal services	D1(c),(d)
4 Batch costing	D1(c),(d)

1 Job costing

FAST FORWARD

Job costing is the costing method used where work is undertaken to customers' special requirements and each order is of comparatively short duration.

The work relating to a job is usually carried out within a factory or workshop and moves through processes and operations as a **continuously identifiable unit**.

Key terms

A **job** is a 'customer order or task of relatively short duration'.

Job costing is a 'form of specific order costing where costs are attributed to individual jobs'. CIMA *Official Terminology*

1.1 Procedure for the performance of jobs

The normal procedure which is adopted in jobbing concerns involves the following.

(a)   The prospective customer approaches the supplier and indicates the requirements of the job.

(b)   A responsible official sees the prospective customer and agrees with him the precise details of the items to be supplied, for example the quantity, quality, size and colour of the goods, the date of delivery and any special requirements.

(c)   The estimating department of the organisation then prepares an estimate for the job. This will include the cost of the materials to be used, the wages expected to be paid, the appropriate amount for factory, administration, selling and distribution overhead, the cost where appropriate of additional equipment needed specially for the job, and finally the supplier's **profit margin**. The total of these items will represent the quoted **selling price**.

(d)   At the appropriate time, the job will be 'loaded' on to the factory floor. This means that as soon as all materials, labour and equipment are available and subject to the scheduling of other orders, the job will be started. In an efficient organisation, the start of the job will be timed to ensure that while it will be ready for the customer by the promised date of delivery it will not be loaded too early, otherwise storage space will have to be found for the product until the date it is required by (and was promised to) the customer.

1.2 Recording job costs

A separate record must be maintained to show the details of individual jobs. In **manual** systems, these are known as **job cost cards** or **job cost sheets**. In **computerised** systems, job costs will be collected in **job accounts**.

1.2.1 Job accounts

Job accounts are very much like the process accounts we encountered in Chapter 12. Inputs to a job are recorded on the left-hand side of the account, outputs on the right-hand side.

1.2.2 Collecting job costs

Key points on the process of collecting job costs are as follows.

(a)   Some labour costs, such as overtime premium, might be charged either directly to a job or else as an overhead cost, depending on the circumstances in which the costs have arisen.

(b)   The relevant costs of materials issued, direct labour performed and direct expenses incurred are charged to a job account in the work in progress ledger, the work in progress ledger recording the cost of all WIP.

(c)   The job account is allocated with the job's share of the factory overhead, based on the absorption rate(s) in operation. If the job is incomplete at the end of an accounting period, it is valued at factory cost in the closing statement of financial position (where a system of absorption costing is in operation).

(d)   On completion of the job, the job account is charged with the appropriate administration, selling and distribution overhead, after which the total cost of the job can be ascertained. The job is transferred to finished goods.

(e)   The difference between the agreed selling price and the total actual cost will be the supplier's profit (or loss).

(f)   When delivery is made to the customer, the costs become a cost of sale.

Question   Job costing

Twist and Tern Co is a company that carries out jobbing work. One of the jobs carried out in February was job 1357, to which the following information relates.

Direct material Y: 400 kilos were issued from stores at a cost of $5 per kilo.
Direct material Z: 800 kilos were issued from stores at a cost of $6 per kilo.
                            60 kilos were returned.
Department P: 320 labour hours were worked, of which 100 hours were done in overtime.
Department Q: 200 labour hours were worked, of which 100 hours were done in overtime.

Overtime work is not normal in Department P, where basic pay is $8 per hour plus an overtime premium of $2 per hour. Overtime work was done in Department Q in February because of a request by the customer of another job to complete his job quickly. Basic pay in Department Q is $10 per hour and overtime premium is $3 per hour.

Overhead is absorbed at the rate of $3 per direct labour hour in both departments.

(a)   The direct materials cost of job 1357 is $ [   ].

(b)   The direct labour cost of job 1357 is $ [   ].

(c)   The full production cost of job 1357 is $ [   ].

Answer

(a)   **The direct materials cost is $ 6,440**

        Workings

	$
Direct material Y (400 kilos × $5)	2,000
Direct material Z (800 – 60 kilos × $6)	4,440
Total direct material cost	6,440

(b)   **The direct labour cost is $ 4,560**

        Workings

	$
Department P (320 hours × $8)	2,560
Department Q (200 hours × $10)	2,000
Total direct labour cost	4,560

In Department P, overtime premium will be charged to overhead. In Department Q, overtime premium will be charged to the job of the customer who asked for overtime to be worked. Go back to chapter 7 Section 5.3 if you have forgotten the principles.

(c)   **The full production cost is $ | 12,560 |**

Workings

	$
Direct material cost	6,440
Direct labour cost	4,560
Production overhead (520 hours × $3)	1,560
	12,560

You may have added the overtime premium for department P here but this would be incorrect.

Remember your absorption costing principles from earlier chapters. The overhead absorption rate is pre-determined using budgeted figures. Actual figures are used to determine over or under absorption at the period end.

1.3 Job costing and computerisation

Job costing cards exist in **manual** systems, but it is increasingly likely that in large organisations the job costing system will be **computerised**, using accounting software specifically designed to deal with job costing requirements. A computerised job accounting system is likely to contain the following features.

(a)   Every job will be given a job code number, which will determine how the data relating to the job is stored.

(b)   A separate set of codes will be given for the type of costs that any job is likely to incur. Thus, 'direct wages', say, will have the same code whichever job they are allocated to.

(c)   In a sophisticated system, costs can be analysed both by job (for example all costs related to Job 456), but also by type (for example direct wages incurred on all jobs). It is thus easy to perform variance analysis and to make comparisons between jobs.

(d)   A job costing system might have facilities built into it which incorporate other factors relating to the performance of the job. In complex jobs, sophisticated planning techniques might be employed to ensure that the job is performed in the minimum time possible. Time management features therefore may be incorporated into job costing software.

1.4 Cost plus pricing

The usual method of fixing prices within a jobbing concern is **cost plus pricing**.

As you know from Chapter 5, cost plus pricing is where a desired profit margin is added to total costs to arrive at the selling price.

The **disadvantages** of cost plus pricing are as follows.

(a)   There are no incentives to **control costs** as a profit is guaranteed.

(b)   There is no motive to tackle **inefficiencies** or **waste**.

(c)   It does not take into account any significant differences in actual and estimated volumes of activity. Since the overhead absorption rate is based upon estimated volumes, there may be **under-/over-absorbed overheads** not taken into account.

(d)   Because overheads are apportioned in an arbitrary way, this may lead to **under and over pricing**.

Assessment focus point

Assessment questions may require you to accumulate costs to arrive at a job cost, and then to determine a **job price** by adding a profit of, say, 30 per cent **on sales**. To do this, you need to jot down the following crucial formula.

	%
Sales price	100
Profit	30
Cost	70

Once the job costs have been accumulated, the profit margin can be added as (cost × 30/70). A common error would be to simply add 30 per cent to cost, so it is vital that you read any assessment question carefully.

Question

Selling prices

The total cost of job 259 is $4,200.

(a) When profit is calculated as 25 per cent of sales, the correct selling price for the job is $ ☐

(b) When profit is calculated as 25 per cent of cost, the correct selling price for the job is $ ☐

Answer

If you have difficulty working out the correct amount, simply jot down the cost and selling price structures as percentages in each case.

(a) **The correct selling price is $ 5,600 .**

Workings

Profit is calculated as a percentage of sales, so selling price must be written as 100%.

	%
Cost	75
Profit	25
Selling price	100

Selling price = $4,200 × 100/75 = $5,600

(b) **The correct selling price is $ 5,250 .**

Workings

Profit is calculated as a percentage of cost, so cost must be written as 100%.

	%
Cost	100
Profit	25
Selling price	125

Selling price = $4,200 × 125/100 = $5,250

2 Job costing example

An example may help to illustrate the principles of job costing.

FM Co is a jobbing company. On 1 June 20X2, there was one uncompleted job in the factory. The job card for this work is summarised as follows.

Job card, job no 6832

	$
Costs to date	
Direct materials	630
Direct labour (120 hours)	840
Factory overhead ($2 per direct labour hour)	240
Factory cost to date	1,710

During June, three new jobs were started in the factory, and costs of production were as follows.

		$
Direct materials		
Issued to:	Job 6832	2,390
	Job 6833	1,680
	Job 6834	3,950
	Job 6835	4,420
Damaged inventory written off from stores		2,300

Material transfers	$
Job 6834 to Job 6833	250
Job 6832 to 6834	620

Materials returned to store	$
From Job 6832	870
From Job 6835	170

Direct labour hours recorded	Hours
Job 6832	430
Job 6833	650
Job 6834	280
Job 6835	410

The cost of labour hours during June 20X2 was $8 per hour, and production overhead is absorbed at the rate of $2 per direct labour hour. Production overheads incurred during the month amounted to $3,800. Completed jobs were delivered to customers as soon as they were completed, and the invoiced amounts were as follows.

Job 6832	$8,500
Job 6834	$9,000
Job 6835	$9,500

Administration and marketing overheads are added to the cost of sales at the rate of 20% of factory cost. Actual costs incurred during June 20X2 amounted to $4,418.

Required

(a) Prepare the job accounts for each individual job during June 20X2. (Remember inputs to the job go on the left-hand side of the account, outputs on the right-hand side.)

(b) Prepare the summarised job cost cards for each job, and calculate the profit on each completed job.

Solution

(a)   **Job accounts**

JOB 6832

	$		$
Balance b/f	1,710	Job 6834 a/c	620
Materials (stores a/c)	2,390	(materials transfer)	
Labour (wages a/c)	3,440	To stores (materials returned)	870
Production overhead (o'hd a/c)	860	Cost of sales (balance)	6,910
	8,400		8,400

JOB 6833

	$		$
Materials (stores a/c)	1,680	Balance c/f	8,430
Labour (wages a/c)	5,200		
Production overhead (o'hd a/c)	1,300		
Job 6834 a/c (materials transfer)	250		
	8,430		8,430

JOB 6834

	$		$
Materials (stores a/c)	3,950	Job 6833 a/c (materials transfer)	250
Labour (wages a/c)	2,240		
Production overhead (o'hd a/c)	560	Cost of sales (balance)	7,120
Job 6832 a/c (materials transfer)	620		
	7,370		7,370

JOB 6835

	$		$
Materials (stores a/c)	4,420	To stores (materials returned)	170
Labour (wages a/c)	3,280		
Production overhead (o'hd a/c)	820	Cost of sales (balance)	8,350
	8,520		8,520

Note that the accounts to which the double entry is made are shown in brackets.

(b)   **Job cards, summarised**

	Job 6832	Job 6833	Job 6834	Job 6835
	$	$	$	$
Materials	1,530*	1,930	4,320 **	4,250
Labour	4,280	5,200	2,240	3,280
Production overhead	1,100	1,300	560	820
Factory cost	6,910	(c/f) 8,430	7,120	8,350
Admin & marketing o'hd (20%)	1,382		1,424	1,670
Cost of sale	8,292		8,544	10,020
Invoice value	8,500		9,000	9,500
Profit/(loss) on job	208		456	(520)

* $(630 + 2,390 – 620 – 870)   ** $(3,950 + 620 – 250)

2.1 Example: job costing and cost bookkeeping

This example will show you how to integrate job costing with your cost bookkeeping knowledge.

Required

Show how the costs recorded in the job accounts in the above example would be shown in the company's cost control accounts.

Solution

STORES CONTROL (incomplete)

	$		$
WIP a/c (returns)	1,040	WIP a/c	
		(2,390 + 1,680 + 3,950 + 4,420)	12,440
		Income statement:	
		inventory written off	2,300

WORK IN PROGRESS CONTROL

	$		$
Balance b/f	1,710	Stores control a/c (returns)	1,040
Stores control a/c	12,440	Cost of sales a/c	
Wages control a/c	*14,160	(6,910 + 7,120 + 8,350)	22,380
Production o'hd control a/c	**3,540	Balance c/f (Job No 6833)	8,430
	31,850		31,850

* 1,770 hours at $8 per hour
** 1,770 hours at $2 per hour

COST OF SALES CONTROL

	$		$
WIP control a/c	22,380	Income statement	26,856
Admin & marketing o'hd a/c			
(1,382 + 1,424 + 1,670)	4,476		
	26,856		26,856

SALES

	$		$
Income statement	27,000	Receivables	27,000
		(8,500 + 9,000 + 9,500)	
	27,000		27,000

PRODUCTION OVERHEAD CONTROL

	$		$
Overhead incurred – payables	3,800	WIP a/c	3,540
		Under-absorbed o'hd a/c	260
	3,800		3,800

UNDER-/OVER-ABSORBED OVERHEADS

	$		$
Production o'hd control a/c	260	Admin & marketing o'hd a/c	58
		Income statement	202
	260		260

ADMIN & MARKETING OVERHEAD CONTROL

	$		$
Overhead incurred – payables	4,418	Cost of sales a/c	4,476
Over absorbed o'hd a/c	58		
	4,476		4,476

INCOME STATEMENT

	$		$
Cost of sales a/c	26,856	Sales a/c	27,000
Stores a/c (inventory written off)	2,300	Loss	2,358
Under-absorbed overhead a/c	202		
	29,358		29,358

The loss of $2,358 is the sum of the profits/losses on each completed job $(208 + 456 – 520) = $144, minus the total of under-absorbed overhead ($202) and the inventory write-off ($2,300).

Question

Selling price of jobs

A furniture-making business manufactures quality furniture to customers' orders. It has three production departments (A, B and C) which have overhead absorption rates (per direct labour hour) of $12.86, $12.40 and $14.03 respectively.

Two pieces of furniture are to be manufactured for customers. Direct costs are as follows.

	Job XYZ	*Job MNO*
Direct material	$154	$108
Direct labour	20 hours dept A	16 hours dept A
	12 hours dept B	10 hours dept B
	10 hours dept C	14 hours dept C

Labour rates are as follows: $7.60(A); $7.00 (B); $6.80 (C)

The firm quotes prices to customers that reflect a required profit of 25% on selling price.

(a) (i) The total cost of job XYZ is $ [   ]. (b) (i) The total cost of job MNO is $ [   ]

(ii) The selling price of job XYZ is $ [   ]. (ii) The selling price of job MNO is $ [   ].

Answer

(a) (i) **The total cost of job XYZ is $ | 1,004.30 |** (b) (i) **The total cost of job MNO is $ | 920.98 |**

(ii) **The selling price of job XYZ is $ | 1,339.07 |** (ii) **The selling price of job MNO is $ | 1,227.97 |**

Workings

		Job XYZ		Job MNO
		$		$
Direct material		154.00		108.00
Direct labour: dept A	(20 × 7.60)	152.00	(16 × 7.60)	121.60
dept B	(12 × 7.00)	84.00	(10 × 7.00)	70.00
dept C	(10 × 6.80)	68.00	(14 × 6.80)	95.20
Total direct cost		458.00		394.80
Overhead: dept A	(20 × 12.86)	257.20	(16 × 12.86)	205.76
dept B	(12 × 12.40)	148.80	(10 × 12.40)	124.00
dept C	(10 × 14.03)	140.30	(14 × 14.03)	196.42
Total cost		1,004.30		920.98
Profit (note)		334.77		306.99
Quoted selling price		1,339.07		1,227.97

Note. If profit is 25% on selling price, this is the same as $33^1/_3$% (25/75) on cost:

	%
Selling price	100
Cost	75
Profit	25

Question

Closing work in progress

A firm uses job costing and recovers overheads on direct labour.

Three jobs were worked on during a period, the details of which are as follows.

	Job 1	Job 2	Job 3
	$	$	$
Opening work in progress	8,500	0	46,000
Material in period	17,150	29,025	0
Labour for period	12,500	23,000	4,500

The overheads for the period were exactly as budgeted, $140,000.

Jobs 1 and 2 were the only incomplete jobs.

What was the value of closing work in progress?

A $81,900   B $90,175   C $140,675   D $214,425

Answer

The correct answer is D.

Total labour cost = $12,500 + $23,000 + $4,500 = $40,000

Overhead absorption rate = $\dfrac{\$140,000}{\$40,000}$ × 100% = 350% of direct labour cost

Closing work in progress valuation

		Job 1		Job 2	Total
		$		$	$
Costs given in question		38,150		52,025	90,175
Overhead absorbed	(12,500 × 350%)	43,750	(23,000 × 350%)	80,500	124,250
					214,425

We can eliminate **option B** because $90,175 is simply the total of the costs allocated to Jobs 1 and 2, with no absorption of overheads. **Option A** is an even lower cost figure, therefore it can also be eliminated.

Option C is wrong because it is a simple total of all allocated costs, including Job 3 which is complete and therefore not WIP.

3 Job costing for internal services

FAST FORWARD

> An **internal job costing** system can be used for costing the work of service departments.

Job costing systems may be used to **control the costs** of **internal service departments**, such as the maintenance department. A job costing system enables the cost of a specific job to be charged to a user department. Therefore instead of apportioning the total costs of service departments, each job done is charged to the individual user department.

3.1 Advantages of internal job costing systems

An **internal job costing system** for service departments will have the following advantages.

(a) **Realistic apportionment**. The identification of expenses with jobs and the subsequent charging of these to the department(s) responsible means that costs are borne by those who incurred them.

(b) **Increased responsibility and awareness**. User departments will be aware that they are charged for the specific services used and may be more careful to use the facility more efficiently. They will also appreciate the true cost of the facilities that they are using and can take decisions accordingly.

(c) **Control of service department costs**. The service department may be restricted to charging a standard cost to user departments for specific jobs carried out. It will then be possible to measure the efficiency or inefficiency of the service department by recording the difference between the standard charges and the actual expenditure.

(d) **Budget information**. This information will ease the budgeting process, as the purpose and cost of service department expenditure can be separately identified.

4 Batch costing

FAST FORWARD

> **Batch costing** is similar to job costing in that each batch of similar articles is separately identifiable. The **cost per unit** manufactured in a batch is the total batch cost divided by the number of units in the batch.

Key term

> **Batch costing** is a 'form of specific order costing where costs are attributed to batches of product (unit costs can be calculated by dividing by the number of products in the batch)'.
> CIMA *Official Terminology*

4.1 Example: batch costing

A company manufactures widgets to order and has the following budgeted overheads for the year, based on normal activity levels.

Department	Budgeted overheads $	Budgeted activity
Welding	6,000	1,500 labour hours
Assembly	10,000	1,000 labour hours

Selling and administrative overheads are 20% of factory cost. An order for 250 widgets type X128, made as Batch 5997, incurred the following costs.

Materials $12,000

Labour   100 hours welding shop at $10/hour; 200 hours assembly shop at $8/hour

$500 was paid for the hire of special X-ray equipment for testing the welds.

Required

Calculate the cost per unit for Batch 5997.

Solution

The first step is to calculate the overhead absorption rate for the production departments.

$$\text{Welding} = \frac{\$6,000}{1,500} = \$4 \text{ per labour hour} \qquad \text{Assembly} = \frac{\$10,000}{1,000} = \$10 \text{ per labour hour}$$

		Total cost – Batch no 5997	
		$	$
Direct material			12,000
Direct expense			500
Direct labour	100 × $10.00	1,000	
	200 × $8.00	1,600	
			2,600
Prime cost			15,100
Overheads	100 × $4	400	
	200 × $10	2,000	
			2,400
Factory cost			17,500
Selling and administrative cost (20% of factory cost)			3,500
Total cost			21,000

$$\text{Cost per unit} = \frac{\$21,000}{250} = \$84.00$$

Question

25% profit on selling price

A printing firm is proposing offering a leaflet advertising service to local traders.

The following costs have been estimated for a batch of 10,000 leaflets.

Setting up machine	6 hours at $10 per hour
Artwork	$20 per batch
Paper	$1.80 per 100 sheets
Other printing materials	$15
Direct labour cost	4 hours at $6 per hour

Fixed overheads allocated to this side of the business are $1,000 per annum incurred at an even rate throughout the year. Overheads are recovered on the basis of orders received, which are expected to be two per week for 50 weeks in the year.

The management requires 25% profit on selling price.

(a) The selling price, to the nearest cent, per thousand leaflets, for quantities of:

     (i)   5,000 leaflets is $ ☐

     (ii)   10,000 leaflets is $ ☐

(b) During the latest week, the firm sold two batches of 10,000 leaflets and one batch of 5,000 leaflets. All costs and selling prices were as estimated.

     The profit for the week was $ ☐

Answer

(a)   (i)   **The selling price is $ 53.20**

       (ii)   **The selling price is $ 41.20**

Workings

Expected orders per annum = 2 orders × 50 weeks = 100 orders

$\therefore$ Fixed overhead per order = $\dfrac{\$1,000}{100}$ = $10

Calculation of price per 1,000 leaflets

Batch size: (leaflets)	5,000	10,000
	$	$
Setting up machine	60.00	60.00
Artwork	20.00	20.00
Paper	90.00	180.00
Other printing materials	7.50	15.00
Direct labour cost	12.00	24.00
Fixed overhead	10.00	10.00
Total cost	199.50	309.00
Profit	66.50	103.00
Selling price	266.00	412.00
Price per 1,000 leaflets	53.20	41.20

The profit is 25% on selling price ie cost (75) + profit (25) = selling price (100), and thus profit = 1/3 cost

(b)   **The profit for the week was $ | 282.50 |**

Workings

	$	$
Batch profit $66.50 × 1		66.50
$103.00 × 2		206.00
		272.50
Plus over-absorbed overhead:		
Overhead absorbed 3 batches × $10	30.00	
Overhead incurred $1,000/50 weeks	20.00	
		10.00
Profit for the week		282.50

Chapter Roundup

- **Job costing** is the costing method used where work is undertaken to customers' special requirements and each order is of comparatively short duration.

- The usual method of fixing prices within a jobbing concern is **cost plus pricing**.

- An **internal job costing system** can be used for costing the work of service departments.

- **Batch costing** is similar to job costing in that each batch of similar articles is separately identifiable. The **cost per unit** manufactured in a batch is the total batch cost divided by the number of units in the batch.

Quick Quiz

1   Which of the following are not characteristics of job costing?

    I   Customer driven production
    II   Complete production possible within a single accounting period
    III   Homogeneous products

    A   I and II only   C II and III only
    B   I and III only   D III only

2   The cost of a job is $100,000

    (a)   If profit is 25% of the job cost, the price of the job = $ ☐

    (b)   If there is a 25% margin, the price of the job = $ ☐

3   Job costing would be most appropriate for which of the following businesses?

    A   A pizza manufacturer   C   A manufacturer of sugar
    B   An architect designing a new school   D   A manufacturer of screws

4   What is a batch?

5   How would you calculate the cost per unit of a completed batch?

6   A job cost estimate includes 630 productive labour hours. In addition, it is anticipated that idle time will be 10% of the total hours paid for the job. The wage rate is $12 per hour.

    What is the total estimated labour cost for the job?

    A $6,804
    B $7,560
    C $8,316
    D $8,400

7   A firm uses job costing. Details of the three jobs worked on during a period are:

	Job BA	Job DC	Job FE
	$	$	$
Opening work-in-progress	22,760	3,190	–
Direct materials in the period	4,620	11,660	14,335
Direct labour in the period	12,125	10,520	7,695

Overheads are absorbed at 40% of prime cost in each period. Jobs DC and FE remained incomplete at the end of the period.

What is the value of the closing work-in-progress?

A $61,894
B $65,084
C $66,360
D $68,952

8   A technical writer is to set up her own business. She anticipates working a 40-hour week and taking four weeks' holiday per year. General expenses of the business are expected to be $10,000 per year, and she has set herself a target of $40,000 a year salary.

Assuming that only 90% of her time worked will be chargeable to customers, her charge for each hour of writing (to the nearest cent) should be $ ☐

9   Which of the following is/are characteristics of job costing?

☐   Customer-driven production
☐   Complete production possible within a single accounting period
☐   Homogeneous products

1   D

2   (a) $100,000 + (25% × $100,000) = $100,000 + $25,000 = $125,000

     (b)   Profit is 25 per cent of the selling price, therefore selling price should be written as 100%:

	%
Selling price	100
Profit	25
Cost	75

∴ Price = $100,000 × 100/75 = $133,333.

3   B   A pizza manufacturer would probably use batch costing. A manufacturer of sugar would probably use process costing, as would a manufacturer of screws.

4   A group of similar articles which maintains its identity during one or more stages of production and is treated as a cost unit.

5    $$\frac{\text{Total batch cost}}{\text{Number of units in the batch}}$$

6   D   (630 ÷ 0·9 hours) x $12/hour) = $8,400.

7   B   Job BA is completed so can be ignored

Total costs = (11,660 + 10,520 + 14,335 + 7,695) × 1.4

= $61,894

Closing work in progress value = 61,894 + 3,190

= $65,084

8   Charge for each hour of writing (to the nearest penny) should be $ [28.94]

Weeks worked per year   = 52 − 4 = 48

Hours worked per year   = 48 × 40 hrs

= 1,920

Hours chargeable to clients   = 1,920 × 90% = 1,728

Total expenses = $10,000 + $40,000 = $50,000

Hourly rate = $\dfrac{\$50,000}{1,728}$ = $28.94 per hour

9   ☑ Customer-driven production

     ☑ Complete production possible within a single accounting period

Each job is separately identifiable, according to a customer's requirements. Therefore the first characteristic is correct.

Jobs are usually of comparatively short duration, compared to situations where contract costing is applied. Therefore the second characteristic is correct.

The third characteristic is incorrect because each job is separately identifiable.

Now try the questions below from the Question Bank

Question numbers
77–82

Service costing

Introduction

So far in this Study Text we have looked at different types of cost and different cost accounting systems and the inference has been that we have been discussing a **manufacturing** organisation. Most of the cost accounting principles we have looked at so far can also be applied to **service organisations**, however.

In this chapter we will therefore look at the costing method used by service organisations which we will call **service costing**. As you study this chapter, you will see how the knowledge you have built up can be applied easily to service organisations.

In the final section of this chapter we'll think about managerial reports, and the type of information managers of a range of organisations require.

Topic list	Syllabus references
1 Service costing	D2(b)
2 Management reports	D2(a),(b)

1 Service costing

Service organisations do not make or sell tangible goods.

1.1 What are service organisations?

Profit-seeking service organisations include accountancy firms, law firms, management consultants, transport companies, banks, insurance companies and hotels. **The majority of not-for-profit organisations** including **charities** and the **public sector** are also service organisations. Examples of these are hospitals, advice agencies, libraries and training organisations.

1.2 Service costing versus other costing methods

(a) With many services, the **cost of direct materials consumed will be relatively small** compared to the labour, direct expenses and overheads cost. In product costing the direct materials are often a greater proportion of the total cost.

(b) Because of the difficulty of identifying costs with specific cost units in service costing, the **indirect costs tend to represent a higher proportion** of total cost compared with product costing.

(c) The **output** of most service organisations is often **intangible** and hence difficult to define. It is therefore **difficult to establish a measurable cost unit**.

(d) The service industry includes such a **wide range of organisations** which provide such different services and have such **different cost structures** that **costing will vary** considerably from one service to another.

(e) There is often a **high fixed cost of maintaining an organisation's total capacity**, which may be **very under utilised at certain times**. Consider the demand for railway and bus services, for example. Demand at midday is likely to be much lower than demand during the rush hours. The costing system must therefore be comprehensive enough to show the effects of this type of demand on the costs of operation. This often involves the analysis of costs into fixed and variable components, and the use of marginal costing techniques and breakeven analysis. **'Cut-price' prices** can then be offered, which might produce a low but still positive contribution to the organisation's high operational fixed costs.

You should bear in mind, however, that service organisations often have **large-scale operations** (think about power stations, large city hospitals) that require **sophisticated cost control techniques to manage the very high level of costs involved**. One such technique is control using flexible budgets, which we looked at in Chapter 10, and which can apply equally to service organisations as to manufacturing ones.

1.3 Characteristics of services

Specific characteristics of services

- Intangibility
- Simultaneity
- Perishability
- Heterogeneity

Assessment focus point

Make sure you learn the four specific characteristics of services. This will help you identify organisations that might use service costing.

Consider the service of providing a haircut.

(a) A haircut is **intangible** in itself, and the performance of the service comprises many other intangible factors, like the music in the salon, the personality of the hairdresser, the quality of the coffee.

(b) The production and consumption of a haircut are **simultaneous,** and therefore it cannot be inspected for quality in advance, nor can it be returned if it is not what was required.

(c) Haircuts are **perishable,** that is, they cannot be stored. You cannot buy them in bulk, and the hairdresser cannot do them in advance and keep them stocked away in case of heavy demand. The incidence of work in progress in service organisations is less frequent than in other types of organisation.

(d) A haircut is **heterogeneous** and so the exact service received will vary each time: not only will two hairdressers cut hair differently, but a hairdresser will not consistently deliver the same standard of haircut.

1.4 Cost units and service costing

FAST FORWARD

One main problem with service costing is being able to define a **realistic cost unit** that represents a suitable measure of the service provided. If the service is a function of two activity variables, a **composite cost unit** may be more appropriate.

A particular problem with service costing is the difficulty in defining a realistic cost unit that represents a suitable measure of the service provided. Frequently, a **composite cost unit** may be deemed more appropriate if the service is a function of two activity variables. Hotels, for example, may use the **'occupied bed-night'** as an appropriate unit for cost ascertainment and control. You may remember that we discussed such cost units in Chapter 2.

Assessment focus point

An objective test question in a previous syllabus assessment asked candidates to identify characteristics of service costing from a number of different characteristics listed. The two relevant characteristics in the particular list provided were:

- High levels of indirect cost as a proportion of total cost
- Use of composite cost units

A similar question may come up in your computer-based assessment: be prepared!

1.4.1 Typical cost units used by companies operating in a service industry

Service	Cost unit
Road, rail and air transport services	Passenger-kilometre, tonne-kilometre
Hotels	Occupied bed-night
Education	Full-time student
Hospitals	Patient-day
Catering establishments	Meal served

Each organisation will need to ascertain the cost unit most appropriate to its activities.

Assessment focus point

Make sure that you are familiar with suitable composite cost units for common forms of service operation such as transport.

1.4.2 Cost per unit

$$\text{Average cost per unit of service} = \frac{\text{Total costs incurred in the period}}{\text{Number of service units supplied in the period}}$$

1.4.3 The use of unit cost measures in not-for-profit organisations

The success of not-for-profit organisations cannot be judged in terms of profitability, nor against competition.

Not-for-profit organisations include **private sector** organisations such as charities and churches and **much of the public sector** (the National Health Service, the police, schools and so on).

Commercial organisations generally have profit or market competition as the objectives which guide the process of managing resources economically, efficiently and effectively. However, **not-for-profit organisations cannot** by definition **be judged by profitability nor do they generally have to be successful against competition**, so other methods of assessing performance have to be used.

Most **financial measures** of performance for not-for-profits therefore tend to be **cost based**. Costs are collected relative to some measure of output and a **unit cost** calculated as described above.

Unit cost measures in not-for-profit organisations have three main **uses**.

(a)   **As a measure of relative efficiency**

Efficiency means **getting out as much as possible for what goes in.**

Most not-for-profit organisations do not face competition but this does not mean that all not-for-profit organisations are unique. Bodies like local governments, health services and so on can **compare** their performance **against each other. Unit cost measurements** like 'cost per patient day' or 'cost of borrowing one library book' can be established to allow organisations to assess whether they are doing better or worse than their counterparts.

Bear in mind, however, that the comparisons are only valid if, say, the hospitals cater for broadly the same type of patients, the same illnesses, are similarly equipped and so on. **Cost comparisons are only valid if like is being compared with like**.

(b)   **As a measure of efficiency over time**

Unit costs of the same organisation can be compared from period to period. This will help to highlight whether efficiency is increasing or decreasing over time.

(c)   **As an aid to cost control**

If unit costs are produced on a regular basis and compared with other similar organisations, this will help to control costs and should engender a more cost-conscious attitude.

1.4.4 Example: cost units in not-for-profit organisations

Suppose that at a cost of $40,000 and 4,000 hours (**inputs**) in an average year, two policemen travel 8,000 miles and are instrumental in 200 arrests (**outputs**). A large number of **possibly meaningful measures** can be derived from these few figures.

		$40,000	4,000 hours	8,000 miles	200 arrests
Cost	$40,000		$40,000/4,000 = $10 per hour	$40,000/8,000 = $5 per mile	$40,000/200 = $200 per arrest
Time	4,000 hrs	4,000/$40,000 = 6 minutes patrolling per $1 spent		4,000/8,000 = ½ hour to patrol 1 mile	4,000/200 = 20 hours per arrest
Miles	8,000	8,000/$40,000 = 0.2 of a mile per $1	8,000/4,000 = 2 miles patrolled per hour		8,000/200 = 40 miles per arrest
Arrests	200	200/$40,000 = 1 arrest per $200	200/4,000 = 1 arrest every 20 hours	200/8,000 = 1 arrest every 40 miles	

These measures do not necessarily identify cause and effect or personal responsibility and accountability. Actual performance needs to be **compared** to the following.

- **Standards**, if there are any
- Similar external activities
- Similar internal activities
- **Targets**
- Over time – ie as trends

1.4.5 Limitations of using unit costs

(a) **Quality of performance is ignored**. Cost per patient day tells us nothing about the quality of the care provided, whether the patients are cured and so on.

(b) **The input mix will vary**. For example, the average cost per patient in a intensive care ward is likely to be higher than the average cost per patient in a post-operative recovery ward.

(c) **Inputs rather than objectives are measured**. Inputs might be the number of eye operations carried out in a hospital but cost per eye operation does not give any indication of the objective of the eye department in a hospital, which might be something along the lines of improving the quality of life of people with eye problems.

(d) **Regional differences are not taken into consideration**. For example, the cost of refuse collection in rural areas will probably be higher than in towns and cities because of the distance to be travelled.

The following examples will illustrate the principles involved in service costing and the further considerations to bear in mind when costing services.

Question | Service costing companies

Which of the following organisations should not be advised to use service costing.

A   Freight rail company
B   IT department of a company
C   Catering company
D   Clothing company

D   All of the activities would use service costing except the clothing manufacturer which will provide products not services.

1.5 Example: costing an educational establishment

A university offers a range of degree courses. The university organisation structure consists of three faculties each with a number of teaching departments. In addition, there is a university administrative/management function and a central services function.

(a)   The following cost information is available for the year ended 30 June 20X3.

(i)   **Occupancy costs**

Total $1,500,000

Such costs are apportioned on the basis of area used which is as follows.

	Square metres
Faculties	7,500
Teaching departments	20,000
Administration/management	7,000
Central services	3,000

(ii)   **Administrative/management costs**

Direct costs: $1,775,000
Indirect costs: an apportionment of occupancy costs

Direct and indirect costs are charged to degree courses on a percentage basis.

(iii)   **Faculty costs**

Direct costs: $700,000
Indirect costs: an apportionment of occupancy costs and central service costs

Direct and indirect costs are charged to teaching departments.

(iv)   **Teaching departments**

Direct costs: $5,525,000
Indirect costs: an apportionment of occupancy costs and central service costs plus all faculty costs

Direct and indirect costs are charged to degree courses on a percentage basis.

(v)   **Central services**

Direct costs: $1,000,000
Indirect costs: an apportionment of occupancy costs

(b)   Direct and indirect costs of central services have, in previous years, been charged to users on a percentage basis. A study has now been completed which has estimated what user areas would have paid external suppliers for the same services on an individual basis. For the year ended 30 June 20X3, the apportionment of the central services cost is to be recalculated in a manner which recognises the cost savings achieved by using the central services facilities instead of using external service companies. This is to be done by apportioning the overall savings to user areas in proportion to their share of the estimated external costs.

The estimated external costs of service provision are as follows.

	$'000
Faculties	240
Teaching departments	800
Degree courses:	
Business studies	32
Mechanical engineering	48
Catering studies	32
All other degrees	448
	1,600

(c)   Additional data relating to the degree courses is as follows.

		Degree course	
	Business studies	Mechanical engineering	Catering studies
Number of graduates	80	50	120
Apportioned costs (as % of totals)			
Teaching departments	3.0%	2.5%	7%
Administration/management	2.5%	5.0%	4%

Central services are to be apportioned as detailed in (b) above.

The total number of undergraduates from the university in the year to 30 June 20X3 was 2,500.

Required

(a)   Calculate the average cost per undergraduate for the year ended 30 June 20X3.

(b)   Calculate the average cost per undergraduate for each of the degrees in business studies, mechanical engineering and catering studies, showing all relevant cost analysis.

Solution

(a)   The average cost per undergraduate is as follows.

	Total costs for university
	$'000
Occupancy	1,500
Admin/management	1,775
Faculty	700
Teaching departments	5,525
Central services	1,000
	10,500
Number of undergraduates	2,500
Average cost per undergraduate for year ended 30 June 20X3	$4,200

(b)   Average cost per undergraduate for each course is as follows.

	Business studies $	Mechanical engineering $	Catering studies $
Teaching department costs			
(W1 and using % in question)	241,590	201,325	563,710
Admin/management costs			
(W1 and using % in question)	51,375	102,750	82,200
Central services (W2)	22,400	33,600	22,400
	315,365	337,675	668,310
Number of undergraduates	80	50	120
Average cost per undergraduate for year			
ended 30 June 20X3	$3,942	$6,754	$5,569

Workings

1   Cost allocation and apportionment

Cost item	Basis of apportionment	Teaching departments $'000	Admin/ management $'000	Central services $'000	Faculties $'000
Direct costs	allocation	5,525	1,775	1,000	700
Occupancy costs	area used	800	280	120	300
Central services					
reapportioned	(W2)	560	–	(1,120)	168
Faculty costs					
reallocated	allocation	1,168	–	–	(1,168)
		8,053	2,055		

2   Apportioning savings to user areas on the basis given in the question gives the same result as apportioning internal costs in proportion to the external costs.

	External costs $'000	Apportionment of internal central service costs $'000
Faculties	240	168.0
Teaching	800	560.0
Degree courses:		
Business studies	32	22.4
Mechanical engineering	48	33.6
Catering studies	32	22.4
All other degrees	448	313.6
	1,600	1,120.0

Question   Service cost units

Briefly describe cost units that are appropriate to a transport business.

The cost unit is the basic measure of control in an organisation, used to monitor cost and activity levels. The cost unit selected must be measurable and appropriate for the type of cost and activity. Possible cost units which could be suggested are as follows.

Cost per kilometre

- Variable cost per kilometre

- Fixed cost per kilometre – however this is not particularly useful for control purposes because it will tend to vary with the kilometres run.

- Total cost of each vehicle per kilometre – this suffers from the same problem as above

- Maintenance cost of each vehicle per kilometre

Cost per tonne-kilometre

This can be more useful than a cost per kilometre for control purposes, because it combines the distance travelled and the load carried, both of which affect cost.

Cost per operating hour

Once again, many costs can be related to this cost unit, including the following.

- Total cost of each vehicle per operating hour

- Variable costs per operating hour

- Fixed costs per operating hour – this suffers from the same problems as the fixed cost per kilometre in terms of its usefulness for control purposes.

Question   Cost per tonne – kilometre

Carry Co operates a small fleet of delivery vehicles. Expected costs are as follows.

Loading	1 hour per tonne loaded
Loading costs:	
Labour (casual)	$2 per hour
Equipment depreciation	$80 per week
Supervision	$80 per week
Drivers' wages (fixed)	$100 per man per week
Petrol	10c per kilometre
Repairs	5c per kilometre
Depreciation	$80 per week per vehicle
Supervision	$120 per week
Other general expenses (fixed)	$200 per week

There are two drivers and two vehicles in the fleet.

During a slack week, only six journeys were made.

Journey	Tonnes carried (one way)	One-way distance of journey Kilometres
1	5	100
2	8	20
3	2	60
4	4	50
5	6	200
6	5	300

The expected average full cost per tonne-kilometre for the week is $ [   ] .

Answer

The expected average full cost per tonne-kilometre for the week is $ 0.304

Workings

Variable costs

Journey	1	2	3	4	5	6
	$	$	$	$	$	$
Loading labour	10	16	4	8	12	10
Petrol (both ways)	20	4	12	10	40	60
Repairs (both ways)	10	2	6	5	20	30
	40	22	22	23	72	100

Total costs

	$
Variable costs (total for journeys 1 to 6)	279
Loading equipment depreciation	80
Loading supervision	80
Drivers' wages	200
Vehicles depreciation	160
Drivers' supervision	120
Other costs	200
	1,119

Journey	Tonnes	One-way distance Kilometres	Tonne-kilometres
1	5	100	500
2	8	20	160
3	2	60	120
4	4	50	200
5	6	200	1,200
6	5	300	1,500
			3,680

Cost per tonne-kilometre $\dfrac{\$1,119}{3,680} = \$0.304$

Note that the large element of fixed costs may distort this measure but that a variable cost per tonne-kilometre of $279/3,680 = $0.076 may be useful for budgetary control.

Mr G and Mrs H have recently formed a consultancy business, and have sought your advice concerning costs and fees. Both wish to receive a salary of $20,000 in the first year of trading. They have purchased two cars at a cost of $13,000 each and expect to use them for three years. At the end of this time each of the cars has an expected resale value of $4,000. Straight-line depreciation is to be applied.

Mr G and Mrs H expect to work for eight hours per day, five days per week for 45 weeks per year. They refer to this as *available time*. 25% of the available time is expected to be used for dealing with administrative matters related to their own business, and in the first year it is expected that there will be idle time which will average 22.5% of the available time. The remainder of the available time is expected to be chargeable to clients.

Mr G and Mrs H agreed that their fee structure should comprise the following.

- An hourly rate for productive client work
- An hourly rate for travelling to/from clients
- A rate per mile travelled to/from clients

They expect that the travelling time will equal 25% of their chargeable time, and will amount to a total of 18,000 miles. They have agreed that this time should be charged at one-third of their normal hourly rate.

Apart from the costs referred to above, Mr G and Mrs H have estimated their other costs for the first twelve months as follows.

	$
Electricity	1,200
Fuel for vehicles	1,800
Insurance – professional liability and office	600
Insurance – vehicles	800
Mobile telephones	1,200
Office rent and rates	8,400
Office telephone/facsimile	1,800
Postage and stationery	500
Secretarial costs	8,400
Servicing and repairs of vehicles	1,200
Vehicle road tax	280

The consultancy business should break even after paying the required salaries.

If costs are classified as either professional services costs or vehicle costs, then, on the basis of the above data and costs,

(a)   the hourly rate for productive client work is $ ☐

(b)   the hourly rate for travelling to/from clients is $ ☐

(c)   the rate per mile travelled to/from clients is $ ☐

Answer

(a) The rate is $ [39.43]

(b) The rate is $ [13.14]

(c) The rate is $ [0.56]

Workings

Cost analysis

	Professional services costs $	Vehicle costs $
Electricity	1,200	
Fuel for vehicles		1,800
Insurance: professional liability and office	600	
vehicles		800
Mobile telephones (note 1)	1,200	
Office rent and rates	8,400	
Office telephone/fax	1,800	
Postage and stationery	500	
Secretarial costs	8,400	
Servicing and repairs of vehicles		1,200
Vehicle road tax		280
Vehicle depreciation (note 2)		6,000
Salaries	40,000	
	62,100	10,080

Notes

1   It is assumed that mobile telephones are used in providing professional services and that their use is not consequent on travelling.

2   Annual depreciation = $\dfrac{\$13,000 - \$4,000}{3} \times 2 \text{ cars} = \$6,000$

Analysis of available time

Total hours per annum	$(8 \times 5 \times 45) \times 2$ people =	3,600 available hours
Less: administration	25.0%	
idle time	22.5%	
	47.5% × 3,600 =	(1,710) hours
		1,890 hours
Travelling time (25%)		427.5 hours
Productive time (75%)		1,417.5 hours

Rates

Travelling time is to be charged at one third of the normal hourly rate.

'Weighted' chargeable time	=	1,417.5 + (472.5/3)
	=	1,575 hours
∴ Rate per productive hour	=	$62,100/1,575

(a) Hourly rate for productive client work = $39.43
(b) Hourly rate for travelling (÷ 3) = $13.14
(c) Rate per mile travelled = $10,080/18,000
   = $0.56

1.6 Job costing and services

Remember that job costing applies where work is undertaken to customers' special requirements. An organisation may therefore be working in the service sector but may supply one-off services which meet particular customers' special requirements; in such a situation job costing may be more appropriate than service costing. For example, a consultancy business, although part of the service sector, could use job costing.

2 Management reports

FAST FORWARD

Management reports based on cost accounting information should be formatted to aid management to cost products and services, and to plan, control and make decisions.

We finish this Study Text by referring you back to the very first sections of the very first chapter.

Cost accounting provides **information** for management to enable them to **cost products or services**, and to **plan**, **control** and **make decisions**.

The **format of cost accounting reports** is entirely at **management discretion**. Each organisation can devise its own management accounting system and format of reports.

So, whatever the type of organisation, be it production or service, commercial or not-for-profit, private sector or public sector, the **cost accounting management reports should be formatted in the most appropriate way so as to provide information to management to enable them to cost products/services, plan, control and make decision**.

As you have worked through this part of the Study Text in particular you should have noticed the sort of information management of organisations in job, batch, process and service industries need.

2.1 Information for management

For example, suppose a private hospital has three main revenue earning departments – maternity, surgical and orthopaedic. These departments are supported by many other departments, some of which also earn revenue by charging for services undertaken for external customers.

The radiology department is one of these departments. In addition to undertaking x-ray work for the above three hospital departments, it charges for external work involved in carrying out x-rays on patients who have been referred to it by doctors in general practice. After this work has been done, patients may continue their treatment within the hospital.

Let's have a think about the **type of information** which ought to be provided within the hospital for **operational control** and for **making proper charges for services**.

2.1.1 Information for operational control

(a) **Responsibility centres**

For effective operational control each department within the hospital should be a **separate cost** or **profit centre** with a manager responsible for the performance of each centre.

Those centres which have a measurable output, such as the maternity, surgical, orthopaedic and radiology departments, can be designated as profit centres since it is possible to determine their **revenue** and therefore their **profit**. Other departments would operate as cost centres, responsible for the **control of their own costs**.

(b) **Coding systems**

The information system should contain an efficient coding system to ensure that all costs and revenues are charged and credited to the **correct responsibility centre**.

(c) **Control reports**

The costs and revenues collected for each centre should be reported to the manager of the centre on a **regular basis**, at least **monthly**.

The reports should show separately **controllable** and **uncontrollable** items. For example the costs directly incurred by the department, which are under the control of the **responsibility centre** manager, should be separated from the **uncontrollable costs**. The latter would include items such as central administration charges. Although there is an argument for excluding these charges altogether, it can be useful to show them on the **control reports** so that managers are aware of the cost of providing them with administrative support services.

(d) **Establishing a basis for comparison**

The most effective way of achieving **operational control** is to **compare** each department's **costs**, and **revenues** if appropriate, with some form of yardstick.

The best basis of comparison is a **budget**, which should be divided into **time periods** according to the frequency with which **control reports** will be prepared.

Variances can then be calculated and analysed. A system of **exception reporting** should be adopted so that the busy manager's attention is drawn to those areas where management action is most urgently needed.

(e) **Determining appropriate cost units**

For those departments with measurable activity a suitable **cost unit** or a series of cost units should be established. This is particularly applicable where **output** can be **standardised**, or where **activities** can be **analysed** into a series of standard tasks such as taking an x-ray.

The cost units can be used to **control costs** by establishing a **standard cost** and providing mangers with information which compares actual unit cost with standard and which identifies any **variances**.

(f) **Flexible budgets**

Control information can be improved if it is based on a system of **flexible budgets**. This is particularly relevant if **activity levels fluctuate** and a significant proportion of costs is **variable**.

Once a cost unit has been established the budget cost allowance for the period can be determined based on the actual activity achieved. This will enable a more **realistic budget comparison** for more **effective operational control**.

(g)   **Ad hoc reports and future projections**

As well as routine reports, the hospital information system should be capable of providing **ad hoc advice** for managers on the cost and revenue affects of **proposed activities**. For example it should be possible to project future costs for the purpose of tendering for work.

2.1.2 Information for charging for services

A well designed information system will provide the basis for making **proper charges** for services.

Once a suitable cost unit has been established the system should be capable of accurately measuring the **units of activity** so that the correct charge is made for services provided.

For tendering and quotation purposes it will be necessary to be able to **project costs** in order to determine a **reasonable price** to be charged. This will require an understanding of the **cost behaviour pattern** for each department.

The **standard cost** used for **operational control** could provide the basis for charging for services. An activity based analysis may provide a better understanding of the cost of services provided. For example the process of taking an x-ray could be broken down into a series of activities with a separate **cost driver** for each (the cost per patient transported to x-ray, and the cost per film processed for example).

Once a realistic standard cost has been established, management can decide on the required margin to be added to achieve a price for the service provided.

2.2 Figures for management

Here are some figures that might be highlighted in some (or many) management reports.

(a)   **Gross revenue** is income (at invoice values) received for goods and services over some given period of time. It is used as an indicator of the level of demand for the organisation's product or services.

(b)   **Value-added** is **sales less cost of bought-in materials and services**, and represents the wealth or value created by an organisation's operations. It is affected only by costs incurred internally, such as labour, and is therefore useful as a target. (Sometimes value added is calculated as profit plus interest plus all conversion costs).

(c)   **Contribution** is the difference between sales revenue and variable costs of sale. It is used in decision making as fixed costs are not relevant to many business decisions.

(d)   **Gross margin** is the ratio of gross profit to sales revenue and is used to look into the relationship between production/purchasing costs and sales revenues and to analyse the pure trading activities of an organisation. It can be increased by raising prices and/or by negotiating lower prices with suppliers. It is calculated as ((sales − cost of sales)/sales for the period) × 100%.

(e)   **Marketing expense** may be compared to revenue on a period by period basis to see whether the expenditure has produced the desired increase in sales and in which areas.

(f)   **General and administrative expenses** need to be carefully controlled in order to keep net profit margins at an acceptable level. They may be targeted as an area for cost reduction if the organisation is trying to improve its profitability.

Chapter Roundup

- **Service organisations** do not make or sell tangible goods.

- **Specific characteristics of services**

    - Intangibility
    - Simultaneity
    - Perishability
    - Heterogeneity

- One main problem with service costing is being able to define a **realistic cost unit** that represents a suitable measure of the service provided. If the service is a function of two activity variables, a **composite cost unit** may be more appropriate.

- **Average cost per unit of service** = $\dfrac{\text{Total costs incurred in the period}}{\text{Number of service units supplied in the period}}$

- **The success of not-for-profit organisations** cannot be judged in terms of profitability, nor against competition.

- **Management reports** based on cost accounting information should be formatted to aid management to cost products and services, and to plan, control and make decisions.

Quick Quiz

1   With many services the cost of direct materials will be relatively high.

     True   ☐

     False   ☐

2   Match up the following services with their typical cost units

Service		Cost unit
Hotels		Patient-day
Education	?	Meal served
Hospitals		Full-time student
Catering organisations		Occupied bed-night

3   What are the specific characteristics of services.

     I   Intangibility
     II   Heterogeneity
     III   Perishability
     IV   Consistency
     V   Regularity
     VI   Simultaneity

     A   I, III, V and VI
     B   II, III, IV and V
     C   I, II, III and VI
     D   II, IV, V and VI

4   Average cost per unit of service = $\dfrac{.............................}{.............................}$

5   Value added is:

A   Sales less cost of materials and services
B   Sales less labour cost
C   Sales less internally generated costs
D   Sales less cost of bought-in materials and services

6   Which two of the following might be characteristic of a hospital?

☐   Use of composite cost units

☐   Use of equivalent units

☐   High levels of indirect costs as a proportion of total cost

☐   Calculation of profit per patient

7   Which of the following are characteristics of service costing?

☐   High levels of indirect costs as a proportion of total cost

☐   Cost units are often intangible

☐   Use of composite cost units

☐   Use of equivalent units

8   Which of the following would be suitable cost units for a hospital?

☐   Patient/day

☐   Operating theatre hour

☐   Ward

☐   X-ray department

☐   Outpatient visit

1   False. Labour, direct expenses and overheads will be a greater proportion of total cost.

2
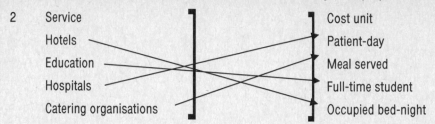

Service	Cost unit
Hotels	Patient-day
Education	Meal served
Hospitals	Full-time student
Catering organisations	Occupied bed-night

3   C

4   $$\text{Average cost per unit of service} = \frac{\text{Total costs incurred in the period}}{\text{Number of service units supplied in the period}}$$

5   D

6   Service costing characteristics include composite cost units and high levels of indirect costs as a proportion of total cost. Not-for-profit organisations such as hospitals would not measure performance on profit so profit per patient would be inappropriate. Equivalent units are used in process costing, not service costing.

7   ☑ High levels of indirect costs as a proportion of total cost

   ☑ Cost units are often intangible

   ☑ Use of composite cost units

In service costing it is difficult to identify many attributable direct costs. Many costs must be treated as **indirect costs** and **shared over several cost units**, therefore the first characteristic does apply. Many services are **intangible**, for example a haircut or a cleaning service provide no physical, tangible product. Therefore the second characteristic does apply. **Composite cost units** such as passenger-mile or bed-night are often used in service costing, therefore the third characteristic does apply. The fourth characteristic does not apply because equivalent units are more often used in **costing for tangible products.**

8   ☑ Patient/day

   ☑ Operating theatre hour

   ☑ Outpatient visit

All of the above would be **measurable** and would be **useful for control purposes.** A ward and an x-ray department are more likely to be used as **cost centres** for the purpose of cost collection and analysis.

Now try the questions below from the Question Bank

Question numbers
83–88

Part E

Decision making

15

Decision making and investment appraisal

Introduction

Another other decision that organisations face is how to compare costs and benefits. Some simple approaches take no account of when costs or revenues are incurred or received. However **discounted cash flow approaches** (net present value and payback) take a more sophisticated approach, being based on the principle that a pound received in the future is not worth as much as a pound received today. We shall explain how each of these approaches work, and have a look at their advantages and limitations.

The final part of the chapter looks at short-term decision making where there is a choice between **making or buying** in components for production.

Topic list	Syllabus references
1 Relevant costs	E2(a)
2 Make or buy decisions	E2(b)
3 Steps in project appraisal	E3(a)
4 Methods of project appraisal	E3(a)
5 The payback period	E3(a),(b)
6 The time value of money	E3(a),(b)
7 Discounted cash flow	E3(a),(b)
8 Public sector capital budgeting decisions	E3(a)

1 Relevant costs

FAST FORWARD

> **Relevant costs** are future cash flows arising as a direct consequence of a decision.
>
> Relevant costs are **future**, **incremental cashflows**.

1.1 Relevant costs

Key term

> A **relevant cost** is a cost that is incurred incrementally as a result of a possible future course of action that would not be incurred if the course of action is not chosen.

Decision making should be based on relevant costs.

(a)   **Relevant costs are future incremental costs**. A decision is about the future and it cannot alter what has been done already. Costs that have been incurred in the past are totally irrelevant to any decision that is being made 'now'. Such costs are **past costs** or **sunk costs**.

An example of a sunk cost is development costs which have already been incurred. Suppose that a company has spent $250,000 in developing a new service for customers, but the marketing department's most recent findings are that the service might not gain customer acceptance and could be a commercial failure. The decision whether or not to abandon the development of the new service would have to be taken, but the $250,000 spent so far should be ignored by the decision makers because it is a sunk cost.

Costs that have been incurred include not only costs that have already been paid, but also costs that have been **committed**. A **committed cost** is a future cash flow that will be incurred anyway, regardless of the decision taken now.

(b)   **Relevant costs are cash flows**. Only cash flow information is required. This means that costs or charges which do not reflect **additional cash spending** (such as depreciation and notional costs) should be ignored for the purpose of decision making.

Other terms are sometimes used to describe relevant costs.

Key term

> An **opportunity cost.** The value of the benefit sacrificed when one course of action is chosen, in preference to an alternative.
>
> **Avoidable costs** are costs that could be avoided if the activity or sector of the business is discontinued. These costs are usually associated with shutdown or divestment decisions.

The following example will help you to understand opportunity cost, which is a concept you will come across repeatedly in your future studies.

Suppose that there are three options, A, B and C, only one of which can be chosen. The net profit from each would be $80, $100 and $70 respectively.

Since only one option can be selected option B would be chosen because it offers the biggest benefit.

	$
Profit from option B	100
Less opportunity cost (ie the benefit from the most profitable alternative, A)	80
Differential benefit of option B	20

The decision to choose option B would not be taken simply because it offers a profit of $100, but because it offers a differential profit of $20 in excess of the next best alternative.

1.2 Non-relevant variable costs

There might be occasions when a variable cost is in fact a sunk cost (and therefore a **non-relevant variable cost**). For example, suppose that a company has some units of raw material in inventory. They have been paid for already, and originally cost $2,000. They are now obsolete and are no longer used in regular production, and they have no scrap value. However, they could be used in a special job which the company is trying to decide whether to undertake. The special job is a 'one-off' customer order, and would use up all these materials in inventory.

(a)   In deciding whether the job should be undertaken, the relevant cost of the materials to the special job is nil. Their original cost of $2,000 is a **sunk cost**, and should be ignored in the decision.

(b)   However, if the materials did have a scrap value of, say, $300, then their relevant cost to the job would be the **opportunity cost** of being unable to sell them for scrap, ie $300.

1.3 Attributable fixed costs

There might be occasions when a fixed cost is a relevant cost, and you must be aware of the distinction between **'specific'** or **'directly attributable' fixed costs**, and general fixed overheads.

Directly attributable fixed costs are those costs which, although fixed within a relevant range of activity level are relevant to a decision for either of the following reasons.

(a)   They could increase if certain extra activities were undertaken. For example, it may be necessary to employ an extra supervisor if a particular order is accepted. The extra salary would be an **attributable fixed cost**.

(b)   They would decrease or be eliminated entirely if a decision were taken either to reduce the scale of operations or shut down entirely.

General fixed overheads are those fixed overheads which will be unaffected by decisions to increase or decrease the scale of operations, perhaps because they are an apportioned share of the fixed costs of items which would be completely unaffected by the decisions. General fixed overheads are unlikely to be relevant in decision making.

1.4 Absorbed overhead

Absorbed overhead is a **notional** accounting cost and hence should be ignored for decision-making purposes. It is **overhead incurred** which may be relevant to a decision.

1.5 The relevant cost of materials

The relevant cost of raw materials is generally their **current replacement cost**, *unless* the materials have already been purchased and would not be replaced once used. In this case the relevant cost of using them is the **higher** of the following.

• Their current resale value
• The value they would obtain if they were put to an alternative use

If the materials have no resale value and no other possible use, then the relevant cost of using them for the opportunity under consideration would be nil.

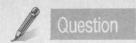

Question

Relevant cost of materials

O'Reilly Co has been approached by a customer who would like a special job to be done for him, and who is willing to pay $22,000 for it. The job would require the following materials.

Material	Total units required	Units already in inventory	Book value of units in inventory $/unit	Realisable value $/unit	Replacement cost $/unit
A	1,000	0	–	–	6
B	1,000	600	2	2.50	5
C	1,000	700	3	2.50	4
D	200	200	4	6.00	9

Material B is used regularly by O'Reilly Co, and if units of B are required for this job, they would need to be replaced to meet other production demand.

Materials C and D are in inventory as the result of previous over-buying, and they have a restricted use. No other use could be found for material C, but the units of material D could be used in another job as substitute for 300 units of material E, which currently costs $5 per unit (of which the company has no units in inventory at the moment).

Required

Calculate the relevant costs of material for deciding whether or not to accept the contract.

Answer

(a) **Material A** is not yet owned. It would have to be bought in full at the replacement cost of $6 per unit.

(b) **Material B** is used regularly by the company. There are existing inventories (600 units) but if these are used on the contract under review a further 600 units would be bought to replace them. Relevant costs are therefore 1,000 units at the replacement cost of $5 per unit.

(c) 1,000 units of **material C** are needed and 700 are already in inventory. If used for the contract, a further 300 units must be bought at $4 each. The existing inventories of 700 will not be replaced. If they are used for the contract, they could not be sold at $2.50 each. The realisable value of these 700 units is an opportunity cost of sales revenue forgone.

(d) The required units of **material D** are already in inventory and will not be replaced. There is an opportunity cost of using D in the contract because there are alternative opportunities either to sell the existing inventories for $6 per unit ($1,200 in total) or avoid other purchases (of material E), which would cost 300 x $5 = $1,500. Since substitution for E is more beneficial, $1,500 is the opportunity cost.

(e) **Summary of relevant costs**

	$
Material A (1,000 × $6)	6,000
Material B (1,000 × $5)	5,000
Material C (300 × $4) plus (700 × $2.50)	2,950
Material D	1,500
Total	15,450

1.6 The relevant cost of labour

The relevant cost of labour, in different situations, is best explained by means of an example.

1.6.1 Example: Relevant cost of labour

LW Co is currently deciding whether to undertake a new contract. 15 hours of labour will be required for the contract. LW Co currently produces product L, the standard cost details of which are shown below.

STANDARD COST CARD
PRODUCT L

	$/unit
Direct materials (10kg @ $2)	20
Direct labour (5 hrs @ $6)	30
	50
Selling price	72
Contribution	22

(a)   What is the relevant cost of labour if the labour must be hired from outside the organisation?

(b)   What is the relevant cost of labour if LW Co expects to have 5 hours spare capacity?

(c)   What is the relevant cost of labour if labour is in short supply?

Solution

(a)   Where labour must be hired from outside the organisation, the relevant cost of labour will be the variable costs incurred.

Relevant cost of labour on new contract = 15 hours @ $6 = $90

(b)   It is assumed that the 5 hours spare capacity will be paid anyway, and so if these 5 hours are used on another contract, there is no additional cost to LW plc.

Relevant cost of labour on new contract

	$
Direct labour (10 hours @ $6)	60
Spare capacity (5 hours @ $0)	0
	60

(c)   Contribution earned per unit of Product L produced = $22

If it requires 5 hours of labour to make one unit of product L, the contribution earned per labour hour = $22/5 = $4.40.

Relevant cost of labour on new contract

	$
Direct labour (15 hours @ $6)	90
Contribution lost by not making product L ($4.40 × 15 hours)	66
	154

It is important that you should be able to identify the relevant costs which are appropriate to a decision. In many cases, this is a fairly straightforward problem, but there are cases where great care should be taken.

Assessment focus point

In NPV calculations, finance costs are irrelevant as interest is taken into account in the discounting process.

2 Make or buy decisions

Make or buy analysis involves calculating whether it **is cheaper to produce** a component internally **or to purchase** it from an external source.

A **make or buy problem** involves a decision by an organisation about whether it should make a product/carry out an activity with its own internal resources, or whether it should pay another organisation to make the product/carry out the activity. Examples of make or buy decisions would be as follows.

(a)   Whether a company should manufacture its own components, or buy the components from an outside supplier.

(b)   Whether a construction company should do some work with its own employees, or whether it should subcontract the work to another company.

(c)   Whether the design and development of a new computer system should be entrusted to in-house data processing staff or whether an external software house should be hired to do the work.

The 'make' option should give management more direct control over the work, but the 'buy' option often has the benefit that the external organisation has a specialist skill and expertise in the work. Make or buy decisions should certainly not be based exclusively on cost considerations.

If an organisation has the freedom of choice about whether to make internally or buy externally and has no scarce resources that put a restriction on what it can do itself, the relevant costs for the decision will be the **differential costs** between the two options.

2.1 Example: make or buy

Buster Co makes four components, W, X, Y and Z, for which costs in the forthcoming year are expected to be as follows.

	W	X	Y	Z
Production (units)	1,000	2,000	4,000	3,000
Unit marginal costs	$	$	$	$
Direct materials	4	5	2	4
Direct labour	8	9	4	6
Variable production overheads	2	3	1	2
	14	17	7	12

Directly attributable fixed costs per annum and committed fixed costs are as follows.

	$
Incurred as a direct consequence of making W	1,000
Incurred as a direct consequence of making X	5,000
Incurred as a direct consequence of making Y	6,000
Incurred as a direct consequence of making Z	8,000
Other fixed costs (committed)	30,000
	50,000

A subcontractor has offered to supply units of W, X, Y and Z for $12, $21, $10 and $14 respectively.

Required

Decide whether Buster Co should make or buy the components.

Solution

(a) The relevant costs are the differential costs between making and buying, and they consist of differences in unit variable costs plus differences in directly attributable fixed costs. Subcontracting will result in some fixed cost savings.

	W	X	Y	Z
	$	$	$	$
Unit variable cost of making	14	17	7	12
Unit variable cost of buying	12	21	10	14
	(2)	4	3	2
Annual requirements (units)	1,000	2,000	4,000	3,000
Extra variable cost of buying (per annum)	(2,000)	8,000	12,000	6,000
Fixed costs saved by buying	1,000	5,000	6,000	8,000
Extra total cost of buying	(3,000)	3,000	6,000	(2,000)

(b) The company would save $3,000 pa by subcontracting component W (where the purchase cost would be less than the marginal cost per unit to make internally) and would save $2,000 pa by subcontracting component Z (because of the saving in fixed costs of $8,000).

(c) In this example, relevant costs are the variable costs of In-house manufacture, the variable costs of subcontracted units, and the saving in fixed costs.

(d) Important further considerations would be as follows.

   (i) If components W and Z are subcontracted, the company will have spare capacity. How should that spare capacity be profitably used? Are there hidden benefits to be obtained from subcontracting? Would the company's workforce resent the loss of work to an outside subcontractor, and might such a decision cause an industrial dispute?

   (ii) Would the subcontractor be reliable with delivery times, and would he supply components of the same quality as those manufactured internally?

   (iii) Does the company wish to be flexible and maintain better control over operations by making everything itself?

   (iv) Are the estimates of fixed cost savings reliable? In the case of Product W, buying is clearly cheaper than making in-house. In the case of product Z, the decision to buy rather than make would only be financially beneficial if the fixed cost savings of $8,000 could really be 'delivered' by management. All too often in practice, promised savings fail to materialise!

Question	Make or buy

BB Co makes three components – S, T and W. The following costs have been recorded.

	Component S Unit cost	Component T Unit cost	Component W Unit cost
	$	$	$
Variable cost	2.50	8.00	5.00
Fixed cost	2.00	8.30	3.75
Total cost	4.50	16.30	8.75

Another company has offered to supply the components to BB Co at the following prices.

	Component S	Component T	Component W
Price each	$4	$7	$5.50

Which component(s), if any, should BB Co consider buying in?

A   Buy in all three components   C   Buy in S and W

B   Do not buy any   D   Buy in T only

Answer

BB Co should buy the component if the variable cost of making the component is more than the variable cost of buying the component.

	Component S $	Component T $	Component W $
Variable cost of making	2.50	8.00	5.00
Variable cost of buying	4.00	7.00	5.50
	(1.50)	1.00	(0.50)

The variable cost of making component T is greater than the variable cost of buying it.

Therefore, BB Co should consider buying in component T only.

The correct answer is D.

3 Steps in project appraisal

FAST FORWARD

The **steps involved** in **project appraisal** are:

- Initial investigation
- Detailed evaluation
- Authorisation

- Implementation
- Project monitoring
- Post-completion audit

We have already discussed the nature of capital expenditure. **Proper appraisal of projects involving capital expenditure** is important for the following reasons.

(a)   A relatively significant amount of the resources of the business will be involved.

(b)   A capital investment decision may be difficult to reverse, and on any reversal considerable costs may have been incurred for little benefit.

(c)   Investment decisions need to be considered in the light of strategic and tactical decisions of the company. The decision made should be consistent with the company's long-term objective, which will usually be the maximisation of the wealth of shareholders.

(d)   Future benefits need detailed evaluation since they are often difficult to predict. Consequently, there may be a high degree of risk and uncertainty.

3.1 Decision making and control cycle

The **decision making and control cycle** in appraisal or evaluation of a capital project has the following key stages.

(a)   **Initial investigation of the proposal**
Is it feasible, technically and commercially? What are its main risks? Does it match the firm's long-term strategic objectives?

(b) **Detailed evaluation**

Once the feasibility of the project has been established, a detailed investigation will examine expected cash flows. The effects of risk **may** be analysed by evaluating the effects on the cash flows of different 'What if…?' outcomes occurring: this is called **sensitivity analysis**. Sources of necessary **finance** will need to be considered. If there are not enough funds to undertake all proposals, they should be ranked in order of priority.

(c) **Authorisation**

For capital projects that are significant relative to the size of the company, authorisation rules will require that the decision to go ahead is made by senior management or by the board of directors. Those making the decision must be satisfied that an appropriately **detailed evaluation** has been carried out, that the proposal meets the **necessary criteria** to **contribute to profitability**, and that it is **consistent** with the **overall strategy** of the enterprise.

(d) **Implementation**

Once the decision has been made that the project will be undertaken, responsibility for the project should be assigned to a **project manager** or other responsible person. The required resources will need to be made available to this manager, who should be given specific targets to achieve.

(e) **Project monitoring**

After the start of the project, **progress** should be **monitored** and **senior management** should be **informed** on the progress of the project regularly. The project can be monitored more effectively if the costs and benefits originally expected are reassessed in the light of unforeseen events happening in the course of the project.

(f) **Post-completion audit**

At the end of the project, or at least several years after it has started, a post-completion audit should be carried out in order to make use of what can be learned from the experience in the planning of future projects. As far as possible, the actual cash flows should be measured and compared with the estimates contained in the original capital expenditure appraisal. The manager **responsible** for the project should be asked to explain any **significant variances**.

Key term

> A **post-completion audit** is an objective, independent assessment of the success of a capital project in relation to plan. It covers the whole life of the project and provides feedback to managers to aid the implementation and control of future projects.

3.2 Post-completion audits

Advantages of post-completion audits include the following.

(a) **Better forecasting techniques**

The post-completion audit can identify **weaknesses** in the forecasting and estimating techniques used to evaluate projects, and should help to improve the **discipline and quality** of forecasting.

(b) **Better future investment decisions**

The post-completion audit can identify where **mistakes** have been made, so that similar mistakes can be avoided in the future. It may also identify **successes** that might be created in future projects.

(c) **Better current investment decisions**

Awareness that a post-completion audit will be carried out at a later date may encourage managers involved to be more realistic and not unduly optimistic in their judgements.

(d) **Contribution to performance evaluation**

A post-completion audit can provide feedback to project managers and to senior management which is of use in the process of management control and performance assessment.

The procedures to be adopted will depend on the type of project being considered. However, key features to be addressed include the following:

(a) **Staff**

Staff involved in the audit should be **independent** of those involved in carrying out the project. They should also have the technical and market **competence** to carry out the review.

(b) **Performance evaluation**

The original **objectives** of the project should be identified, and performance should be evaluated against these objectives. This may mean that the audit concentrates on those aspects that have been identified as particularly **sensitive** or **critical. Financial performance** should be compared with the original plan, and **material deviations** should be **investigated**. In particular **significant variations** from the forecast costs and revenues should be investigated to improve the way in which risk is handled in project evaluation.

(c) **Recommendations**

The audit team should make specific **recommendations** at the end of the audit that will **improve** the **cost effectiveness** of future project management. Benefits of the process should exceed its costs.

(d) **Communication**

Communication with those directly involved in the project is important throughout the process. If the audit team is seen as the 'hit squad' there will be little incentive to learn from the process. Audit should not be about apportioning blame. There should be **feedback** of the outcomes to all the relevant personnel to ensure that the maximum is learned from the exercise and that project management is improved as a result.

Sometimes it will be useful to undertake an audit **during**, rather than after the end of, an investment's useful life. Such an audit may **identify inefficiencies** which could be corrected during the remainder of the investment's useful life, or be corrected sooner on other projects. Alternatively the audit may suggest that it is better to **abandon** the investment rather than incur more costs on it.

3.3 Non-financial factors

A decision maker should always bear in mind **non-financial factors** that affect a decision, and you may be asked to identify these from a case described in an exam question. Such 'non-financial' factors may have indirect financial implications, for example at a later stage.

3.4 Possible non-financial factors

(a) **Legal issues**. Possible legal actions should be considered.

(b) **Ethical issues**. Unethical actions by a company could be damaging if not illegal.

(c) **Changes to regulations.** Many governments have regulations designed to promote competition, for example.

(d) **Political issues**. A future change of government in the country concerned could affect plans.

(e) **Quality implications.** Poorer quality materials or equipment may be cheaper but may lead to problems later on, for example problems relating to breakdowns and warranty claims by customers.

(f) **Level of competition.** Investment in a new product may be matched by a competitor during the product's life-time, affecting revenues

3.5 Cash flow forecasting

Before looking at the methods of appraising projects in turn, it is worth emphasising one problem common to all of them, that of estimating future cash flows. **Cash flow forecasting** is never easy, but in capital budgeting the problems are particularly acute. This is because the period under consideration may not be merely a year or two, but five, ten, perhaps twenty years.

4 Methods of project appraisal

FAST FORWARD

The **key methods of project appraisal** are:

- The payback period
- Net present value
- Internal rate of return (IRR)

The following four sections consider the different methods of project appraisal – the tools you can use when deciding whether or not to make an investment.

5 The payback period

FAST FORWARD

The **payback period** is the time taken for the initial investment to be recovered in the cash inflows from the project. The payback method is particularly relevant if there are liquidity problems, or if distant forecasts are very uncertain.

The **payback period** method is one which gives greater weight to cash flows generated in earlier years. The payback period is the length of time required before the total cash inflows received from the project is equal to the original cash outlay. In other words, it is the length of time the investment takes to pay itself back.

The payback method has obvious disadvantages. Consider the case of two machines for which the following information is available.

		Machine P	Machine Q
		$	$
Cost		10,000	10,000
Cash inflows year	1	1,000	5,000
	2	2,000	5,000
	3	6,000	1,000
	4	7,000	500
	5	8,000	500
		24,000	12,000

Machine Q pays back at the end of year two and machine P not until early in year four. Using the payback method machine Q is to be preferred, but this ignores the fact that the total profitability of P ($24,000) is double that of Q.

Advantages of payback method	Disadvantages of payback method
It is easy to calculate and understand	Total profitability is ignored.
It is widely used in practice as a first screening method.	The **time value of money is ignored**
Its use will tend to minimise the effects of **risk** and help liquidity, because greater weight is given to	It ignores any cash flows that occur after the project has paid for itself. A project that takes time

Advantages of payback method	Disadvantages of payback method
earlier cash flows which can probably be predicted more accurately than distant cash flows.	to get off the ground but earns substantial profits once established might be rejected if the payback method is used, whereas a smaller project, paying back more quickly, may be accepted.
It identifies quick cash generators.	The **cut-off period** for deciding what is acceptable is **arbitrary.**

A more scientific method of investment appraisal is the use of **discounted cash flow** (DCF) approaches. Before DCF can be understood it is necessary to know something about the **time value of money**.

Question
Payback period

Project X has the following cash flows.

Year	Cash flow
	$
0	(105,000)
1	25,000
2	35,000
3	35,000
4	40,000
5	50,000

What is project X's payback period?

A	3 years	C	3.75 years
B	3.25 years	D	4 years

Answer

B (25,000 + 35,000 + 35,000) = 95,000 will be paid back at the end of year 3 leaving 10,000 to be repaid in year 4.

$\dfrac{10,000}{40,000}$ = 0.25 Therefore payback occurs after 3.25 years.

6 The time value of money

FAST FORWARD

The **time value of money** is based on the concept that money received now is worth more than the same sum received in one year's time or at another time in the future.

Money is spent to earn a profit. For example, if an item of machinery costs $6,000 and would earn profits (ignoring depreciation) of $2,000 per year for three years, it would not be worth buying because its total profit ($6,000) would only just cover its cost.

In addition the size of profits or return must be sufficiently large to justify the investment. In the example given in the previous paragraph, if the machinery costing $6,000 made total profits of $6,300 over three years, the return on the

investment would be $300, or an average of $100 per year. This would be a very low return, because it would be much more profitable to invest the $6,000 somewhere else (eg in a bank).

We must therefore recognise that if a capital investment is to be worthwhile, it must earn at least a **minimum profit or return** so that the size of the return will compensate the investor (the business) for the **length of time** which the investor must wait before the profits are made.

When capital expenditure projects are evaluated, it is therefore appropriate to decide whether the investment will make enough profits to allow for the 'time value' of capital tied up. The time value of money reflects people's **time preference** for $100 now over $100 at some time in the future. DCF is an evaluation approach which takes into account the time value of money.

6.1 The time value of money concept

Discounted cash flow (DCF) is a project appraisal approach that is based on the concept of the time value of money, that $1 earned or spent sooner is worth more than $1 earned or spent later. Various reasons could be suggested as to **why a present $1 is worth more than a future $1**.

(a) **Uncertainty.** The business world is full of risk and uncertainty, and although there might be the promise of money to come in the future, it can never be certain that the money will be received until it has actually been paid. This is an important argument, and risk and uncertainty must always be considered in investment appraisal. But this argument does not explain why the discounted cash flow approach should be used to reflect the time value of money.

(b) **Inflation.** Because of inflation it is common sense that $1 now is worth more than $1 in the future. It is important, however, that the problem of inflation should not be confused with the meaning of DCF, and the following points should be noted.

  (i) If there were no inflation at all, discounted cash flow approaches would still be used for investment appraisal.

  (ii) Inflation, for the moment, has been completely ignored.

  (iii) It is obviously necessary to allow for inflation.

(c) **An individual attaches more weight to current pleasures than to future ones, and would rather have $1 to spend now than $1 in a year's time**. Individuals have the choice of consuming or investing their wealth and so the return from projects must be sufficient to persuade individuals to prefer to invest now. Discounting is a measure of this time preference.

(d) Money is invested now to make profits (more money or wealth) in the future. **Discounted cash flow approaches** can therefore be used to **measure** either of two things.

  (i) **What alternative uses of the money would earn (NPV method)** (assuming that money can be invested elsewhere at the cost of capital)

  (ii) **What the money is expected to earn (IRR method)**

6.2 Discounting and compound interest

If we were to invest $1,000 now in a bank account which pays interest of 10% per annum, with interest calculated once each year at the end of the year, we would expect the following returns.

(a)   After one year, the investment would rise in value to:

$1,000 plus 10% = $1,000 (1 + 10%) = $1,000 × (1.10) = $1,100

Interest for the year would be $100. We can say that the rate of **simple interest** is 10%.

(b)   If we keep all our money in the bank account, after two years the investment would now be worth:

$1,100 × 1.10 = $1,210

Interest in year two would be $(1,210 − 1,100) = $110.

Another way of writing this would be to show how the original investment has earned interest over two years as follows.

$1,000 × (1.10) × (1.10) = $1,000 × $(1.10)^2$ = $1,210

(c)   Similarly, if we keep the money invested for a further year, the investment would grow to $1,000 × (1.10) × (1.10) × (1.10) = $1,000 × $(1.10)^3$ = $1,331 at the end of the third year. Interest in year three would be $(1,331 − 1,210) = $121.

6.3 Compound interest

This example shows how **compound interest** works. The amount of interest earned each year gets larger because we earn interest on both the original capital and also on the interest now earned in earlier years.

A formula which can be used to show the value of an investment after several years which earns compound interest is:

$S = P(1 + r)^n$

where   S   = future value of the investment after n years
        P   = the amount invested now
        r   = the rate of interest, as a proportion. For example, 10% = 0.10, 25% = 0.25, 8% = 0.08
        n   = the number of years of the investment

For example, suppose that we invest $2,000 now at 10%. What would the investment be worth after the following number of years?

(a)   Five years
(b)   Six years

The future value of $1 after n years at 10% interest is given in the following table.

n	$(1 + r)^n$ with r = 0.10
1	1.100
2	1.210
3	1.331
4	1.464
5	1.611
6	1.772
7	1.949

The solution is as follows.

(a)   After five years: (b)   After six years:

S = $2,000 (1.611) = $3,222   S = $2,000 (1.772) = $3,544

The principles of compound interest are used in discounted cash flow, except that discounting is compounding in reverse.

6.4 Discounting

With **discounting**, we look at the size of an investment after a certain number of years, and calculate how much we would need to invest now to build up the investment to that size, given a certain rate of interest. This may seem complicated at first, and an example might help to make the point clear. With discounting, we can calculate how much we would need to invest now at an interest rate, of say, 6% to build up the investment to (say) $5,000 after four years.

The compound interest formula shows how we calculate a future sum S from a known current investment P, so that if S = P (1 + r)^n, then:

$$P = \frac{S}{(1+r)^n} = S \times \frac{1}{(1+r)^n}$$

This is the basic formula for discounting, which is sometimes written as: $P = S(1 + r)^{-n}$

[$(1 + r)^{-n}$ and $\frac{1}{(1+r)^n}$ mean exactly the same thing.]

To build up an investment to $5,000 after four years at 6% interest, we would need to invest now:

$$P = \$5,000 \times \frac{1}{(1+0.06)^4} = \$5,000 \times 0.792 = \$3,960$$

6.4.1 Further examples of discounting

If you have never done any discounting before, the basic principle and mathematical techniques might take some time to get used to. The following examples might help to make them clearer.

(a)   A business person wants to have $13,310 in three years' time, and has decided to put some money aside now which will earn interest of 10% per annum. How much money must he put aside in order to build up the investment to $13,310 as required?

Solution $P = \$13,310 \times \dfrac{1}{(1.10)^3} = \$10,000$

Proof   After one year the investment would be worth $10,000 × 1.10 = $11,000; after two years it would be $11,000 × 1.10 = $12,100; and after three years it would be $12,100 × 1.10 = $13,310.

(b)   Another businessman has two sons who are just 18 years and 17 years old. He wishes to give them $10,000 each on their 20th birthdays and he wants to know how much he must invest now at 8% interest to pay this amount.

The following table is relevant, giving values r = 8% or 0.08. Note that you can read the figures in the 'present value' column from the **Present Value Table** in the Appendix to this Study Text: look down the 8% column.

Year n	Future value of $1 $(1 + r)^n$	Present value of $1 $(1 + r)^{-n}$
1	1.080	0.926
2	1.166	0.857
3	1.260	0.794
4	1.360	0.735

The investment must provide $10,000 after two years for the elder son and $10,000 after three years for the younger son.

	After n years n =	Discount factor 8%		Amount provided $	Present value $
Elder son	2	0.857	×	10,000	8,570
Younger son	3	0.794	×	10,000	7,940
Total investment required					16,510

Proof   After two years the investment of $16,510 will be worth $16,510 × 1.166 = $19,251. After paying $10,000 to the elder son, $9,251 will be left after two years. This will earn interest of 8% in year three, to be worth $9,251 × 1.08 = $9,991 at the end of the year. This is almost enough to pay $10,000 to the younger son. The difference ($9) is caused by rounding errors in the table of discount (present value) factors and compound (future value) factors.

(c)   A company is wondering whether to invest $15,000 in a project which will pay $20,000 after two years. It will not invest unless the return from the investment is at least 10% per annum. Is the investment worthwhile? The present value of $1 in two years time at 10% interest is 0.826.

Solution

The return of $20,000 after two years is equivalent to an investment now at 10% of $20,000 × 0.826 = $16,520.

In other words, in order to obtain $20,000 after two years, the company would have to invest $16,520 now at an interest rate of 10%. The project offers the same payment at a cost of only $15,000, so that it must provide a return in excess of 10% and it is therefore worthwhile.

	$
Present value of future profits at 10%	16,520
Cost of investment	15,000
The investment in the project offers the same return, but at a cost lower by	1,520

7 Discounted cash flow

FAST FORWARD   **Discounted cash flow approaches** take account of the time value of money – the fact that $1 received now is worth more because it could be invested to become a greater sum at the end of a year, and even more after the end of two years, and so on. As with payback, discounted cash flow approaches use cash figures before depreciation in the calculations.

Key term   **Discounted cash flow** is an approach of evaluating capital investment projects, using discounting arithmetic to determine whether or not they will provide a satisfactory return.

A typical investment project involves a payment of capital for non-current assets at the start of the project and then there will be returns coming in from the investment over a number of years.

As we noted earlier, DCF can be used in either of two ways: the **net present value method,** or the **internal rate of return** (sometimes called DCF yield, DCF rate of return) method. We will now look at each method in turn.

7.1 The net present value (NPV) method of DCF

FAST FORWARD   The **net present value method** calculates the present value of all cash flows, and sums them to give the net present value. If this is positive, then the project is acceptable.

The **net present value (NPV) method** of evaluation is as follows.

(a) **Determine the present value of costs**

In other words, decide how much capital must be set aside to pay for the project. Let this be $C.

(b) **Calculate the present value of future cash benefits from the project**

To do this we take the cash benefit in each year and discount it to a present value. This shows how much we would have to invest now to earn the future benefits, if our rate of return were equal to the cost of capital. ('Cost of capital' is explained below.) By adding up the present value of benefits for each future year, we obtain the total present value of benefits from the project. Let this be $B.

(c) **Compare the present value of costs $C with the present value of benefits $B**

The net present value is the difference between them: $(B − C).

(d) **NPV is positive**

The present value of benefits exceeds the present value of costs. This in turn means that the project will earn a return in excess of the cost of capital. Therefore, the project should be accepted.

(e) **NPV is negative**

This means that it would cost us more to invest in the project to obtain the future cash receipts than it would cost us to invest somewhere else, at a rate of interest equal to the cost of capital, to obtain an equal amount of future receipts. The project would earn a return lower than the cost of capital and would not be worth investing in.

7.1.1 Example: The NPV method

Suppose that a company is wondering whether to invest $18,000 in a project which would make extra profits (before depreciation is deducted) of $10,000 in the first year, $8,000 in the second year and $6,000 in the third year. Its cost of capital is 10% (in other words, it would require a return of at least 10% on its investment). You are required to evaluate the project.

Solution

In DCF we make several assumptions. One such assumption is that discounted cash flows (payments or receipts) occur on the last day of each year. For example, although profits are $10,000 during the course of year 1, we assume that the $10,000 is not received until the last day of year 1. Similarly, the profits of $8,000 and $6,000 in years 2 and 3 are assumed to occur on the last day of years 2 and 3 respectively. The cash payment of $18,000 occurs 'now' at the start of year 1. To be consistent, we say that this payment occurs on the last day of the current year which is often referred to as year 0.

The NPV is now calculated with discounting arithmetic. Note that the Present Value Table in the Appendix to this Text gives us the following values.

Year	Present value of $1	
n	$(1 + r)^{-n}$	where r = 0.10
1	0.909	
2	0.826	
3	0.751	

Year	Cash flow $	Present value factor	Present value $
0	(18,000)	1.000	(18,000)
1	10,000	0.909	9,090
2	8,000	0.826	6,608
3	6,000	0.751	4,506
		NPV	2,204

The NPV is positive, which means that the project will earn more than 10%. ($20,204 would have to be invested now at 10% to earn the future cash flows; since the project will earn these returns at a cost of only $18,000 it must earn a return in excess of 10%.)

Question

A project would involve a capital outlay of $24,000. Profits (before depreciation) each year would be $5,000 for six years. The cost of capital is 12%. Is the project worthwhile?

(Use the Present Value Table in the Appendix.)

Answer

Years	Cash flow $	Present value factor	Present value $
0	(24,000)	1.000	(24,000)
1	5,000	0.893	4,465
2	5,000	0.797	3,985
3	5,000	0.712	3,560
4	5,000	0.636	3,180
5	5,000	0.567	2,835
6	5,000	0.507	2,535
		NPV	(3,440)

The NPV is negative and so the project is not worthwhile.

7.1.2 Advantages and disadvantages of NPV

Advantages of NPV	Disadvantages of NPV
Shareholder wealth is **maximised**.	It can be difficult to identify an **appropriate discount rate**.
It takes into account the **time value of money**.	For simplicity, cash flows are sometimes all assumed to occur at **year ends**: this assumption may be unrealistic.
It is based on **cash flows** which are less subjective than profit.	Some managers are **unfamiliar** with the concept of NPV.
Shareholders will **benefit** if a project with a positive NPV is accepted.	

7.2 The cost of capital

We have mentioned that the appropriate discount rate to use in investment appraisal is the company's **cost of capital**. In practice this is difficult to determine. It is often suggested that the discount rate which a company should use as its cost of capital is one that reflects the return expected by its investors in shares and loan notes, the **opportunity cost of finance**.

Shareholders expect dividends and capital gains; loan notes investors expect interest payments. A company must make enough profits from its own operations (including capital expenditure projects) to pay dividends and interest. The average return is the weighted average of the return required by shareholders and loan note investors. The cost of capital is therefore the **weighted average cost** of all the sources of capital.

7.3 Annuities

FAST FORWARD

Annuities are an annual cash payment or receipt which is the same amount every year for a number of years.

In DCF the term **'annuities'** refers to an annual cash payment which is the same amount every year for a number of years, or else an annual receipt of cash which is the same amount every year for a number of years.

In the question above, the profits are an annuity of $5,000 per annum for six years. The present value of profits is the present value of an annuity of $5,000 per annum for six years at a discount rate of 12%.

When there is an annuity to be discounted, there is a shortcut method of calculation. You may already have seen what it is. Instead of multiplying the cash flow each year by the present value factor for that year, and then adding up all the present values (as shown in the solution above), we can **multiply** the **annuity** by the **sum of the present value factors**.

Thus we could have multiplied $5,000 by the sum of (0.893 + 0.797 + 0.712 + 0.636 + 0.567 + 0.507) = 4.112. We then have $5,000 × 4.112 = $20,560.

This quick calculation is made even quicker by the use of 'annuity' tables. These show the sum of the present value factors each year from year one to year n.

The Annuity Table in the Appendix to this Text shows the following.

Years n	Present value of $1 received per year $\dfrac{[1-(1+r)^{-n}]}{r}$	Notes
1	0.893	PV factor for year 1 only
2	1.690	(0.893 + 0.797)
3	2.402	(add 0.712)
4	3.038	(add 0.636)
5	3.605	(add 0.567)
6	4.112	(add 0.507)

7.3.1 Example: Annuities

A project would involve a capital outlay of $50,000. Profits (before depreciation) would be $12,000 per year. The cost of capital is 10%. Would the project be worthwhile if it lasts:

(a)   Five years
(b)   Seven years

Solution

We can find the discount factors from the Annuity Table in the Appendix.

(a)   If the project lasts five years

Years	Cash flow $	Discount factor 10%	Present value $
0	(50,000)	1.000	(50,000)
1 – 5	12,000 pa	3.791	45,492
		NPV	(4,508)

(b)   If the project lasts seven years

Years	Cash flow $	Discount factor 10%	Present value $
0	(50,000)	1.000	(50,000)
1 – 7	12,000 pa	4.868	58,416
		NPV	8,416

The project is not worthwhile if it last only five years, but it would be worthwhile if it lasted for seven years. The decision to accept or to reject the project must depend on management's view about its duration.

Question   Two projects

(a)   A project costs $39,500. It would earn $10,000 per year for the first three years and then $8,000 per year for the next three. Cost of capital is 10%. Is the project worth undertaking?

(b)   Another project would cost $75,820. If its life is expected to be five years and the cost of capital is 10%, what are the minimum annual savings required to make the project worthwhile?

Use the Annuity Table in the Appendix to derive your answers.

Answer

(a)

Present value of $1 per annum, years 1-6	4.355
Less present value of $1 per annum, years 1-3	2.487
Gives present value of $1 per annum, years 4-6	1.868

Year	Cash flow $	Discount factor 10%	Present value $
0	(39,500)	1.000	(39,500)
1 – 3	10,000 pa	2.487	24,870
4 – 6	8,000 pa	1.868	14,944
		NPV	314

The **NPV is positive**, but only just ($314). The project therefore promises a return a little above 10%. If we are confident that the estimates of cost and benefits for the next six years are accurate, the project is worth undertaking. However, if there is some suspicion that earnings may be a little less than the figures shown, it might be prudent to reject it.

(b)   The project will just be worthwhile if the NPV is 0. For the NPV to be 0 the present value of benefits must equal the present value of costs, $75,820.

PV of benefits   = annual savings × present value of $1 per year for 5 years (at 10%)
$75,820   = annual savings × 3.791

$$= \frac{\$75,820}{3.791}$$

Annual savings   = $20,000

This example shows that annuity tables can be used to calculate an annual cash flow from a given investment.

7.4 Calculating a 'breakeven' NPV

You might be asked to calculate how much income would need to be generated for the NPV of a project to be zero. This must be referred to as in **breakeven NPV**.

7.4.1 Example: Breakeven NPV

For the project in the example above, calculate how much the annual income from the project could reduce before the NPV would reach a 'breakeven' zero level.

Solution

For every $1 reduction in the annual income of $12,000, the NPV will fall by $1 × 4.868 = $4.868.

'Breakeven' fall in income = $8,416 ÷ 4.868 = $1,729

Annual income of $12,000 − $1,729 = $10,271 will result in a 'break-even' NPV of zero.

7.5 Internal rate of return (IRR)

FAST FORWARD

The **Internal rate of return technique** uses a trial and error method to discover the discount rate which produces the NPV of zero. This discount rate will be the annual return forecast for the project.

The **internal rate of return method** of DCF involves two steps.

- Calculating the rate of return which is expected from a project
- Comparing the rate of return with the cost of capital

If a project earns a **higher rate of return** than the cost of capital, it will be worth undertaking (and its **NPV** would be **positive**). If it earns a **lower rate of return**, it is not worthwhile (and its **NPV** would be **negative**). If a project earns a return which is exactly equal to the cost of capital, its NPV will be 0 and it will only just be worthwhile.

7.5.1 Calculating the internal rate of return

You may find the method of calculating the rate of return to be rather unsatisfactory because it involves some guesswork and approximation. An example will help to illustrate the technique.

Suppose that a project would cost $20,000 and the annual net cash inflows are expected to be as follows. What is the internal rate of return of the project?

Year	Cash flow
	$
1	8,000
2	10,000
3	6,000
4	4,000

The IRR is a rate of interest at which the NPV is 0 and the discounted (present) values of benefits add up to $20,000. We need to find out what interest rate or cost of capital would give an NPV of 0.

We are after two rates of return.

(a)   One at which the NPV is a **small positive value**. The actual IRR will be higher than this rate of return.

(b)   One at which the NPV is a **small negative value**. The actual IRR will be lower than this rate of return.

The actual IRR will then be found (approximately) by using the two rates in (a) and (b).

In our example, we might begin by trying discount rates of 10%, 15% and 20%.

Year	Cash flow	Discount factor at 10%	Present value at 10%	Discount factor at 15%	Present value at 15%	Discount factor at 20%	Present value at 20%
	$		$		$		$
0	(20,000)	1.000	(20,000)	1.000	(20,000)	1.000	(20,000)
1	8,000	0.909	7,272	0.870	6,960	0.833	6,664
2	10,000	0.826	8,260	0.756	7,560	0.694	6,940
3	6,000	0.751	4,506	0.658	3,948	0.579	3,474
4	4,000	0.683	2,732	0.572	2,288	0.482	1,928
Net present value			2,770		756		(994)

The IRR is more than 15% but less than 20%. We could try to be more accurate by trying a discount rate of 16%, 17%, 18% or 19%, but in this solution we will use the values for 15% and 20% to estimate the IRR.

To estimate the IRR, we now assume that the NPV falls steadily and at a constant rate between $756 at 15% and $(994) at 20%. This represents a fall of $(756 + 994) = $1,750 in NPV between 15% and 20%. This is an average fall of:

$$\frac{\$1,750}{(20-15)\%} = \$350 \text{ in NPV for each 1\% increase in the discount rate}$$

Since the IRR is where the NPV is 0, it must be $\frac{\$756}{\$350} \times 1\%$ above 15%

ie about 2.2% above 15% = 17.2%

7.5.2 A formula for the IRR

A formula for making this calculation (which is known as **interpolation**) is as follows

$$IRR = A + \left[\frac{a}{a - b} \times (B - A) \right]$$

where A   is the discount rate which provides the positive NPV
      a   is the amount of the positive NPV
      B   is the discount rate which provides the negative NPV
      b   is the amount of the negative NPV

In our example, using this formula, the IRR would be calculated as follows

$$15\% + \left[\frac{756}{756 - 994} \times (20 - 15) \right]\% \; = \; 15\% + [\, 0.432 \times 5 \,]\%$$

$$= 15\% + \quad 2.16\%$$
$$= 17.16\%, \text{ say } 17.2\%$$

7.5.3 Advantages of the IRR method

The following are advantages of using IRR.

(a)   It takes into account the **time value of money**, unlike other approaches such as payback.

(b)   Results are expressed as a **simple percentage**, and are more easily understood than some other methods.

(c)   It indicates how **sensitive** calculations are to changes in interest rates.

7.5.4 Problems with the IRR method

The following are problems of using IRR.

(a)   Projects with unconventional cash flows can produce **negative** or **multiple IRRs**.

(b)   IRR may be **confused** with return on capital employed (ROCE), since all give answers in percentage terms.

(c)   It may give **conflicting recommendations** with mutually exclusive projects, because the result is given in relative terms (percentages), and not in absolute terms ($s) as with NPV.

(d)   Some **managers** are **unfamiliar** with the IRR method.

(e)   It cannot accommodate **changing interest rates**.

(f)   It assumes that funds can be **re-invested** at a rate equivalent to the IRR, which may be too high.

Question

Machine purchase

LCH Co manufactures product X which it sells for $5 per unit. Variable costs of production are currently $3 per unit, and fixed costs 50c per unit. A new machine is available which would cost $90,000 but which could be used to make product X for a variable cost of only $2.50 per unit. Fixed costs, however, would increase by $7,500 per annum as a direct result of purchasing the machine. The machine would have an expected life of 4 years and a resale value after that time of $10,000. Sales of product X are estimated to be 75,000 units per annum. LCH Co expects to earn at least 12% per annum from its investments. Ignore taxation.

You are required to decide whether LCH Co should purchase the machine.

Answer

Savings are 75,000 × ($3 – $2.50) = $37,500 per annum.

Additional costs are $7,500 per annum.

Net cash savings are therefore $30,000 per annum. (Remember, depreciation is not a cash flow and must be ignored as a 'cost'.)

The first step in calculating an NPV is to establish the relevant costs year by year. All future cash flows arising as a direct consequence of the decision should be taken into account. It is assumed that the machine will be sold for $10,000 at the end of year 4.

Year	Cash flow	PV factor	PV of cash flow
	$	12%	$
0	(90,000)	1.000	(90,000)
1	30,000	0.893	26,790
2	30,000	0.797	23,910
3	30,000	0.712	21,360
4	40,000	0.636	25,440
			7,500

The NPV is positive and so the project is expected to earn more than 12% per annum and is therefore acceptable.

Question   IRR

Find the IRR of the project given below and state whether the project should be accepted if the company requires a minimum return of 17%.

Time		$
0	Investment	(4,000)
1	Receipts	1,200
2	"	1,410
3	"	1,875
4	"	1,150

Answer

The initial estimate of the IRR that we shall try is 14%.

Time	Cash flow	Try 14% Discount factor	PV	Try 16% Discount factor	PV
	$		$		$
0	(4,000)	1.000	(4,000)	1.000	(4,000)
1	1,200	0.877	1,052	0.862	1,034
2	1,410	0.769	1,084	0.743	1,048
3	1,875	0.675	1,266	0.641	1,202
4	1,150	0.592	681	0.552	635
		NPV	83	NPV	(81)

The IRR must be less than 16%, but higher than 14%. The NPVs at these two costs of capital will be used to estimate the IRR.

Using the interpolation formula:

$$IRR = 14\% + \left[\frac{83}{83--81} \times (16\% - 14\%) \right] = 15.01\%$$

The IRR is, in fact, almost exactly 15%. The project should be rejected as the IRR is less than the minimum return demanded.

7.6 Advantages of DCF methods of appraisal

Taking account of the time value of money (by discounting) is one of the principal advantages of the DCF appraisal method. Other advantages include:

(a)   The method uses all cash flows relating to the project (unlike payback).

(b)   It allows for the timing of the cash flows (unlike payback).

(c)   There are universally accepted methods of calculating the NPV and IRR.

8 Public sector capital budgeting decisions

FAST FORWARD

Capital budgeting decisions in the **public sector** are not often made with the intention of earning profits. Social costs and social benefits can be very important in public sector investment appraisals.

Capital budgeting in **the public sector** differs from capital budgeting in the private sector for several reasons.

(a)   Relatively few public sector capital investments are made with the intention of earning a **financial return**.

(b)   Rather than considering financial costs and benefits alone, public sector capital budgeting decisions will often have regard to the **social costs** and the **social benefits** of investments. Social costs and benefits include non-financial aspects such as pollution (a cost) and better health (a benefit).

(c)   The cost of capital that is applied to project cash flows will not be a commercial rate of return, but one that is **determined** by the **Treasury** on behalf of the government.

For capital budgeting decisions in the public sector, where social costs and benefits are thought to be significant elements in the decision the following points should be noted.

(a)   An attempt can be made to **quantify** the **social costs** and **social benefits** in monetary terms, and to treat them as cash flows.

(b)   In choosing between mutually exclusive options (such as sites for a new airport) the **option** with the **lowest total of PV** of costs would be preferred. For optional investments, the decision would be to go ahead with the investment if it had a positive NPV, taking both financial and social costs and benefits into account.

Chapter Roundup

- **Relevant costs** are future cash flows arising as a direct consequence of a decision.

- Relevant costs are **future, incremental cashflows**.

- Make or buy analysis involves calculating whether it is **cheaper to produce** a component internally **or to purchase** it from an external source.

- The **steps involved** in **project appraisal** are:

    - Initial investigation
    - Detailed evaluation
    - Authorisation

    - Implementation
    - Project monitoring
    - Post-completion audit

- The **key methods of project appraisal** are:

    - The payback period
    - Net present value
    - Internal rate of return (IRR)

- The **payback period** is the time taken for the initial investment to be recovered in the cash inflows from the project. The payback method is particularly relevant if there are liquidity problems, or if distant forecasts are very uncertain.

- The **time value of money** is based on the concept that money received now is worth more than the same sum received in one year's time or at another time in the future.

- **Discounted cash flow approaches** take account of the time value of money – the fact that $1 received now is worth more because it could be invested to become a greater sum at the end of a year, and even more after the end of two years, and so on. As with payback, discounted cash flow approaches use cash figures before depreciation in the calculations.

- The **net present value method** calculates the present value of all cash flows, and sums them to give the net present value. If this is positive, then the project is acceptable.

- **Annuities** are an annual cash payment or receipt which is the same amount every year for a number of years.

- The **internal rate of return technique** uses a trial and error method to discover the discount rate which produces the NPV of zero. This discount rate will be the return forecast for the project.

- Capital budgeting decisions in the **public sector** are not often made with the intention of earning profits. Social costs and social benefits can be very important in public sector investment appraisals.

1   .... is the length of time required before the total of the cash inflows received from a project equals the original cash outlay.

2   Which of the following statements is incorrect?

    A   Committed costs are relevant costs   C   Incremental costs are relevant costs

    B   Future costs are relevant costs   D   Cash flows are relevant costs

3   If materials have already been purchased but will not be replaced, what is their relevant cost?

4   Depreciation should be included in DCF calculation.

    True ☐   False ☐

5   What is the yardstick for acceptance of projects when using the net present value method?

    A   Accept if a profit is made

    B   Accept if the present value of future cash flows is positive

    C   Accept if payback occurs within an reasonable timeframe

    D   Accept if the discount rate that achieves a breakeven return is greater than the company's cost of capital

6   The .... is the weighted average cost of all sources of capital for an enterprise, used as the discount rate in investment appraisal.

7   What are the two steps involved in assessing whether the internal rate of return of a project is sufficient?

    Step 1 –   Step 2 –

8   A firm has some material which originally cost $45,000. It has a scrap value of $12,500 but if reworked at a cost of $7,500, it could be sold for $17,500. There is no other foreseen use for the material.

    The relevant cost of using the material for a special job is $ ☐

9   A company is considering its options with regard to a machine which cost $120,000 four years ago.

    If sold, the machine would generate scrap proceeds of $150,000. If kept, this machine would generate net income of $180,000.

    The current replacement cost for this machine is $210,000.

    The relevant cost of the machine is:

    ☐ $120,000   ☐ $180,000

    ☐ $150,000   ☐ $210,000

10   Tick the correct box to indicate whether or not the following items are included in the cash flows when determining the net present value of a project.

		Included	Not included
(a)	The disposal value of equipment at the end of its life	☐	☐
(b)	Depreciation charges for the equipment	☐	☐
(c)	Research costs incurred prior to the appraisal	☐	☐
(d)	Interest payments on the loan to finance the investment	☐	☐

1   **Payback** is the length of time required before the total of the cash inflows received from a project is equal to the original cash outlay.

2   A   Committed costs are not relevant costs.

3   The relevant cost will be the higher of their current resale value and the value they would obtain if they were put to an alternative use.

4   False. Depreciation does not reflect additional cash spent, and so is not a relevant cost.

5   B   Accept the project if the net present value is positive.

6   The time after which the net present value of an investment becomes positive.

7   The **cost of capital** is the weighted average cost of all sources of capital for an enterprise, used as the discount rate in investment appraisal.

   Step 1 – Calculate the rate of return expected.

   Step 2 – Compare the rate of return with the cost of capital.

8   The relevant cost of using the material for a special job is $ $\boxed{12,500}$

   The original cost of $45,000 is a non-relevant sunk or past cost. The material would not be reworked, since its value would increase by only $5,000 ($17,500 – $12,500) for a cost of $7,500.

   The relevant cost of using the material for the special job is therefore the opportunity cost of the $12,500 scrap sale forgone.

9   The relevant cost (deprival value) of the machine is:

   $\boxed{\checkmark}$ $180,000

10 (a)   Included

   (b)   Not included (non-cash)

   (c)   Not included (past cost)

   (d)   Not included (included in the discount rate).

   Now try the questions below from the Question Bank

Question numbers
89–94

Appendix
Present value tables

Present value table

Present value of $1 ie $(1+r)^{-n}$ where r = interest rate, n = number of periods until payment or receipt.

Periods					Interest rates (r)					
(n)	1%	2%	3%	4%	5%	6%	7%	8%	9%	10%
1	0.990	0.980	0.971	0.962	0.952	0.943	0.935	0.926	0.917	0.909
2	0.980	0.961	0.943	0.925	0.907	0.890	0.873	0.857	0.842	0.826
3	0.971	0.942	0.915	0.889	0.864	0.840	0.816	0.794	0.772	0.751
4	0.961	0.924	0.888	0.855	0.823	0.792	0.763	0.735	0.708	0.683
5	0.951	0.906	0.863	0.822	0.784	0.747	0.713	0.681	0.650	0.621
6	0.942	0.888	0.837	0.790	0.746	0.705	0.666	0.630	0.596	0.564
7	0.933	0.871	0.813	0.760	0.711	0.665	0.623	0.583	0.547	0.513
8	0.923	0.853	0.789	0.731	0.677	0.627	0.582	0.540	0.502	0.467
9	0.914	0.837	0.766	0.703	0.645	0.592	0.544	0.500	0.460	0.424
10	0.905	0.820	0.744	0.676	0.614	0.558	0.508	0.463	0.422	0.386
11	0.896	0.804	0.722	0.650	0.585	0.527	0.475	0.429	0.388	0.350
12	0.887	0.788	0.701	0.625	0.557	0.497	0.444	0.397	0.356	0.319
13	0.879	0.773	0.681	0.601	0.530	0.469	0.415	0.368	0.326	0.290
14	0.870	0.758	0.661	0.577	0.505	0.442	0.388	0.340	0.299	0.263
15	0.861	0.743	0.642	0.555	0.481	0.417	0.362	0.315	0.275	0.239
16	0.853	0.728	0.623	0.534	0.458	0.394	0.339	0.292	0.252	0.218
17	0.844	0.714	0.605	0.513	0.436	0.371	0.317	0.270	0.231	0.198
18	0.836	0.700	0.587	0.494	0.416	0.350	0.296	0.250	0.212	0.180
19	0.828	0.686	0.570	0.475	0.396	0.331	0.277	0.232	0.194	0.164
20	0.820	0.673	0.554	0.456	0.377	0.312	0.258	0.215	0.178	0.149

Periods					Interest rates (r)					
(n)	11%	12%	13%	14%	15%	16%	17%	18%	19%	20%
1	0.901	0.893	0.885	0.877	0.870	0.862	0.855	0.847	0.840	0.833
2	0.812	0.797	0.783	0.769	0.756	0.743	0.731	0.718	0.706	0.694
3	0.731	0.712	0.693	0.675	0.658	0.641	0.624	0.609	0.593	0.579
4	0.659	0.636	0.613	0.592	0.572	0.552	0.534	0.516	0.499	0.482
5	0.593	0.567	0.543	0.519	0.497	0.476	0.456	0.437	0.419	0.402
6	0.535	0.507	0.480	0.456	0.432	0.410	0.390	0.370	0.352	0.335
7	0.482	0.452	0.425	0.400	0.376	0.354	0.333	0.314	0.296	0.279
8	0.434	0.404	0.376	0.351	0.327	0.305	0.285	0.266	0.249	0.233
9	0.391	0.361	0.333	0.308	0.284	0.263	0.243	0.225	0.209	0.194
10	0.352	0.322	0.295	0.270	0.247	0.227	0.208	0.191	0.176	0.162
11	0.317	0.287	0.261	0.237	0.215	0.195	0.178	0.162	0.148	0.135
12	0.286	0.257	0.231	0.208	0.187	0.168	0.152	0.137	0.124	0.112
13	0.258	0.229	0.204	0.182	0.163	0.145	0.130	0.116	0.104	0.093
14	0.232	0.205	0.181	0.160	0.141	0.125	0.111	0.099	0.088	0.078
15	0.209	0.183	0.160	0.140	0.123	0.108	0.095	0.084	0.074	0.065
16	0.188	0.163	0.141	0.123	0.107	0.093	0.081	0.071	0.062	0.054
17	0.170	0.146	0.125	0.108	0.093	0.080	0.069	0.060	0.052	0.045
18	0.153	0.130	0.111	0.095	0.081	0.069	0.059	0.051	0.044	0.038
19	0.138	0.116	0.098	0.083	0.070	0.060	0.051	0.043	0.037	0.031
20	0.124	0.104	0.087	0.073	0.061	0.051	0.043	0.037	0.031	0.026

Cumulative present value table

This table shows the present value of $1 per annum, receivable or payable at the end of each year for n years $\frac{1-(1+r)^{-n}}{r}$.

Periods					Interest rates (r)					
(n)	1%	2%	3%	4%	5%	6%	7%	8%	9%	10%
1	0.990	0.980	0.971	0.962	0.952	0.943	0.935	0.926	0.917	0.909
2	1.970	1.942	1.913	1.886	1.859	1.833	1.808	1.783	1.759	1.736
3	2.941	2.884	2.829	2.775	2.723	2.673	2.624	2.577	2.531	2.487
4	3.902	3.808	3.717	3.630	3.546	3.465	3.387	3.312	3.240	3.170
5	4.853	4.713	4.580	4.452	4.329	4.212	4.100	3.993	3.890	3.791
6	5.795	5.601	5.417	5.242	5.076	4.917	4.767	4.623	4.486	4.355
7	6.728	6.472	6.230	6.002	5.786	5.582	5.389	5.206	5.033	4.868
8	7.652	7.325	7.020	6.733	6.463	6.210	5.971	5.747	5.535	5.335
9	8.566	8.162	7.786	7.435	7.108	6.802	6.515	6.247	5.995	5.759
10	9.471	8.983	8.530	8.111	7.722	7.360	7.024	6.710	6.418	6.145
11	10.368	9.787	9.253	8.760	8.306	7.887	7.499	7.139	6.805	6.495
12	11.255	10.575	9.954	9.385	8.863	8.384	7.943	7.536	7.161	6.814
13	12.134	11.348	10.635	9.986	9.394	8.853	8.358	7.904	7.487	7.103
14	13.004	12.106	11.296	10.563	9.899	9.295	8.745	8.244	7.786	7.367
15	13.865	12.849	11.938	11.118	10.380	9.712	9.108	8.559	8.061	7.606
16	14.718	13.578	12.561	11.652	10.838	10.106	9.447	8.851	8.313	7.824
17	15.562	14.292	13.166	12.166	11.274	10.477	9.763	9.122	8.544	8.022
18	16.398	14.992	13.754	12.659	11.690	10.828	10.059	9.372	8.756	8.201
19	17.226	15.679	14.324	13.134	12.085	11.158	10.336	9.604	8.950	8.365
20	18.046	16.351	14.878	13.590	12.462	11.470	10.594	9.818	9.129	8.514

Periods					Interest rates (r)					
(n)	11%	12%	13%	14%	15%	16%	17%	18%	19%	20%
1	0.901	0.893	0.885	0.877	0.870	0.862	0.855	0.847	0.840	0.833
2	1.713	1.690	1.668	1.647	1.626	1.605	1.585	1.566	1.547	1.528
3	2.444	2.402	2.361	2.322	2.283	2.246	2.210	2.174	2.140	2.106
4	3.102	3.037	2.974	2.914	2.855	2.798	2.743	2.690	2.639	2.589
5	3.696	3.605	3.517	3.433	3.352	3.274	3.199	3.127	3.058	2.991
6	4.231	4.111	3.998	3.889	3.784	3.685	3.589	3.498	3.410	3.326
7	4.712	4.564	4.423	4.288	4.160	4.039	3.922	3.812	3.706	3.605
8	5.146	4.968	4.799	4.639	4.487	4.344	4.207	4.078	3.954	3.837
9	5.537	5.328	5.132	4.946	4.772	4.607	4.451	4.303	4.163	4.031
10	5.889	5.650	5.426	5.216	5.019	4.833	4.659	4.494	4.339	4.192
11	6.207	5.938	5.687	5.453	5.234	5.029	4.836	4.656	4.486	4.327
12	6.492	6.194	5.918	5.660	5.421	5.197	4.988	4.793	4.611	4.439
13	6.750	6.424	6.122	5.842	5.583	5.342	5.118	4.910	4.715	4.533
14	6.982	6.628	6.302	6.002	5.724	5.468	5.229	5.008	4.802	4.611
15	7.191	6.811	6.462	6.142	5.847	5.575	5.324	5.092	4.876	4.675
16	7.379	6.974	6.604	6.265	5.954	5.668	5.405	5.162	4.938	4.730
17	7.549	7.120	6.729	6.373	6.047	5.749	5.475	5.222	4.990	4.775
18	7.702	7.250	6.840	6.467	6.128	5.818	5.534	5.273	5.033	4.812
19	7.839	7.366	6.938	6.550	6.198	5.877	5.584	5.316	5.070	4.843
20	7.963	7.469	7.025	6.623	6.259	5.929	5.628	5.353	5.101	4.870

Question bank

1   Which of the following would be data rather than information?

    A   Sales increase/decrease per product in last quarter
    B   Total sales value per product
    C   Sales made per salesman as a percentage of total sales
    D   Salesmen's' commission as a percentage of total sales

2   Which is an example of internal information for the wages department of a large company?

    A   A Code of Practice issued by the Institute of Directors
    B   A new national minimum wage
    C   Changes to tax arrangements issued by the tax authorities
    D   The company's employees' schedule of hours worked

3   Which **one** of the following is **not** a quality of good information?

    A   Accuracy
    B   Completeness
    C   Complexity
    D   Relevance

4   For whom are management accounts prepared?

    A   Employees
    B   Internal managers
    C   Shareholders
    D   Suppliers

5   Which of the following statements is/are correct?   True   False

    1   **Strategic planning** is carried out by front-line managers.   ☐   ☑
    2   Non-financial information is relevant to management accounting.   ☑   ☐

6   Which of the following are part of the prime cost for a manufacturing company?

    A   Maintenance cost of a machine used in production
    B   Salary cost of a supervisor overseeing direct employees
    C   Cost of a canteen used by production employees
    D   Royalties payable to the designer of the basic product

7   Employee A is a carpenter and normally works 36 hours per week, which is treated as direct labour. The standard rate of pay Is $7.00 per hour. A premium of 50% of his basic hourly rate is paid for all overtime hours worked. During the last week of October, Employee A worked for 42 hours. The overtime hours worked were for the following reasons:

    Machine breakdown: 4 hours
    To complete a special job at the request of a customer: 2 hours

    How much of Employee A's earnings for the last week of October would have been treated as direct wages?

    A $315.00   B $252.00   C $273.00   D $294.00

8   **Fill in the blanks** in the statements below, using the words in the box:

- Costs can be divided into the following three categories (1)................; (2)............... ; (3) ....

- There are a number of different ways in which costs can be classified.

  - (4)............ and (5)............ (or overhead) costs

  - (6)................................costs (production costs, distribution and selling costs, administration costs and financing costs)

- A (7).............. is a unit of product which has costs attached to it. A (8) .... is a type of responsibility centre where managers are responsible for expenses only.

• Cost centre	• Direct	• Labour	• Cost unit
• Material	• Functional	• Indirect	• Other costs

9   Direct costs are:

A   costs which can neither be identified with a cost centre nor identified with a single cost unit
B   costs which can be identified with a single cost unit
C   costs incurred as a direct result of a particular decision
D   costs incurred which can be attributed to a particular accounting period

10   A system of accounting that segregates revenue and costs into areas of personal responsibility in order to monitor and assess the performance of each part of the organisation is known as:

A   Control accounting   C   Controllable accounting
B   Responsibility accounting   D   Centre accounting

11   DP Co is preparing its estimate of distribution costs for the next period. Based on previous experience, a linear relationship has been identified between sales volume and distribution costs. The following information has been collected concerning distribution costs.

Sales volume	Distribution cost
Units	$
22,000	58,600
34,000	73,000

What would be the estimated distribution costs for a sales volume of 28,000 units?

A $32,200   B $33,600   C $65,800   D $74,582

12   A delivery driver for a courier company is paid a salary of $1,000 per month, plus an extra 12 cents per delivery made. This labour cost is best described as:

A   a variable cost   C   a fixed cost
B   a step cost   D   a semi-variable cost

13   The following is a graph of cost against level of activity

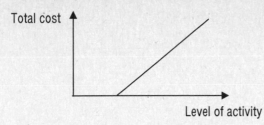

Total cost

Level of activity

To which one of the following costs does the graph correspond?

A   Sales commission payable per unit up to a maximum amount of commission

B   Electricity bills made up of a standing charge and a variable charge

C   Bonus payments to employees, paid per unit when production reaches a certain level

D   Machine rental costs, where a fixed amount is payable up to a certain level of output, and thereafter an additional rate per unit is payable

14   Identify which type of cost is being described in (a)-(d) below.

VARIABLE COST	FIXED COST	STEPPED FIXED COST	SEMI-VARIABLE COST

(a)   This type of cost stays the same, no matter how many products you produce

(b)   This type of cost increases as you produce more products. The sum of these costs are also known as the marginal cost of a product

(c)   This type of cost is fixed but only within certain levels of activity

(d)   This type of cost contains both fixed and variable elements

15   Total cost

Level of activity

Which of the following costs is depicted by this graph?

A   Labour costs where employees are paid a guaranteed wage. When output exceeds an agreed level a bonus is paid for each additional unit produced.

B   Labour costs where employees are paid a guaranteed wage plus a bonus per unit for all units produced.

C   Gas costs which comprise a standing charge each period and an additional charge for each unit of gas consumed.

D   Rental of a car which comprises a fixed charge per month plus an additional charge for mileage.

16   Factory overheads can be absorbed by which of the following methods?

1   Direct labour hours
2   Machine hours
3   As a % of prime cost
4    $x per unit

A   1, 2, 3 or 4
B   1 and 2 only
C   1, 2 or 3 only
D   2, 3 or 4 only

17   Which of the following would be the most appropriate basis for apportioning machinery insurance costs to cost centres within a factory?

A   The number of machines in each cost centre
B   The floor area occupied by the machinery in each cost centre
C   The value of the machinery in each cost centre
D   The operating hours of the machinery in each cost centre

18   Department L production overheads are absorbed using a direct labour hour rate. Budgeted production overheads for the department were $480,000 and the actual labour hours were 100,000. Actual production overheads amounted to $516,000.

Based on the above data, and assuming that the production overheads were over absorbed by $24,000, what was the overhead absorption rate per labour hour?

A $4.80
B $4.92
C $5.16
D $5.40

19   AC Co absorbs production overhead in the assembly department on the basis of direct labour hours. Budgeted direct labour hours for the period were 200,000. The production overhead absorption rate for the period was $2 per direct labour hour.

Actual results for the period were as follows.

Direct labour hours worked	220,000
Production overheads incurred	$480,000

Which one of the following statements is correct?

A   Production overheads were $40,000 over absorbed
B   Production overheads were $40,000 under absorbed
C   Production overheads were $80,000 under absorbed
D   No under or over absorption occurred

20   The budgeted production overheads and other budget data of Eiffel Co are as follows.

Budget	Production dept X
Overhead cost	$36,000
Direct materials cost	$32,000
Direct labour cost	$40,000
Machine hours	10,000
Direct labour hours	18,000

What would be the absorption rate for Department X using the various bases of apportionment?

(a)   % of direct material cost = ☐

(b)   % of direct labour cost = ☐

(c)   % of total direct cost = ☐

(d)   Rate per machine hour = ☐

(e)   Rate per direct labour hour = ☐

21   Cost and selling price details for product Q are as follows.

	$ per unit
Direct material	4.20
Direct labour	3.00
Variable overhead	1.00
Fixed overhead	2.80
	11.00
Profit	4.00
Selling price	15.00

Budgeted production for month	10,000 units
Actual production for month	12,000 units
Actual sales for month	11,200 units
Actual fixed overhead cost incurred during month	$31,000

(a)   Based on the above data, the marginal costing profit for the month is

       A $44,800   B $45,160   C $50,600   D $76,160

(b)   Based on the above data, the absorption costing profit for the month is

       A $42,200   B $44,800   C $45,160   D $47,400

22   B Company makes a product which has a variable production cost of $21 per unit and a sales price of $39 per unit. At the beginning of 20X5, there was no opening inventory and sales during the year were 50,000 units. Fixed costs (production, administration, sales and distribution) totalled $328,000. Production was 70,000 units.

(a)   The contribution per unit is $ ☐ .

(b)   The profit per unit is $ ☐ .

23   A Co requires a 25% return on sales. The full cost of product R is $27.

The selling price of product R should be $ ☐ .

24   R Co expects to sell 10,000 units of product Y in the coming year. The organisation makes an annual investment of $1,700,000 in production of product Y and requires a return of 22% on its investment. The full cost of product Y is $15.

The required selling price of product Y is $ ☐ .

25   (a)   Product S's unit cost is $5. A selling price is based on a margin of 25%. The selling price is $ ☐ to the nearest cent.

(b)   Product H sells for $175. The mark-up is 12%. The unit cost of product H is $ ☐ to the nearest cent.

26   J Co manufactures three products, details of which are as follows.

	Product K $ per unit	Product L $ per unit	Product M $ per unit
Selling price	105	133	133
Direct materials ($3/litre)	15	6	21
Direct labour ($8/hour)	24	32	24
Variable overhead	9	12	9
Fixed overhead	23	50	42

In a period when direct labour is restricted in supply, the most and least profitable use of labour are:

	Most profitable	Least profitable
A	K	M
B	L	K
C	M	K
D	M	L

27   V Co manufactures three products which have the following selling prices and costs per unit.

	V1 $	V2 $	V3 $
Selling price	30.00	36.00	34.00
Costs per unit			
Direct materials	8.00	10.00	20.00
Direct labour	4.00	8.00	3.60
Overhead			
Variable	2.00	4.00	1.80
Fixed	9.00	6.00	2.70
	23.00	28.00	28.10
Profit per unit	7.00	8.00	5.90

All three products use the same type of labour.

In a period in which labour is in short supply, the rank order of production is:

V1   ....

V2   ....

V3   ....

28   Product N generates a contribution to sales ratio of 20%. Annual fixed costs are $80,000.

The breakeven point, in terms of units sold per annum,

A   is 96,000
B   is 400,000
C   is 480,000
D   cannot be calculated without more information

29

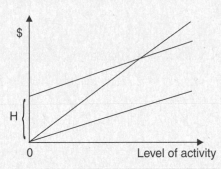

(a)   H on the graph indicates the value of

A   contribution   B   fixed cost   C   sales value   D   variable cost

(b)   This graph is known as a

A   contribution breakeven chart   C   profit-volume chart
B   conventional breakeven chart   D   semi-variable cost chart

30   S Co manufactures a single product, V. Data for the product are as follows.

	$ per unit
Selling price	40
Direct material cost	8
Direct labour cost	6
Variable production overhead cost	4
Variable selling overhead cost	2
Fixed overhead cost	10
Profit per unit	10

The profit/volume ratio for product V is [   ]

31   Fast Fandango Co manufactures a single product, the FF, which sells for $10. At 75% capacity, which is the normal level of activity for the factory, sales are $600,000 per period.

The cost of these sales are as follows.

Direct cost per unit	$3
Production overhead	$156,000 (including variable costs of $30,000)
Sales costs	$ 80,000
Distribution costs	$ 60,000 (including variable costs of $15,000)
Administration overhead	$ 40,000 (including variable costs of $9,000)

The sales costs are fixed with the exception of sales commission which is 5% of sales value.

(a)   The contribution per unit of product FF is $ [   ]

(b)   The fixed cost per period is $ [   ]

(c)   The breakeven volume of sales per period is [   ] units

32   A factory manufactures three components A, B and C.

During week 26, the following data were recorded.

Labour grade	Number of employees	Rate per hour $	Individual hours worked
I	6	12.00	40
II	18	9.60	42
III	4	8.40	40
IV	1	4.80	44

Output and standard times during the same week were as follows.

Component	Output	Standard minutes (each)
A	444	30
B	900	54
C	480	66

The normal working week is 38 hours. Overtime is paid at a premium of 50% of the normal hourly rate.

A group incentive scheme is in operation. The time saved is expressed as a percentage of hours worked and is shared between the group as a proportion of the hours worked by each grade.

The bonus rate paid is 75% of the normal hourly rate.

(a)   The overtime premium payable to each grade of labour is:

Grade I $ ▢

Grade II $ ▢

Grade III $ ▢

Grade IV $ ▢

(b)   The number of standard hours produced is ▢

(c)   The amount of bonus payable in total to all employees is $ ▢

33   Standard costing provides which of the following? Tick all that apply.

(a)   Targets and measures of performance   ▢

(b)   Information for budgeting   ▢

(c)   Simplification of inventory control systems   ▢

(d)   Actual future costs   ▢

34   CC Co manufactures a carbonated drink, which is sold in 1 litre bottles. During the bottling process there is a 20% loss of liquid input due to spillage and evaporation. The standard usage of liquid per bottle is

A   0.80 litres   B   1.00 litres   C   1.20 litres   D   1.25 litres

35   PM Co is in the process of setting standard unit costs for next period. Period J uses two types of material, P and S. 7 kg of material P and 3 kg of material S are needed, at a standard price of $4 per kg and $9 per kg respectively.

Direct labour will cost $7 per hour and each unit of J requires 5 hours of labour.

Production overheads are to be recovered at the rate of $6 per direct labour hour, and general overhead is to be absorbed at a rate of ten per cent of production cost.

The standard prime cost for one unit of product J will be:

A $55   B $90   C $120   D $132

36   Calculate the standard cost of producing 100 wheels for a toy car using the information given below. Fill in the shaded box.

	Bending	Cutting	Assembly
Standard labour rates of pay per hour $	4	6	5
Standard labour rates per 100 wheels (hours)	0.8	0.5	1.2

STANDARD COST CARD			
Toy car wheels	Part number 5917B - 100 wheels		Date:
	Quantity	Rate/price	Total $
Direct materials			
Tyres	100	10c each	
Steel strip	50	$10.40 per 100	
Wire	1000	2c each	
Direct labour	hours	$	
Bending			
Cutting			
Assembly			
STANDARD COST			

37   SG Co has extracted the following details from the standard cost card of one of its products.

Direct labour 3.5 hours @ $9.20 per hour

During period 4, SG Co produced 1,600 units of product and incurred direct labour cost of $55,100 for 5,800 hours.

The direct labour rate and efficiency variances for period 4 were

	Rate $	Efficiency $
A	1,740 adverse	1,840 adverse
B	1,740 adverse	1,900 adverse
C	1,740 adverse	1,840 favourable
D	1,740 favourable	1,840 favourable

38   Which of the following would help to explain a favourable direct material price variance?

		Would help to explain variance	Would not help to explain variance
(a)	The standard price per unit of direct material was unrealistically high	☐	☐
(b)	Output quantity was greater than budgeted and it was possible to obtain bulk purchase discounts	☐	☐
(c)	The material purchased was of a higher quality than standard	☐	☐

39   SL Co has budgeted to make and sell 4,200 units of product S during the period.

The standard variable overhead cost per unit is $4.

During the period covered by the budget, the actual results were as follows.

Production and sales   5,000 units
Variable overhead incurred $17,500

The variable overhead total variance for the period was

A $2,500 favourable   C $2,500 adverse
B $700 favourable   D $700 adverse

Questions 40 and 41 are based on the following data

Standard costing is used to control the material costs of product Alpha. No material inventories are held.

The following data are available for product Alpha during May.

	Budget	Actual
Production units	6,000	6,300
Material usage	48,000 kg	51,150 kg
Material cost	$576,000	$562,650

40   The material usage variance for May is:

A $750 (A)   C $9,000 (A)
B $6,000 (A)   D $28,800 (F)

41   The material price variance for May is:

A $8,900 (F)   C $62,000 (F)
B $51,150 (F)   D $64,100 (F)

42   Standard and budgeted data for the latest period for a company's single product are as follows:

Budgeted sales volume	19,680 units
Actual sales volume	18,780 units
Standard selling price per unit	$27.10
Standard variable cost per unit	$21.70
Actual sales revenue	$529,596

The sales price variance for the period is:

A $3,732 (A)   C $20,658 (F)
B $20,658 (A)   D $24,390 (A)

43   P Co has the following data relating to its budgeted sales for October 20X7:

Budgeted sales	$100,000
Budgeted selling price per unit	$8.00
Budgeted contribution per unit	$2.50

During October 20X7, actual sales were 11,000 units for a sales revenue of $99,000.

P Co uses a marginal costing system.

The sales variances for October 20X7 were:

	Price	Volume
	$	$
A	11,000 (F)	3,750 (A)
B	11,000 (F)	6,000 (A)
C	12,500 (F)	12,000 (A)
D	12,500 (A)	12,000 (A)

44   J Co uses a standard costing system and has the following data relating to one of its products.

	$	$
Selling price		9.00
Variable cost	4.00	
Fixed costs	3.00	
		7.00
Profit per unit		2.00

Its budgeted sales for October 20X5 were 800 units, but the actual sales were 850 units. The revenue earned from these sales was $7,480.

If a profit reconciliation statement were to be drawn up using marginal costing principles, the sales variances would be

	Price	Volume
A	$160 (A)	$100 (F)
B	$160 (A)	$250 (F)
C	$170 (A)	$240 (F)
D	$170 (A)	$250 (F)

45   J Co operates a standard cost accounting system. The following information has been extracted from its standard cost card and budgets.

Budgeted sales volume	5,000 units
Standard sales price	$10.00 per unit
Standard variable cost	$5.60 per unit
Standard total cost	$7.50 per unit

If it used a standard marginal cost accounting system and its actual sales were 4,500 units at a selling price of $12.00, its sales volume variance would be

A	$1,250 adverse	C	$2,250 adverse
B	$2,200 adverse	D	$3,200 adverse

46 Which of the following would help to explain a favourable sales volume variance?

   (i)   Increased competitor activity led to a reduction in the number of units sold.

   (ii)   Customers were given discounts at a higher level than standard in order to encourage increased sales.

   (iii)   The unit cost of production was lower than standard and selling prices were maintained at the standard level, so that a higher contribution was achieved per unit sold.

   (iv)   Higher quality material supplies led to improvements in the quality of the final output, which customers found attractive.

   A   (i), (ii) and (iv) only
   B   (ii), (iii) and (iv) only
   C   (ii) and (iv) only
   D   (ii) only

47 PG Co makes a single product and is preparing its material usage budget for next year. Each unit of product requires 2 kg of material, and 5,000 units of product are to be produced next year.

Opening inventory of material is budgeted to be 800 kg and PG Co budgets to increase material inventory at the end of next year by 20%.

The material usage budget for next year is

   A   8,000 kg   C   10,000 kg
   B   9,840 kg   D   10,160 kg

48 In a situation where there are no production resource limitations, which of the following must be available for the material usage budget to be completed? Tick all that apply.

   (a)   Production volume from the production budget   ☐

   (b)   Budgeted change in materials inventory   ☐

   (c)   Standard material usage per unit   ☐

49 The following details have been extracted from the accounts receivable records of PR Co.

Invoices paid in the month after sale	80%
Invoices paid in the second month after sale	10%
Invoices paid in the third month after sale	5%
Bad debts (irrecoverable debts)	5%

Invoices are issued on the last day of each month, and customers paying in the month after sale are entitled to deduct a 1% settlement discount.

Credit sales values for January to April are budgeted as follows.

January	February	March	April
$35,000	$40,000	$60,000	$45,000

The amount budgeted to be received from credit sales in April is

   A $43,640   C $53,750
   B $53,270   D $55,020

50   If a company has no production resource limitations, in which order would the following budgets be prepared?

Order

Material usage budget	
Sales budget	
Material purchase budget	
Finished goods inventory budget	
Production budget	
Material inventory budget	

51   When preparing a production budget, the quantity to be produced equals

A   sales quantity + opening inventory + closing inventory
B   sales quantity − opening inventory + closing inventory
C   sales quantity − opening inventory − closing inventory
D   sales quantity + opening inventory − closing inventory

52   The following extract is taken from the distribution cost budget of DC Co:

Volume delivered (units)	8,000	14,000
Distribution cost	$7,200	$10,500

The budgeted cost allowance for distribution cost for a delivery volume of 12,000 units is

A $6,600   B $9,000   C $9,400   D $10,800

53   Which of the following best describes a flexible budget?

A   A budget which is designed to be easily updated to reflect recent changes in unit costs or selling prices

B   A budget which can be flexed when actual costs are known, to provide a realistic forecast for the forthcoming period

C   A budget which, by recognising different cost behaviour patterns, is designed to change as the volume of activity changes

D   A budget which is prepared on a spreadsheet, with the flexibility to add new costs items to prepare new forecasts as circumstances change during the year

54

		True	False
(a)	Budgetary control procedures are useful only to maintain control over an organisation's expenditure		
(b)	A prerequisite of flexible budgeting is a knowledge of cost behaviour patterns		
(c)	Fixed budgets are not useful for control purposes		

55   A flexible budget is

A   a budget comprising variable production costs only
B   a budget which is updated with actual costs and revenues as they occur during the budget period
C   a budget which shows the costs and revenues at different levels of activity
D   a budget which is prepared using a computer spreadsheet model

56 The following extract is taken from the production cost budget of W Co:

Production units	2,000	3,000
Production cost	$17,760	$20,640

The budget cost allowance for an activity level of 4,000 units is

A $11,520   B $23,520   C $27,520   D $35,520

57 In a standard cost bookkeeping system, when the actual wage rate paid per hour is higher than the standard wage rate per hour, the accounting entries to record this are

	Debit	Credit
A	Labour rate variance account	Wages control account
B	Labour rate variance account	Work in progress control account
C	Wages control account	Labour rate variance account
D	Work in progress control account	Labour rate variance account

58 Which of the following statements is correct?

A   An adverse direct material cost variance will always be a combination of an adverse material price variance and an adverse material usage variance

B   An adverse direct material cost variance will always be a combination of an adverse material price variance and a favourable material usage variance

C   An adverse direct material cost variance can be a combination of a favourable material price variance and a favourable material usage variance

D   An adverse direct material cost variance can be a combination of a favourable material price variance and an adverse material usage variance

59 PB Co maintains a standard cost bookkeeping system. The work in progress account for the latest period is as follows.

WORK IN PROGRESS CONTROL ACCOUNT

	$'000		$'000
Stores account	724	Finished goods control	3,004
Wages control	1,210	Material usage variance	180
Production overhead control	1,050		
Labour efficiency variance	200		
	3,184		3,184

Which of the following statements is/are consistent with the entries in the work in progress account?

		Consistent with the account entries	Not consistent with the account entries
(a)	The material used in production was more than the standard allowed for the number of units produced		
(b)	All of the material issued to production was completely processed during the period		
(c)	The number of labour hours worked was greater than the standard allowed for the number of units produced		

60 Libra Co uses standard costing and an integrated accounting system. The double entry for a favourable labour efficiency variance is (delete as appropriate):

DR

DIRECT LABOUR EFFICIENCY VARIANCE ACCOUNT
WORK IN PROGRESS CONTROL ACCOUNT
DIRECT LABOUR CONTROL ACCOUNT
DIRECT LABOUR RATE VARIANCE ACCOUNT

CR

DIRECT LABOUR EFFICIENCY VARIANCE ACCOUNT
WORK IN PROGRESS CONTROL ACCOUNT
DIRECT LABOUR CONTROL ACCOUNT
DIRECT LABOUR RATE VARIANCE ACCOUNT

61 A firm operates an integrated cost and financial accounting system. The accounting entries for direct wages incurred would be:

	Debit	Credit
A	Wages control account	Work in progress account
B	Wages control account	Bank account
C	Work in progress account	Wages control account
D	Bank account	Wages control account

62 In the same integrated system, the firm's entries for production overhead absorbed would be:

	Debit	Credit
A	Finished goods inventory account	Overhead control account
B	Income statement	Overhead control account
C	Work in progress control account	Overhead control account
D	Overhead control account	Work in progress control account

63 LE Co operates an integrated accounting system. The raw materials control account at 31 May is as follows.

RAW MATERIALS CONTROL

	$		$
Balance b/f	18,000	?	71,000
Bank	76,000	Production overhead control	6,000
		Balance c/f	17,000
	94,000		94,000

The $71,000 credit entry is the value of the transfer to the

A	cost of sales account	C	finished goods control account
B	account payable control account	D	work in progress control account

64 In cost bookkeeping, when material costs are debited to the materials account, the corresponding credit entry is to which of the following accounts?

Cash [   ]

Suppliers [   ]

Work-in-progress [   ]

65   PC Co makes a product in two processes. The following data is available for the latest period, for process 1.

Opening work in progress of 200 units was valued as follows.

Material	$2,400
Labour	$1,200
Overhead	$400

No losses occur in the process.

Units added and costs incurred during the period:

Material	$6,000 (500 units)
Labour	$3,350
Overhead	$1,490

Closing work in progress of 100 units had reached the following degrees of completion:

Material	100%
Labour	50%
Overhead	30%

PC Co uses the weighted average method of inventory valuation.

(a)   How many equivalent units are used when calculating the cost per unit in relation to overhead?

   A   500   B   600   C   630   D   700

(b)   The value of the units transferred to process 2 was

   A $7,200   B $13,200   C $14,840   D $15,400

66   A company needs to produce 340 litres of Chemical X. There is a normal loss of 10% of the material input into the process. During a given month the company did produce 340 litres of good production, although there was an abnormal loss of 5% of the material input into the process.

How many litres of material were input into the process during the month?

   A   357 litres
   B   374 litres
   C   391 litres
   D   400 litres

67   20,000 litres of liquid were put into a process at the beginning of the month at a cost of $4,400. The output of finished product was 17,000 litres. The normal level of waste in this process is 20% and the waste which is identified at the end of the process can be sold at $0.50 per litre. Use this information to complete the process account below.

PROCESS ACCOUNT

	Litres	$		Litres	$
Materials			Normal waste		
Abnormal gains			Finished goods		

68   Bonto Co produces a simple product in two processes, process R and process X. The following information relates to process X for period 4.

Work in progress at start of period - nil.
Material transferred from process R during the period - 2,500 kgs valued at $7,145.
Wages paid - 234½ hours at $4 per hour.
Other direct costs allocated - $463.

Normal waste during processing - 5% of process R input. This has a scrap value of 16c per kg.

At the end of period 4 there were 2,100 kgs transferred to finished inventory, and 150 kgs remained in work in progress.

The work in progress is 100% complete so far as materials are concerned, but only 80% of labour costs and 60% of other direct costs have been incurred.

(a)   During the period there was an abnormal ⬚ of ⬚ kg

(b)   The cost per equivalent unit of each cost element during the period was:

Materials $ ⬚

Labour $ ⬚

Other direct costs $ ⬚

69   What is an equivalent unit?

A   A unit of output which is identical to all others manufactured in the same process
B   Notional whole units used to represent uncompleted work
C   A unit of product in relation to which costs are ascertained
D   The amount of work achievable, at standard efficiency levels, in an hour

The following information relates to questions 70 and 71

Patacake Co produces a certain food item in a manufacturing process. On 1 November, there was no opening inventory of work in process. During November, 500 units of material were input to the process, with a cost of $9,000. Direct labour costs in November were $3,840. Production overhead is absorbed at the rate of 200% of direct labour costs. Closing inventory on 30 November consisted of 100 units which were 100% complete as to materials and 80% complete as to labour and overhead. There was no loss in process.

70   The full production cost of completed units during November was

A $10,400   B $16,416   C $16,800   D $20,520

71   The value of the closing work in progress on 30 November is

A $2,440   B $3,720   C $4,200   D $20,520

72   In process costing, if an abnormal loss arises, the process account is generally

A   debited with the scrap value of the abnormal loss units
B   debited with the full production cost of the abnormal loss units
C   credited with the scrap value of the abnormal loss units
D   credited with the full production cost of the abnormal loss units

73   A food manufacturing process has a normal wastage of 10% of input. In a period, 3,000 kgs of material were input and there was an abnormal loss of 75 kg. No inventories are held at the beginning or end of the process.

The quantity of good production achieved was [   ] kg.

74   A company makes a product, which passes through a single process.

Details of the process for the last period are as follows.

Materials   5,000 kg at 50c per kg
Labour $700
Production overheads   200% of labour

Normal losses are 10% of input in the process, and without further processing any losses can be sold as scrap for 20c per kg.

The output for the period was 4,200 kg from the process.

There was no work in progress at the beginning or end of the period.

The value credited to the process account for the scrap value of the normal loss for the period will be $ [   ]

75   A company makes a product, which passes through a single process.

Details of the process for the last period are as follows.

Materials   5,000 kg at 50c per kg
Labour $700
Production overheads   200% of labour

Normal losses are 10% of input in the process, and without further processing any losses can be sold as scrap for 20c per kg.

The output for the period was 4,200 kg from the process.

There was no work in progress at the beginning or end of the period.

The value of the abnormal loss for the period is $ [   ]

76   A product is manufactured as a result of two processes, 1 and 2. Details of process 2 for the latest period were as follows.

Opening work in progress   Nil
Materials transferred from process 1 10,000 kg valued at $40,800
Labour and overhead costs $8,424
Output transferred to finished goods 8,000 kg
Closing work in progress   900 kg

Normal loss is 10% of input and losses have a scrap value of $0.30 per kg.

Closing work in progress is 100% complete for material, and 75% complete for both labour and overheads.

The value of the closing work in progress for the period was $ [   ]

77   PA Co operates a job costing system. The company's standard net profit margin is 20 per cent of sales.

The estimated costs for job 173 are as follows.

Direct materials   5 metres @ $20 per metre
Direct labour   14 hours @ $8 per hour

Variable production overheads are recovered at the rate of $3 per direct labour hour.

Fixed production overheads for the year are budgeted to be $200,000 and are to be recovered on the basis of the total of 40,000 direct labour hours for the year.

Other overheads, in relation to selling, distribution and administration, are recovered at the rate of $80 per job.

The price to be quoted for job 173 is, to the nearest $

A $404   B $424   C $485   D $505

78   Which of the following is a feature of job costing?

A   Production is carried out in accordance with the wishes of the customer
B   Associated with continuous production of large volumes of low-cost items
C   Establishes the cost of services rendered
D   Costs are charged over the units produced in the period

79   A firm uses job costing and recovers overheads as a percentage of direct labour cost.

Three jobs were worked on during a period, the details of which are as follows.

	Job 1 $	Job 2 $	Job 3 $
Opening work in progress	8,500	0	46,000
Material in period	17,150	29,025	0
Labour for period	12,500	23,000	4,500

The overheads for the period were exactly as budgeted, $140,000.

Job 3 was completed during the period and consisted of 2,400 identical circuit boards. The firm adds 50% to total production costs to arrive at a selling price.

What is the selling price of a circuit board?

A   It cannot be calculated without more information
B $31.56
C $41.41
D $55.21

80   P Co manufactures ring binders which are embossed with the customer's own logo. A customer has ordered a batch of 300 binders. The following data illustrate the cost for a typical batch of 100 binders.

	$
Direct materials	30
Direct wages	10
Machine set up	3
Design and artwork	15
	58

Direct employees are paid on a piecework basis.

P Co absorbs production overhead at a rate of 20 per cent of direct wages cost. Five per cent is added to the total production cost of each batch to allow for selling, distribution and administration overhead.

P Co requires a profit margin of 25 per cent of sales value.

The selling price for a batch of 300 binders (to the nearest cent) will be

A $189.00   B $193.20   C $201.60   D $252.00

81   JC Co operates a job costing system. The company's standard net profit margin is 20 per cent of sales value.

The estimated costs for job B124 are as follows.

Direct materials   3 kg @ $5 per kg

Direct labour   4 hours @ $9 per hour

Production overheads are budgeted to be $240,000 for the period, to be recovered on the basis of a total of 30,000 labour hours.

Other overheads, related to selling, distribution and administration, are budgeted to be $150,000 for the period. They are to be recovered on the basis of the total budgeted production cost of $750,000 for the period.

The price to be quoted for job B124 is $ [_____]

82   In which of the following situation(s) will job costing normally be used?

[_____] Production is continuous

[_____] Production of the product can be completed in a single accounting period

[_____] Production relates to a single special order

83   Which of the following would be appropriate cost units for a passenger coach company?

		Appropriate	Not appropriate
(a)	Vehicle cost per passenger-kilometre	[____]	[____]
(b)	Fuel cost for each vehicle per kilometre	[____]	[____]
(c)	Fixed cost per kilometre	[____]	[____]

84   The following information is available for the Whiteley Hotel for the latest thirty day period.

Number of rooms available per night	40
Percentage occupancy achieved	65%
Room servicing cost incurred	$3,900

The room servicing cost per occupied room-night last period, to the nearest cent, was:

A $3.25   B $5.00   C $97.50   D $150.00

85   Consider the following features and identify whether they relate to job costing, service costing or none of these costing methods.

J =   Job costing
S =   Service costing
N =   None of these costing methods

(i)   Production is carried out in accordance with the wishes of the customer [_____]

(ii)   Work is usually undertaken on the contractor's premises [_____]

(iii)   Costs are averaged over the units produced in the period [_____]

(iv)   It establishes the costs of services rendered [_____]

86   The following information relates to two hospitals for the year ended 31 December 20X5.

	St Matthew's	St Mark's
Number of in-patients	15,400	710
Average stay per in-patient	10 days	156 days
Total number of out-patient attendances	130,000	3,500
Number of available beds	510	320
Average number of beds occupied	402	307

Cost analysis	In- patients $	Out- patients $	In- patients $	Out- patients $
Patient care services				
Direct treatment services and supplies (eg nursing staff)	6,213,900	1,076,400	1,793,204	70,490
Medical supporting services:				
Diagnostic (eg pathology)	480,480	312,000	22,152	20,650
Other services (eg occupational therapy)	237,160	288,600	77,532	27,790
General services				
Patient related (eg catering)	634,480	15,600	399,843	7,700
General (eg administration)	2,196,760	947,700	1,412,900	56,700

Note. In-patients are those who receive treatment while remaining in hospital. Out-patients visit hospital during the day to receive treatment.

(a)   The cost per in-patient day at each hospital is (to the nearest cent):

      (i)   St Matthew's $ [   ]   (ii)   St Mark's $ [   ]

(b)   The cost per out-patient attendance at each hospital is (to the nearest cent):

      (i)   St Matthew's $ [   ]   (ii)   St Mark's $ [   ]

(c)   The bed occupation percentage at each hospital is (to one decimal place):

      (i)   St Matthew's   % [   ]   (ii)   St Mark's   % [   ]

The following information relates to questions 87 and 88.

Happy Returns Co operates a haulage business with three vehicles. During week 26 it is expected that all three vehicles will be used at a total cost of $10,390; 3,950 kilometres will be travelled (including return journeys when empty) as shown in the following table.

Journey	Tonnes carried (one way)	Kilometres (one way)
1	34	180
2	28	265
3	40	390
4	32	115
5	26	220
6	40	480
7	29	90
8	26	100
9	25	135
	280	1,975

87   The total of tonne-kilometres in week 26 = [   ]

88   The average cost per tonne-kilometre for week 26 = $ [   ] per tonne-kilometre (to the nearest cent).

89   What is the present value of $5,000 in perpetuity at a discount rate of 10%?

A $500
B $5,500
C $4,545
D $50,000

90   Which of the following is a disadvantage of the payback method of investment appraisal?

A   It tends to maximise financial and business risk.
B   It is a fairly complex technique and not easy to understand.
C   It cannot be used when there are limited funds available.
D   It doesn't account for the cost of capital in making investment decisions.

91   A company is considering investing in a manufacturing project that would have a three-year life span. The investment would involve an immediate cash outflow of $50,000. In each of the three years, 4,000 units would be produced and sold. The contribution per unit, based on current prices, is $5. The company has an annual cost of capital of 8%.

Year	Discount factor 8%
0	1.000
1	0.926
2	0.857
3	0.794

Calculate the net present value of the project $ [   ]

92   A company is considering investing $100,000 now to receive five annual sums of $25,000, commencing in a year's time. The company has a cost of capital of 10%. The annuity factor for 10% over 5 years is 3.791.

Calculate the net present value of the investment $ [   ]

93   Top Co's accountant has worked out the following NPVs for an investment in machinery. Use the data below to work out the internal rate of return for the investment.

NPV at 5%	$350
NPV at 10%	$(1,750)

[   ]

94   Which TWO of the following are relevant costs for decision making?

A   A sunk cost
B   A committed cost
C   A differential cost
D   A future cost

Answer bank

1	B	The other three items have been processed in some way to provide meaningful information whereas total sales value per product is the basic data for further processing.
2	D	Only this option refers to internal information.
3	C	Good information should be as simple as possible – remember ACCURATE.
4	B	Management accounts are produced for the internal managers of an organisation. The other groups of people would use the financial accounts of an organisation.

5

True	False	
☐	✓	**Strategic planning** is carried out by senior management. Front line managers will be concerned with **operational planning**.
✓	☐	The management accountant may frequently have to take into account non-financial information

6	D	Royalty costs can be traced directly to cost units and are therefore direct expenses and a part of prime cost.

Options A, B and C are all **indirect costs** which cannot be traced directly to cost units. They would be classified as **production overheads** and are not a part of prime cost.

7	C	The overtime premium paid at the specific request of a customer would be treated as a direct cost because it can be traced to a specific cost unit.

The four hours of machine breakdown time is idle time. It cannot be traced to a specific cost unit therefore it is an indirect cost.

The direct wages cost is as follows.

	$
Basic pay for active hours: 38 hours × $7.00	266.00
Overtime premium re: customer request 2 hours × $3.50	7.00
	273.00

Option A is incorrect because it is the employee's total wages for the week, both direct and indirect.

Option B is the basic pay for a 36 hour week, making no allowance for the overtime worked at the customer's request.

If you selected **option D** you calculated the basic pay for all of the hours worked, but you made no allowance for either the idle time or the overtime premium.

8	(1)	Material	(5)	Indirect
	(2)	Labour	(6)	Functional
	(3)	Other costs	(7)	Cost unit
	(4)	Direct	(8)	Cost centre

9	B	You need to learn this definition.
10	B	Responsibility accounting requires costs to be classified as controllable or uncontrollable.

11 **C** Using the high-low method.

	Units	$
High sales	34,000	73,000
Low sales	22,000	58,600
Variable cost of	12,000	14,400

Variable cost per unit $14,400/12,000 = $1.20

$$\text{Fixed cost} = \$73,000 - (34,000 \times \$1.20)$$
$$= \$32,200$$

Estimated distribution costs for a sales volume of 28,000 units:

	$
Fixed cost	32,200
Variable cost (28,000 × $1.20)	33,600
	65,800

Options A and B are the fixed cost and variable cost respectively, rather than the total cost. If you selected **option D** you simply calculated an average unit cost rate without allowing for the constant nature of the fixed costs.

12 **D** The driver's wages are part fixed ($1,000 per month) and part variable (12 cents per delivery). Therefore the wages are a semi-variable cost.

If you chose options A or C you were considering only part of the cost.

Option B, a step cost, is a cost which remains constant up to a certain level and then increases to a higher, constant level of fixed cost.

13 **C** The depicted cost is zero up to a certain level of output, then it increases at a constant rate per unit of output. The description of bonus payments fits this pattern.

Graphs for the other options would look like this.

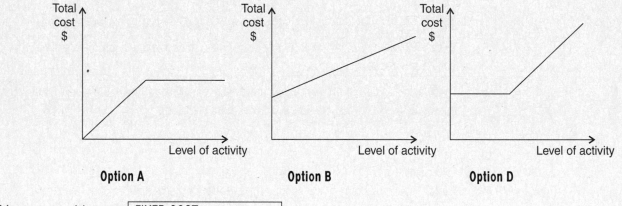

14

(a)	FIXED COST
(b)	VARIABLE COST
(c)	STEPPED FIXED COST
(d)	SEMI-VARIABLE COST

15 A   Costs B, C and D would be depicted as follows.

Total cost $

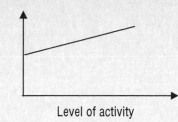

Level of activity

16 A   All of the overhead absorption methods are suitable, depending on the circumstances.

Method 1, direct labour hours, is suitable in a labour-intensive environment. **Method 2**, machine hours, is suitable in a machine-intensive environment. **Method 3**, a percentage of prime cost, can be used if it is difficult to obtain the necessary information to use a time-based method. **Method 4**, a rate per unit, is suitable if all cost units are identical.

17 C   The insurance cost is likely to be linked to the cost of replacing the machines, therefore the most appropriate basis for apportionment is the value of machinery.

Options A, **B and D** would all be possible apportionment bases in the absence of better information, but option C is preferable.

18 D

	$
Actual overheads	516,000
Over absorbed overheads	24,000
Overheads absorbed by 100,000 hours	540,000

∴ Overhead absorption rate = $540,000/100,000 = $5.40 per labour hour

Option A is incorrect because it is based on the budgeted overhead and the actual labour hours.

If you selected **option B** you deducted the over absorbed overheads by mistake, at the beginning of the calculation. If overhead is over absorbed, then the overhead absorbed must be higher than the actual overhead incurred.

Option C is incorrect because it is the actual overhead per direct labour hour.

19 B

	$
Overhead absorbed 220,000 hours × $2	440,000
Overhead incurred	480,000
Overhead under absorbed	40,000

Option A is the correct monetary amount, but the overhead incurred is more than the overhead absorbed, therefore there is an under absorption. **Option C** is the difference between the original budgeted overhead and the actual overhead incurred. This takes no account of the amount of overhead absorbed based on the activity achieved.

Option D is incorrect because there is a difference between the overhead incurred and the overhead absorbed.

20 (a) % of direct material cost = $\boxed{112.5\%}$

(b) % of direct labour cost = $\boxed{90\%}$

(c) % of total direct cost = $\boxed{50\%}$

(d) Rate per machine hour = $\boxed{\$3.60}$

(e) Rate per direct labour hour = $\boxed{\$2}$

Workings

(a) % of direct materials cost $\dfrac{\$36,000}{\$32,000} \times 100\% = 112.5\%$

(b) % of direct labour cost $\dfrac{\$36,000}{\$40,000} \times 100\% = 90\%$

(c) % of total direct cost $\dfrac{\$36,000}{\$72,000} \times 100\% = 50\%$

(d) Rate per machine hour $\dfrac{\$36,000}{10,000\,\text{hrs}} = \$3.60$ per machine hour

(e) Rate per direct labour hour $\dfrac{\$36,000}{18,000\,\text{hrs}} = \$2$ per direct labour hour

21 (a) B

Contribution per unit	=	$15 – $(4.20 + 3.00 + 1.00)
	=	$6.80
Contribution for month	=	$6.80 × 11,200 units
	=	$76,160
Less fixed costs incurred	=	$31,000
Marginal costing profit		$45,160

Option A bases the profit on the actual sales volume at $4 per unit profit. This utilises a unit rate for fixed overhead which is not valid under marginal costing.

If you selected option C you used the correct method but you based your calculations on the units produced rather than the units sold.

If you selected option D you calculated the correct contribution but you forgot to deduct the fixed overhead.

(b) D

	$
Sales 11,200 units × $15	168,000
Absorption costs for 11,200 units (× $11)	123,200
	44,800
Over absorbed fixed overhead for month (see working)	2,600
Absorption costing profit	47,400

Working	$
Overhead absorbed into production (12,000 units × $2.80)	33,600
Overhead incurred	31,000
Overhead over absorbed	2,600

If you selected **option A** you calculated all the figures correctly but you subtracted the over absorbed overhead instead of adding it to profit.

Option B makes no allowance for the over absorbed overhead, and **option C** is the marginal costing profit.

22 (a) The contribution per unit is $900,000/50,000 = \$ \boxed{18}$

(b) The profit per unit is $572,000/50,000 = \$ \boxed{11.44}$

	$'000	$'000
Sales (at $39 per unit)		1,950
Opening inventory	–	
Variable production cost ($21 × 70,000)	1,470	
Less closing inventory ($21 × 20,000)	420	
Variable cost of sales		1,050
Contribution		900
Less fixed costs		328
Profit		572

23 The selling price is $ \boxed{36}$

Selling price = $27/0.75 = $36

24 The selling price is $ \boxed{52.40}$

Required return = 0.22 × $1.7m = $374,000

Expected cost = 10,000 × $15 = $150,000

Expected revenue = $(374,000 + 150,000)
= $524,000

∴ Selling price = $524,000/10,000 = $52.40

25 (a) The selling price is $ \boxed{6.67}$

Selling price = $5/0.75 = $6.67

(b) The cost is $ \boxed{156.25}$

Cost = $175/1.12 = $156.25

26 C

	Product K	Product L	Product M
Contribution per unit	$57	$83	$79
Labour hours per unit	3	4	3
Contribution per labour hour	$19	$20.75	$26.33
Ranking	3	2	1

Therefore M is the most profitable and K is the least profitable.

If you selected **option A** you reversed the ranking. **Option B** ranks the products according to the contribution per unit, but this takes no account of the **limiting factor**. If you selected **option D** you ranked the products according to their profit per unit, but this takes no account of the **limiting factor** and is **distorted by the fixed costs**.

27   V1 = 1st
      V2 = 3rd
      V3 = 2nd

	V1	V2	V3
	$	$	$
Selling price per unit	30	36	34.00
Variable costs per unit	14	22	25.40
Contribution per unit	16	14	8.60
Labour cost per unit	$4	$8	$3.60
Contribution per $ of labour cost	$4	$1.75	$2.39
Rank order of production	1	3	2

28   D   The breakeven point cannot be calculated in terms of units because we do not know the unit selling price.

           Option C gives the breakeven point in terms of sales value:

           $$\frac{\$80,000}{0.2} = 400,000$$

           To convert this to a number of units we would need to divide by the selling price per unit.

29   (a)   B   The distance H is the total cost at zero activity, ie the fixed cost. **Option A**, contribution, is the distance between the sales line and the variable cost line, which are the two lines that pass through the origin. Sales value (**option C**) is represented by the steepest of the two lines passing through the origin. Variable cost (**option D**) is represented by the less steep of the two lines passing through the origin.

      (b)   A   The chart shows the variable cost line and the contribution can be read directly as the distance between this and the sales value line. Therefore this is a contribution breakeven chart.

                 A conventional breakeven chart (**option B**) shows the fixed cost line instead of the variable cost line. A profit volume chart (**option C**) plots a single line to indicate the profit at any level of activity. **Option D** is not a generally recognised description of a chart used for breakeven analysis.

30   The profit/volume ratio for product V is [50] %

      The profit/volume ratio (P/V ratio) is another term used to describe the contribution/sales ratio (C/S ratio)

      $$P/V \ ratio \ = \frac{Contribution \ per \ unit}{Selling \ price \ per \ unit}$$

      $$= \frac{\$(40-8-6-4-2)}{\$40} \times 100\% = 50\%$$

31 (a) The contribution per unit of product FF is $5.60.

Workings

Sales are 60,000 units at the normal level of activity. Variable costs at 60,000 units of production/sales are as follows.

	$	$ per unit
Production overhead	30,000	0.50
Sales costs (5% of $600,000)	30,000	0.50
Distribution costs	15,000	0.25
Administration overhead	9,000	0.15
	84,000	1.40
Direct costs	180,000	3.00
Total variable costs	264,000	4.40
Sales revenue	600,000	10.00
Contribution	336,000	5.60

(b) The fixed cost per period is $252,000.

Fixed costs	$
Production overhead	126,000
Sales oosts	50,000
Distribution costs	45,000
Administration overhead	31,000
	252,000

(c) The breakeven volume of sales per period is 45,000 units.

Workings

$$\text{Breakeven point} = \frac{\text{fixed costs}}{\text{contribution per unit}}$$

$$= \frac{\$252,000}{\$5.60}$$

$$= 45,000 \text{ units}$$

32 (a)
Grade I $72.00
Grade II $345.60
Grade III $33.60
Grade IV $14.40

Workings

Grade	Overtime premium (50% of basic rate) $/hour (a)	Overtime hours payable (b)	Overtime premium $ ((a) × (b))
I	6.00	2 hrs × 6 = 12	72.00
II	4.80	4 hrs × 18 = 72	345.60
III	4.20	2 hrs × 4 = 8	33.60
IV	2.40	6 hrs × 1 = 6	14.40

(b) The number of standard hours produced is 1,560.

Workings

Component		Standard hours
A	$444 \times \dfrac{30}{60}$ hours	222
B	$900 \times \dfrac{54}{60}$ hours	810
C	$480 \times \dfrac{66}{60}$ hours	528
		1,560

(c) The amount of bonus payable in total to all employees is $2,630.88.

Workings

Actual time taken

Grade		Hours
I	6×40 hrs	240
II	18×42 hrs	756
III	4×40 hrs	160
IV	1×44 hrs	44
		1,200

∴ Time saved = (1,560 − 1,200) hrs = 360 hrs

Time saved as a percentage of hours worked = $\dfrac{360}{1,200} \times 100\% = 30\%$

Calculation of bonus payable

Grade	Bonus hours		75% basic rate $	Bonus payable $
I	$240 \times 30\%$	= 72.0	× 9.00	648.00
II	$756 \times 30\%$	= 226.8	× 7.20	1,632.96
III	$160 \times 30\%$	= 48.0	× 6.30	302.40
IV	$44 \times 30\%$	= 13.2	× 3.60	47.52
				2,630.88

33 (a) Targets and measures of performance ✓

(b) Information for budgeting ✓

(c) Simplification of inventory control systems ✓

(d) Actual future costs ☐

Standard costing provides targets for achievement, and yardsticks against which actual performance can be monitored (**item (a)**). It also provides the unit cost information for evaluating the volume figures contained in a budget (**item (b)**). Inventory control systems are simplified with standard costing. Once the variances have been eliminated, all inventory units are evaluated at standard price (**item (c)**).

Item (d) is incorrect because standard costs are an estimate of what will happen in the future, and a unit cost target that the organisation is aiming to achieve.

34   D   Required liquid input = 1 litre $\times \dfrac{100}{80}$ = 1.25 litres

If you selected **option A** you **deducted** 20 per cent from the required output, instead of **adding extra** to allow for losses, whereas **option B** makes **no allowance** for losses.

Option C simply adds an extra 20 per cent to the completed output, but the wastage is 20 per cent of the liquid input, not 20 per cent of output.

35   B

		$ per unit	$ per unit
Material P	7 kg × $4	28	
Material S	3 kg × $9	<u>27</u>	
			55
Direct labour 5hr × $7			<u>35</u>
Standard prime cost of product J			<u><u>90</u></u>

Option A is the **standard material cost** and **option C** is the **standard total production cost**, including overheads which are not part of prime cost.

Option D includes the absorption of **general overhead**; always **read the question carefully**!

36

STANDARD COST CARD			
Toy car wheels	Part number 5917B - 100 wheels		Date:
	Quantity	*Rate/price*	*Total* $
Direct materials			
Tyres	100	10c each	10.00
Steel strip	50	$10.40 per 100	5.20
Wire	1000	2c each	20.00
			35.20
Direct labour	hours	$	
Bending	4	0.8	3.20
Cutting	6	0.5	3.00
Assembly	5	1.2	6.00
			12.20
STANDARD COST			47.40

37 A

	$
5,800 hours should have cost (× $9.20)	53,360
but did cost	55,100
Labour rate variance	1,740 (A)
1,600 units should take (× 3.5 hours)	5,600 hrs
but did take	5,800 hrs
Variance in hours	200 hrs (A)
× standard rate per hour	× $9.20
Labour efficiency variance	$1,840 (A)

If you selected option B you valued the efficiency variance in hours at the actual rate per hour instead of the standard rate per hour.

If you selected option C or option D you calculated the money values of the variances correctly but misinterpreted their direction.

38

		Would help to explain variance	Would not help to explain variance
(a)	The standard price per unit of direct material was unrealistically high	✓	☐
(b)	Output quantity was greater than budgeted and it was possible to obtain bulk purchase discounts	✓	☐
(c)	The material purchased was of a higher quality than standard	☐	✓

Statement (a) is consistent with a favourable material price variance. If the standard is high then actual prices are likely to be below the standard.

Statement (b) is consistent with a favourable material price variance. Bulk purchase discounts would not have been allowed at the same level in the standard, because purchases were greater than expected.

Statement (c) is not consistent with a favourable material price variance. Higher quality material is likely to cost more than standard, resulting in an adverse material price variance.

39 A   **Variable overhead total variance**

	$
Budgeted 5,000 units should cost (× $4)	20,000
But did cost	17,500
Variable overhead total variance	2,500 (F)

The variance is favourable because the actual expenditure was less than the amount budgeted.

If you selected an incorrect option you misinterpreted the direction of the variance or calculated one element of it only.

40 C   Standard price per kg of material = $576,000/48,000 = $12

Standard material usage per unit = 48,000 kg/6,000 = 8 kg per unit

6,300 units should have used (× 8 kg)	50,400	kg
but did use	51,150	kg
Usage variance in kg	750	kg (A)
× standard price per kg	× $12	
Material usage variance	$9,000	(A)

41 B

	$
51,150 kg of material should have cost (× $12 (from question 40))	613,800
but did cost	562,650
Material price variance	51,150 (F)

42 C

	$
18,780 units should sell for (× $27.10)	508,938
but did sell for	529,596
Sales price variance	20,658 (F)

43 A

	$
11,000 units should have sold for (× $8)	88,000
but did sell for	99,000
Selling price variance	11,000 (F)

Budgeted sales volume ($100,000 ÷ $8)	12,500 units
Actual sales volume	11,000 units
Sales volume variance in units	1,500 units (A)
× standard contribution per unit	× $2.50
Sales volume contribution variance	$3,750 (A)

44 D

Actual sales	850 units
Budgeted sales	800 units
Variance in units	50 units (F)
× standard contribution per unit ($(9 − 4))	× $5
Sales volume contribution variance	$250 (F)

	$
Revenue for 850 units should have been (× $9)	7,650
but was	7,480
Selling price variance	170 (A)

45 B Since J Co uses a standard marginal costing system, the sales volume variance will be valued at the standard contribution of $4.40 per unit ($10.00 − $5.60).

Budgeted sales volume	5,000 units
Actual sales volume	4,500 units
Sales volume variance in units	500 units (A)
× standard contribution per unit	× $4.40
Sales volume contribution variance in $	$2,200 (A)

46 C **Situation (i)** would result in an adverse sales volume variance because volumes were reduced.

Situation (ii) would result in a favourable sales volume variance, evaluated at the standard contribution achievable on the extra sales volume above standard.

A higher contribution per unit (**situation (iii)**) would not affect the sales volume variance because the variance is evaluated at standard contribution per unit.

Situation (iv) would lead to an increased sales volume and hence a favourable sales volume variance.

47   C   Material usage budget = 5,000 units produced × 2 kg per unit
                                  = 10,000 kg

Option D is the material purchases budget. If you selected this you need to read the question more carefully. If you selected **option B** you adjusted incorrectly for the inventory change in attempting to calculate the purchases budget, but the material usage budget was required. If you selected **option A** you seem to have taken 20 per cent of the usage budget as the correct answer: the change in material inventory will have no effect at all on the usage budget for the year.

48   (a)   Production volume from the production budget ✓

         (b)   Budgeted change in materials inventory ☐

         (c)   Standard material usage per unit ✓

Since there are no production resource limitations, the production budget would be prepared before the material usage budget (a). The standard material usage per unit (c) would then indicate the total material usage required to produce the budgeted production volume.

It would not be necessary to know the budgeted change in materials inventory (b) since this would affect the material purchases, rather than the material usage.

49   B

		Received in April
		$
March sales	$60,000 × 80% × 99%*	47,520
February sales	$40,000 × 10%	4,000
January sales	$35,000 × 5%	1,750
		53,270

*This reduction allows for the 1% settlement discount.

If you selected **option A** you misinterpreted 'month **after** sale' to be the month the sale was made. The invoices are issued on the last day of each month, therefore cash receipts in respect of each month's sales will begin in the following month.

Option C makes no allowance for the settlement discount and **option D** includes the receipt of bad debts; those amounts will never be received cash.

50

	Order
Material usage budget	4
Sales budget	1
Material purchase budget	6
Finished goods inventory budget	2
Production budget	3
Material inventory budget	5

51   B   Sales = opening inventory + production − closing inventory

            ∴ Production = sales − opening inventory + closing inventory

52 C

	Units	$
High activity	14,000	10,500
Low activity	8,000	7,200
Increase	6,000	3,300

Variable cost per unit = $3,300/6,000 = $0.55

Fixed cost, substituting in high activity = $10,500 – (14,000 × 0.55)
= $2,800

Budget cost allowance to distribute 12,000 units:

	$
Variable cost (12,000 × $0.55)	6,600
Fixed cost	2,800
	9,400

If you selected **option A** you did not include an allowance for fixed cost, and if you selected **option B** or **D** you calculated the answer on a pro rata basis from the data given. This does not take account of the fixed element of the distribution cost.

53 C   A flexible budget identifies fixed costs separately from variable costs. The allowance for variable costs can be flexed to derive a realistic target in the light of the actual activity level achieved.

54

		True	False
(a)	Budgetary control procedures are useful only to maintain control over an organisation's expenditure	☐	☑
(b)	A prerequisite of flexible budgeting is a knowledge of cost behaviour patterns	☑	☐
(c)	Fixed budgets are not useful for control purposes	☐	☑

Comments

(a)   Budgetary control procedures can also be useful to maintain control over an organisation's revenue.

(b)   A knowledge of cost behaviour patterns is necessary so that the variable cost allowance can be flexed in line with changes in activity.

(c)   Fixed budgets may be useful for control purposes when:

(i)   Variable costs are negligible or non-existent
(ii)   Activity levels are not subject to change

55 C   Learn this definition.

56 B

			Change
Production units	2,000	3,000	+1,000
Production cost	$17,760	$20,640	$2,880

Variable cost per unit = $\dfrac{\$2,880}{1,000}$ = $2.88; Fixed costs = $17,760 – (2,000 × $2.88) = $12,000

Therefore, budget cost allowance for activity level of 4,000 units = $12,000 + (4,000 × $2.88) = $23,520

57 A   The labour rate variance is recorded in the wages control account. Since the actual rate paid was higher than the standard rate, the labour rate variance is adverse. Therefore the variance will be debited in the labour rate variance account.

Options B and D are incorrect because it is the labour efficiency variance that is recorded in the work in progress account, not the labour rate variance.

If you selected option C you identified the correct accounts, but you reversed the debit and credit.

58 D   Direct material cost variance = material price variance + material usage variance

The adverse material usage variance could be larger than the favourable material price variance. The total of the two variances would therefore represent a net result of an adverse total direct material cost variance.

The situation in option A would sometimes arise, but not always, because of the possibility of the situation described in option D.

Option B could sometimes be correct, depending on the magnitude of each of the variances. However it will not always be correct as stated in the wording.

Option C is incorrect because the sum of the two favourable variances would always be a larger favourable variance.

59

		Consistent with the account entries	Not consistent with the account entries
(a)	The material used in production was more than the standard allowed for the number of units produced	✓	☐
(b)	All of the material issued to production was completely processed during the period	✓	☐
(c)	The number of labour hours worked was greater than the standard allowed for the number of units produced	☐	✓

Statement (a) is correct because the resulting adverse usage variance is a debit in the variance account.

Statement (b) is correct because there is no opening or closing balance on the work in progress account.

Statement (c) is incorrect because the labour efficiency variance will be transferred as a credit in the variance account. Therefore it is a favourable variance and the number of labour hours worked was actually lower than the standard allowed.

60 DR | WORK IN PROGRESS CONTROL ACCOUNT |

    CR | DIRECT LABOUR EFFICIENCY VARIANCE ACCOUNT |

61 C   The **direct costs of production**, of which direct wages are a part, are **debited to the work in progress account**. The credit entry is made in the **wages control account**, where the wages cost has been 'collected', as it is paid or accrued, prior to **its analysis** between direct and indirect wages.

If you selected option A you identified the correct accounts but your **entries were reversed**.

Option B represents the entries for direct wages paid, and option D is the (incorrect) reversal of these entries.

62   C   Overhead is absorbed into the cost of production for the period by debiting the work in progress account with the appropriate amount of overhead based on the predetermined overhead absorption rate. The credit entry is made in the overhead control account, where the overhead has been 'collected' in the debit side, as it is paid or accrued.

If you selected **option D** you identified the correct accounts but your **entries were reversed**.

Option A is incorrect because the cost of production must first be 'collected' in the **work in progress account** before the final transfer of the cost of completed production to the finished goods account.

Option B represents the entries, usually made at the end of a period, to account for any production overhead under absorbed.

63   D   There are two possible transfers from the raw materials control account:

- the cost of direct materials is transferred to the work in progress account
- the cost of indirect materials is transferred to the production overhead control account

The transfer of the cost of indirect materials to the production overhead control account is already shown as $6,000. Therefore the $71,000 must represent the issue of direct materials to work in progress.

64   Cash ✓

Payables ✓

Work-in-progress ☐

Note. When materials are purchased, they are either paid for in cash (credit cash account) or purchased on credit (credit/supplier account)

65   (a)   C   STATEMENT OF EQUIVALENT UNITS

	Total Units		Materials	Equivalent units Labour		Overheads
Output to process 2*	600		600	600		600
Closing WIP	100	(100%)	100	(50%) 50	(30%)	30
	700		700	650		630

*500 units input + opening WIP 200 units – closing WIP 100 units.

Option A is incorrect because it is the number of units input to the process, taking no account of opening and closing work in progress. **Option B** is the completed output, taking no account of the work done on the closing inventory.

Option D is the total number of units worked on during the period, but they are not all complete in respect of overhead cost.

(b)　B　STATEMENT OF COSTS PER EQUIVALENT UNIT

	Materials $	Labour $	Overheads $	Total
Opening inventory	2,400	1,200	400	
Added during period	6,000	3,350	1,490	
Total cost	8,400	4,550	1,890	
Equivalent units	700	650	630	
Cost per equivalent unit	$12	$7	$3	$22

Value of units transferred to process 2 = 600 units × $22 = $13,200

Option A is incorrect because it represents only the material cost of the units transferred. **Option C** is all of the costs incurred in the process during the period, but some of these costs must be allocated to the closing work in progress. **Option D** is the value of 700 completed units: but only 600 units were transferred to the next process.

66　D　The total loss was 15% of the material input. The 340 litres of good output therefore represents 85% of the total material input.

Therefore, material input = $\dfrac{340}{0.85}$ = 400 litres

Options A and B are incorrect because they represent a further five per cent and ten per cent respectively, added to the units of good production.

If you selected **option C** you simply added 15 per cent to the 340 litres of good production. However, the losses are stated as a percentage of input, not as a percentage of output.

67

PROCESS ACCOUNT

	Litres	$		Litres	$
Materials	20,000	4,400	Normal waste		
			(4,000 × $0.50)	4,000	2,000
			Finished goods	17,000	2,550
Abnormal gain	1,000	150			
	21,000	4,550		21,000	4,550

Workings

Normal loss = 20% × 20,000 litres = 4,000 litres

Expected output = 20,000 − 4,000 = 16,000 litres

Cost per unit $= \dfrac{\text{Process costs} - \text{scrap proceeds of normal loss}}{\text{Expected output}}$

$= \dfrac{\$4,400 - (4,000 \times \$0.50)}{16,000\,\text{litres}}$

$= \dfrac{\$4,400 - \$2,000}{16,000\,\text{litres}}$

$= \dfrac{\$2,400}{16,000\,\text{litres}}$

$= \$0.15$

68   (a)   During the period there was an abnormal loss of 125 kg.

Workings

Loss in process	2,500 kg – (2,100 + 150)kg	= 250 kg
Normal loss	5% × 2,500 kg	= 125 kg
∴ Abnormal loss		= 125 kg

(b)

Materials	$3.00
Labour	$0.40
Other direct costs	$0.20

Workings

STATEMENT OF EQUIVALENT UNITS OF PRODUCTION

		Equivalent units					
	Total	Materials		Labour		Other direct costs	
	Units	Units	%	Units	%	Units	%
Normal loss	125	0		0		0	
Abnormal loss	125	125	100	125	100	125	100
Finished inventory	2,100	2,100	100	2,100	100	2,100	100
Work In progress	150	150	100	120	80	90	60
	2,500	2,375		2,345		2,315	
Costs		*$7,125		$938		$463	
Cost per equivalent unit	$3.60	$3.00		$0.40		$0.20	

* $7,145 less scrap value of normal loss $20 = $7,125.

69   B   This is the correct definition of an equivalent unit.

70   C   **Step 1**   Determine output

			Equivalent units			
Input	*Output*	*Total*	*Materials*		*Labour and overhead*	
Units		Units	Units	%	Units	%
	Finished units (balance)	400	400	100	400	100
500	Closing inventory	100	100	100	80	80
500		500	500		480	

Step 2   Calculate the cost per equivalent unit

Input	*Cost*	*Equivalent production in units*	*Cost per unit*
	$		$
Materials	9,000	500	18
Labour and overhead	11,520	480	24
			42

Step 3   Calculate total cost of output

Cost of completed units = $42 × 400 units = $16,800

If you selected option A you omitted the absorption of overhead at the rate of 200 per cent of direct labour costs. If you selected option B you did not allow for the fact that the work in progress was incomplete. Option D is the total process cost for the period, some of which must be allocated to the work in progress.

71   B   Using the data from answer 70 above, extend **step 3** to calculate the value of the work in progress.

	Cost element	Number of equivalent units	Cost per equivalent unit $	Total $
Work in progress:	Materials	100	18	1,800
	Labour and overhead	80	24	1,920
				3,720

If you selected option A you omitted the absorption of overhead into the process costs. If you selected option C you did not allow for the fact that the work in progress was incomplete. Option D is the total process cost for the period, some of which must be allocated to the completed output.

72   D   The abnormal loss units are valued at their **full production cost** and **credited** to the process account, so that their occurrence does not affect the cost of good production. Therefore the correct answer is D.

Options A and C are incorrect because the scrap value of the abnormal loss is debited to the **scrap account** and credited to the **abnormal loss account**, it has no impact on the process account.

73   The quantity of good production achieved was $\boxed{2,625}$ kg.

Good production   = input – normal loss – abnormal loss
                = 3,000 – (10% × 3,000) – 75
                = 3,000 – 300 – 75
                = 2,635 kg

74   The value credited to the process account for the scrap value of the normal loss for the period will be $ $\boxed{100}$

Normal loss   = 10% × input
          = 10% × 5,000 kg
          = 500 kg

When scrap has a value, normal loss is valued at the value of the scrap ie 20p per kg.

Normal loss   = $0.20 × 500 kg
          = $100

75   The value of the abnormal loss for the period is $ $\boxed{300}$

	kg
Input	5,000
Normal loss (10% × 5,000 kg)	(500)
Abnormal loss	(300)
Output	4,200

$$\text{Cost per kg} = \frac{\text{Input costs} - \text{scrap value of normal loss}}{\text{Expected output}}$$

$$= \frac{\$4,600^* - \$100}{5,000 - 500}$$

$$= \frac{\$4,500}{4,500} = \$1.00$$

Value of abnormal loss = 300 × $1.00 = $300

*Materials (5,000 kg × 0.5)   2,500

Labour   700
Production overhead   1,400
                                                                   ─────
                                                                   4,600

76   The value of the closing work in progress for the period was $ | 4,698 |

STATEMENT OF EQUIVALENT UNITS

	Total units	Materials units		Labour and overhead units	
Completed output	8,000	(100%)	8,000	(100%)	8,000
Normal loss	1,000	(0%)	–	(0%)	–
Abnormal loss	100	(100%)	100	(100%)	100
Closing WIP	900	(100%)	900	(75%)	675
	10,000		9,000		8,775

STATEMENT OF COST PER EQUIVALENT UNIT

	Materials	Labour and overhead
Total costs	*$40,500	$8,424
Equivalent units	9,000	8,775
Cost per equivalent unit	$4.50	$0.96

* $40,800 less scrap value normal loss $300 = $40,500

Value of work in progress:

	$
Materials 900 equivalent units × $4.50	4,050
Labour and overhead 675 equivalent units × $0.96	648
	4,698

77   D

	$
Direct materials (5 × $20)	100
Direct labour (14 × $8)	112
Variable overhead (14 × $3)	42
Fixed overhead (14 × $5*)	70
Other overhead	80
Total cost of job 173	404
Profit margin (× 20/80)	101
Selling price	505

*Fixed production overhead absorption rate = $\dfrac{\$200,000}{40,000}$ = $5 per direct labour hour

Option A is the total cost, but a profit margin should be added to this to determine the selling price. If you selected **option B** you added only $5 for fixed production overhead: but this is the hourly rate, which must be multiplied by the number of direct labour hours. If you selected **option C** you calculated 20 per cent of cost to determine the profit: but the data states that profit is calculated as 20 per cent of the sales value.

78   A   Job costing is a costing method applied where work is **undertaken to customers' special requirements.** Option B describes process costing, C describes service costing and D describes absorption costing.

79 C Workings

Total labour cost incurred during period = $(12,500 + 23,000 + 4,500)
$$= \$40,000$$

∴ Overhead absorption rate = ($140,000/$40,000) × 100%
$$= 350\% \text{ of labour cost}$$

	$
Opening WIP	46,000
Labour for period	4,500
Overhead absorbed ($4,500 × 350%)	15,750
Total production cost	66,250
50% mark up	33,125
Sales value of job 3	99,375
Selling price per circuit board = $99,375 ÷ 2,400	$41.41

Option B is the selling price without the inclusion of any overhead absorbed. If you selected option D you calculated a 50 per cent margin based on the selling price, instead of a 50% mark up on cost.

80 C Since wages are paid on a piecework basis they are a variable cost which will increase in line with the number of binders. The machine set-up cost and design costs are fixed costs for each batch which will not be affected by the number of binders in the batch.

For a batch of 300 binders:

	$
Direct materials (30 × 3)	90.00
Direct wages (10 × 3)	30.00
Machine set up	3.00
Design and artwork	15.00
Production overhead (30 × 20%)	6.00
Total production cost	144.00
Selling, distribution and administration overhead (+ 5%)	7.20
Total cost	151.20
Profit (25% margin = 33$\frac{1}{3}$% of cost)	50.40
Selling price for a batch of 300	201.60

If you selected option A you calculated the cost correctly, but added a profit mark up of 25% of cost, instead of a margin of 25% of selling price.

If you selected option B you failed to absorb the appropriate amount of fixed overhead. If you selected option D you treated all of the costs as variable costs.

81   The price to be quoted for job B124 is $ 124.50

Production overhead absorption rate = $240,000/30,000 = $8 per labour hour

Other overhead absorption rate = ($150,000/$750,000) × 100% = 20% of total production cost

Job B124	$
Direct materials (3 kgs × $5)	15.00
Direct labour (4 hours × $9)	36.00
Production overhead (4 hours × $8)	32.00
Total production cost	83.00
Other overhead (20% × $83)	16.60
Total cost	99.60
Profit margin: 20% of sales (× $^{20}/_{80}$)	24.90
Price to be quoted	124.50

82   ☑ Production of the product can be completed in a single accounting period

☑ Production relates to a single special order

Job costing is appropriate where each cost unit is **separately identifiable** and is of relatively **short duration**.

83   *Appropriate*   *Not appropriate*

(a) Vehicle cost per passenger-kilometre   ☑   ☐

(b) Fuel cost for each vehicle per kilometre   ☑   ☐

(c) Fixed cost per kilometre   ☐   ☑

The vehicle cost per passenger-kilometre (a) is appropriate for cost control purposes because it **combines** the distance travelled and the number of passengers carried, **both of which affect cost**.

The fuel cost for each vehicle per kilometre (b) can be useful for control purposes because it **focuses on a particular aspect** of the cost of operating each vehicle.

The fixed cost per kilometre (c) is not particularly useful for control purposes because it **varies with the number of kilometres travelled**.

84   B   Number of occupied room-nights = 40 rooms × 30 nights × 65%
                                           = 780

Room servicing cost per occupied room-night = $\frac{$3,900}{780}$ = $5

Option A is the cost per available room-night. This makes no allowance for the 65% occupancy achieved. If you selected **option C** you simply divided $3,900 by 40 rooms. This does not account for the number of nights in the period, nor the percentage occupancy achieved. If you selected **option D** you calculated the cost per occupied room, rather than the cost per occupied room-night.

85   (i)   Production is carried out in accordance with the wishes of the customer   J

(ii)   Work is usually undertaken on the contractor's premises   N

(iii) Costs are averaged over the units produced in the period   S

(iv)   It establishes the costs of services rendered   S

86   (a)   (i)   St Matthew's $63.40

           (ii)   St Mark's $33.46

Workings

Number of in-patient days = number of in-patients × average stay

St Matthew's = 15,400 × 10 days   = 154,000

St Mark's   = 710 × 156 days   = 110,760

St Matthew's cost per in-patient day   = total cost ÷ 154,000

                                              = $9,762,780 ÷ 154,000

                                              = $63.40

St Mark's cost per in-patient day   = $3,705,631 ÷ 110,760

                                              = $33.46

    (b)   (i)   St Matthew's $20.31   (Total cost $2,640,300 ÷ 130,000)

           (ii)   St Mark's $52.38   (Total cost $183,330 ÷ 3,500)

    (c)   (i)   St Matthew's   78.8%

           (ii)   St Mark's   95.9%

Workings

St Matthew's = $\dfrac{402}{510}$ × 100% = 78.8%

St Mark's   = $\dfrac{307}{320}$ × 100% = 95.9%

87 | 66,325 |

Working

Calculation of tonne-km

Journey	Tonnes	Km	Tonne-km
1	34	180	6,120
2	28	265	7,420
3	40	390	15,600
4	32	115	3,680
5	26	220	5,720
6	40	480	19,200
7	29	90	2,610
8	26	100	2,600
9	25	135	3,375
	280	1,975	66,325

88    $ | 0.16 | per tonne-kilometre (to the nearest cent).

Working

Average cost per tonne-kilometre = $\dfrac{\text{Total cost}}{\text{Total tonne - kilometres}}$

                                          = $\dfrac{\$10,390}{66,325}$

                                          = $0.16 per tonne-kilometre (to the nearest cent)

89 D The present value of $5,000 in perpetuity is calculated as $5,000/0.1.

If you selected **option A**, you might have calculated $5,000 × 10%.

If you selected **option B**, you might have calculated $5,000 × 110%.

If you selected **option C**, you might have calculated $5,000/110%.

90 D **A** is not a disadvantage because the fact that it tends to bias in favour of short-term projects means that it tends to minimise both financial and business risk.

B is untrue. It is simple to calculate the simple to understand, which may be important when management resources are limited.

C is not a disadvantage because it helps to identify those projects which generate additional cash for investment quickly.

D is a disadvantage because the firm needs to make a minimum return to cover the cost of raising funds and what investors are expecting as a return on their funds invested in the company.

91 $1,540

Year		Annual cash flow	Discount factor	PV
		$	8%	$
0		(50,000)	1.000	(50,000)
1	(4,000 × $5)	20,000	0.926	18,520
2	(4,000 × $5)	20,000	0.857	17,140
3	(4,000 × $5)	20,000	0.794	15,880
				1,540

92 $(5,225)

$100,000 − ($25,000 × 3.791) = $(5,225)

93 5.83%

$$IRR = 5\% + \frac{350}{(350+1,750)} \times (10\text{-}5) \ \%$$

$$= 5\% + 0.83\%$$
$$= 5.83\%$$

94 C,D A **differential cost** is the difference in cost between two alternatives and is therefore a relevant cost for decision making. Relevant costs are also future costs. Costs incurred in the past are irrelevant to any decision being made now.

Index

Review Form – Paper C01 Fundamentals of Management Accounting

Please help us to ensure that the CIMA learning materials we produce remain as accurate and user-friendly as possible. We cannot promise to answer every submission we receive, but we do promise that it will be read and taken into account when we up-date this Study Text.

Name: _____   Address: _____

_____

_____

How have you used this Interactive Text?
(Tick one box only)

☐ Home study (book only)

☐ On a course: college _____

☐ With 'correspondence' package

☐ Other _____

Why did you decide to purchase this Interactive Text? *(Tick one box only)*

☐ Have used BPP Texts in the past

☐ Recommendation by friend/colleague

☐ Recommendation by a lecturer at college

☐ Saw information on BPP website

☐ Saw advertising

☐ Other _____

Which BPP products have you used?

Text	☑	Home Study Package	☐
Kit	☐	Interactive Passcard	☐
Passcard	☐	i-Pass	☐

During the past six months do you recall seeing/receiving any of the following?
(Tick as many boxes as are relevant)

☐ Our advertisement in *Financial Management*

☐ Our advertisement in *PQ*

☐ Our brochure with a letter through the post

☐ Our website www.bpp.com

Which (if any) aspects of our advertising do you find useful?
(Tick as many boxes as are relevant)

☐ Prices and publication dates of new editions

☐ Information on Text content

☐ Facility to order books off-the-page

☐ None of the above

Your ratings, comments and suggestions would be appreciated on the following areas.

	Very useful	Useful	Not useful
Introductory section (Key study steps, personal study)	☐	☐	☐
Chapter introductions	☐	☐	☐
Key terms	☐	☐	☐
Quality of explanations	☐	☐	☐
Case studies and other examples	☐	☐	☐
Assessment focus points	☐	☐	☐
Questions and answers in each chapter	☐	☐	☐
Fast forwards and chapter roundups	☐	☐	☐
Quick quizzes	☐	☐	☐
Question Bank	☐	☐	☐
Answer Bank	☐	☐	☐
Index	☐	☐	☐
Icons	☐	☐	☐

Overall opinion of this Study Text	Excellent ☐	Good ☐	Adequate ☐	Poor ☐

Do you intend to continue using BPP products?   Yes ☐   No ☐

On the reverse of this page are noted particular areas of the text about which we would welcome your feedback.

The BPP author of this edition can be e-mailed at: vallirajagopal@bpp.com

Please return this form to: Adrian Sims, CIMA Publishing Director, BPP Professional Education, FREEPOST, London, W12 8BR

Review Form (continued)

TELL US WHAT YOU THINK

Please note any further comments and suggestions/errors below